African perspectives in international investment law

Manchester University Press

Melland Schill Perspectives on International Law

General Editors
Jean d'Aspremont
Iain Scobbie
Sufyan Droubi

Building on the history of Melland Schill Classics and Melland Schill Studies at Manchester University Press, Melland Schill Perspectives on International Law was established to reflect the diversity of international legal scholarship worldwide. This inclusive, accessible series aims to offer a platform for scholars from different regions who adopt innovative approaches to new and old topics.

Melland Schill Perspectives on International Law is founded on the idea that every international legal issue should be debated from various and, at times, incommensurable perspectives. Though there is a great deal of diversity in international legal debates and practice, this diversity is often obfuscated by prevailing Euro-centric and positivist narratives, which not only creates difficulties for non-Western scholars to be heard but hinders the development of different approaches.

Previously published

International organisations, non-State actors and the formation of customary international law
Edited by Sufyan Droubi and Jean d'Aspremont

African perspectives in international investment law

Edited by
Yenkong Ngangjoh Hodu
and Makane Moïse Mbengue

Assisted by Parveen Morris

Manchester University Press

Published by Manchester University Press
Oxford Road, Manchester M13 9PL
www.manchesteruniversitypress.co.uk

British Library Cataloguing-in-Publication Data
A catalogue record for this book is available from the British Library

ISBN 978 1 5261 5127 8 hardback
ISBN 978 1 5261 8247 0 paperback

First published 2020
Paperback published 2024

Typeset by Newgen Publishing UK

Contents

Contents

Notes on contributors

Victor Adetula is Head of Research at the Nordic Africa Institute, Sweden, and Professor of International Relations and Development Studies at the University of Jos, Nigeria.

Collins C. Ajibo holds both an LLM and PhD in international business and commercial law from the University of Manchester, and is currently a lecturer in law, at the Faculty of Law, University of Nigeria. He is a member of many professional affiliations, including the African Society of International Law (AfSIL), the Society of Legal Scholars, among others. He acts as the External Consultant for the publishing outfit of the African Development Bank (*African Development Review*). Dr Collins has published a number of peer-reviewed articles and book chapters, cutting across different areas of international business law. He has also delivered papers in diverse areas of international business law, particularly international investment law.

Jean d'Aspremont is Professor of Public International Law at the University of Manchester, where he founded the Manchester International Law Centre (MILC). He also is Professor of International Legal Theory at the University of Amsterdam. He is General Editor of the *Cambridge Studies in International and Comparative Law* and co-Editor-in-Chief of *Oxford International Organizations* (OXIO). He is a member of the Scientific Advisory Board of the *European Journal of International Law* and Series Editor of the Melland Schill Studies in International Law. He has acted as counsel in proceedings before the International Court of Justice. Professor d'Aspremont has published widely in the field of international law, having authored several books and edited volumes, as well as more than 90 peer-reviewed articles and book chapters. Some of his articles have been translated into several languages including Spanish, Hindi and Persian. He has delivered more than 100 talks in academic institutions around the world over the last 10 years.

Mahamat Atteib is a lecturer at Gaston Berger University in Saint-Louis, where he is preparing a joint doctoral thesis in law with the University of Geneva. For several years now, he has been interested in regulating extractive activities in Africa and the rest of the world in its theoretical and practical aspects. He is the author of *Stabilization Clauses in Mining and Oil Contracts. Analysis of Legal and Fiscal Aspects in the Light of Positive Chadian Law* (Saarbrücken: European University Publishing, 2013), p. 136.

Francis N. Botchway is a professor of law and Sir William Blair Chair in Alternative Dispute Resolution at the College of Law, Qatar University, where he also served as Associate Dean of Research and Graduate Studies for five years. He obtained law degrees from leading universities in Ghana, Canada, the United States of America (US) and the United Kingdom (UK). He teaches and researches in international investment law, international law, natural resources law, comparative law, and arbitration and negotiations. He also taught at the University of Warwick School of Law for six years and briefly at the University of Hull, both in the UK. Formerly, he was Adjunct Professor at Leuven University in Belgium, Assistant Professor/Lecturer at the University of Warwick, and Visiting Professor at the University of Puerto Rico. He is a consultant on TradeLab, providing legal services to governments, non-governmental organizations and businesses. He is consulted by law firms in the UK and the US on litigation, arbitration as well as international business transactions. He has published books and dozens of articles in leading international journals in Europe, the US, Australia, Asia and Africa. He is the Editor-in-Chief of the *Global Journal of Comparative Law* and served as Vice President of AfSIL for six years. His latest edited book is entitled *Natural Resource Investment and Africa's Development*. His forthcoming book is entitled *Defences in International Investment Law*, to be published by Routledge, UK.

Laurence Boisson de Chazournes is a professor of international law at the University of Geneva School of Law. Her writings and practice cover various fields such as international economic law, international dispute settlement, international environmental law and the law of international organizations. She is a recognized practitioner for her role as an advisor to many international organizations, States, and non-State entities both public and private, as well as being an arbitrator and counsel in various dispute settlement fora. Professor Boisson de Chazournes is an associate member of Matrix. She advises and litigates on a wide range of international law issues. She has served as Chairperson of WTO arbitration panels on pre-shipment inspections, as an arbitrator for the International Centre for Settlement of Investment Disputes (ICSID) and other arbitration fora, such as the Permanent Court of Arbitration (PCA) and the Court of Arbitration for Sport (CAS). She has also acted as counsel before the International Court of Justice (ICJ) and in other fora. She is a member of the PCA, the WTO indicative list of governmental and non-governmental panelists, a member of the ICSID Panel of Conciliators, the list of arbitrators under Annex VII of the United Nations Convention on the Law of the Sea, the list of arbitrators of the French Arbitration Committee, International Chamber of Commerce (ICC), the general list of arbitrators of the Court of Arbitration for Sport, and the Panel of Experts for the Trade and Sustainable Development Chapter of the EU–Korea Free Trade Agreement. She has been a member of the United Nations Human Rights Council Advisory Committee since 2011. Between 1995 and 1999 she was Senior Counsel to the World Bank.

Dominic Npoanlari Dagbanja is a senior lecturer in law at The University of Western Australia Law School and Research Fellow, African Public Procurement Law Unit, Department of Mercantile Law, Stellenbosch University South Africa. He previously worked at the University of Manchester Law School in the UK as a post-doctoral research associate. He also served as a lecturer in law at the Ghana Institute of Management and Public Administration, and practised law in both public and private institutions in Ghana. His teaching and research interests include company law, contract law, international commercial law, international investment law and arbitration, international trade law and public procurement law. Dr Dagbanja is the author of *The Law of Public Procurement in Ghana: Law, Policy and Practice* (Saarbrücken: Lap Lambert Academic Publishing AG & Co. Kg, 2011) and has published articles in reputable peer-reviewed journals, including *African Journal of International and Comparative Law*, *Arizona Journal of International and Comparative Law*, *Journal of African Law*, *Transnational Legal Theory* and *The Oxford University Commonwealth Law Journal*. Dr Dagbanja holds the following degrees: BA (Hons), University of Ghana, 2000; LLB (Hons), University of Ghana, 2003; Qualifying Certificate and Certificate of Enrolment on the Roll of Lawyers, Ghana School of Law, 2005; LLM in transnational business practice, University of the Pacific, USA, 2008; LLM in government procurement law, George Washington University, USA, 2009; and PhD in law, University of Auckland, New Zealand, 2016.

Mohamed Salem Abou El Farag is Associate Professor of Law and Assistant Professor of Law at Cairo University, and Manager of the Innovation and Intellectual Property Office, Qatar University.

Notes on contributors

Tarcisio Gazzini is Professor of Law at the University of East Anglia. Between 2014 and 2017 he was responsible for the research project 'Foreign Investment in Africa: Gaining Development Momentum' supported by the Swiss National Science Foundation and jointly run by the Universities of Lausanne and Geneva. He has previously taught at the Universities of Padua, Glasgow and VU University Amsterdam. He is a member of the International Law Association Committee on the Role of International Law in Sustainable Natural Resource Management for Development. He also serves on the Editorial Board of the book series *International Investment Law* published by Brill Nijhoff. His publications include *The Interpretation of International Investment Treaties* (Oxford: Hart Publishing, 2016).

Yenkong Ngangjoh Hodu is a professor of international economic law and Head of the University of Manchester Law School. Before coming to Manchester, he was a senior researcher and a programme coordinator on global trade and regional integration at the Nordic Africa Institute (NAI) in Uppsala, Sweden. He is regularly consulted by many governments, regional organizations and United Nations agencies on international trade and investment law. He has published broadly on international trade law, especially in the area of dispute resolution. Some of his publications include: 'ICSID Annulment Procedure and the WTO Appellate System: The Case for an Appellate System for Investment Arbitration' 6 (2) (2015) *Journal of International Dispute Settlement*, 308–31; *The Political Economy of WTO Implementation and China's Approach to Litigation in the WTO* (Cheltenham: Edward Elgar, 2016).

Olugbemi Jaiyebo is Senior Lecturer at the College of Law, Osun State University, Ifetedo, Nigeria. He is enrolled as a solicitor and advocate of the Supreme Court of Nigeria and is admitted to the Appellate Division of the Supreme Court of the State of New York, First Judicial Department, and the United States District Court, Southern District of New York.

Maurice Kamto is a professor of international law at the Faculty of Law and Political Science, University of Yaounde 2, Soa, Cameroon. Professor Kamto has published several books and over fifty peer-reviewed articles. He was a member of the International Law Commission (ILC) of the United Nations from 1999 to 2016, as well as Special Rapporteur of the ILC on the subject '*Expulsion of aliens*' from 2004 to 2016. He has been led Counsel to many countries before the ICJ. He successfully led the Cameroonian delegation during the negotiations to resolve the matter of Bakassi, a peninsula disputed with neighbouring Nigeria. His contribution was instrumental in Cameroon winning the case. He is a member of the Curatorium of the Hague Academy of International Law.

Notes on contributors

Alicia Köppen is a PhD candidate within the Intlaw Research Group 'The International Rule of Law – Rise or Decline?'. She finished her law studies which she conducted in Bonn, Paris and Berlin in 2015 after successfully passing her first exams. She also holds a Bachelors degree in political science from the University of Bonn, obtained in 2009. In the course of her law studies she specialized in public international law. She took part in the Philip C. Jessup Moot Court Competition in international law as a participant, coach and judge. Since November 2014, she has been part of the service team of the *Voelkerrechtsblog*, a blog on international law and international legal thought.

Richard Albert Makon Ma Mbeb is a lecturer and research associate at the University of Yaoundé II, Cameroon. He obtained his PhD in public law from the University of Yaoundé II on 10 December 2016. He teaches public international law at the Faculty of Law and Political Science (FLPS) at the University of Yaoundé II. He has been an expert/consultant in the setting up, analysis and evaluation of research and development projects since 2010. He is also a specialist in investment law. He has been a consultant at Media & Law Conseils (MLC) since 2015, specializing in investment law, mining, oil and gas law, public-private partnership law and public procurement law.

Makane Moïse Mbengue is Associate Professor of International Law at the Faculty of Law of the University of Geneva. Professor Mbengue is also a Visiting Professor at Sciences Po Paris (School of Law). He holds a PhD in public international law from the University of Geneva. He acts as a professor for courses in international law organized by the United Nations Office of Legal Affairs (OLA) and by the United Nations Institute for Training and Research (UNITAR). Professor Mbengue acts as counsel in disputes before international courts and tribunals.

Justice Osei-Afriyie is Assistant Lecturer in Law at Kwame Nkrumah University of Science and Technology (KNUST), Kumasi, Ghana. He holds a degree in political science and philosophy from the University of Ghana and a Bachelor of Laws (LLB) and Master of Laws (LLM) from Queen Mary University of London. Before joining KNUST Faculty of Law, he was a teaching instructor for the LLM programme at the University of Liverpool, where he taught legal methodology, foreign investment law and the law of the World Trade Organization (WTO). His main areas of research interests are in jurisprudence and legal theory, public law, international economic law and international investment law. Currently, he teaches jurisprudence and the

Ghanaian legal system and method, and is also in charge of examinations, at the KNUST Faculty of Law.

Stefanie Schacherer is a dual PhD candidate in international public law at the University of Vienna and the University of Geneva. She is specialized in international and European investment law. Her research focuses in particular on investment and trade agreements concluded by the European Union and their nexus with sustainable development. Mrs Schacherer holds a Masters degree in international and European law from the University of Geneva, as well as an LLM in international business law from King's College London. She is currently working as a teaching and research assistant at the Faculty of Law of the University of Geneva. She has been working with Professor Makane Moïse Mbengue on the elaboration of the Pan-African Investment Code (PAIC).

Alain-Guy Sipowo holds a doctorate in Law from Laval University (LLD, 2014). His dissertation on the International Criminal Court and the protection of secrets won the René Cassin Thesis Prize from the International Institute of Human Rights in 2015. He is a lecturer at the Department of Political Science at the Faculty of Law, McGill University, and has conducted postdoctoral research on the responsibility of multinational corporations for human rights violations abroad. He is now a consultant with a Montreal law firm and Deputy Secretary General for AfSIL Canada.

List of abbreviations

AfSIL	African Society of International Law
ATCA	1789 Alien Tort Claims Act
ATS	Alien Tort Statute
AU	African Union
BIT	Bilateral investment treaty
CEMAC	Economic and Monetary Community of Central Africa
CETA	European Union–Canada Comprehensive Economic Trade Agreement
CFTA	Continental Free Trade Area
EAC	East African Community
EC	European Community
ECOWAS	Economic Community of West African States
EITI	Extractive Industries Transparency Initiative
EU	European Union
FDI	Foreign direct investment
FNC	Treaty of Friendship, Commerce and Navigation
FTA	Free trade agreement
GATT	General Agreement on Tariffs and Trade
HDI	Human Development Index
ICJ	International Court of Justice
ICSID	International Centre for Settlement of Investment Disputes
IFC	International Finance Corporation
IIA	International investment agreement
IMF	International Monetary Fund
ISDS	Investor-State dispute settlement
ITO	International Trade Organization

List of abbreviations

MIA	Multilateral investment agreement
MOSOP	Movement for the Survival of the Ogoni People
NAFTA	North American Free Trade Agreement
NGBIT	New generation of bilateral investment treaty
NIEO	Declaration on the Establishment of a New International Economic Order
NNPC	Nigerian National Petroleum Corporation
OAU	Organisation for African Unity
OECD	Organisation for Economic Co-operation and Development
OHADA	Organisation pour l'Harmonisation en Afrique du Droit des Affaires
PAIC	Pan-African Investment Code
SADC	Southern African Development Community
TPP	Trans-Pacific Partnership Agreement
TRIPS	Agreement on Trade-Related Aspects of Intellectual Property Rights
TTIP	Transatlantic Trade and Investment Partnership
TVPA	Torture Victim Protection Act
UNCITRAL	United Nations Commission on International Trade Law
UNCTAD	United Nations Conference on Trade and Development
UNDAF	United Nations Development Assistance Framework
UNECA	United Nations Economic Commission for Africa
UNEP	United Nations Environment Programme
UNESCO	United Nations Educational, Scientific and Cultural Organization
USA	United States of America
WTO	World Trade Organization

Introduction

Yenkong Ngangjoh Hodu and Makane Moïse Mbengue

The last decade has seen tremendous growth in foreign direct investment (FDI) in Africa, and a significant increase in greenfield investment from emerging economies like China, India, Turkey and the Gulf States. According to African Economic Outlook 2018, foreign investment in Africa was expected to reach over USD 60 billion.[1] What is more, FDI into Africa is diversifying away from mineral resources into consumer goods and services. Sadly, FDI in Africa has not always translated into sustainable development. In many countries on the continent, evidence of the so-called 'resource curse' abound.[2] FDI in Africa comes at a time when the field of international investment law and arbitration is witnessing a renewal. It is under intense public scrutiny and has become the focus of heated debates. The investment has led to big business for law firms in the area of investment arbitration. In this regard, the last decade witnessed an increased number of investment treaties, proliferating investment disputes, the rise of mega-regional trade agreements and the negotiation of mega-regional infrastructure projects. Yet, while the argument in support of investment treaties as instruments to attract FDI is highly contested,

1 African Development Bank, 'African Economic Outlook 2018' (2018) www.afdb.org/fileadmin/uploads/afdb/Documents/Publications/African_Economic_Outlook_2018_-_EN.pdf, accessed November 2018.

2 Nomathemba Mhlanga, Garrick Blalock, Ralph Christie, 'Understanding Foreign Direct Investment in the Southern African Development Community: An Analysis Based on Project-Level Data' (2010) 41:3–4 *Agricultural Economics* 337; Yin-Wong Cheung *et al.*, 'China's Outward Direct Investment in Africa' (2012) 20:2 *Review of International Economics* 201; Dominic Dagbanja, 'The Limitation on Sovereign Regulatory Autonomy and Internationalization of Investment Protection by Treaty: An African Perspective' (2016) 60 (1) *Journal of African Law* 56.

many African countries are no doubt becoming more aware of the need to reshape the international investment architecture.

These changing fundamentals also come with renewed expectations from African governments and citizens. With the hope of attracting and benefiting from increased FDI, almost all African countries have adopted a development vision. Since almost all of these development visions are anchored on increased FDI, there is currently intense competition among African countries to attract FDI. All this is happening at a time when there is a renewed call from both practitioners and academics for the recalibration of the nature of the international investment relationship between African host States and foreign investors. On the one hand, there are calls for the reform of international investment rules that have largely been seen as pro investors. On the other hand, many countries have taken steps to adjust what they have long perceived to be unfair international investment agreements. With this in mind, this volume will respond to the fundamental question regarding the continuous perception that the international investment regime is skewed against African host States.

Indeed, if international law is seen as a breeding ground for academic and policy contestations,[3] the law regulating foreign investment is undoubtedly one of the epicentres of such contestations.[4] The fact that politics cannot be disentangled from normative construction of international law means that the socioeconomic environment within which foreign investments flourish in Africa cannot be discounted when the normative framework governing foreign investment is being formulated. Any attempt to construct/deconstruct international investment agreements in isolation of the socioeconomic environment in African host States is undoubtedly bound to generate contestations. It is, therefore, no news that the manner in which foreign investments should be regulated has pitted capital exporting countries against capital importing developing countries in an ideological battle for many decades.[5]

3 On the nature of international legal arguments, see Martti Koskenniemi, *From Apology to Utopia: The Structure of International Legal Argument* (Cambridge University Press, 2006).

4 On this, see M. Sornarajah, *The International Law on Foreign Investment* (Cambridge University Press, 4th edn, 2017) 1, citing J. Harlan, in *Banco Nacional de Cuba* v. *Sabbatino* (1964) 374 US 398.

5 For the place of investment law within international law, see Christian Tams, 'Sources of International Investment Law' in Tarcisio Gazzini and Eric De Brabandere (eds), *International Investment law: Sources of Rights and Obligations* (Brill, 2012). For a comprehensive discussion on the ideological divide on international investment law, see M. Sornarajah, *The International Law on Foreign Investment*.

With unequivocal expression of disdain in the notion of international minimum standards of protection as adumbrated in the Hull formula, developing host States, many of which are African States, through their overwhelming endorsement of the Calvo Doctrine and the Declaration on the Establishment of a New International Economic Order (NIEO), have, to this date, continued to express unease with the modus operandi of traditional bilateral investment treaties (BITs).[6] This explains why since 2015 South Africa, as well as other African countries as will be seen in Chapter 8 by Gazzini, has taken the lead in overhauling its investment treaty regime. Some other States party to the new generation of investment agreements have also reformulated the preambular language to investment treaties, as well as added interpretative clauses to such treaties.[7]

The polemics surrounding the current architecture of foreign investment law have reigned over the years, although in the last few decades some of the traditional capital importing countries have become capital exporting countries themselves. In this regard, expression of unease with the traditional nature of BITS and the nature of protection associated with them, including investor-State dispute settlements, are nowadays commonplace in both developing and developed countries. To this end, the notion of reforms of the whole international investment system have become hot topics in contemporary international law discussions.

However, against the backdrop of intense contestations with the nature of international investment law, tremendous growth in foreign investment in Africa and the increased relevance of international investment law, this volume explores trends in FDI in the African continent, the benefits and challenges that FDI presents for African States, and Africa's participation in the international investment law regime more generally. It is one of the purposes of this monograph to revisit the claim that African countries have been at the receiving end of poor treatment in the international investment system for decades. Such analyses will be done bearing in mind the possible successes/lack of successes of African countries with the NIEO in the 1970s. This volume, with contributions from prominent academics, jurists, and international arbitration and litigation experts, offers insights and comments on challenges in Africa's foreign investment climate and international investment law more generally. This timely

6 For more discussion on this ideological battle, see M. Sornarajah, *The International Law on Foreign Investment*; Surya P. Subedi QC, *International Investment Law: Reconciling Policy and Principle* (Hart Publishing, 3rd edn, 2016).

7 For a discussion on the nature of policy considerations that should be taken into account in the new-generation of investment treaties, see Suzanne A. Spears, 'The Quest for Policy Space in a New Generation of International Investment Agreements' (2010) 13 (4) *Journal of International Economic Law* 1037.

volume succinctly analyses key conceptual issues of international investment law, as well as practical issues relating to investment disputes.

Before engaging in such discussion, it is important to first revisit the more crucial question of what investment is and some of the contestations that are at the forefront of the debate on the reform of the international investment regime.[8] These two issues which the African Society of International Law (AfSIL) attempted to deal with in the 2016 AfSIL Principles on International Investment for Sustainable Development in Africa may sound belated or even modest. Despite the numerous scholarships on the subject, it is indeed very timely to revisit the subject, especially with the benefit of lessons learned from some domestic practices and the changing economic/legal landscape in Africa. It is not unusual in many African countries to hear contestations that challenge the current investment architecture as providing little or no policy space for governments to exercise their constitutional duties.

The identification and analyses of human rights practices of investors in Africa, the implementation of technological transfer clauses included in investment treaties, and the handling of the consequences in investment arbitration deserve to be put into perspective. When we ask ourselves if the current BITs between Africa and third parties is balanced, we are indirectly questioning whether the BIT protects the interests of investors while also reflecting the development aspirations of those African countries. In other words, is there room for policy space in such agreements that would not hinder African governments from fulfilling their constitutional rights? The contributions made in this book by prominent international lawyers in the field are precisely aimed at helping readers to get a better understanding of answers to these questions, including some of the key challenges facing the international investment law regime from the vantage point of African countries.

8 On reform of international investment law, see Stephan W. Schill, 'Reforming Investor–State Dispute Settlement: A (Comparative and International) Constitutional Law Framework' (2017) 20 (3) *Journal of International Economic Law* 649; UNCTAD, 'Taking Stock of IIA Reform' (IIA Issues Note No. 1 March 2016) http://investmentpolicyhub.unctad.org/Upload/Taking_Stock_of_IIA_Reform_IIA_Issues_Note.pdf, accessed August 2018.

Part I

Sustainable development and the changing fundamentals of international investment law in Africa

1
The development of international investment law in Africa

Maurice Kamto

Introduction

The fast development of major countries in Asia, particularly China, has fuelled the imagination of many African countries and the expectations of their peoples.[1] Each of them has set its own deadline to become an emerging economy. To meet such a target, they all expect to attract more and more foreign direct investment (FDI). There is, therefore, fierce competition to get the largest share of FDI. Taking into account this situation and the topic of this present monograph, this chapter will respond to the following fundamental questions: firstly, what is an investment in investment law?; secondly, are there justifications in support of the arguments that Africa has been unfairly treated in international investment terms since decolonisation?; thirdly, did the 1970s new international economic order bring any investment successes to Africa?; fourthly, what is the position of Africa post-1990s and beyond?

1 What is an investment in investment law?

It is important to start with a definition of investment because its definition determines the jurisdiction of arbitral tribunals and any other mechanism entrusted with the jurisdiction to settle disputes between investors and the receiving State of the investment.

The term 'investment' seems to have appeared after the Second World War to address the foreign property contribution, either through the creation of new companies in the territory of the host State, with the foreign investor being the

1 See Kaitlyn DeGhetto, Jacob R. Gray and Moses N. Kiggundu, 'The African Union's Agenda 2063: Aspirations, Challenges, and Opportunities for Management Research' (2016) 2 (1) *Africa Journal of Management* 93–116.

major shareholder, or by taking a share (generally the majority) of the capital of a company that already existed in that country.

There is no general definition of the term 'investment'. An investigation of the codes and treaties in the domain of investment shows a 'pragmatic' or 'functional' approach, where every definition is made for the purpose of each legal instrument and is not meant to be a general definition of investment as such. For instance, the definition of investment in the Convention on the Settlement of Investment Disputes between States and Nationals of Other States (known as the Washington Convention), which created the International Centre for Settlement of Investment Disputes (ICSID), is relevant only for the purpose of assessing the jurisdiction of arbitral tribunals. These tribunals assess only the scope of the legal instrument brought to their consideration or their jurisdiction, which depends partly on the contentious operation being qualified as an investment, and is only assessed in the context of that legal instrument.[2]

According to traditional conception, the criteria for an investment are: the contribution of the investor in the territory of the foreign State, whether financial, material or know-how; the contribution must last a certain time, meaning that it should not be a purely financial speculation or an instant commercial transaction; there must be some economic risk for the investor who should be ready to face lost or make or maximise profit; and if it is not included in the first three criteria, the investor must be in position to influence or control the management of the economic operation, namely a local company if the investment consists of buying shares in such a company or creating a new company. However, this conception that can be found in the United States model bilateral investment treaty (BIT) is no more relevant to account accurately the definition of investment as can be derived from new treaties for protection of investments, investment codes and arbitration practice.[3] Indeed, new forms of economic operations are qualified as 'investments'. The definition has expanded beyond property investment to a series of contributions without having an interest in the company's capital and without a minimum interest in the company. Yet, is it desirable to dilute the notion of investment in that of property, interest or whether investment is linked to a commercial transaction, for it will lead to the merging of different regimes, which might not be easy to manage in

2 Jean Matringe, 'La notion d'investissement' in Charles Leben (ed), *Droit international des investissements et de l'arbitrage transnational* (Paris: Editions Pedone, 2015) 139.

3 *Ibid.* 144.

practice? Finally, the definition of investment under the ICSID Convention is not very precise.[4]

Although at certain periods focus has been put on the contribution of the investment to the development of the host countries, some scholars think that it is not the main purpose of the investment law.[5] Roughly, there are two approaches in defining investment in the process of ascertaining jurisdiction in a particular dispute: on the one hand, the objective definition of investment, and on the other hand, the normative qualifications of investment.

It is unnecessary to delve into normative qualifications because they are subjective, meaning they depend on the parties to a particular BIT. Indeed, to overcome the hurdle of defining investment, many BITs, while refraining to state exactly what constitutes an investment – and even when they do – would define a list of operations the parties consider as 'investment'. Normative qualifications are distinct from the definition because of their combination of concepts and concrete cases. It is a mental operation of linkage and connection of a notion with its materialisation. The qualification would set the appropriate applicable legal regime, for instance, whether the matter is one of international investment law or not. Qualification will therefore determine the jurisdiction of the arbitral tribunal.

For the Parties to the BIT to consider an operation as an investment does not prejudge the same qualification, later on, by the ICSID Tribunal.[6] In *Ceskoslovenska Obchodni Banka, A.S.* v. *The Slovak Republic* (1999) the Tribunal considered that a 'two-fold test' 'must ... be applied in determining whether this Tribunal has the competence to consider the merits of the claim: whether the dispute arises out of an investment within the meaning of the Convention and, if so, whether the dispute relates to an investment as defined in the Parties' consent to ICSID arbitration, in their reference to the BIT and the pertinent definitions contained in Article 1 of the BIT'[7] In *MHS* v. *Malaysia* (2007) the ICSID Arbitration Tribunal recognised that: 'Under the double-barrelled test, a finding that the Contract satisfied the definition of "investment" under the BIT would not be sufficient for this Tribunal to assume jurisdiction, if the Contract failed to satisfy the objective criterion of an "investment" within the meaning of Article 25 … .'[8]

4 *Ibid.* 156.
5 *Ibid.* 157.
6 See *Joy Mining* v. *Egypt* (2004); *Romak* v. *Uzbekistan.*
7 *Ceskoslovenska Obchodni Banka, A.S.* v. *The Slovak Republic* (24 May 1999) ARB/97/4, 68.
8 *Malaysian Historical Salvors SDN BHD v. the Government of* Malaysia (17 May 2007) ICSID Case No. ARB/05/10, Award on Jurisdiction 55.

Paragraph 27 of the report of the ICSID administrators[9] provides that it has not been found useful to define the term 'investment', since the consent of the parties are an essential condition, taking into consideration the mechanism by which the contracting parties can decide in advance, if they so wish, the categories of dispute they would be ready to submit to the ISCID. The subjective theory goes along this line. According to this theory, the definition of 'investment' depends only on the applicable law, as it derives from Article 25(1) of the Washington Convention on the consent to arbitration.[10]

It is to be noted that normative qualifications do not define investment but confine themselves to specify the legal forms that investments can have. For instance, in some cases, the purchase of shares can be considered an investment. One advantage of the subjective approach is that it can attract investments, thanks to its very broad conception of this notion.

The criteria of the objective definition of investment are rather controversial among arbitral tribunals. In *Salini* v. *Morocco*,[11] Morocco argued that the road construction contracts allocated to two Italian companies were not an investment under the Washington Convention; but the BIT included the rights to a contractual service with an economic value, meaning that the contract fell within that definition of investment. In a landmark decision in that case, the Tribunal rejected this subjective definition and looked for objective criteria of investment. It stated that academics generally consider that investment supposes contributions, the execution of the contract for a certain period of time (or durability) and a participation in the risk of operation. It added that the consideration of the Preamble of the Washington Convention allows the addition of the criterion of 'contribution to economic development'.

These criteria can be independent of each other. Thus, the risk of operation may depend on the contributions to and the duration of the execution of the contract. However, the criteria may also be considered globally even though the Tribunal considered them separately. The post-*Salini* jurisprudence is characterised by the

9 Reports compiled in *The History of the ICSID Convention*, Volumes I–IV, available at https://icsid.worldbank.org/en/Pages/resources/The-History-of-the-ICSID-Convention.aspx.

10 For ISCID jurisprudence on this concept, see for instance: *Fedax N.V.* v. *The Republic of Venezuela* (9 March 1998) ICSID Case No. ARB/96/3; *Lanco International Inc* v. The *Argentine Republic* (8 December 1998), Jurisdiction of the Arbitral Tribunal, ICSID Case No. ARB/97/6.

11 *Salini Costruttori S.p.A. and Italstrade S.p.A.* v. *Kingdom of Morocco [I]*, ICSID Case No. ARB/00/4, Decision on Jurisdiction 52.

will to suppress the contribution to development in the host state because it is more difficult to establish and is implicitly covered by the three other criteria.[12] In *Patrick Mitchell* v. *Congo*, the issue was the contribution of a law firm to the development of the host country. The Arbitral Tribunal held that the contribution should be 'positive and significant'; on the contrary, the Ad Hoc Committee annulled the award on the grounds that such contribution 'shall not necessarily be important and successful'.[13]

Indeed, although the Ad Hoc Committee specified that the existence of a contribution to economic development of the host State is 'an essential – although not sufficient – characteristic or unquestionable criterion of the investment', it added that this 'does not mean that this contribution must always be sizable or successful; and, of course, ICSID tribunals do not have to evaluate the real contribution in one way or another to the economic development of the host State, and this concept of economic development is, in any event, extremely broad but also variable depending on the case'.[14]

Critics of the *Salini* award say that its criteria are rigid and not provided by the Washington Convention; that they contradict the choice to let the parties decide in the BITs and therefore might exclude certain operations from the protection of the investments. The preference was clearly therefore to go back to a more economic-oriented conception of the investment, focused on the contribution, profit, durability and risk, but, such an approach is based essentially on the conduct of an individual, whereas from a legal perspective, an investment must be considered in terms of bilateral relationships. For instance, when an aircraft manufacturer sells an aircraft, it is true that it makes a sale, but at the same time it is an investment for the purchasing state.

In the framework of the economic approach, international economic and financial institutions like the World Bank, the International Monetary Fund (IMF) and the Organisation for Economic Co-operation and Development (OECD) promote more operative definitions of investment, putting emphasis on the notions of enterprise, financial operation, economic control, and the idea of durability. It is in this light that the notion of 'direct investment' has been introduced. Their preference

12 *Consortium Groupement L.E.S.I.-DIPENTA v. People's Democratic Republic of Algeria* (10 January 2005) ICSID Case No. ARB/03/8, Award 3.

13 *Mr. Patrick Mitchell* v. *Democratic Republic of the Congo* (1 November 2006) ICSID Case No. ARB/99/7, Annulment Proceedings Regarding the Award 31, footnote 15.

14 *Patrick Mitchell* v. *Democratic Republic of the Congo* (November 2006) ICSID Case No. ARB/99/7, Decision on the Application for Annulment of the Award 33.

goes clearly for a restrictive definition of 'investment'.[15] In summary, the jurisprudence retains the following criteria for the definition of 'investment', while qualifying some as characteristic or essential: contribution, management, profit, risk, durability and contribution to development of the host State.

- *Contribution* is not controversial. It can be in cash, in nature or in industry (see *Bayindir* v. *Pakistan),* and also reputation (management of luxury hotels): *Holiday Inns* v. *Morocco;* but know-how and financial contribution are considered sufficient.
- *Management* implies that the investor must be able to influence significantly the decisions; involvement in the decision-making depends on whether the investment is made, for instance, through a company or state contract.
- *Profit* is essentially contingent and not cannot be considered a true criterion, for there is no obligation to make profit and no guarantee that an investment will absolutely be profitable.
- *Risk* is a characteristic of all economic operations, but political risks are specific to investment, and no legal mechanism can protect it against such risks. Risk is not only for the investor. It can be on both sides, as was the case in *Klöckner* v. *Cameroon*, but very often only the risk borne by the investor is compensatable.
- *Durability* is more a characteristic than a criterion. It refers to the duration of the investment: short-, medium- or long-term investment. It is the opposite of volatility. In Draft Article 30 of the Washington Convention, an investment was considered to be any contribution in money or other assets with an economic dedicated value for an unlimited period of time or for a minimum of five years. In *Salini*, the Tribunal retained a maximum of two years; and so does ICSID jurisprudence in general, as well as the definitions of investment by IMF and OCED. This does not mean that there is a unique duration; some commercial operations may take many years.
- Lastly, the *contribution to economic development of the host State,* which means that investment must have a significant economic and financial impact for the host State: it is a controversial element, mainly because development is a complex notion, with economic, financial, social, cultural aspects, transfer of technology

15 See, for instance, Article 12, Convention Establishing the Multilateral Investment Guarantee Agency; see also UNCTAD, *Scope and Definition. UNCTAD Series on Issues in International Investment Agreements* (UNCTAD/ITE/IIT/11 Vol. II) (New York: United Nations, 1999) 8.

> and know-how, etc. According to some opinion, although at certain periods the focus has been put on the contribution of the investment to the development of the host countries, the main purpose of investment law is not to achieve such an objective.[16]

Nevertheless, one cannot easily come to such a conclusion regarding the 'jurisprudence' of arbitration tribunals. In Malaysian Historical Salvors, SDN, BHD v. Malaysia, the Tribunal stated that the contribution must be substantial, for an investment might be profitable for the investor, but has no impact on the development of the host country. The awards under ICSID are divided between those that consider the contribution to economic development as a criterion for a definition of investment and those for which it is a mere circumstantial characteristic.

This overview of the definition of investment in investment law aimed to show how the most important criterion of such a definition for the host countries, which are essentially from the developing areas of the world, has declined. Nowadays the extremist conception of liberalism in economics triumphs. It is with that in mind that I will now give you some thoughts from a historical perspective of investment in Africa.

2 Investment in Africa from the colonial era to the modern day: from lawless investment to unfair investment law

Having discussed the criteria for defining investment, I would like to put to the forefront the criterion of the contribution to development of host States and see how this contribution has shaped the development of international investment law in Africa. I believe, I am sure you will agree with me, that, though arbitral tribunals may not systematically apply this criterion, it remains the intended purpose, be it in the south or in the north, for attracting FDI. In that regard, to me, investment law should be a balanced one, meaning in essence that it should take into account the interests of host States, as well as the interests of the investor. Historically, the host State's interest for development, or for any other concern, has unsystematically been taken care of; international investment law has mainly developed as a legal regime for protecting foreigners' property. While that paradigm was understandable in the context of European, American and Canadian sovereign States, the particular history – colonial history – of Africa begs the question as to whether that

16 Jean Matringe, 'La notion d'investissement' in Charles Leben, *Droit international des investissements et de l'arbitrage transnational.*

logic should continue to predominate in international investment law. Indeed, it seems that foreign investors have always been dominant over African States, to the extent that international investment law has rather been seen as unfair and unjust, therefore calling for 'international development law'. In fact, whereas investment law is known to be about protecting 'private property', why should the fate of public property not be a concern?

Colonial empires have had an impact on the development path of former colonies through a number of attitudes and operations: the nature of the legal system imported to the colonies. While English common law has been efficient, it is commonly considered that French institutions were not. The model of colonisation was as follows:

- There were colonial settlements as opposed to extractive colonies. Colonial settlements are known to have better protected private property rights.
- The indirect versus direct rule systems imply different administrative and institutional structures with different impacts on development.

In terms of investment law, these approaches to colonial domination have had tremendous consequences. Where Europeans settled, they set up 'institutions encouraging investments', while 'in regions that were not suitable for heavy settlement, they set up extractive colonies with little protection of private property and little checks and balances against government expropriation. At the other extreme, in regions where many Europeans settled, the settlers replicated European institutions with strong emphasis on private property and checks against government power'.[17] 'General European preference was to settle in more prosperous pre-colonial areas, though political factors disturbed this general pattern: … colonised areas that received more Europeans settlers have performed better than colonised areas that received less Europeans settlers. … the negative impact of settlers on institutions was locally overwhelmed by their positive impact on capital investment.'[18]

In any event, be it settlement colonies or extractive colonies, the fact is that the capital remained abundantly within the hands of the colonialist powers, therefore preventing African States to gain their economic independence after the departure of the colonialists in the 1960s. A period of lawless investment was replaced by a system

17 Elise Huillery, 'The Impact of European Settlement within French West Africa: Did Pre-colonial Prosperous Areas Fall Behind?' (2011) 20 (2) *Journal of African Economies* 263.
18 *Ibid.* 267.

of unfair international investment law, whereby African countries found themselves obliged to provide for the protection of those real 'investors' exploiting them.

3 The new economic order of the 1970s: honourable battle for meaningless results?

'Most scholars attribute much of the cause of African underdevelopment to the colonial period and to the political and economic institutions inherited from colonialism.'[19] After independence in the 1960s, Africa discovered the profound inequality of the international economic order in which it was marginalised, with around 2% of the global economy, despite being a resource-rich area. The perpetuation of the inequalities of the colonial era had led to an asymmetrical relationship with the international order and perpetuation of economic dependency. That is why African states largely voted for the demands of a New International Economic Order (NIEO).

Many African countries were then engaged in ambitious development programmes and were very enthusiastic about attracting as many foreign investors as possible. For instance, in 1970 Cameroon, with its large forest resources, decided to build a pulp mill plant, one of the largest in the world. It partnered with a European company, named Klöckner & Co., who claimed to be specialised in that area. The partnership was a total failure, as the plant never functioned: not a single kilogram of pulp came out of that plant which cost Cameroon over 100 billion CFA, a huge amount of money even nowadays. This failure led to the famous *Klöckner* v. *Cameroon* (1990) case before an ICSID Arbitral Tribunal. Cameroon lost the case, mainly because the contract with the foreign investor was not properly drafted and gave room to a very contested interpretation by the Tribunal, but also Cameroon was blamed for not mastering the technological aspects of the contract and relying completely on its foreign partner. In short, there was a double lack of skilled people: lack of skill in contract drafting and a lack of skill in technology transfer. When the case was brought before the Tribunal, there was no-one from Cameroon or indeed from Africa as a judge in that Tribunal. This time it was not because of a lack of skilled people in Africa, but because the African leadership does not trust African skill. A lesson has to be learnt from that.

19 Hugh M. Arnold, 'Africa and the New International Economic Order' (1980) 2 (2) *Third World Quarterly* 296.

Despite the NIEO Declaration and Programme of Action in the 1970s, measures conceded as part of that NIEO had not produced the awaited results. One can argue that NIEO measures have failed to produce the intended results, not least because they were not good measures, but rather because Africa was not ready to engage in the type of economy those measures were purported for.

Having stressed that investment should be intended, at least politically, to contribute to the development of host States, it is hard to see how the NIEO measures have contributed to improving living conditions of many Africans. Not so many FDIs are interested in investing in agriculture, education, health, those very areas where African basic needs are not met. Instead, they concentrate on production of services and products, which are less fit for the consumption of the majority of the rural population.

4 The 1990s and entry into the globalisation era: has Africa missed the boat?

From the 1990s, a fierce competition between African States, whether considered individually or at a regional level, has led to a multiplicity of BITs and regional agreements. As a result, the international legal framework for investment in Africa now consists of over 840 BITs, of which 155 are intra-African and a myriad of regional instruments.[20] Such a situation can only benefit foreign investors, as they are likely to play one country against another or one region against another to obtain the highest standards for the protection of their investment and the lowest tax rates.

Indeed, as has been pointed out by a commentator: 'The provisions included in these investment treaties limit the right of host States to regulate investment; promote investment only indirectly through investment protection; have been drafted on the basis of developed countries' models with little or no modifications (this also holds true for intra-African BITs), and include broad investor-State dispute settlement mechanisms allowing foreign investors to bypass domestic courts and bring international arbitration proceedings that may impact African countries' right to regulate key public policies, such as health, the environment or other social policies.' It is time for African countries to think regionally, and more so, continentally, at least in some areas. Since the economic competition is not mainly bilateral like from

20 See Hamed El-Kady, 'Towards a more effective International Investment Policy Framework in Africa' (2016) 13 (4) *Transnational Dispute Management* www.transnational-dispute-management.com.

the 1960s to the 1980s, the competition is global, meaning with immensely powerful countries like China, India, Indonesia, etc. Therefore, coordination of investment policies between African countries has become imperative.

Concluding remarks

We can praise initiatives like the Organization for the Harmonization of Business Law in Africa (OHADA), although again it is a foreign initiative. It offers supranational mechanisms for settlement of investment disputes based in Abidjan, Côte d'Ivoire, with two branches: one judicial and the other arbitration. Both mechanisms are composed of African judges and arbitrators. Its main weakness is probably that it is mainly based on the civil law system and its membership is, at least for now, made up of only francophone African countries, although it is open to all other countries on the continent.

In any case, intra-African initiatives should be encouraged with the view to settle most investment disputes involving African states or companies in Africa. Above all, African countries should learn from the past and adapt their investment policies to the current international economic context. Firstly, investment is both about the legal framework and access to technology taking part in the world economic fierce competition. As regards access to technology, one cannot expect an investor to give its technology for free. One buys it or one accesses it otherwise. Secondly, investment is being part of the economic competition through economic intelligence. African countries have to build up economic intelligence capacities to make sure, for instance, a plant they want to build will be competitive and will survive competition from other competitors. In short, when we think investment in Africa we should think economic intelligence and strategy. Thirdly, African countries should develop expertise both in drafting investment contracts and in transfer of technology in order to better protect their interests. In the 1980s, most African countries lacked national expertise in these fields. This is not the case anymore. Yet, African states will have recourse to foreign lawyers for the drafting of their contract, and it is extremely rare to see Africans, either as arbitrators or even as lawyers in most international arbitration involving African states or companies. It is not because of a lack of skill, but because of a lack of confidence by African leadership in African skill. This is sad, especially at a moment where young and talented African scholars are known for their expertise throughout the world, including in the developed world. This must be corrected because African self-confidence is a pre-condition for the continent to emerge after Asia as a global player in the world economy in the next half century to come.

2

Global reform versus regional emancipation: the principles on international investment for sustainable development in Africa

*Jean d'Aspremont and Alicia Köppen**

International investment law has been weathering contestation since its inception. It suffices to recall the opposition of capital-importing States to the idea of an international minimum standard expressed in the famous Calvo Doctrine which rejected the standards of compensations for expropriation. Contestation also flared with the rejection of an obligation to provide compensation for the expropriation of foreigners that accompanied the Declaration on the Establishment of the New International Economic Order (NIEO). In that sense, contestation has always been part of investment law practice and discourses. Nowadays, such continuous defiance is even voiced by various actors in capital-exporting States. After all, one of the most publicized instances of criticism came from Europe on the occasion of the Transatlantic Trade and Investment Partnership and the European Union–Canada Comprehensive Economic and Trade Agreement (CETA) negotiations[1] – criticism that arguably resulted in the European Commission's proposal of an investment court system.

As illustrated by these examples, it seems possible to distil two main modes of contestation. On the one hand, contestation can be directed at a reform of the universal investment protection regime as a whole and the adjustment of its rules. This is what is called in this chapter *global reform*. On the other hand, contestation has manifested itself in attempts by certain countries or regions to emancipate themselves from the universal regime with a view to establishing a distinct regional or

* The authors are grateful to Emma Nyhan for her assistance.

1 European Commission, 'Online Public Consultation on Investment Protection and Investor-to-State Dispute Settlement (ISDS) in the Transatlantic Trade and Investment Partnership Agreement' (13 January 2015) http://trade.ec.europa.eu/doclib/docs/2015/january/tradoc_153044.pdf, accessed 20 January 2017, 14.

national practice. This is what is called in this chapter *regional emancipation*. It must be acknowledged that it is not always possible to distinguish neatly between these two modes of contestation, as the challenges of the international investment protection regime may simultaneously borrow from both. Yet, the distinction bears some didactic and cognitive virtues which justify its use in the following paragraphs. In particular, the distinction helps introduce (and delineate the breath of) a remarkable initiative that has been overlooked by the investment law community, namely the adoption by the African Society of International Law (AfSIL) of the Principles on International Investment for Sustainable Development in Africa[2] (hereafter referred to as the AfSIL Principles) on 29 October 2016. It is the ambition of this chapter to discuss and situate the specific mode of contestation of the international investment regime espoused by AfSIL.

The AfSIL Principles boil down to a series of recommendations on international investment law that call for a recalibration of the ways in which international investment law is applied to the African continent. It is submitted in this chapter that the AfSIL Principles constitute an emancipatory form of contestation, whereby the application of the rules of international investment law is tailored to serve political projects valued highly by AfSIL, while falling short of the ambition to revamp the universal investment protection regime.

The following observations shed light on the extent of the emancipation from the international investment protection regime contemplated by AfSIL and situate them against the backdrop of some recent contestations of international investment law. After recalling the drafting history of the AfSIL Principles (Section 1) and some concurrent recent contestations (Section 2), the attention turns to the content and possible adjustment to the international investment protection regime vindicated by AfSIL (Section 3). This short chapter ends with a few concluding remarks on the choice for an emancipatory mode of contestation rather than a reformist type thereof (Section 4).

A preliminary caveat is necessary regarding the formal status of both the rules that are the object of the contestations discussed here and the means through which contestation is articulated. It is important to emphasize that the contestations of the investment protection regime are discussed in the following paragraphs irrespective of the possible customary or conventional nature of the standards being contested or of the measures through which the contestation is raised. Looking at the

2 The Principles can be accessed here: www.cdiph.ulaval.ca/sites/cdiph.ulaval.ca/files/2016_afsil_principles_on_international_investment_for_sustainable_development_in_africa.pdf, accessed 26 February 2019.

contestations of the international investment protection regime from the vantage point of the sources of international law is a project for another day. It must also be stressed that although it evolved towards a very conventional regime in the second half of the twentieth century, international investment law continues to accommodate customary law, thereby making the distinction between conventional investment law and customary investment law very porous.[3]

1 The adoption of the AfSIL Principles

In 2015, AfSIL set up a high-level task force to reflect on recent investment practices within the African continent and prepare recommendations on investment law in Africa. The task force was composed of five renowned international legal scholars who had been advisors to African governments in investment disputes as well as arbitrators. At AfSIL's fifth Annual Conference held in Accra, Ghana, in October 2016, the high-level task force presented a set of fifteen recommendations to AfSIL's Executive Board. On 29 October 2016 at the conclusion of its fifth Annual Conference, the AfSIL General Assembly adopted carefully drafted recommendations enunciating some common ambitions of African countries in their approach to investment on the African continent, i.e. the so-called AfSIL Principles.

2 The AfSIL Principles and concurrent contestations of the investment protection regime

Needless to say that the AfSIL Principles have not been adopted in a vacuum and must be examined against the backdrop of a complex and overlapping web of bilateral, regional and global investment instruments. Looking at the sheer number of instruments designed to influence investment policy in Africa, it becomes clear that the continent is increasingly active in formulating its own preferences regarding investment policy and protection.[4] This is why, before focusing on the contents of

3 On the place of customary law in international investment law, see Jean d'Aspremont, 'International Customary Investment Law: Story of a Paradox' in E. de Brabandere and T. Gazzini (eds.), *Sources of Transnational Investment Law* (Nijhoff, 2012), 5.

4 Makane Mbengue, 'The Quest for a Pan-African Investment Code to Promote Sustainable Development' International Centre for Trade and Sustainable Development, 21 June 2016 www.ictsd.org/bridges-news/bridges-africa/news/the-quest-for-a-pan-african-investment-code-to-promote-sustainable, accessed 20 January 2017; Francesco Seatzu and Paolo Vargiu, 'Africanizing Bilateral Investment Treaties ('BITs'): Some Case Studies and Future Prospects of a Pro-Active African Approach to International Investment' (2015) 30 *Connecticut Journal of International Law* 143.

the AfSIL Principles, attention should turn to a few concurrent contestations of the international investment protection regime with a view to situating the AfSIL Principles and highlighting the specificities of the emancipation they envisage.

(a) UNCTAD's Investment Policy Framework for Sustainable Development

Before examining efforts by African countries and the continent as a whole to reform the international investment protection regime, the global reform envisaged under the Investment Policy Framework for Sustainable Development of the United Nations Conference on Trade and Development (UNCTAD) (hereafter referred to as the UNCTAD Framework) should be mentioned. This is particularly warranted since the UNCTAD Framework served as an inspiration for the AfSIL Principles, which is demonstrated in its preamble.

The UNCTAD Framework was launched in 2012, and updated in 2015, to address the challenge of implementing sustainable development objectives through investment policy at the national and international level.[5] Placing emphasis on but not confined to developing countries' needs, it represents comprehensive expert guidance, detailing different policy options for policymakers and negotiators.[6] The expressed aim of the UNCTAD Framework at the international level is to encourage 'sustainable-development-friendly [International Investment Agreements]'.[7] This broad objective is broken down into ten core principles, one example being 'balanced rights and obligations' for States and investors.[8] Subsequently, corresponding policy options are deduced. Regarding investor obligations, for example, these range from the non-inclusion of any obligations to clauses that deny investors treaty protection under certain circumstances.[9] It is noteworthy, for the sake of argument made here, that the UNCTAD Framework enables both global reform and regional emancipation. Indeed, it aims at ensuring that, on the one hand, investment policy worldwide

5 UNCTAD, *World Investment Report 2012* http://unctad.org/en/PublicationsLibrary/wir2012_embargoed_en.pdf, accessed 7 February 2017, 97; UNCTAD, *World Investment Report 2016* https://unctad.org/en/PublicationsLibrary/wir2012_embargoed_en.pdf, accessed 20 January 2017, 108.

6 UNCTAD, *Investment Policy Framework for Sustainable Development (2015 Edition)* http://unctad.org/en/pages/PublicationWebflyer.aspx?publicationid=1437, accessed 7 February 2017, 25.

7 *Ibid.* 77.

8 *Ibid.* 30.

9 *Ibid.* 109f.

fosters sustainable development and, on the other hand, it simultaneously allows States to cherry-pick from a wide variety of options and tailor investment policy to their individual needs. In this sense, the UNCTAD Framework can be construed as a tool that allows both global reform and regional emancipation.

(b) South Africa's National Investment Policy

South Africa is traditionally among the top recipient countries of foreign investment in Africa.[10] In a move unexpected by many commentators, it chose to shift investment protection from the international to the national sphere by passing the Investment Protection Act (IPA), enacted in December 2015.[11] According to the IPA, foreign investors do not enjoy any access to international arbitration. Instead, their protection is, apart from inter-State arbitration, 'nationalized': investors can either refer a dispute to a single mediator or to the domestic courts. Substantively, the IPA contains several typical investor and investment protections but aligns them with South Africa's laws and its constitution, which translates to a narrower protection, most notably with regard to expropriation. The IPA applies to foreign and domestic investors alike.

The enactment of the IPA was the culmination of a policy review process initiated in 2008. One of the central reasons for South Africa's policy shift was the clash of substantial investor protection as enshrined in bilateral investment treaties (BITs) with its Black Economic Empowerment programme. The conflict between domestic law and international obligations had until then largely gone unnoticed. One of the reasons for this was that many BITs, especially those between South Africa and European countries , were signed from 1994 onwards, even before the South African constitution came into force in 1997.

In *Foresti* v. *South Africa*, [12] one of two notable arbitration cases against South Africa, this clash was exemplified. The dispute was filed under the Belgium-Luxemburg–South Africa BIT in 2006 following the enactment of a new mining

10 UNCTAD, *World Investment Report 2015* http://unctad.org/en/PublicationsLibrary/wir2015_en.pdf, accessed 20 January 2017, 32; but there was a significant decrease in foreign direct investment inflows to South Africa in 2016, see UNCTAD, *World Investment Report 2016* https://unctad.org/en/PublicationsLibrary/wir2016_en.pdf 40, 41.

11 Protection of Investment Act 22 of 2015 www.thedti.gov.za/gazzettes/39514.pdf, accessed 20 January 2017.

12 *Piero Foresti, Laura de Carli* et al. v. *The Republic of South Africa* (4 August 2010) ICSID Case No. ARB(AF)/07/1 59.

and drilling law in 2002, which was designed to, *inter alia*, 'substantially and meaningfully expand opportunities for historically disadvantaged persons … to enter the mineral and petroleum industries and to benefit from the exploitation of the nation's mineral and petroleum resources'.[13] The investor company claimed it was expropriated by the law which converted private ownership of mineral resources into State ownership accompanied by a licensing system through which the previous owners could apply for so-called 'new order rights'. The law also required that at least 26% of the ownership stake in the applying enterprise must be held by black South Africans. The case was eventually settled at the expense of South Africa, as the company was not required to fully meet the ownership stake requirements (5% instead of 26%).[14]

The *Foresti* case constituted one of the main drivers for the ensuing investment policy review process. Indeed, the South African government decided not to renew or renegotiate but to terminate numerous elapsing BITs.[15] The government also decided to refrain from entering into future BITs and instead to develop a domestic framework for investment protection with the enactment of the IPA. By doing away with international standards of foreign investment protection, both procedurally and substantively, South Africa sent out a signal that the best way to ensure a balance between foreign investment protection and the host State's policy interests is to prioritize national (constitutional) law. Until now, no other (African) country seems to have chosen a similar path. This reform, albeit solely focused on the national sphere, represents a specific attempt of emancipation from the global investment protection regime that falls short of any amendment of the latter.

(c) Regional and continent-wide investment peculiarities: SADC Model BIT 2012 and the Draft Pan-African Investment Code

Germane examples for a less radical emancipatory approach are found in the 2012 Southern African Development Community Model Bilateral Investment Treaty (SADC Model BIT), as well as in the 2015 Draft Pan-African Investment Code

13 Article 2d of the Mineral and Petroleum Resources Development Act No. 28 of 2002.

14 Engela C. Schlemmer, 'An Overview of South Africa's Bilateral Investment Treaties and Investment Policy' (2016) 31 (1) *ICSID Review* 167, 186.

15 See UNCTAD Investment Policy Hub International Investment Agreements Navigator http://investmentpolicyhub.unctad.org/IIA/CountryBits/195, accessed 26 February 2019; and Engela C. Schlemmer, 'An Overview of South Africa's Bilateral Investment Treaties and Investment Policy' 189.

(PAIC).[16] SADC is one of fourteen regional economic communities that coexist in Africa. In this elaborate web, the vast majority of African countries retain at least dual membership,[17] while most of these regional economic communities have issued instruments regarding the regulation of foreign investment.

The SADC Model BIT of 2012 is one of the most prominent regional economic instruments. Drafted by representatives from nine of the fifteen SADC Member States with technical support from the International Institute for Sustainable Development (IISD),[18] the SADC template is not a legally binding document. It is intended to serve as a tool that provides a coherent option to SADC Member States in future investment treaty negotiations. For this reason, the SADC Model BIT does not opt for specific policy decisions but presents different choices for each element of an investment treaty. Among the options presented, however, the treaty template indicates clear preferences.

Drafted by independent African experts and reviewed by African Union (AU) experts, the legal status of the PAIC is still unclear. It is formulated as a binding treaty and as such would need to be signed and ratified by the AU Member States in order to enter into force. Moreover, it would complicate its relationship with existing investment treaties, although the PAIC addresses this issue in Article 2. Not unlike the SADC Model BIT, it might remain a draft and, therefore, serve as a treaty template.

A central innovative feature of both instruments is the strong emphasis on the linkage between investment and sustainable development. For instance, Article 1 of the SADC Model BIT provides:

> *The Main objective of this Agreement is to encourage and increase investments ... that support the sustainable development of each Party, and in particular the Host State where an investment is to be located.*

Article 1 of the PAIC provides for a similar objective. In both instruments, the focus on sustainable development serves as a benchmark for streamlining all other draft provisions. Differences between the two may be found in nuances: regarding investor-State dispute settlement (ISDS), for example, the drafters of the SADC

16 SADC, *SADC Model Bilateral Investment Treaty Template with Commentary*, www.iisd.org/itn/wp-content/uploads/2012/10/SADC-Model-BIT-Template-Final.pdf, accessed 20 January 2017; PAIC, *Draft Pan-African Investment Code*, http://repository.uneca.org/handle/10855/23009, accessed 20 January 2017.

17 Makane Mbengue, 'The Quest for a Pan-African Investment Code.

18 SADC, 'SADC Model Bilateral Investment Treaty Template with Commentary' 3.

Model BIT advise treaty negotiators to not include any ISDS provisions in future investment treaties.[19] This recommendation, however, is followed by an acknowledgement that States might decide otherwise and draft ISDS provisions are presented which, *inter alia*, include the obligation to exhaust local remedies. In the PAIC, ISDS is included without any particular reservation but it codifies the exhaustion of local remedies and places an emphasis on an African seat of arbitration.[20] Both instruments include numerous provisions regarding investor obligations enforceable via counterclaims and stress the host State's right to regulate.[21]

The PAIC and the SADC Model BIT both reject the traditional approach of BITs popular in the 1990s and in the 2000s. At the same time, they represent an earlier emancipatory attempt by African countries to tailor investment protection to the overall objective of sustainable development. The primary addressees of the two instruments are, in SADC's case, a regional sub-group of African States and, in the PAIC's case, the AU Member States. Consequently, they can be seen as 'an attempt by African countries to shape an international investment treaty according to their own priorities'.[22]

3 The AfSIL Principles as a mild regional emancipation from the investment protection regime

As mentioned above, reformist projects can be of two kinds: they aim to reform the universal regime as a whole or seek to provide for some regional adjustment. The AfSIL Principles dispel some ambiguity in this respect, as they claim from the outset that their ambition is to soften the universal regime as it is applied to the African continent but not to reform it universally.

It is worth noting that the emancipatory contestation of the AfSIL Principles is not carried out through formal channels. First, the Principles are not legally binding. They are not drafted in treaty language but rather in the form of a

19 SADC, *SADC Model Bilateral Investment Treaty Template with Commentary* (2012) Article 29 'Special Note'.

20 PAIC, *Draft Pan-African Investment Code*, Article 42.

21 SADC. *SADC Model Bilateral Investment Treaty Template with Commentary*, Articles 10–9, Articles 19–24; PAIC. *Draft Pan-African Investment Code*, Article 43.

22 Makane Mbengue, 'The Quest for a Pan-African Investment Code'.

declaration. As such, they are meant to complement the previously presented instruments by formulating the underlying rationales in a more abstract and general way.

Given their non-binding nature, the value of these principles must be found elsewhere. They do not as such derogate from any existing rule of investment law but seek to contribute to a specific interpretation thereof that is more attuned to what is perceived as the needs, priorities and agendas of the African continent. In that sense, they constitute an intervention by AfSIL to steer the making and the interpretation of the rules of the international investment regime in a way that is deemed more favourable to the dominant agenda of Africa.[23]

The principles are not only meant to inform authoritative interpretation of the current investment regime. They also seek to guide African States in the ongoing negotiations of BITs and multilateral investment treaties. As noted by H.E. Marietta Brew Appiah-Oppong, the former Attorney-General and Minister of Justice of Ghana, at the fifth annual conference of AfSIL, the adoption of the Principles marks an important milestone and 'will undoubtedly serve as a useful guide for investment negotiations in the continent'.

Although many of the AfSIL Principles are not norm-creating, the ways in which the AfSIL Principles substantially depart from the common investment protection regime can be summarized as follows. Even the title '2016 AFSIL Principles on International Investment for Sustainable Development in Africa' indicates that sustainable development goals and the interests of the host States should play a central role. This focus fits squarely within the goals of the SADC Model BIT and the Draft Pan-African Investment Code. Principle 1, according to which 'Foreign investment must contribute to the sustainable development of African states', as well as Principles 2 and 3 – linking the right to regulate to the United Nations Sustainable Development Goals and calling for the promotion of only investment that fosters sustainable development – reinforce this commitment.

The overall orientation and concept of AfSIL is a balanced emancipatory reform effort. This is expressly acknowledged in Principle 5, which reads that 'Investment agreements and laws should seek an overall balance of the rights and obligations between states and investors', thereby presuming that no such balance currently exists. In that sense, the AfSIL Principles are more reminiscent of the SADC Model BIT and the PAIC, and differ from the South African contestation which prioritizes the host State's interests in a much more radical way. Nonetheless, the

23 See, for instance, Agenda 2063 of the African Union https://au.int/agenda2063/about, accessed 26 February 2019.

AfSIL Principles place a great emphasis on the State's sovereign right to regulate (Principle 2). Interestingly, such expressed reference to this 'right' – apart from both instruments previously mentioned – is similarly found in recent investment-related treaties, such as European Union–Canada Comprehensive and Economic Trade Agreement (CETA) or the European Union–Vietnam Free Trade agreement. Considerable weight is given to investor obligations, with four of the fifteen principles dedicated to this question (Principles 6–10) – again, one of the innovative features of newer-generation investment treaties mirrored in the AfSIL Principles.[24] Remarkably, the Principles mention ISDS only in passing, with Principle 11 calling for dispute settlement mechanisms that are 'fair, open and transparent, with appropriate safeguards to prevent abuse'. No particular stance is taken on the desirability of ISDS or restrictions to it, which differs from the SADC template or the PAIC.[25]

Another emancipatory feature can be found in the AfSIL Principles' distinction between 'States' in general and 'African States' when formulating duties and obligations towards them. Such differentiation does not appear either in the SADC template or in the PAIC. In the Principles, some provisions, such as the call for a reliable and transparent regulatory framework for investment and a warning against the lowering of standards to attract investment, are directed at States in general (Principles 4 and 6).[26] Other provisions are expressly directed at African States (Principles 12–15), including, *inter alia*, the call for cooperation and coordination of investment policies and for strengthening domestic judicial systems. Moreover, these provisions add an African academic perspective to the project of investment policy reform: Principles 12 and 13 call for the participation of African lawyers and experts in the drafting of investment agreements and for the inclusion of investment law and policy expertise in academic curricula, respectively.

It is expected the AfSIL Principles, irrespective of the absence of formal bindingness and their unpredictable interpretive effects on existing conventional instruments, will prove germane in the continuation of current debates on the investment protection regime, especially in relation to Africa. This is so, even if African

24 SADC, *SADC Model Bilateral Investment Treaty Template with Commentary*, Articles 10–9, Articles 19–24; PAIC, *Draft Pan-African Investment Code*, Article 43.

25 SADC, *SADC Model Bilateral Investment Treaty Template with Commentary*, Article 29 'Special Note'; PAIC, *Draft Pan-African Investment Code*, Article 42.

26 These provisions mirror similar ones in the SADC Model BIT and the PAIC: *SADC Model Bilateral Investment Treaty Template with Commentary*, Article 22.2; PAIC, *Draft Pan-African Investment Code*, Article 37.

States do not have the same weight in the global investment landscape.[27] Indeed, while one of the goals of the AfSIL Principles is to promote harmonization of investment policies and legislation within the continent, they simultaneously capture and formalize the aspiration of many African countries to shape the investment regime in the region, according to their needs and priorities, and constitute another step towards a greater assertiveness of African States in the negotiations and drafting of future investment treaties.

Concluding remarks: regional emancipation rather than global reform

Contestation of the international investment protection regime seems ubiquitous nowadays. As noted earlier, contestation is also heard in capital-exporting States. It even seems to have become a defining practice in international investment law as a whole. It must be acknowledged that contestations, while being located in both the Global North and the Global South, seem more genuine and earnest when they emanate from the latter.[28] This is confirmed by the African contestation that has been discussed here. Indeed, however moderate the emancipation envisaged by the AfSIL Principles may be, it appears much more resolute and considerate than the fashionable dissent also heard in the Global North.

It has been submitted here that contemporary contestations of the investment protection regime can manifest themselves in attempts to reform the global regime as a whole or quests for more regional autonomy, with some contestations borrowing from both modes without making a neat distinction. It has been argued that the mode of contestation chosen by AfSIL, as discussed above, has favoured regional emancipation over global reform. This specific mode of contestation obviously has its merits. At least it seems to reinforce an African identity of some sort, while not alienating the major capital-exporting States. This choice simultaneously vindicates the hope of an investment protection regime that is tailored to regional sensibilities

27 UNCTAD, *World Investment Report 2016*, 39ff.

28 See the renunciation of the ICSID Convention and numerous BITs by Bolivia, Venezuela and Ecuador and the attempts to create regional institutions; KF Gomez, 'Latin America and ICSID: David versus Goliath?' (12 November 2010) SSRN Paper https://papers.ssrn.com/sol3/papers.cfm?abstract_id=1708325, accessed 20 January 2017; Katia Fach Gomez and Catharine Titi, 'UNASUR Centre for the Settlement of Investment Disputes: Comments on the Draft Constitutive Agreement' (2016) 7 (3) *Investment Treaty News Quarterly*. See also the South African investment reform presented above.

and specificities. It remains that the choice for regional emancipation, instead of a global reform, inevitably comes down to a choice by some leading international lawyers of the African continent about how capital flows, how interventions into global inequalities should be designed, and how environmental degradation of the planet should be prevented. Whether this is the best choice for prosperity, distributive justice and environmental protection does not need to be discussed here. The architects of the AfSIL Principles know too well that both global reform and regional emancipation have their distinct costs. They should be credited for standing up for what they believe to be good for Africa and the environment. The debate will go on. And so will the contestation of the international investment protection regime.

3

Foreign investment treaties and the sovereignty of developing host States: ants riding elephants?

Justice Osei-Afriyie

Introduction and background

Foreign investment treaties[1] are one of the key international law mechanisms through which State parties protect and secure the investment of their citizens abroad. Foreign investment treaties set basic standards of legal protection for the investment of foreign investors in the host State. Foreign investment treaties have evolved over the years and as such have taken different forms in their stages of development.[2] The first generation of foreign investment treaties were treaties on Friendship, Commerce and Navigation (FNCs). The second generation of foreign investment agreements developed by home States (capital-exporting countries) has been framed in the form of bilateral investment treaties (BITS), regional and multilateral investment agreements as well as free trade agreements. In recent years there has been an astronomical increase in the number of investment treaties concluded between capital-exporting States and capital-importing States, the majority of which are developing countries. A plethora of reasons have been attributed to the massive increase in the number of foreign investment treaties concluded between developed capital-exporting countries and developing host States. The common rationale is that such agreements promote social and economic development for developing host States.[3]

1 Also known as international investment agreements (IIAs).

2 For a general overview of the historical development of investment treaties, see M. Sornarajah, *The International Law on Foreign Investment* (Cambridge University Press, 2004) Chapter 2. On bilateral investment treaties see S. P. Subedi, *International Investment Law: Reconciling Policy and Principle* (Hart Publishing, 2008) 83.

3 United Nations Conference on Trade and Development, *The Role of International Investment Agreements in Attracting Foreign Direct Investment to Developing Countries* UNCTAD Series on International Investment Policies for Development (New York and Geneva: United Nations, 2009).

Justice Osei-Afriyie

States are the primary subjects of international law. However, the emergence of foreign investment treaties characterised by a vortex of investment protection measures vested in foreign investors have raised certain fundamental issues regarding the rules on customary international law and international relations. Through the use of investor-state dispute settlement clauses in foreign investment treaties paralleled with the granting of most-favoured-nation (MFN) treatment and fair and equitable treatment (FET) clauses, the rights of foreign investors have been strengthened significantly at the expense of developing host States. Trends in the jurisprudence of various arbitral tribunals encapsulate the nature and extent of the conundrum. The interpretations by various investment arbitral tribunals, particularly the World Bank's International Centre for the Settlement of Investment Disputes (ICSID), often go beyond the settled frontiers of customary international rules of standard treatment of foreign investors. In an assiduous attempt to entrench the private rights of investors and promote foreign investment, arbitral tribunals have given expansive and very broad interpretations to the meaning and scope of MFN and FET clauses without taking cognisance of the public policy space of host States. It is the basic contention of this chapter that the legal regime of foreign investment only imposes obligation on sovereign host States without imposing corresponding duties on foreign investors. This makes the relationship between foreign investors and host States unbalanced and, as a result, has undermined the sovereignty of host States. This threatens the legitimacy of the international investment regime.

This chapter is divided into four parts. The first part examines how the international investment law regime resolves competing interests of foreign investors and host States. In order to ascertain the balanced or unbalanced nature of the legal regime of foreign investment, Part 2 looks into some of the substantive rights and obligations of foreign investment treaties and how they have been interpreted by investment arbitral tribunals. The main concern of the penultimate section of the chapter is to find out whether the international investment regime provides a level playing field for both foreign investors and host States. The final part, – the conclusion – discusses the way forward for developing host States in Africa vis-à-vis the international investment law regime. It concludes that South Africa's recent legislation – the Promotion of Investment Act, 2015 – should provide a model for developing States in Africa who aim to achieve a balanced relationship between foreign investors and host States.

1 The architecture of international investment law: balancing competing interests

Foreign investment law is characterised as a regime that seeks to protect two competing interests in linear relationships. Among such competition of interests and relationships are: the protection of interest between the developed home State (capital-exporting country) and the developing host State (capital-importing country) or the North–South divide;[4] and the protection of interest between the private rights of foreign investors and the legitimate public interests of host States. The latter of the underlined relationships is the focus of this chapter. The object is to examine how the international investment law regime balances the private rights and public interests with respect to developing host States' capacity to regulate. It has been argued that treaties on foreign investment in their traditional and current versions place obligations solely on the host State without equal commitments on the part of the foreign investor[5] and this has resulted in restricting the national policy space of sovereign host States to implement their socioeconomic and developmental goals. Some have also argued that the existing law is 'shockingly unsuited to the task of balancing private rights against the interest of the public'.[6] This raises two essential questions. One, do the rights of foreign investors as provided by foreign investment treaties override the sovereign capacity of host States to regulate? The second question, which is seminal to the first, is this: to what extent do the substantive rights and obligations of investment treaties balance the relationship between foreign investors and host States? In order to address both questions, it is essential to consider some of the theoretical arguments that have been put forward to explain the relationship between foreign investors and host States.

According to Professor Brigitte Stern,[7] foreign investment treaties are reciprocal agreements and their objectives are not unidimensional. These traits can be

4 This has been the traditional cause of concern about foreign investment law. See, for example, Roberto Echandi, 'What Do Developing Countries Expect from the International Investment Regime?' in Jose E. Alvarez and Karl P. Sauvant, *The Evolving International Investment Regime: Expectations, Realities, Options* (Oxford University Press, 2011) 3.

5 Rudolf Dolzer and Christoph Schreuer, *Principles of International Investment Law* (2nd edn, Oxford University Press, 2012) 20.

6 Campbell McLachlan, Laurence Shore and Matthew Weinige, *International Investment Arbitration: Substantive Principles* (Oxford University Press, 2008) 21.

7 Brigitte Stern, 'The Future of International Investment Law: A Balance Between the Protection of Investors and the States' Capacity to Regulate' in Jose E. Alvarez and Karl P. Sauvant, *The Evolving International Investment Regime: Expectations, Realities, Options.*

found in the preambles of foreign investment treaties.[8] To Professor Stern, it is the objective of investment treaties to protect the interests of both foreign investor and host States. Through the use of various interpretive techniques, the investment arbitration system has always sought to balance the competing interests of both parties. In the words of Stern: 'it is clear that such preambles can be interpreted to take into account different aspects, and indeed, different approaches have already been used so far to interpret BITs. Such interpretive techniques range from favouring State sovereignty to protecting exclusively private investors 'economic interests'.[9] It can be said that Stern would rebut the argument that foreign investment treaties invest enormous rights in the hands of foreign investors at the expense of host States. Stern would also disagree with the idea that the sovereignty of host States is undermined as a result of the foreign investment law regime. To this end, Stern would conclude that foreign investment law balances the relationship between foreign investors and host States. To Stern, there is no zero-sum game and the foreign investment law regime is a level playing field.

Another interesting theoretical perspective has been espoused by two renowned leading experts of international investment law, namely Professor Rudolf Dolzer and Professor Christoph Schreuer. To them, foreign investment treaties are balanced in terms of seeking the protection of interests between foreign investors and host States. It is their contention that: 'investment treaties do not pit the interests and benefits of the host State against those of the investor. Instead, the motivation underlying such treaties assumes that the parties share a joint purpose … The mode and spirit of investment treaties is to understand the two interests as mutually compatible and reinforcing, held together by the joint purpose of implementing investments consistent with the business plan of the investor and the legal order of the host State.'[10] Dolzer and Schreuer are of the view that the foreign investment law architecture provides a balanced relationship between foreign investors and host States. Similar to the thoughts of Stern, both Dolzer and Schreuer believe that investment treaty law addresses the balance between the recognition of the legitimate public sphere of operation of the host State and the protection of the rights of foreign investors. It is also their firm conviction that the sovereignty of host States is not undermined if the traditional notion of the concept of sovereignty is to be interpreted or seen through the prism of contemporary international economic relations. To Dolzer

8 See the Preamble of the France 2006 Model BIT for an example.

9 Brigitte Stern, 'The Future of International Investment Law: A Balance Between the Protection of Investors and the States' Capacity to Regulate' 191.

10 Rudolf Dolzer and Christoph Schreuer, *Principles of International Investment Law* 21.

and Schreuer, the creation of an investment-friendly climate by States is part and parcel of the modern-day conception of the concept of sovereignty[11] and it should be understood as such. In their words, 'a traditional understanding of the concept of sovereignty detached from current international economic realities may lead to the view that the international rules on foreign investment reach or even cross the lines of what is considered acceptable'.[12] In an investment treaty, the host State deliberately renounces an element of its sovereignty in return for a new opportunity: the chance to better attract new foreign investments which it would not have acquired in the absence of a treaty.[13] Thus according to them, the concept of sovereignty, seen through the lens of modern-day international economic relations and architecture,[14] should not be considered as being eroded by foreign investment treaties. This view is similar to the thinking of Stern, for Dolzer and Schreuer perceive the foreign investment regime as a legal framework that balances the competing interests of foreign investors and host States, but not only that: the regime does not pose a threat to the sovereignty of host States, nor does it constitute a zero-sum game.

The underlined theoretical expositions provide fascinating perspectives on how international law on foreign investment simultaneously resolves competing interests between foreign investors and host States. They all seem to suggest that there is reciprocity of the obligations in investment treaties and that there are mutual benefits that arise from foreign investment treaties. The above indicates that international investment law architecture provides a balanced relationship between host States and foreign investors. In view of this contention, it is important to examine the substantive rights and obligations of foreign investment treaties against the backdrop of the jurisprudence of the investment arbitral tribunals.

11 See, for example, J.E. Vinuales, 'Sovereignty in Foreign Investment Law' in Zachary Douglas, Joost Pauwelyn and Jorge E. Viñuales (eds), *The Foundations of International Investment Law: Bringing Theory into Practice* (Oxford University Press, 2014) 317.

12 R. Dolzer and C. Schreuer, *Principles of International Investment Law* 9.

13 *Ibid.* Similar thinking can be found in the jurisprudence of the Permanent Court of International Justice in the S.S. 'Wimbledon' case in 1923, where the Court held that entry into a treaty is an exercise of a State's right of self-determination: it is in effect an exercise of sovereignty, not a renunciation of it.

14 The threat to sovereignty posed by international economic agreements was one of the issues raised in the recent Comprehensive Economic and Trade Agreement (CETA) between the European Union and Canada. See *The Economist*, 'Hot-air Walloons' (print edition, 22 October 2016).

2 The investor-State dispute settlement mechanism and the substantive rights and obligations of foreign investment treaties

In the light of the aforementioned arguments advanced by Dolzer, Schreuer and Stern, it is important at this stage to identify some of the cardinal features of the investment treaty regime. Apart from the investor-state dispute settlement (ISDS) clauses provided for in foreign investment treaties, the regime also bestows on foreign investors a deluge of substantive rights such as provisions on FET, full protection and security, MFN, the right against/prohibition of expropriation,[15] and legitimate expectation. However, careful examination of arbitral awards with respect to the underlined substantive rights and obligation in foreign investment treaties will assist us in our assessment of the balancing nature or otherwise of the foreign investment law regime.

(a) Fair and equitable treatment

According to Professor Subedi, '[t]he concept of fair and equitable treatment is a major, if not the most important, principle of foreign investment law, and is deeply rooted in customary international law'.[16] The FET principle seems to have originated from the treaty practice of the United States of America (US) in the era of FNCs.[17] Article 1, Section 1, of the 1954 Treaty of Friendship, Commerce and Navigation between the US and the Federal Republic of Germany reads: 'Each Party shall at all times accord fair and equitable treatment to the nationals and companies of the other Party and to their property, enterprise and other interests.'[18] Generally speaking, the purpose of the FET in foreign investment treaties is to require host States to provide a minimum level of protection for investment of foreign investors. Although the FET principle is considered to be emanating from customary international law and foreign investment treaties, its precise meaning as to what it actually amounts to has generated considerable controversies. The

15 See, for example, Graham Mayeda, 'Sustainable International Investment Agreements: Challenges and Solutions for Developing Countries' in Marie-Claire Cordonier Segger, Markus W. Gehring and Andrew Newcombe, (eds) *Sustainable Development in World Investment Law* (Kluwer Law International, 2011) 548.

16 Surya P. Subedi, *International Investment Law: Reconciling Policy and Principle* 63.

17 Rudolf Dolzer and Christoph Schreuer, *Principles of International Investment Law* 130.

18 United States of America and Federal Republic of Germany, *Treaty of Friendship, Commerce and Navigation (with Protocol and exchange of notes)* https://treaties.un.org/doc/publication/unts/volume%20273/volume-273-i-3943-english.pdf.

exercise of the fair and equitable treatment principle has caused and continues to cause challenges for host States. As noted by Professor Subedi, 'violation of the fair and equitable treatment principle by the host state … is the most common allegation made by foreign investors before international investment tribunals'.[19] This is due to the fact that investment treaty law does not provide the precise definition of the concept of the FET principle. This has resulted in considerable and charged debates among law students, legal academics, jurists, international law experts, international law lawyers, as well as the various stakeholders of the investment arbitration system. Investment arbitrators have also been involved in these debates in an attempt to ascertain whether the FET measure contained in foreign investment treaties is the same as espoused by the customary international law principle of international minimum standard or whether it offers an autonomous standard that is additional and higher than general international law.[20] Some argue that FET constitutes an independent treaty standard that goes beyond a mere restatement of customary international law.[21] Notable among them is the distinguished international lawyer, Dr Francis A. Mann who, when writing about the British investment treaty with the Philippines in the early eighties, wrote:

> It is submitted that nothing is gained by introducing the conception of a minimum standard and, more than this, it is positively misleading to introduce it. The terms 'fair and equitable treatment' envisage conduct which goes far beyond the minimum standard and afford protection to a greater extent and according to a much more objective standard than any previously employed form of words. A tribunal would not be concerned with a minimum, maximum or average standard. It will have to decide whether in all circumstances the conduct in issue is fair and equitable or unfair and inequitable. No standard defined by other words is likely to be material. The terms are to be understood and applied independently and autonomously.[22]

19 Surya P. Subedi, *International Investment Law: Reconciling Policy and Principle* 63.

20 For critical discussion on this point see M. Sornarajah, 'The Fair and Equitable Standard of Treatment: Whose Fairness? Whose Equity?' in Federico Ortino *et al.* (eds) *Investment Treaty Law: Current Issues II. Nationality and Investment Treaty Claims. Fair and Equitable Treatment in Investment Treaty Law* (British Institute of International and Comparative Law, 2007) 167.

21 See Rudolf Dolzer and Christoph Schreuer, *Principles of International Investment Law* 134; *Pope & Talbot Inc.* v. *The Government of Canada*, UNCITRAL (2002) 122 ILR 293.

22 *Ibid.* 135. For a full review of Dr. Mann's argument, see F.A. Mann C.B.E, F.B.A., 'British Treaties for the Promotion and Protection of Investments' (1982) 52 (1) *British Yearbook of International Law* 241.

On the other hand, some have argued persuasively that the FET standard is set by customary international law.[23] In this camp, the FET measure contained in various investment treaties is nothing more than what has been espoused by principles of international law. Represented in this camp are the Note and Comments to OECD Draft Convention on the Protection of Foreign Property 1967, the European Parliament Resolution of 6 April 2011 on the Future European International Investment Policy (paragraph 19), Article 1105 of the North American Free Trade Agreement, as well as Article 5, paragraph 1, of the 2012 US Model BIT.

However, it is by far developing host States that have borne the brunt of the exercise of FET rights by foreign investors. This can be seen in the broad and expansive interpretations given by the investor-State dispute settlement system. According to Professor Mayeda of the University of Ottawa, Canada:

> investment tribunals are continually raising the floor that defines the protection that states must provide. Historically, case law and provisions in particular IIAs have identified the floor with the customary international law minimum standard of treatment, which has its origin in The Neer Claim … However, recent investment tribunals have interpreted the fair and equitable treatment standard as entailing a higher level of protection than provided in customary international law. They have done so by requiring the host state to protect the basic business expectations of investors when they invested in the host state and to provide a stable and predictable investment environment.[24]

The following two cases illustrate how arbitral tribunals have interpreted the FET standard against host States. The awards highlight the plight of host States in their encounter with the dispute settlement mechanism of the international investment law regime. The cases underline as well the nature of the relationship between foreign investors and host States as bequeathed by the international investment law regime. The also cases undermine the sovereign capacity of the host State to regulate.

The case of *MTD* v. *Chile*[25] concerned a foreign investment contract signed on behalf of Chile for the construction of a large planned community which failed because it turned out to be inconsistent with zoning regulations in Chile. The Tribunal applied a provision in the BIT between Chile and Malaysia requiring that 'investments of investors of either Contracting Party shall at all times be

23 Rudolf Dolzer and Christoph Schreuer, *Principles of International Investment Law* 135.

24 Graham Mayeda, 'Sustainable International Investment Agreements: Challenges and Solutions for Developing Countries'.

25 *MTD Equity Sdn. Bhd. and MTD Chile S.A.* v. *Republic of Chile* (25 May 2004) ICSID Case No. ARB/01/7, Award.

accorded fair and equitable treatment'. Relying on the standard of FET as defined in *Tecmed* v. *Mexico*,[26] the Tribunal emphasised a duty by the host State to adopt proactive behaviour in favour of the foreign investor and held that: 'fair and equitable treatment should be understood to be treatment in an even-handed and just manner, conducive to fostering the promotion of foreign investment'. The Tribunal emphasised that the BIT terms are framed as a proactive statement – 'to promote', 'to create', 'to stimulate' – rather than prescriptions for passive behaviour by the state or avoidance of prejudicial conduct to the investors.[27] On this basis, the Tribunal found that the FET standard had been violated by the host State, namely, Chile.[28]

The case of *Desert Line* v. *Yemen*[29] concerned contracts for the construction of asphalt roads. A dispute between the parties involved armed threats and the arrest of some of the investor's personnel. Local arbitration resulted in an award of certain sums to the claimant who was, however, subsequently given a much reduced amount in a settlement agreement. The Tribunal found that the settlement agreement had been imposed upon the claimant under physical and financial duress. In the resulting award, the Tribunal took the unusual step of awarding not only damages for the alleged violation of the FET standard by the host State but additionally, the Tribunal awarded moral damages in the amount of USD 1 million.[30]

The above cases indicate that the application of the fair and equitable standard do not take into consideration the public interests of host States. It also highlights the fact that in arbitral awards, the private rights of foreign investors override the public interests of host States. It must be stressed that the interpretation of the FET standard by the investment arbitration does not exhaust the theoretical picture painted earlier on by Dolzer, Schreuer and Stern. This is because the majority of the arbitral awards appear to give prominence to private rights of foreign investors at the expense of the regulatory powers of host States. Some host States have begun to learn lessons from the expansive interpretation of the FET standard by investment arbitral tribunals. For example, the US and Canada have withdrawn from the

26 *Técnicas Medioambientales Tecmed, S.A.* v. *The United Mexican States* (29 May 2003) ARB (AF)/00/2.

27 *Ibid.* 113.

28 See Rudolf Dolzer and Christoph Schreuer, *Principles of International Investment Law* 143.

29 *Desert Line Projects LLC* v. *The Republic of Yemen* (6 February 2008) ICSID Case No. ARB/05/17, Award 48.

30 Rudolf Dolzer and Christoph Schreuer, *Principles of International Investment Law* 159–60.

expansive standard and reinterpreted the fair and equitable standard to ensure that the standard is construed narrowly.[31] Other States have avoided reference to the FET standard in their foreign investment treaties. For example, the investment provisions of the Comprehensive Economic Cooperation Agreement between India and Singapore contain no reference the FET standard. India, South Africa and China have also avoided references to the FET standard.

(b) *Most-favoured-nation treatment*

MFN treatment is one of the substantive obligations that forms part of the international investment law architecture. Like the FET standard, it is one of the oldest and most important principles of both foreign investment law and the law of international trade.[32] MFN clauses in foreign investment treaties basically require host States to treat investors in similar ways without discrimination on the basis of nationality. As held in the arbitral award in *Tza Yap Shum* v. *Peru*,[33] the effect of an MFN clause in a bilateral investment treaty is to widen the rights of the investor.[34] It is a right enjoyed by the foreign investor in its relationship with the host State. It is a relative standard because it depends for its reach and scope on the conduct of the particular State. The MFN clause may not have any practical significance if the State concerned fails to grant any relevant benefit to a third party.[35] However, as soon as the State confers a relevant benefit, it is automatically extended to the beneficiary of the MFN clause. Put differently, if a host State is party to many different investment agreements, MFN provisions may import the standards from other agreements into the investment treaty if the provisions of those agreements provide for higher levels of protection than the later investment treaty. The ICSID award in *Maffezini* v. *Spain*[36] spelt out the nature and scope of the MFN rights. The Tribunal held, *inter alia*, that an investor may be entitled to the most favourable dispute resolution process in all foreign investment treaties signed by the host State even if the

31 See M Sornarajah, 'The Fair and Equitable Standard of Treatment: Whose Fairness? Whose Equity?' 167.

32 The MFN clauses have formed part of international economic treaties for centuries. See Rudolf Dolzer and Christoph Schreuer, *Principles of International Investment Law* 143.

33 *Tza Yap Shum* v. *The Republic of Peru* (19 June 2009) ICSID Case No. ARB/07/6, Decision on Jurisdiction 196.

34 Rudolf Dolzer and Christoph Schreuer, *Principles of International Investment Law* 143.

35 *Ibid.* 206.

36 *Emilio Agustín Maffezini* v. *The Kingdom of Spain* (13 November 2000) ICSID Case No. ARB/97/7, Award.

process differs from that provided for by the investment treaty with the State of which the investor is a national. What is found to be enigmatic about MFN rights in investment treaties is their scope of application. As held by the ICSID Tribunal in the *Maffezini* case, the MFN right is not limited only to substantive rights[37] found in investment treaties but its reach also encompasses international dispute settlement mechanisms. The Tribunal in the *Maffezini* case held that: unless it appears clearly that the State party to a BIT, or the parties to a particular investment agreement, settled on a different method to resolve any dispute that may arise, MFN provisions in BITs should be understood to be applicable to dispute settlement.[38]

The decision in the *Maffezini* case has given foreign investors unilateral and undemocratic powers to drag host States into dispute settlement mechanisms that were not stated or even contemplated in the investment treaty between the home and host States concerned. This concern has been expressed by Professor Subedi, who states that 'such extension of the application of the MFN principle to dispute settlement provisions had allowed foreign investors to resort to dispute settlement mechanisms that were not stipulated or envisaged in the BIT between the home and host States concerned, but rather had been provided for in another BIT to which the host State was a party'.[39] It can be said that, as far as the interpretation of the MFN clauses in investment treaties by arbitral tribunals are concerned, the host State is put at the receiving end in its relationship with the foreign investor. This goes to indicate the unbalanced nature of the relationship between foreign investors and host States.

(c) Full protection and security

One of the substantive obligations that has evolved in foreign investment treaties is the concept of 'full protection and security'. The principle of full protection and security puts the burden of responsibility on host States to ensure that reasonable steps are taken by the host State to protect the investment of foreign investors in its territory. However, as a norm, the principle of full protection and security lacks a universally accepted definition. Different parties have claimed different levels of protection under this principle[40] and as a result this has led to different

37 In *Bayindir Insaat Turizm Ticaret Ve Sanayi A.S.* v. *Islamic Republic of Pakistan*, ICSID Case No. ARB/03/29, Decision on Jurisdiction, (14 November 2005), the Arbitral Tribunal found that an MFN clause would permit the invocation of an FET clause contained in another BIT.

38 *Ibid.* 49.

39 Surya P. Subedi, *International Investment Law: Reconciling Policy and Principle* 69.

40 Surya P. Subedi, *International Investment Law: Reconciling Policy and Principle* 66.

interpretations by investment arbitral tribunals. Nevertheless, there is broad consensus that the standard does not provide absolute protection against physical or legal infringement.[41] Under the international law principle of State responsibility, host States are not placed under an obligation of strict liability to prevent such violations. Instead, it is generally accepted that host States will have to exercise 'due diligence' and will have to take such measures to protect the foreign investment as are reasonable under the circumstances.[42]

In *Noble Ventures* v. *Romania* (2005),[43] the Tribunal held that the phrase 'full protection and security' should not be understood as being wider in scope than the general duty to provide protection and security of foreign nationals found in the customary international law of aliens, which was limited to requiring due diligence to be exercised by the State.[44] The thinking in *Noble Ventures* and the International Court of Justice decision in the *ELSI* case[45] generally reflect the position of foreign investment treaties. Some of the treaties have emphasised that what is expected under 'full protection and security' is the level of police protection required under customary international law.[46] Notwithstanding this position, host States have been punished by foreign investors as a result of the interpretation of the principle by investment tribunals. In *AAPL* v. *Republic of Sri Lanka*,[47] the ICSID Tribunal held that the counter-insurgency operation by the Sri Lanka security forces were unwarranted and excessive and thus violated the foreign investor's right to full protection and security within the territory of Sri Lanka. To the Tribunal, Sri Lanka had breached the standard by failing to take precautionary measures, including the removal of employees from the farm, before launching the offensive.[48] In *Wena Hotels* v. *Egypt*,[49] the Tribunal found Egypt liable under the standard of full protection and security because employees of a State entity had seized the hotel in question and because the police authorities had been aware

41 Rudolf Dolzer and Christoph Schreuer, *Principles of International Investment Law* 161.

42 *Ibid.*

43 *Noble Ventures, Inc.* v. *Romania* (12 October 2005) ICSID Case No. ARB/01/11, Award.

44 *Ibid.*

45 *Elettronica Sicula S.p.A. (ELSI) (USA* v. *Italy)* (1989) *ICJ Reports* 15.

46 Surya P. Subedi, *International Investment Law: Reconciling Policy and Principle* 67.

47 *Asian Agricultural Products Ltd.* v. *The Republic of Sri Lanka* (27 June 1990) ARB/87/3.

48 *Ibid.* 284.

49 *Wena Hotels Ltd.* v. Arab Republic of *Egypt* (8 December 2000) ICSID Case No. ARB/98/4, Award.

of the seizure and had not acted to protect the investor before or after the invasive action.[50] The last straw in this respect is the ICSID Tribunal decision in *Biwater Gauff* v. *Tanzania*.[51] In this case, the Tribunal confirmed that the guarantee of 'full security' extends to actions both of the host State and of third parties.[52] According to the ICSID Tribunal, 'full protection' implies 'a State's guarantee to stability in a secure environment, both physical commercial and legal'.[53] These cases confirm the claim that the foreign investment regime has increasingly undermined the sovereignty of host States. If a host State can be dragged to an unaccountable foreign court[54] by foreign investors for exercising its regulatory functions, including the police powers of the State, then there is more to be said about the sovereign capacity of States in international law.

(d) Expropriation

By international law standards, States have the right to lawful expropriation. That is to say, host States can interfere with the proprietary interests of foreign investors without adequate compensation. Expropriation constitutes one of the major substantive obligations of the international investment law regime. Expropriation has been defined as 'the taking of assets of foreign companies or investors by a host State against the wishes or without the consent of the company or investor concerned. It includes deprivation of the right to property owned by foreign companies'.[55] Both customary international law and investment treaty law[56] empowers host States to

50 *Ibid.* 84.

51 *Biwater Gauff (Tanzania) Ltd.* v. *United Republic of Tanzania*, (24 July 2008) ICSID Case No. ARB/05/22, Award.

52 *Ibid.* 730.

53 *Ibid.* 729.

54 For a critical review of the legitimacy of the investor-State dispute settlement mechanism, see, for example, the comment by M. Sornarajah, 'The Fair and Equitable Standard of Treatment: Whose Fairness? Whose Equity?' 173.

55 Surya P. Subedi, *International Investment Law: Reconciling Policy and Principle* 120.

56 State practice has considered this right to be so fundamental that even modern investment treaties (often entitled agreements 'for the promotion and protection of foreign investment') respect this position. See Rudolf Dolzer and Christoph Schreuer, *Principles of International Investment Law* 89.

exercise such rights provided certain basic conditions are satisfied cumulatively,[57] namely: the host State measure is for a public purpose; it is non-discriminatory; and payment of prompt, adequate and effective compensation is made once the measure is carried out by the host State. It must be noted that the exercise of this right by host States is in consonance with the classical rules on international law with respect to the notion of territorial sovereignty. However, as noted by Professor Subedi, international law imposes certain restrictions on the exercise of economic sovereignty by States.[58] By the very act of inviting and admitting foreign investors into the country, the State concerned voluntarily accepts limitation on its sovereignty and subjects itself to the rules of international investment law.[59]

It is worth mentioning at this juncture that recent decisions of international investment tribunals have interpreted the protection against expropriation broadly in a way that restrict the host State's capacity to regulate. Such broad interpretation highlights the fact that private interests override the regulatory space of host States. The meaning of expropriation was broadly defined in *Middle East Cement Shipping* v. *Egypt.*[60] This award concerned the revocation of a free zone license through the prohibition of import of cement into Egyptian territory. The Tribunal found that the import prohibition by the Egyptian Government amounted to an indirect taking of the foreign investor's investment. Equally in *Goetz* v. *Burundi*[61], an ICSID Tribunal had to rule on the revocation by the host State of a free-zone status accorded to a foreign investor. Although there had been no formal taking of property, the Tribunal had no difficulty in finding that the actions of the Government of Burundi constituted a measure that had an effect similar to expropriation.

57 *ADC Affiliate Limited and ADC & ADMC Management Limited* v. *The Republic of Hungary*, Award (2 October 2006) ARB/03/16; James Crawford and Karen Lee (eds) *ICSID Reports Volume 15* (Cambridge University Press, 2010) 429–33.

58 Surya P. Subedi, *International Investment Law: Reconciling Policy and Principle* 122.

59 *Ibid.*

60 *Middle East Cement Shipping and Handling Co. S.A.* v. *Arab Republic of Egypt*, (12 April 2002) ICSID Case No. ARB/99/6, Award; James Crawford and Karen Lee (eds) *ICSID Reports Volume 7* (Cambridge University Press, 2005) 178.

61 *Antoine Goetz* et al. v. *The Republic of Burundi*, ICSID Case No. ARB/95/3, Award (10 February 1999); Meg Kinnear and Campbell McLachlan QC (eds) *ICSID Review Foreign Investment Law Journal*, 15 (Oxford University Press, 2000) 457.

(e) Legitimate expectation

The concept of 'legitimate expectation' has evolved as one of the principal pillars of the international investment law regime. Unlike substantive obligations found in foreign investment treaties, such as the protection of full security and the FET requirements, the notion of legitimate expectation has received recognition in international investment regime through the workings of the investment dispute settlement mechanism. As a concept, legitimate expectation was introduced into the legal relations between foreign investors and host country governments to denote that the latter cannot act contrary to certain expectations they have set in the past.[62] However, there is no clear-cut framework that spells out what those expectations actually amount to before foreign investors can assert the violation of such rights by host States. Nevertheless, the practice of the investment dispute settlement mechanism has emphasised that such expectations can be relevant under certain substantive obligations of foreign investment treaties, such as the principles of fair-and-equitable treatment and indirect expropriation articles in foreign investment treaties.[63] This means that the enjoyment of such rights by foreign investors can be invoked on the basis of a breach of a substantive obligation by the host State. Thus foreign investors can claim breach when host States fail to fulfil expectations based on some sources. Dr Karl P. Sauvant and Dr Günes Ünüvar have identified three of such sources as: host States' written commitments to investors (e.g. contractual commitments beyond mere contractual expectations); host States' representations with respect to specific investments (e.g. direct and public endorsements); or host States' unilateral representations (e.g., favourable regulatory frameworks as existed at the time of an investment).[64]

It is important to note that since the early 2000s, foreign investors have claimed a breach of legitimate expectations by host States in investor-State arbitration. However, Dr Sauvant and Dr Ünüvar raise the question: can host States too have legitimate expectations against foreign investors concerning the latter's behaviour within their economies, absent any specific investor obligations in foreign investment agreements?[65] In raising the question above, both Sauvant and Ünüvar point out that the concept of legitimate expectation in international

62 Karl P. Sauvant and Günes Ünüvar, 'Can Host Countries Have Legitimate Expectations?' (29 November 2016) *Columbia FDI Perspectives* 183.

63 *Ibid.*

64 *Ibid.*

65 *Ibid.*

investment law should be seen as two sides of the same coin. While foreign investors have the right to rely on certain pronouncements made by host States with respect to the investment, host States on the other hand have equal rights to count on investors' written commitments and representations (such as contractual infrastructural commitments concerning the quality of services such as water and sanitation) to the host States.[66] In their words: 'assessing the legitimacy of expectations involve an inherent, context-bound balancing of investors' and States' expectations. Arguably, in fact, even the assessment of investor' legitimate expectations under the current approach should require that a State's legitimate expectations are taken into account.'[67] Just like the other underlined provisions of international investment law, the discourse on the notion of legitimate expectation shows that much is required from host States in their relationship with foreign investors. In order to achieve a balanced relationship with respect to the concept of legitimate expectation, there is the need for the international investment law architecture to reconcile competing public interests of host States and those of foreign investors.

3 A zero-sum game? How level is the level playing field?

The foregoing review of the treatment and interpretation of the substantive rights and obligations by investment arbitration reveals that host States are disadvantaged. The review has also brought to light some of the structural bias of the foreign investment regime. Having identified the structural and substantive biases of the international investment law regime, this chapter will now address the initial issues of concern raised in the introduction, viz, whether the investment regime is unbalanced and as such has reined in the national policy space of host States. To start with, as far as the legal relationship between foreign investors and host States are concerned, the foreign investment regime does not create a level playing field for host States. This bias is not by accident but by design – *the default setting* of the foreign investment regime. Although the elements of reciprocity and mutuality of benefits are clearly spelt out in the preambles of investment treaties, host States have always been disadvantaged when it comes to their engagement with foreign investors in investment arbitration. The investor-State dispute settlement mechanism

66 See, for example, *Sempra Energy International* v. *Argentina* (2005) ICSID Case No ARB/02/16; *Biwater Gauff (Tanzania) Ltd.* v. *United Republic of Tanzania* (24 July 2008) ICSID Case No. ARB/05/22, Award.

67 *Ibid.*

of the regime pits host States that have broader responsibilities beyond those of the investor, against a foreign investor with fewer duties and whose primary focus is on profit maximisation.[68] In the words of Dolzer and Schreuer: 'In deciding between the investor's right to stability and the State's right to regulate, some tribunals have weighed the investor's legitimate expectations against the State's duty to act in the public interests.'[69] Although I share the same view, I, however, found the earlier assertion made by Professor Dolzer and Professor Schreuer regarding the balanced nature of the investment regime to be paradoxical in this respect.

Secondly and closely related to the first point is that the international investment regime restricts the 'policy space' of host States. The regime does not give flexible policy space for governments of host States to respond to the public welfare needs of their local residents.[70] This has generated vitriolic opposition to the investment regime. Such concerns have been highlighted by the public statement issued by the Osgood Hall Law School in 2010. It stated a 'shared concern for the harm done to the public welfare by the international investment regime' and in particular, how it 'hampers the ability of governments to act for their people in response to the concern of human development and environmental sustainability'.[71]

Conclusion

The thesis of this chapter is that the scale of balance of the foreign investment regime is skewed against the legitimate interest of host States. Whilst seeking to protect the interest of foreign investors, the foreign investment regime has stopped host States from effectively discharging their public welfare duties. The regime has also undermined the capacity of developing host States to achieve their developmental goals. These threaten the legitimacy of the international investment law regime. For instance, Indonesia recently refused to accept awards by the investment arbitration.

68 Graham Mayeda, 'Sustainable International Investment Agreements: Challenges and Solutions for Developing Countries' 541.

69 Rudolf Dolzer and Christoph Schreuer, *Principles of International Investment Law* 149, but see José E. Alvarez, *The Public International Law Regime Governing International Investment* (Brill, 2011) 389 where he argues, *inter alia*, that there is much less evidence to support the view that investor-State arbitration is itself necessarily biased in favor of pro-investor outcomes.

70 See, for example, José E. Alvarez, *The Public International Law Regime Governing International Investment* (Brill, 2011) 340.

71 *Ibid.*

Some States have made public pronouncements to withdraw from the ICSID investor-State dispute settlement mechanism. Apart from the refusal of some States to make references to FET clauses in their foreign investment treaties, there have also been a lot of antisuit injunctions being issued against investment arbitrations.

(a) Are there lessons for developing host States?

Developing countries have always been the traditional recipients of foreign investment. They have welcomed it for a variety of reasons – it is considered as an engine of economic growth; it provides capital; it is a source of foreign currency, skills and technology. These notwithstanding, developing host States have faced enormous claims which are, in some instances, in excess of their national reserves as a result of foreign investment treaties. There are reports that the claims made in one year in *Hubco*, *SGS*, *Salineri* and other awards against Pakistan put together, exceeded the national reserves of Pakistan.[72] Moreover, the cases of *Biwater Gauff*,[73] *CMS Gas*[74] and *Piero Foresti*[75] are some of the many instances of the investment regime's blatant disregard for the obligation of developing host States to promote the socioeconomic development of their residents, as well as their sovereign and constitutional capacity to regulate. Furthermore, it has become evident that foreign investment treaties inhibit the ability of governments of developing countries to protect their environment from the nefarious activities of mining companies.[76] The jurisprudence of arbitral awards has also raised questions about the unbalanced nature of the international investment law regime, as well as the notion of Western economic development institutions that foreign investment promotes economic growth for developing countries.

72 M. Sornarajah, 'The Fair and Equitable Standard of Treatment: Whose Fairness? Whose Equity?'180.

73 *Biwater Gauff (Tanzania) Ltd* v. *United Republic of Tanzania*, ICSID Case No. ARB/05/22.

74 *CMS Gas Transmission Company* v. *the Argentine Republic*, ICSID Case No. ARB/01/8.

75 *Piero Foresti, Laura de Carli* et al. v. *The Republic of South Africa*, ICSID Case No. ARB(AF)/07/01.

76 Joseph Stiglitz, 'Investment Bill Marks a Shift in South Africa's Trade Policy', *Business Day* (4 November 2013).

(b) What then is the way forward for developing host States in Africa?

The reappraisal of the international investment law regime has been started by many developing countries in Africa. Some bold initiatives have been taken at the national level, such as South Africa's recently enacted Investment Promotion Act 2015 and there are efforts to formulate investment treaties at the regional level as well. Notable examples include the Economic Community of West African States (ECOWAS) Model BIT and the Southern African Development Community (SADC) Model BIT. However, a very careful approach has to be taken on both fronts of bilateralism and regionalism by developing countries in Africa, for it has been argued, for instance, that the ECOWAS Common Investment Code reflects the same traditional measures contained in the US and Canadian Model BITs that have encumbered developmental goals of developing host States.[77] Nevertheless, it is submitted that the South African Protection of Investment Act 2015 is a step in the right direction. This is because the 2015 Act addresses almost all of the challenges posed by the traditional foreign investment regime. For example, Section 4 balances the competing interests between foreign investors and the host State to ensure that the public interest is given the required priority in investment arbitration. Section 8 also removes the FET provisions. Now in South Africa, it is the elephant that controls the show not the ant.

77 See, for example, Muna Ndulo, *Bilateral Investment Treaties, the Settlement of Investment Disputes, and Developing Countries* (Monograph, 2016).

4

Les contrats miniers déséquilibrés à l'épreuve des Principes d'Unidroit relatifs aux contrats du commerce international

Mahamat Atteib

L'idée d'équilibre est inhérente à la norme juridique. Hérité du droit naturel, promu parfois par le juge en droit positif, au cœur de la technique contractuelle, l'équilibre des prestations est une problématique bien connue en droit des contrats miniers. Les récentes modifications législatives[1] en Afrique et les processus de révision des contrats miniers initiés par certains pays[2] sont largement impulsés par une volonté de rééquilibrage des droits et devoirs des Etats et des entreprises minières.[3]

En droit des investissements miniers, on constate que le déséquilibre contractuel a été d'emblée analysé par rapport au statut de l'Etat. Partant du postulat que l'Etat a des pouvoirs exorbitants pouvant altérer ou anéantir le contrat, on a mis en place un régime juridique renforcé de protection de l'investisseur. Une telle protection s'inscrivait dans l'optique d'atténuer le déséquilibre statutaire présupposé et ses implications corrélatives en oubliant au même moment que l'Etat en question peut être un jeune Etat, politiquement et économiquement fragile (cas des États nouvellement indépendants). Aujourd'hui encore, on se retrouve avec un régime juridique des investissements étrangers impulsé par des théories juridiques à la neutralité suspecte et dominé par un droit conventionnel presque asymétrique.

1 La Guinée en 2011, la Côte d'Ivoire en 2014, le Burkina Faso en juin 2015 et le Sénégal en 2016, ont mis en place de nouveaux codes miniers. Plus récemment, le Tchad (2018), le Mali et le Gabon (2019) ont également mis en place de nouveaux codes miniers.

2 On peut citer les processus entamés par la République Démocratique du Congo à partir de 2007 et la Guinée, presque au même moment, qui ont connu un grand retentissement dans l'actualité continentale. Nous pouvons citer à titre d'illustration, pour la Guinée, le Décret D/2012/045/PRG/SGG portant modalités de mise en œuvre d'un programme de revue des titres et conventions miniers par la Convention Nationale des Mines.

3 Voir notamment Article 2 de la loi L/2011/006/CNT portant Code minier de la Guinée.

Un tel constat est fort justifié en Afrique. En effet, le contexte révèle l'existence des grandes multinationales minières économiquement puissantes et rompues aux techniques de négociation face à des Etats récents économiquement et politiquement instables. Il s'en suit infailliblement des partenariats à l'équilibre précaire et au déséquilibre presque congénital.

La notion de déséquilibre des prestations est généralement définie comme un défaut d'équivalence des droits et devoirs contractuels. Cet état de fait préjudiciable pour une partie et corrélativement profitable à l'autre, peut se rattacher à la période de conclusion du contrat ou se réaliser lors de son exécution. C'est ainsi que l'on retrouve la distinction classique entre la lésion et l'imprévision respectivement comme déséquilibre contemporain de la conclusion du contrat et déséquilibre lié à son exécution. Aujourd'hui, les exigences d'équilibre contractuel traversent toute la vie de la vie du contrat de la phase précontractuelle à la phase post-contractuelle. Initial ou ultérieur, « léger » ou fondamental, psychologique ou matériel, économique ou intellectuel, le déséquilibre n'est pas toujours aisé à saisir de façon concrète. Néanmoins, l'approche analytique et systémique d'obligations contractuelles permet d'apprivoiser ce phénomène à la lisière du droit, de l'économie et de la morale. Ainsi, certaines obligations dans les conventions minières sont dites corrélatives. Il en est ainsi de l'obligation de l'Etat de mettre à la disposition de l'investissement minier la superficie à exploiter, créant corrélativement l'obligation de l'investisseur de lui verser une participation initiale dite « gratuite » en contrepartie du droit d'exploitation concédé.[4]

Ce déséquilibre peut se retrouver dans divers instruments juridiques, parmi lesquels on retrouve les contrats miniers, pouvant lier les Etats aux sociétés minières. Ceux-ci sont appréhendés comme des engagements par lesquels l'Etat s'engage avec une entreprise généralement privée et étrangère chargée d'exploiter ses ressources minières en contrepartie d'un prix. Ces contrats sont généralement désignés comme des contrats d'investissement, des contrats d'Etat, des contrats internationalisés, des contrats administratifs, des 'quasi-traités' internationaux et parfois dans un élan quasi désespéré des contrats sui generis. Si l'exercice de qualification contractuelle est déterminant dans l'analyse du déséquilibre des prestations, il est important de noter que l'objet de cette étude n'est pas de retenir à l'avance une qualification au détriment d'une autre. Il s'agit à tout le moins, à partir d'une approche volontairement fonctionnelle, d'approcher le phénomène partant des règles matériellement applicables.

En effet, pour pallier en effet au déséquilibre contractuel dans les contrats miniers, plusieurs instruments juridiques sont généralement mobilisés. Certains

4 Il est important de noter que cette participation n'est pas systématiquement exigée dans toutes les législations minières.

instruments peuvent être spécifiques au droit minier. Il en est ainsi de la licence de rétention mise en place par le Code minier de la Gambie aux termes de laquelle l'investisseur, nonobstant la découverte d'un gisement commercialement exploitable, peut solliciter et obtenir une autorisation de suspension des activités de développement minier en raison notamment d'un contexte économique défavorable.[5] De façon plus explicite et plus complète, le code minier du Gabon de 2019 consacre le principe d'équilibre qu'il définit en son article premier et dresse le contenu en tant que « principe d'ordre public qui régit l'octroi des avantages dans toute convention minière en phase d'exploitation ». L'article précise que ce principe « requiert que les avantages, notamment juridiques, fiscaux, douaniers et économiques soient accordés dans le strict respect de l'équilibre global entre la rentabilité de l'investissement pour l'opérateur et sa portée économique pour l'État, notamment en termes de contribution aux finances publiques, ainsi qu'au développement socio-économique ». Le principe d'équilibre, précise l'article premier, « interdit l'octroi d'avantage sans cause, excessif et préjudiciables au droit de jouissance inaliénable dans l'exploitation minière ». Dans le même élan, cet article précise enfin que ce principe « garantit le droit, pour tout opérateur, à un régime conventionnel favorable aux conditions de rentabilité de son investissement ». D'autres mécanismes sont tirés du droit commun des contrats et se proposent avec une certaine marge d'adaptation aux contrats miniers. Il en est ainsi de la lésion, l'imprévision, l'obligation essentielle, l'exigence de bonne foi, la théorie des bénéfices excessifs[6] dérivée de l'idée d'abus de droit ou encore les attentes légitimes.[7] Aussi, des engagements anodins a priori de règlement de différends ou de droit applicable, paraissent dans une double perspective d'analyse systémique et substantielle du contrat, comme des données à fort potentiel dans une démarche de conciliation harmonieuse d'intérêts contractuels.

Ces différents mécanismes peuvent être tous capitalisés par les parties contractantes ou le tribunal compétent sous réserve de leur conformité au droit applicable. Ainsi, le test préliminaire auquel sont soumis les contrats miniers déséquilibrés est le droit applicable à ces contrats. C'est à partir de cette variable que l'on pourrait en effet envisager le rejet ou l'admission et la correction le cas échéant du déséquilibre

5 Gambia's Mines and Quarries Act 2005, Section 34, Part 4.

6 Voir Claude Imperiali « Les Bénéfices Excessifs, une Pratique Limitée et Controversée » dans *Annuaire Français de Droit International* (1978) 24 678.

7 Voir Yenkong Ngangjoh Hodu, « The Concept of Legitimate Expectations in Investment Arbitration » (October 2013) *European Journal of International Law*; voir également Karl P. Sauvant and Günes Ünüvar, « Can Host Countries Have Legitimate Expectations? » (29 November 2016) 183 *Columbia FDI Perspectives*.

contractuel. En droit des contrats miniers, la question du droit applicable est ardemment négociée entre les Etats et les investisseurs. Généralement, on retient une formule mixte composée du droit national et des principes généraux du droit (international) confondus ou complétés parfois par les usages de l'industrie minière/ pétrolière ou simplement par les usages du commerce international. Ces derniers n'ont pas toujours été codifiés. Avec l'avènement et le développement fulgurant des Principes d'Unidroit relatifs aux contrats de commerce international (PUCCI)[8] ainsi que leur succès retentissant devant les prétoires et dans la doctrine, on a pu déduire le reflet d'une lex mercatoria codifiée, une certaine expression de principes généraux de droit tout simplement, une synthèse des droits nationaux dans une perspective transystémique, voire l'émergence d' un ordre juridique a-étatique.

Du point de vue de leur origine et de leur portée, les PUCCI ont été d'abord conçus comme un ensemble de règles, d'origine doctrinale et largement partagés dans la communauté juridique, affectés aux contrats du commerce international. Ainsi, ces principes ont à la fois une fonction pédagogique (pour inspirer le législateur national), une fonction réitérative (pour répandre le droit interne dans l'espace international) et une force normative, parfois dite optionnelle.[9] Cette destinée des PUCCI questionne évidemment la théorie des sources du droit et la notion d'ordre juridique, elle-même rattrapée par celle d'« espace juridique » ou « espace normatif »[10] aujourd'hui.

Du point de vue de leur contenu, les PUCCI révèlent un corps de règles et d'instruments juridiques qui retiennent l'attention dans la perspective d'une étude relative à l'équilibre contractuel. Nonobstant le fait que ces principes sont élaborés dans la perspective des contrats commerciaux classiques (d'échanges) notamment. Il n'en demeure pas moins qu'ils soient sollicités de façon non moins heureuse dans les contrats d'investissement et les contrats de longue durée, précisément comme le démontre leur récente orientation depuis 2010 entre autres.[11] Ainsi,

8 Ces principes sont analysés dans ce texte dans leur version de 2016. De plus et pour des raisons de commodité, l'expression « droit commercial transnational » et l'acronyme « PUCCI » sont utilisés de manière alternative pour désigner ces principes.

9 Dans ce sens, voir Pascale Deumier, *Le Droit Spontané: Contribution à l'Etude des Sources du Droit* thèse de doctorat de l'Université de Toulouse 1, 2000.

10 Voir dans ce sens Mireille Delmas-Marty, « La Grande Complexité Juridique du Monde », *Etudes en l'honneur de Gérard Timsit* (Bruylant, 2004), 89 et suivant.

11 Les PUCCI (dans leur version de 2010, puis celle de 2016, précisément les commentaires de l'Article 1.11) disposent clairement que ces principes ont vocation à s'appliquer aux contrats d'investissements et aux contrats de longue durée plus généralement dont les contrats miniers sont une catégorie à part entière. En effet, plusieurs sentences arbitrales

la notion d'attentes légitimes relèverait-elle une préoccupation d'équilibre du contrat au même titre que la théorie des obligations implicites?[12] Plus largement, il convient de constater que le droit des investissements miniers et le droit commercial se convergent de plus en plus, même si la notion juridique d'investissement est régie distinctement de celle de négoce en droit interne notamment. Aujourd'hui, les critères de la commercialité ont largement évolué et les deux domaines se retrouvent sous le couvercle généreux d'activité économique.[13] L'exploitation des ressources minières, opération d'investissement par excellence, est citée à juste titre comme un acte de commerce par nature.[14] Ces deux disciplines partagent au demeurant une rationalité commune de prise en compte des enjeux économiques dans l'appréhension de la norme juridique et promeuvent des normes qui ont vocation à se développer en dehors de l'intervention de l'Etat.

L'application des PUCCI aux contrats miniers en tant qu'outil de rééquilibrage des prestations est dès lors envisageable. Précisément, dans quelles conditions les Principes d'Unidroit s'appliquent-ils aux contrats miniers ? Quels sont les Principes d'Unidroit pertinemment applicables aux contrats miniers déséquilibrés ? Au

rendues par le Centre international pour le règlement des différends relatifs aux investissements (CIRDI) ont pu retenir les activités minières comme un investissement au sens de la Convention CIRDI et, précisément, avec l'exploitation pétrolière, comme la quintessence d'une opération d'investissement. Voir CIRDI, *RSM Production Corporation* c. *République centrafricaine* (7 décembre 2010), Affaire n° ARB/07/02, décision sur la compétence et la responsabilité, 61.

12 Voir l'Article 1.1 et suivants des PUCCI. Ces obligations implicites découleraient de la nature et du but du contrat, des usages, de la bonne foi ou du raisonnable. Une telle disposition pourrait être rapprochée des dispositions de l'Article 1134, alinéa 2, selon laquelle le contrat lie les parties autant à ce qui est prévu expressément convenus ou à ce que tout ce que la bonne foi recommande. Avec la dernière réforme du Code civil, la bonne foi est d'ailleurs consacrée comme un principe directeur du droit des contrats valable autant durant la formation que l'exécution du contrat.

13 Voir Jacques Chapeyre, « Le Code des Activités Economiques: Apport du Professeur Jean Paillusseau à l'Edification d'un Nouveau Droit des Entreprises en République de Guinée », dans Collectif, *Aspects organisationnels du droit des affaires, mélanges en l'honneur de Jean Paillusseau* (Dalloz, 2003) 93 et suivant ; Arnaud de Nanteuil, « Droit de l'Investissement et Droit de l'OMC » dans Charles Leben (dir), *Droit international des investissements et arbitrage transnational*, (Editions Pedone, 2015) 581 et suivant.

14 Voir Article 3 de l'Acte Uniforme OHADA portant sur le droit commercial général de 2010. L'OHADA est l'acronyme de l'Organisation pour l'Harmonisation en Afrique du Droit des Affaires instituée par le Traité de Port Louis de 1993 et regroupant 17 pays africains de la zone franc.

demeurant, quelle configuration possible de l'équilibre dans les relations Etats-investisseurs au regard de la théorie générale du droit et des nouvelles méthodes d'analyse en droit économique ? Quelles stratégies contractuelles et processuelles prévoir pour apprivoiser le risque de déséquilibre des prestations dans les contrats miniers ? Si toutes ces questions demeurent importantes, la portée de cette contribution est moindre en ce qu'elle se limite à l'analyse des contrats miniers déséquilibrés à l'une des PUCCI du point de vue de leur contenu.

Une telle analyse passe d'abord par l'examen de l'approche des PUCCI face au déséquilibre contemporain de la conclusion du contrat minier (Section 1) avant de se poursuivre sur le déséquilibre ultérieur à la conclusion du contrat minier à l'épreuve des mêmes PUCCI (Section 2).

1 Principes d'Unidroit et déséquilibre contemporain de la conclusion du contrat minier

(a) La consécration de la lésion qualifiée en droit commercial transnational

La lésion est classiquement définie comme le préjudice résultant de l'absence d'équivalence des prestations au moment de la conclusion du contrat. Telle que définie, elle n'a pas toujours été admise par le droit, du moins au rang de règle principale. Elle a souvent été admise exceptionnellement en raison du statut de certains sujets de droit ou en considération de certaines situations juridiques.

Des vifs débats ont animé la question de sa nature juridique. Tantôt, il s'agissait d'une conception objectiviste tendant à rattacher la lésion à un vice touchant à l'objet et au contenu du contrat, tantôt, c'est d'une situation de vice de consentement dont il s'agit, selon une lecture subjectiviste. Les PUCCI semblent retenir une conception mixte au regard de la formulation de l'Article 3.2.6:

> La nullité du contrat ou de l'une de ses clauses pour cause de lésion peut être invoquée par une partie lorsqu'au moment de sa conclusion, le contrat ou la clause accorde injustement un avantage excessif à l'autre partie.

Cette disposition est le siège de la lésion en droit commercial transnational.[15] Il s'agit précisément d'une lésion qualifiée, c'est-à-dire une lésion qui proviendrait

15 J.M. Jacquet, « Le Droit Français des Contrats et les Principes d'UNIDROIT », Rapport présenté au Colloque sur « L'harmonisation du Droit OHADA des Contrats » tenu à Ouagadougou (Burkina Faso) du 15 au 17 novembre 2007, Rev. dr. unif. 2008, 185.

d'une forte disproportion entre les droits et devoirs contractuels, résultat de certaines circonstances liées au statut et aux comportements des parties contractantes. La lésion qualifiée, se distinguant alors de la lésion simple, est diversement apprécié en droits internes. En droit belge, une décision de la Cour de Cassation a retenu la théorie de la lésion qualifiée de façon expresse.[16] En droit français, le nouveau Code civil de 2016, reprenant certaines solutions jurisprudentielles relatives à la violence économique, conduisent également à raisonner sur le terrain de la lésion qualifiée,[17] suivant un processus de densification normative.

En définissant le contenu de la lésion qualifiée, le « législateur » Unidroit fait référence à la notion d'avantage excessif injustifié qu'il s'attèle à caractériser. Dans ses commentaires[18] de l'Article 3.2.6, il décrit l'avantage injustifié comme celui qui dénote d'une forte inégalité entre les obligations contractuelles. Pour aboutir à une telle conclusion, il faut dès lors analyser toutes les obligations contractuelles et particulièrement les engagements réciproques et corrélatifs. Dans le cadre des contrats miniers en Afrique, il n'est pas rare d'observer que l'exploitant minier après avoir bénéficié des titres miniers et d'autres facilités administratives soit exonéré de tout impôt à verser à l'État d'accueil dans une certaine période. Il y a vraisemblablement ici un risque d'existence d'un avantage excessif ou d'engagements insuffisamment causés. Le processus de révision des contrats miniers en République Démocratique du Congo a permis de mettre en évidence ces hypothèses d'exonérations fiscales et douanières totale sur plusieurs années. On peut citer la convention minière conclue entre la République Démocratique du Congo et *Anvil Mining* n.l. du 31 janvier 1998. En raison de l'importance de la fiscalité comme revenus miniers contractuels, de telles exonérations sont des sources potentielles de déséquilibre contractuel. Ce constat s'observe aussi dans les joint-ventures où les apports de la partie étatique, essentiels du reste (titres miniers notamment) sont parfois sous évalués. Il s'en suit des titres sociaux faiblement proportionnels aux apports étatiques dans la société d'exploitation minière. Ainsi, la partie étatique se retrouve parfois avec moins de 10% des parts alors que son cocontractant, en plus des avantages fiscaux, bénéficie d'une proportion importante des parts sociales. Tandis que le terme « excessif »

16 Voir notamment Cass., 9 novembre 2012, R.G.D.C., 2013, 129, note M. de Potter de ten Broeck.

17 Voir Article 1139 et suivants du Code civil.

18 Comme le note plusieurs auteurs, les commentaires font partie intégrante des Principes d'Unidroit. Voir notamment Élise Charpentier, « L'Emergence d'un Ordre Public … Privé: une Présentation des Principes d'UNIDROIT » (2002) 36 *Revue Juridique Thémis* 355, 360 et suivant.

exclue une « disparité moyenne des obligations contractuelles ».[19] Dans l'affaire *RSM Production Corporation* c. *la République Centrafricaine*, l'Etat alléguait notamment le fait que :

'la superficie du permis (55 000 km²) est disproportionnée et confère à la demanderesse un monopole sur tout le bassin pétrolier centrafricain en contravention des dispositions d'ordre public du Code pétrolier et du bon sens (à titre de comparaison, dans plusieurs pays la superficie maximum d'un permis pétrolier ne peut dépasser 5 000 km²), le montant de la taxe superficiaire est dérisoire sinon inexistant.'[20]

Cette allégation constitue une tentative d'illustration d'un avantage excessif même si le moyen a été rejeté en l'espèce par le Tribunal au motif que le contrat pétrolier est conforme au modèle type national de contrat minier et qu'il est également approuvé par les autorités étatiques.

Pour son application, la lésion qualifiée est appréciée au regard de certains critères. On note en premier lieu la définition légale des critères d'appréciation de l'avantage unilatéral excessif et injustifié. Ces critères sont liés au statut et au comportement des contractants. Dans un souci de précision et de facilitation de l'interprétation de la règle édictée, l'Article 3.2.6 des Principes d'Unidroit précise l'ensemble de circonstances pertinentes qui doivent être prises en compte dans l'appréciation de l'avantage unilatéral excessif. Ces critères sont relatifs en effet au statut et au comportement des parties contractantes ou du moins à l'une d'entre elles. Il s'agit en effet de la situation économique du contractant désavantagé, à sa personnalité ou encore à ses manques de connaissances professionnelles. Dans l'affaire *RSM Production Corporation* c. *la République Centrafricaine*, la partie étatique rappelle : « Le Ministre André LATOU, qui a signé le Contrat, ne pratiquait pas la langue anglaise. … il ne disposait ni de l'expérience, ni de l'aptitude à la négociation en matière pétrolière ».[21]

En deuxième lieu, un autre élément est pris en compte dans l'appréciation de la lésion qualifiée et se rapporte à la prise en compte de la nature et du but du contrat en cause . Une double lecture du terme « nature du contrat » s'impose. L'idée peut renvoyer à une catégorisation contractuelle basée sur l'objet du contrat ou encore sur les parties contractantes. Ainsi, on pourrait distinguer les contrats de consommation qui sont par essence des contrats inégalitaires ou encore selon le fait que les

19 *RSM Production Corporation* c. *République centrafricaine* (7 décembre 2010) ARB/07/02, 139, 45.

20 *Ibid.*

21 *Ibid.*

contrats permettent ou non de réaliser un transfert de propriété. Dans le cadre des contrats miniers, c'est l'Etat qui semble être en position de force presomptivement mais la double analyse substantielle et systémale conduit à le placer au rang de « consommateur des revenus miniers », dépourvu juridiquement de ses prérogatives de puissance publique[22] face à une partie privée juridiquement, économiquement et techniquement protégée. Le but d'un contrat, quant à lui, peut varier d'un contrat à un autre mais aussi d'une partie à une autre. Aussi, dans un contrat, ne peut-on pas voir dans le cadre des Principes d'Unidroit une référence à la cause commune du contrat pour déterminer si un avantage excessif et unilatéral aurait pu être justifié au regard du but du contrat ? La question du but du contrat questionne assurément celle de la cause du contrat. Dans le cadre des contrats d'investissement de façon générale et des contrats miniers en particulier, il est souvent précisé que le projet d'investissement vise à contribuer au développement économique de l'Etat d'accueil ou dans certain cas à la mise en place d'un partenariat juste et équitable.

Une fois la lésion qualifiée établie, le contrat en cause connaît un traitement particulier.

(b) Le traitement de la lésion qualifiée en droit commercial transnational

La lésion qualifiée, lorsqu'elle est établie, peut être une source d'annulation du contrat tout comme conduire les parties à l'adapter. Dans les rapports entre les parties contractantes, l'annulation peut être parfaitement une solution subsidiaire, mise en œuvre seulement lorsque l'adaptation échoue. De même, devant le tribunal compétent, lorsque celui-ci applique les Principes d'Unidroit comme droit applicable, il peut être tenté de privilégié le maintien du contrat vicié au regard des perspectives *favor contractus* et *in favorem valididatis* dans lesquelles s'inscrivent les Principes d'Unidroit et les tribunaux arbitraux.

Dans tous les cas, lorsque l'annulation devient inéluctable, celle-ci doit se faire suivant une procédure particulière. Une telle annulation peut s'effectuer par voie de notification des contrats miniers déséquilibrés au regard des Principes d'Unidroit qui admettent une telle modalité d'annulation. Il convient de noter que l'annulation est en général une sanction judiciaire.[23] L'Article 3.2.11 établit le principe selon lequel une partie peut annuler un contrat sans qu'un tribunal n'intervienne. Cela signifie

22 Voir Pierre Mayer, « La Neutralisation du Pouvoir Normatif de l'Etat en Matière de Contrats d'Etat », *Journal de Droit International* 1986 I, 5 et suivant.

23 Voir Article 89 du Code des obligations civiles et commerciales du Sénégal.

que l'annulation se fait par voie d'action, par déclaration unilatérale, donc par notification conformément aux règles de la notification prévue par les PUCCI (Article 1.10 et suivant). La partie qui reçoit une notification d'annulation peut saisir le tribunal compétent et demander une adaptation du contrat à la place de l'annulation envisagée. Aussitôt, la partie lésée perd son droit d'annulation.[24]

Aussi, l'action en annulation peut être effectuée autant devant un tribunal arbitral que devant un tribunal judiciaire, saisi par voie d'action ou d'exception. Devant un tribunal judiciaire, il peut se poser un problème d'articulation dans l'application des règles étatiques et des Principes d'Unidroit. Une telle difficulté peut être néanmoins évitée. Certaines législations à l'instar du Code civil québécois prévoit que le droit applicable choisi par les contractants est écarté lorsqu'il a pour effet de provoquer la nullité du contrat.[25] En outre, la procédure implique notamment des règles relatives aux titulaires de l'action en annulation, à la possibilité de confirmation expresse ou tacite du contrat vicié.

Du point de vue de son étendue, l'annulation peut être alors totale ou partielle. D'abord, l'annulation totale est retenue par le juge lorsque les clauses viciées contiennent des engagements déterminants de la volonté des parties. On peut penser ainsi aux clauses de répartition des parts sociales qui occupent une place primordiale dans l'évaluation de l'équilibre des droits et obligations des parties. Ces clauses ne méritent pas un tel intérêt d'autant plus que les apports des partenaires dans le joint-venture ne sont pas identiques. L'Etat apporte souvent des titres miniers tandis que l'investisseur apporte souvent son capital, son industrie et son outil technologique. Ensuite, l'annulation partielle du contrat minier déséquilibré est envisageable dans certains cas et au regard de certains impératifs. En droit sénégalais, par exemple, l'annulation totale est retenue lorsque la clause en cause a été déterminante dans la conclusion du contrat. Les PUCCI s'inscrivent également dans cette dernière perspective en s'appuyant sur le caractère déterminant de la clause concernée.

En tout état de cause, l'anéantissement du contrat déséquilibré est réputé rétroactif conformément aux termes de l'Article 3.2.14 des Principes d'Unidroit. L'effet rétroactif de l'annulation implique une restitution des prestations contractuelles si le contrat annulé a connu un début d'exécution. La restitution qui porte sur une somme d'argent implique que le montant initialement libéré doit être restitué, on peut tenir compte d'une dépréciation monétaire éventuelle. La restitution en nature devient délicate lorsque la chose objet du contrat a pu générer des fruits ou lorsqu'elle a été détruite ou amortie. Dans cette perspective, les Principes

24 Voir Article 3.2.10 et suivant.

25 Voir Article 3112.

d'Unidroit admettent une restitution en valeur à la place de la prestation initiale, si la restitution en nature devient impossible ou inappropriée.[26]

Il arrive en pratique que les prestations réalisées dans le cadre d'une convention minière exécutée durant plusieurs années ne puissent faire l'objet d'une restitution. C'est pour cette raison que les parties peuvent convenir en accord avec le tribunal arbitral ayant prononcé l'annulation, de réduire les effets de cette sanction pour le passé. Un tel choix peut être justifié sur le plan économique. D'ailleurs, l'analyse économique du droit ne serait pas toujours réfractaire à la terminaison d'un contrat profondément déséquilibré. En effet, au regard de la théorie d'*efficient breach*,[27] il peut y avoir des effets économiques positifs avec la fin d'un contrat lorsque sa survie coûte plus qu'elle n'apporte. Cela est davantage confirmé lorsque les effets rétroactifs et notamment les restitutions sont largement réduits. Autant le facteur temps joue dans l'analyse des conséquences de la sanction de la lésion qualifié, autant ce facteur est caractéristique d'un autre type de déséquilibre contractuel.

2 Principes d'Unidroit et déséquilibre durant l'exécution du contrat minier

(a) La consécration de l'imprévision en droit commercial transnational

Le déséquilibre postérieur à la conclusion du contrat est souvent pris en compte par la théorie juridique de l'imprévision. Celle-ci ne constitue pas cependant l'unique moyen juridique mobilisé pour sanctionner ce déséquilibre des prestations. A titre de rappel, on peut retrouver plusieurs Principes d'Unidroit tels que la bonne foi, la théorie des obligations implicites et le devoir de coopération qui peuvent jouer un rôle important en matière de rééquilibrage de contrat.

Il n'y a pas toujours une définition légale qui précise l'imprévision dans les différents droits nationaux en Afrique francophone. En général, l'imprévision se révèle dans le changement de circonstances, extérieures, imprévisibles, insurmontables et postérieures à la conclusion du contrat rendant l'exécution de celui-ci anormalement onéreuse. Après plusieurs années d'indifférence légale (sur le plan principiel) et des hardiesses jurisprudentielles[28] contestées parfois,

26 Voir Article 3.2.14 et suivants.

27 Voir Sophie Le Gac-Pech « Rompre son contrat » (2005) *Revue Trimestrielle de droit civil* 223 et suivant.

28 Voir notamment l'arrêt Huard: Cass. com. fr., 3 novembre 1992, arrêt Huard, Defrénois, 1993, 1377, observations J.-L. Aubert.

l'imprévision est consacrée expressément comme une règle supplétive de volonté en droit privé français des contrats avec la réforme du Code civil de 2016, même si le droit administratif français reconnaît l'imprévision depuis la jurisprudence Compagnie générale d'éclairage de Bordeaux.[29] En droit minier interne, l'Article 88 du Code minier guinéen de 2011 liste un certain nombre d'événements constitutifs de la force majeure, notion que l'Article 88 confond parfois avec l'imprévision.[30] Dans la jurisprudence arbitrale, comme le démontre l'affaire *Ministry of Defense and Support for the Armed Forces of the Islamic Republic of Iran* c. *Cubic Defense Systems*,[31] l'adaptation du contrat en cas de changement de circonstances a été avancé comme principe général de droit international.

Tel qu'appréhendé par les PUCCI, le déséquilibre postérieur à la conclusion du contrat est sanctionné sous le sceau de l'imprévision (avec la consécration du *hardship*) et d'autres principes juridiques tels la bonne foi et l'obligation de coopération.[32] L'Article 6.2.2 des PUCCI précise qu':

Il y a *hardship* lorsque surviennent des événements qui altèrent fondamentalement l'équilibre des prestations, soit que le coût d'exécution des prestations ait augmenté, soit que la valeur de la contreprestation ait diminué.

C'est donc un déséquilibre important par son impact sur la balance des prestations contractuelles qui est visé ; il n'est pas nécessaire que celui-ci ait un caractère économique. Ainsi, ces évènements constitutifs d'imprévision peuvent se rapporter au bouleversement des prix des minerais, à la variation des résultats de l'exploration par rapport aux attentes initiales, à l'augmentation des coûts de production ou encore à la mise en place d'une nouvelle imposition fiscale à la charge de l'investisseur.

29 Conseil d'Etat 30 mars 1916, Compagnie générale d'éclairage de Bordeaux N° 599228, Lebon, 125.

30 Outre cette confusion volontaire du législateur guinéen, il est important de noter qu'en droit du commerce international, il arrive que les opérateurs choisissent d'assimiler les deux notions dans leurs questions même si la question demeure entière sur une définition contractuelle en déphasage avec une définition légale. La question remonte à nouveau sur le droit applicable la hiérarchie des normes y relatives. Voir P. Kahn, « Force Majeure et Contrats Internationaux de Longue Durée » (1975) *Journal de Droit International* 468 et suivant.

31 *Ministry of Defense and Support for the Armed Forces of the Islamic Republic of Iran* c. *Cubic Defense Systems* (ICC, 5 May 1997), dans *Inc.*: Revue de Droit Uniforme, 796. Cette sentence est rappelée également par W.B. Hamida, « Les Principes d'UNIDROIT et l'Arbitrage Transnational: l'Expansion des Principes d'UNIDROIT aux arbitrages opposant des Etats ou des Organisations Internationales à des Personnes Privées » (2012) 4 *Journal de Droit International* 1220 et suivant.

32 Voir Article 5.1.3 des PUCCI.

Selon l'Article 6.2.2(b) des Principes d'Unidroit, ces événements doivent survenir ou être connus au moment de l'exécution du contrat. Ils doivent être extérieurs à la partie lésée, raisonnablement imprévisibles pour elle et dont elle n'en a pas assumé le risque. C'est là une reprise du classique triptyque caractéristique de l'imprévision qui se retrouve ici à savoir, l'extériorité, l'imprévisibilité et l'insurmontabilité. Ces différents critères sont appréciés de façon flexible notamment en tenant compte du standard juridique du raisonnable à défaut d'une définition conventionnelle stricte et adaptée.

Il convient de noter en pratique que l'imprévision est souvent invoquée autant par les Etats que les investisseurs devant les tribunaux, même si ces derniers n'y accèdent pas toujours en l'absence certainement des ressources. Du coté des investisseurs, on peut noter dans une affaire concernant une société minière contre l'Etat du Sénégal suite à l'institution par le Sénégal d'une taxe parafiscale, en l'occurrence la Contribution Spéciale sur les Produits des Mines et Carrières,[33] les sociétés minières concernées ont soulevé le fait que l'application de cette contribution bouleverserait l'équilibre économique du contrat, même si le tribunal n'a pas repris ce motif de droit dans sa décision.[34] Dans le même registre, la société minière Arcelor Mittal a soulevé l'existence d'un contexte économique défavorable due notamment à la baisse des prix des minerais et l'absence de viabilité du projet pour justifier sa suspension et sa renégociation. Le tribunal compétent avait alors conclu en violation substantielle du contrat dont la fin était en définitive actée sur cette base.[35] Du coté de l'Etat cette fois-ci, dans une affaire portée devant le CIRDI, l'Equateur, tente de justifier une modification unilatérale du droit applicable en se basant sur l'évolution du contexte économique en vigueur en rappelant notamment:

33 Cette contribution a été instituée par la loi N°2013-07 du 18 décembre 2013 (Journal Officiel de la République du Sénégal n° 6776 du 22 février 2014). Elle a été confirmée et modifiée par la Loi de finances rectificative du 27 octobre 2014. Cette contribution a eu des difficultés à s'appliquer du fait de l'opposition des sociétés minières qui disposaient des garanties de stabilité fiscale et finalement les parties ont adopté pour une application dégressive par la Loi de finances rectificative sénégalaise du 27 octobre 2014.

34 Voir Tribunal Régional hors classe de Dakar, 28 mai 2014, *ICS* c. *Direction Générale des Impôts et Domaines* ; Tribunal Régional hors classe de Dakar, 23 avril 2014, *Société sénégalaise des phosphates de Thiès* c. *Ministère de l'Economie et de finances et Cie.*

35 La sentence arbitrale partielle rendue le 3 septembre 2013 à cet effet est confidentielle. Voir néanmoins les commentaires de *Global Arbitration Review* à propos de cette affaire, disponible suivant ce lien: https://globalarbitrationreview.com/article/1032629/senegal-wins-first-round-against-arcelormittal.

La loi 42 était une mesure nécessaire et appropriée au regard des circonstances en jeu. En 2002, il y a eu une hausse imprévisible et sans précédent du prix du pétrole. Cette hausse imprévisible a accentué le prix du pétrole et détruit l'équilibre économique des contrats de partage de production. Cet équilibre économique doit refléter l'opinion généralement répandue dans l'industrie pétrolière selon laquelle l'Etat, en tant que propriétaire des ressources non renouvelables, 'doit être le principal bénéficiaire de revenus extraordinaires résultant de la hausse de prix du pétrole.' ... Avec cette augmentation des prix du pétrole importante et imprévisible, l'Equateur n'était plus le principal bénéficiaire des revenus pétroliers. Par conséquent, les contrats de partage de production qui était en cours ne reflétaient plus une répartition équitable de la rente pétrolière entre l'Etat et le contractant.[36]

Dans le domaine des contrats miniers plus que dans tout autre domaine, l'admission de l'imprévision est conforme aux exigences de l'analyse économique du droit qui impliquent que le contrat soit économiquement utile.[37] Il serait dès lors fort préjudiciable aux parties de se lier par une convention aux profits économiques réduits en l'absence d'un accord commun. Celui-ci aurait pu justifier la prise en compte de l'imprévision de même que le droit applicable si celui-ci comprenait les PUCCI. Ces principes prévoient un traitement particulier lorsque l'imprévision est établie.

(b) Le traitement de l'imprévision en droit commercial transnational

Le principe de respect des engagements semble être la règle en matière de contrats internationaux et la règle *clausula rebus sic santibus*, l'exception. Une telle articulation semble participer à une sécurisation et à une stabilisation des rapports

36 Traduction personnelle de: « Law 42 was a necessary and appropriate measure under the circumstances. As of 2002, there was an unprecedented and unforeseen rise of oil prices. This unforeseen increase in the price of oil destroyed the economic equilibrium of the PSCs [production sharing contracts]. This economic equilibrium must reflect the oil industry's widely accepted assumption that the State, as the owner of the non-renewable resource, 'is to be the main beneficiary of extra revenue resulting from high oil prices.' ... With the massive and unforeseen increase of oil prices, Ecuador was no longer the main beneficiary of the oil revenues. As a result, the PSCs no longer reflected a fair division of extractive oil rent between the State and the contractor ». Extraits de la sentence arbitrale *Burlington Resources Inc.* c. *République de l'Ecuador* ICSID Case No. ARB/08/5 (autrefois *Burlington Resources Inc. et autres* c. *République de l'Ecuador et Empresa Estatal Petróleos del Ecuador (Petro Ecuador))* 377.

37 Voir Honoré Le Leuch, « Analyse Economique et Renégociation des Contrats Extractifs », dans A. Ngwanza et G. Lhuilier (dir), *Le Contentieux Extractif*, 30 et suivant.

contractuels. En effet, la prise en compte des faits économiques pertinents (chute des prix dans le marché international par exemple) justifie l'admission de l'imprévision pour permettre une meilleure exécution du contrat.[38]

L'Article 6.2.3 des PUCCI donne d'abord la possibilité aux parties contractantes, à l'initiative de la partie lésée (demande non suspensive de l'exécution du contrat) d'adapter le contrat dans un délai raisonnable. A défaut, après avoir établi l'existence d'une situation constitutive de *hardship*, le tribunal compétent peut mettre fin au contrat ou l'adapter afin de rétablir l'équilibre des prestations. Elle est d'abord convenue et à défaut impliquant l'intervention du tribunal compétent (arbitre, juge, …). Cette renégociation conventionnelle doit être menée de bonne foi tout en respectant le devoir de coopération prévu par les PUCCI. Il en résulte une obligation de renégociation à la charge de deux parties dont la méconnaissance pourrait être sanctionnée par l'allocation des dommages-intérêts en faveur de la partie lésée. Si les parties ne réussissent pas la phase de l'adaptation conventionnelle, les Principes d'Unidroit reconnaissent le pouvoir au juge compétent d'adapter le contrat en cas de *hardship*.[39] Concrètement, il peut s'agir d'une répartition des pertes ou d'une adaptation du prix. Il est important de mentionner que ces principes font référence au tribunal compétent. Celui-ci peut être autant un tribunal arbitral ou un tribunal judiciaire classique. Dans tous les cas, le tribunal compétent, en exerçant les fonctions d'adaptation du contrat, semble s'offrir par la même occasion un pouvoir créateur des normes contestables dans la sphère contractuelle au regard de certains droits applicables où le contrat est opposable (en l'état) au juge.

Globalement, on peut noter que la jurisprudence arbitrale est sensible à l'exigence d'équilibre des prestations. La sentence n°2291 de la C.C.I[40] le rappelle fort opportunément en ces termes:

> Toute transaction commerciale est fondée sur l'équilibre des prestations réciproques et … nier ce principe reviendrait à faire du contrat commercial un contrat aléatoire, fondé sur la spéculation ou le hasard. C'est une règle de la lex mercatoria que les prestations restent équilibrées sur le plan financier.

Une difficulté particulière peut être observée lorsque le règlement instituant le tribunal arbitral limite sa compétence au différend d'ordre juridique. Tel est le cas

38 *Ibid.*

39 Article 6.2.3.

40 Sentence C.C.I. N° 2291 (1975), *Journal de Droit International 1976*, 989. Elle est citée par le Professeur Darankoum. Voir Emmanuel S. Darankoum, « L'Application des Principes d'UNIDROIT par les Arbitres Internationaux et par les Juges Etatiques » (2002) 36 *Revue Juridique Thémis* 421, 425 et suivant.

du CIRDI. En effet, l'Article 25 dispose que la compétence du CIRDI concerne le « différend juridique » tout en s'abstenant de donner une définition précise à la notion de différend juridique. Celui-ci est généralement opposé au conflit d'intérêts.

Les PUCCI ne prévoient pas l'hypothèse de mettre fin au contrat déséquilibré par une partie, soit une possibilité de résiliation unilatérale. Cependant, en pratique, plusieurs Etats africains comme la République Démocratique du Congo et la Guinée se sont engagés dans ce processus. En pareille occurrence, la partie victime de la résiliation prend acte de la fin de la relation contractuelle ou alors conteste la mesure de résiliation devant le tribunal compétent. Cette contestation peut viser la légalité de l'acte de résiliation en se prévalant notamment d'une clause d'intangibilité dans le contrat minier. Elle peut également indexer une irrégularité intrinsèque à l'acte de résiliation tout comme ou dans une perspective autre demander une indemnisation du préjudice consécutif à la résiliation.

Au total, bien que les Principes d'Unidroit prennent une avance sur certains droits internes en consacrant la lésion et l'imprévision, il reste que l'application de ces règles est limitée dans certaines conditions. En l'état actuel, ces principes doivent s'articuler avec les droits internes pour une meilleure application, au risque de ne pas contrarier certaines règles nationales et ainsi compromettre leur application. A terme, un équilibre plus élargi est souhaitable entre les différents acteurs du secteur minier incluant les populations locales impactées pour une exploitation minière durable et inclusivement profitable.

5

The politics of international technology transfer: the imperative of host State measures

Collins C. Ajibo

Introduction

The modalities for transfer of technology to developing countries are far too diverse and encompassing to be covered by this chapter. The literature on technology transfer is diverse and keeps burgeoning.[1] The drive by developing countries for technology, as well as the debate about the transfer is not a new phenomenon.[2] Evidence exists of several strides in the past towards that direction.[3] The issue of

1 See K. Chandrashekhar Iyer and Partha S. Banerjee, 'Facilitators and Inhibitors in Sector Wide Technology Transfer Projects in Developing Economies: An Empirical Study' (2018) 43 (1) *Journal of Technology Transfer* 172; Dietrich Schroeer and Micro Elena, *Technology Transfer* (Routledge, 2019); Tamir Agmon and Mary Ann Von Glinow (eds), *Technology Transfer in International Business* (Oxford Universities Press, 1991); Michael Blakeney, 'Transfer of Technology and Developing Nations' (1987) 11 (4) *Fordham International Law Journal* 690; Karl P. Sauvant, 'The Negotiations of the United Nations Code of Conduct on Transnational Corporations: Experience and Lessons Learned' (2015) 16 *Journal of World Investment & Trade* 11; UNCTAD, *Draft International Code of Conduct on the Transfer of Technology* (UNCTAD, 1985); UNCTAD, *Transfer of Technology. UNCTAD Series on Issues in International Investment Agreements* (UNCTAD, 2001).

2 Technology transfer first came into the limelight as an international issue in 1961 as part of a request to the United Nations Secretary-General to commission studies to ascertain the role of international treaties in the promotion of protection of intellectual property rights in developing countries. See International Centre for Trade and Sustainable Development (ICTSD) 'Unpacking the International Technology Transfer Debate: Fifty Years and Beyond' (2012) 6 www.ictsd.org/downloads/2012/07/unpacking-the-international-technology-transfer-debate-fifty-years-and-beyond.pdf, accessed 4 July 2018.

3 See Article 6 of the 1962 UN General Assembly Resolution on the Permanent Sovereignty over Natural Resources (Resolution 1803 (XVII)) www.ohchr.org/EN/ProfessionalInterest/Pages/NaturalResources.aspx, accessed 4 July 2018; Article 4(p) of the 1974 UN Declaration on the Establishment of a New International Economic Order

international transfer of technology has featured in many multilateral and bilateral frameworks such as, *inter alia*, the United Nations resolutions and conferences; the Agreement on Trade-Related Aspects of Intellectual Property Rights (TRIPS Agreement); multilateral environmental treaties;[4] the World Intellectual Property Organization (WIPO) development agenda;[5] Global Strategy and Plan of Action of the World Health Organization (WHO);[6] free trade agreements (FTAs); and bilateral investment treaties (BITs)[7]. Technology transfer has become necessary in view of the critical and strategic function technology engenders to economic development of every nation;[8] and the unenviable position of African countries in this sphere. Although other factors of production, such as capital, labor, and land, equally constitute important determinants of economic development, the influence of technology remains significant. Indeed, the income gap between developed countries and developing countries is largely attributable to differences in generation, application and diffusion of technology.[9] It was observed sometimes in the

(A/RES/S-6/3201) www.un-documents.net/s6r3201.htm, accessed 4 July 2018. Other efforts at technological transfer include: the first UN General Assembly resolution on patents and technology transfer by Brazil (1961); UNCTAD-WIPO report 'The Role of the Patent System in the Transfer of Technology to Developing Countries' (1975); discussions on the reform of the Paris Convention for the Protection of Industrial Property (1977–1983). For details of the preceding, see 'From the UNCTAD Code of Conduct to the WTO's TRIPS Agreement: Global Efforts for Technology Transfer' (2013) ICTSD 3. www.teknolojitransferi.gov.tr/TeknolojiTransferPlatformu/resources/temp/71EDCEB4-1E26-4BFE-B839-E32FD091DA79.pdf;jsessionid=7D39612467C0B87BBD49D370C3E17B72, accessed 4 July 2018.

4 See Principle 9 of the *1992 Rio Declaration on Environment and Development*; and Paragraph 1(d), *Bali Action Plan*, United Nations Framework Convention on Climate Change (2007), to name just a few, encouraging, *inter alia*, the diffusion and transfer of (innovative) technologies.

5 WIPO, *WIPO Development Agenda* (2016) www.wipo.int/edocs/mdocs/africa/en/wipo_ip_recs_ge_16/wipo_ip_recs_ge_16_t_3_d.pdf, accessed 4 July 2018.

6 WHO, *The Global Strategy and Plan of Action on Public Health, Innovation and Intellectual Property* (2011) www.who.int/phi/publications/Global_Strategy_Plan_Action.pdf, accessed 4 July 2018.

7 See ICTSD, *Unpacking the International Technology Transfer Debate: Fifty Years and Beyond* 39–45.

8 See Article 7 of the TRIPS Agreement.

9 See WIPO, *World Intellectual Property Report: The Changing Face of Innovation* (2011) 168–71, www.wipo.int/edocs/pubdocs/en/intproperty/944/wipo_pub_944_2011.pdf, accessed 4 July 2018.

past that the major capital stock of an industrially advanced nation is 'the body of knowledge amassed from tested findings of empirical science and the capacity and training of its population to use this knowledge effectively'.[10] This is no less an affirmation of a culture of systematic research generation and application of technological know-how, which African countries largely lack.

While the generation of a significant proportion of this technology occurs in industrially developed countries, where a preponderant part of research is situated and conducted, transnational corporations (TNCs) constitute the most significant source of its cross-border transfer. Thus, there is asymmetry between the location where the technology is generated and the place that is seeking the transfer of the technology, coupled with the fact that the TNCs are not necessarily good 'commercializers' of technology. The situation is made more complicated by the emerging regimes of TRIPS-Plus,[11] evidenced in BITs and mega trade agreements.[12] TRIPS-Plus provisions are found in FTAs and are stricter in terms of requirements than the type of flexibility under the provisions of the World Trade Organization Trade-Related Intellectual Property Rights. These are generally called TRIPS-Plus.

These regimes embed even a stronger intellectual property protection, thereby dampening the development aspirations of developing countries. This situation will particularly affect the contour of the technological transfer debate and the position of African countries. Though a number of developing countries, particularly in Asia and South America, have optimized the options for transfer through varied frameworks,[13] African countries have largely failed to catch up.[14] Consequently, it is time

10 See Simon Kuznets, *Toward a Theory of Economic Growth* (New York: Norton, 1968) 34–5.

11 It was noted that by conclusion of the Alien Tort Claims Act (ACTA), the countries have taken 'matters into their own hands to seek solutions outside of the multilateral system to the detriment of inclusiveness of the present system'. See Catherine Saez, 'ACTA a Sign of Weakness in Multilateral System, WIPO Head Says' (2010) *Intellectual Property Watch* www.ip-watch.org/weblog/2010/06/30/acta-a-sign-of-weakness-in-multilateral-system-wipo-head-says, accessed 4 July 2018.

12 The withdrawal of the US from the Trans-Pacific Partnership Agreement (TPP) by the administration of President Donald Trump by no means terminates the regime of the agreement, since other partner countries have signaled their intention to replace the US with China. Countries constituted by TPP arrangement include at the time of writing: Australia, Brunei, Canada, Chile, Japan, Malaysia, Mexico, Peru, Singapore, the United States, Vietnam, and New Zealand.

13 See Article 8 of the TRIPS Agreement on the Principles that underline the Agreement.

14 'Catch up' refers to the process of narrowing of the technological gap between more technologically advanced countries or firms and less technologically advanced countries or firms.

for African countries to look inward, brace themselves for the emerging TRIPS-Plus realities, and properly articulate their trade and investment policies in order to harness opportunities afforded by technological transfer in national and international instruments. Such technological transfer can be accomplished through a carefully formulated and implemented policy intended to build local capacities, optimize transfer opportunities, and foster absorptive capacities. This chapter continues the debate on how African countries can engender technological revolution to alter the equilibrium in favour of development. The chapter does not claim to offer comprehensive facts and solutions in the area of international technological transfer. However, it does provide a guideline on how African countries can leverage their current unenviable position in the technological development ladder.

The chapter is divided into five sections. Apart from the introduction above, Section 1 provides a general overview of the TRIPS Agreement within the context of the technological transfer debate. Section 2 examines the facilitators of transfer involving the modes and means of transfer. Section 3 evaluates the impacts of the TRIPS Agreement on transfer; while Section 4 explores the dynamics of the TRIPS-Plus regime and its impacts on technological transfer to developing countries. Section 5 assesses the imperatives of host country measures, proffering suggestions worth charting by the African countries in order to optimize the transfer opportunities. The chapter ends with concluding remarks.

1 TRIPS Agreement and the transfer debate

The emergence of the regime of the TRIPS Agreement was hailed as a major milestone in the protection of intellectual property, being the most comprehensive multilateral treaty on intellectual property protection. As a part of the larger Uruguay Round of negotiations within the framework of the General Agreement on Tariffs and Trade (GATT), the TRIPS Agreement constitutes a product of the trade-off between developing countries and developed countries on intellectual property protection and development aspirations. On the one hand, intellectual property protection is necessary to enable producers and owners to extract rents or benefits involved in investment in research and development (R&D); such protection provides an incentive for further innovation, the outcomes of which are beneficial to humanity.[15] Failure to accord intellectual property protection may constitute a disincentive for further investment in R&D and, by implication, delay innovation and

15 Matthew Turk, 'Bargaining and Intellectual Property Treaties: The Case for a Pro-Development Interpretation of TRIPS but not TRIPS PLUS' (2010) 42 *New York University. Journal of International Law & Politics* 982–5.

development. In the same vein, failure to accord protection can lead to freeloading by countries who are beneficiaries of the intellectual property. Therefore, there is an altruistic policy consideration in intellectual property protection, in addition to the legal consideration, in order to keep the engine of innovation rolling to foster constant access to essential goods and services. On the other hand, strict intellectual property protection can restrict policy space available to countries at the lower rungs of development ladder.[16] These countries, made up of mostly developing countries and least developed countries, require policy space and flexibilities in order to enhance competitiveness and provide essential services to the populace. African countries are largely caught up in the latter group.

The TRIPS Agreement, for its part, recognizes the foregoing dichotomy by providing for the balance between intellectual property protection and development aspirations of intellectual property recipients. Article 7, entitled 'Objectives', recognizes that the protection and enforcement of intellectual property rights should contribute to the promotion of technological innovation and to the transfer and dissemination of technology for the mutual advantage of producers and users of technological knowledge. It should be done in a manner conducive to social and economic welfare, and to a balance of rights and obligations. In the same vein, Article 8, called 'Principles', entitles members, in formulating or amending their laws and regulations, to adopt measures necessary to protect public health and nutrition, and to promote the public interest in sectors of vital importance to their socioeconomic and technological development, provided that such measures are consistent with the provisions of the TRIPS Agreement. These two provisions are widely acknowledged as evidential of the thrust of the TRIPS Agreement to engender a balance of competing interests between the technological producers and technological recipients.

Despite the apparent balance, the TRIPS Agreement is still somewhat regarded as being biased in favour of developed countries. The vast stretch of rights and interests protected by the Agreement pertain to those owned and possessed by developed countries. In other words, the regime of the TRIPS Agreement preponderantly harbours and protects the interests of industrial countries, mostly developed countries. On the other hand, certain essential interests of developing countries are not completely captured by the Agreement. Equally, a regime of excessive protection

16 *Ibid.*

appears to stifle the growth and development aspirations of countries in the process of industrialisation.[17]

Evidence indicates that countries with weak intellectual property policies can achieve rapid economic growth and development; with the strengthening of intellectual property rights occurring only after the initial stages of increased growth and development.[18] However, it has been contended that adherence to international intellectual property standards of protection is necessary for countries interested in reaching the frontiers of the knowledge economy and converting their economies' nonrivalrous and intangible outputs into tradeable knowledge goods.[19] Be that as it may, an effective balance ought to be drawn between intellectual property protection and development imperatives. It should be borne in mind that experience of successful economic development indicates that, in addition to intellectual property protection, some other relevant factors such as the nature of governance, fiscal policies, education, industrial policy, stability, trade policy, competition, and R&D culture equally shape economic growth and development.[20] Yet, development and intellectual property protection are intertwined. Reverse engineering and imitative engineering are only possible when the extant intellectual property regime makes such a concession. Nevertheless, a number of options that facilitate internalization of transfer are presented hereunder.

2 Facilitators of transfer

African countries may wish to consider the interplay that characterizes transfers based on the regulatory approach, market-based approach and international alliances and partnership. While the regulatory approach is flexible and allows a

17 See Margaret Chon, 'Intellectual Property and the Development Divide' (2006) 27 (6) *Cardozo Law Review* 2815 (noting that '[i]ntellectual property, while purporting to heed the issues of development, often runs rough-shod over the central concerns of development').

18 Such countries include Brazil, India, Korea, Malaysia, Taiwan, and others. See Bryan Mercurio, 'Reconceptualising the Debate on Intellectual Property Rights and Economic Development' (2010) 3 (1) *Law and Development Review* 65–8.

19 Jerome H. Reichman, 'Intellectual Property in the Twenty-First Century: Will the Developing Countries Lead or Follow?' (2009) 46 (4) *Houston Law Review* 1118.

20 K.E. Maskus, 'Intellectual Property Rights and Economic Development' (2000) 32 *Case Western Reserve Journal of International Law* 476; Bryan Mercurio, 'Growth and Development: Economic and Legal Conditions' (2007) 30 (2) *University of New South Wales Law Journal* 437.

country to structure transfer based on its development status and aspiration, the market-based approach is hinged purely on a competitive market for technology, operating mainly based on arm's length dealing. International alliances and partnerships are better utilized if they involve countries with higher technological growth stage and another country at the low technological growth stage. African countries must look inward and take a position based on the country's peculiarity and interest.

Foreign direct investment (FDI) constitutes the main driver of transfer, since a number of other transfer options are closely related to it. For instance, other transfer arrangements closely intertwined with FDI include: performance requirements; licensing agreements; joint ventures; management contracts; and turnkey contracts, among others. Therefore, countries can leverage FDI to facilitate the spillover of other transfer arrangements.

There is already an African Science and Technology Consolidated Plan of Action structured around three main areas: knowledge production, capacity building and technological innovation. Article 51 of African Economic Community urges mutual cooperation for the development, acquisition and dissemination of appropriate technologies among the African Union (AU) Member States. Similarly, Article 27 of the Economic Community of West African States (ECOWAS) Treaty and Article 21 of the Southern African Development Community (SADC) embody science and technology cooperation between their members. Collaborative or cooperative arrangements of this nature also exist in other regions such as Asia and Latin America.[21] Though this approach could be relevant for groupings with a significant proportion of their membership made up of countries with technologically advanced economies, it is hardly appropriate for countries that are not in such a position. While the aforementioned should not be totally jettisoned, African countries should seek more collaboration with more technologically advanced countries. Such an option becomes even more compelling in the light of the prevailing TRIPS regime and its impact on transfers.

3 Impacts of the TRIPS Agreement on transfer

The TRIPS Agreement constitutes a watershed in intellectual property protection in a multilateral setting but it is not a perfect document. As noted by a commentator, the TRIPS Agreement: … 'limits the extent to which developing countries can learn and incrementally innovate, by limiting their ability to reverse engineer. It also expands the

21 UNCTAD, *Technology and Innovation Report 2012: Innovation, Technology and South-South Collaboration* (UNCTAD, 2012) 61.

scope and application of IPRs [intellectual property rights] to newer areas and subject matters … This circumscribes their ability to promote technological and economic catch-up.'[22]

Nevertheless, the TRIPS Agreement is not totally devoid of technological transfer utility. Indeed, it does make some provisions for technological transfers in return for stronger intellectual property protection from the developing countries. Accordingly, members accepts that some licensing practices or conditions relating to intellectual property rights that restrain competition may have adverse effects on trade and may impede the transfer and dissemination of technology.[23] Therefore, members may adopt, consistently with the other provisions of the TRIPS Agreement, appropriate measures to prevent or control restrictive business practices.[24] These measures may include, for example, exclusive grant back conditions, conditions preventing challenges to validity and coercive package licensing, in the context of the relevant laws and regulations of that country member.[25] Not only are restrictive business practices prohibited,[26] developed countries are

22 See ICTSD, *Unpacking the International Technology Transfer Debate: Fifty Years and Beyond* 36.

23 Article 40(1) of the TRIPS Agreement.

24 The United Nations Conference on Restrictive Business Practices (UNCRBP) was convened by the General Assembly in its resolution 33/153 of 20 December 1978 under the auspices of UNCTAD. It concluded on 22 April 1980, adopting a resolution approving a 'Set of Multilaterally Agreed Equitable Principles and Rules for the Control of Restrictive Business Practices' (agreed principles and rules). This was subsequently adopted by the General Assembly, at its thirty-fifth session in its resolution 35/63 of 5 December 1980. See UNCTAD, *UN Set of Principles and Rules on Competition: The Set of Multilaterally Agreed Equitable Principles and Rules for the Control of Restrictive Business Practices* (UNCTAD, 2000). See also Paul Kuruk, 'Controls on Technology Transfer: an Analysis of the Southern Response to Northern Technological Protectionism' (1989) 13 (2) *Maryland Journal of International Law* 309.

25 Article 40(2) of the TRIPS Agreement.

26 The UN Set of Principles and Rules on Competition defines restrictive business practices as 'acts or behaviour of enterprises which, through an abuse or acquisition and abuse of a dominant position of market power, limit access to markets or otherwise unduly restrain competition, having or being likely to have adverse effects on international trade, particularly that of developing countries, and on the economic development of these countries, or which through formal, informal, written or unwritten agreements or arrangements among enterprises, have the same impact.' The 'dominant position of market power' is similarly defined as a situation where 'an enterprise, either by itself or acting together with a few other enterprises, is in a position to control the relevant

obliged to provide incentives to enterprises and institutions in their territories for the purpose of promoting and encouraging technology transfer to least-developed country members in order to enable them to create a sound and viable technological base.[27]

Moreover, the developed country members shall provide, on request and on mutually agreed terms and conditions, technical and financial cooperation in favour of developing and least-developed country members.[28] Such cooperation shall include assistance in the preparation of laws and regulations on the protection and enforcement of intellectual property rights, as well as on the prevention of their abuse, and shall include support regarding the establishment or reinforcement of domestic offices and agencies relevant to these matters, including the training of personnel.

In respect of the latter provisions, the TRIPS Agreement was genuine and perceptive in making provision to tackle the core problems in developing countries by targeting precisely the need to strengthen the technical capabilities of the least developed countries.[29] Despite these provisions, evidence indicates that no significant successful transfers have been made to developing countries.[30] The situation is made even more complicated now that the dynamics of the TRIPS-Plus regime hold sway, which practically constitute a significant barrier to the transfer, use and availability of technologies to firms from the developing countries.[31]

4 The dynamics of the TRIPS-Plus regime

It should be noted that Article 1 stipulates that the TRIPS Agreement provides merely for a minimum standard. Therefore, members are entitled to conclude more stringent standards otherwise known as TRIPS-Plus. Nevertheless, the imposition of a regime of more stringent standards, as evidenced by TRIPS-Plus, not only results in more intellectual property protection, but circumscribes the technological transfer

market for a particular good or service or group of goods or services'. See UNCTAD, *UN Set of Principles and Rules on Competition: The Set of Multilaterally Agreed Equitable Principles and Rules for the Control of Restrictive Business Practices* 10.

27 Article 66(2) of the TRIPS Agreement.

28 Article 67 of the TRIPS Agreement.

29 See ICTSD, *Unpacking the International Technology Transfer Debate: Fifty Years and Beyond* 39.

30 *Ibid.* 40.

31 *Ibid.* 39.

options available to developing countries.[32] The emergence of the TRIPS-Plus era portends a great danger to the flexibilities epitomized by the TRIPS Agreement. It entails a progressive erosion and derogation of the flexibilities afforded to developing countries by the TRIPS Agreement.[33] Such erosion will have far-reaching implications on the development objectives of developing countries. Referring to the negative effect of TRIPS-Plus on developing countries, it was stated that:

> Recent PTAs [preferential trade agreements] have … altered in a significant way the TRIPS original "grand bargain" that was achieved at the end of the Uruguay Round. What stands out is that the important flexibilities, including transitional adjustment periods, policy space in implementation, and the underlying public policy objectives of national systems, including developmental and technological objectives, are now largely foregone in different ways as a result of the PTAs.[34]

The TRIPS-Plus regime is being aggressively extended and consolidated by evolving alliances and partnerships expected to even trigger and embed further deterioration in the technological development initiatives of developing countries. According to the United Nations Development Programme (UNDP), the European Union (EU) and the United States of America (US) have employed 'a combination of unilateral pressure and forum shifting from bilateral agreements to multilateral standard setting and then back to bilaterals again as a way of securing trade concessions … including stronger intellectual property protection' from developing countries.[35] The aforementioned undermines the legitimacy of multilateralism, as well as raises imputations on the motive of the proponents of the TRIPS-Plus regime. Put differently, it appears that the proponents of the TRIPS-Plus regime crave and

32 The UN Human Rights Council reiterates that 'flexibilities were included in TRIPS to allow States to take into consideration their economic and development needs. States need to take steps to facilitate the use of TRIPS flexibilities.' See UN Human Rights Council, *Report of the Special Rapporteur on the Right of Everyone to the Enjoyment of the Highest Attainable Standard of Physical and Mental Health, Anand Grover* (2009) A/HRC/11/12.

33 For a discussion of the flexibilities and their implication on the TRIPS Agreement, see J.H. Reichman, 'The TRIPs Agreement Comes of Age: Conflict or Cooperation With the Developing Countries?' (2000) 32 *Case Western Reserve Journal of International Law* 459.

34 See ICTSD, *Unpacking the International Technology Transfer Debate: Fifty Years and Beyond* 41.

35 Ruth Mayne, 'Regionalism, Bilateralism, and "TRIP Plus" Agreements: The Threat to Developing Countries' (2005) Human Development Report Office Occasional Paper http://hdr.undp.org/sites/default/files/hdr2005_mayne_ruth_18.pdf, accessed 4 July 2018.

surreptitiously implement an agenda that entails a progressive erosion of the efficacy of a multilateral regime that affords flexibilities to developing countries, in favour of a stronger regime that eschews those flexibilities. The current dynamics are likely to have a significant drawback on the technological aspirations of developing countries, particularly African countries.

In the light of the foregoing, it is imperative for African countries to readjust their tactics and strategies, paying attention to local dynamics and available options at the international level in order to harness the opportunities available to foster transfer.

5 Imperatives of host State measures

Although it is not going to be easy for African technological aspirations in view of the alliances and partnerships mentioned above, they have to chart their own destinies. No country will have more of their interests at heart than themselves. After all, the evolving alliances are determined by the pursuit and protection of trade and the investment interests of the signatories. African countries may need to pay attention to a number of options to optimize their development interests, which are discussed in the subsections below.

(a) The negotiating template

Most developed countries have a negotiating template or model agreement for trade and investment agreements.[36] Where there is derogation from the text, it does not, in most cases, substantially deviate in substance from the model template or agreement. African countries need to develop trade and investment negotiating templates to protect their interests. Such templates should embody credible and workable technological transfer provisions commensurate with the level of intellectual property protection espoused in an agreement. By having such a boilerplate, African countries will be better positioned to stem the tide of being ambushed by superior negotiating and bargaining power. Although the aforementioned is not going to be easy, mainly because of covert coercion and asymmetrical bargaining power, an existing boilerplate will have a more credible chance of withstanding pressure from the opposite party than a non-existent template.

36 See 2012 US Model BIT and Model BIT of major capital exporting countries in the European Union, such as Germany, France and the United Kingdom.

Alternatively, African countries may wish to resist entry into and conclusion of trade and investment agreements that undermine their technological development agendas. Evidence already indicates that a stringent post-TRIPS regime does not advance the development agendas of developing countries. Such evidence should constitute authoritative guidance for African countries to be circumspect in the conclusion of agreements and promulgation of law with intellectual property protection standards more stringent than the TRIPS Agreement. The UN Special Rapporteur on the right to health advised that developing countries and least developed countries (LDCs) 'should not introduce TRIPS-plus standards in their national laws. Developed countries should not encourage developing countries and LDCs to enter into TRIPS-plus FTAs and should be mindful of actions which may infringe upon the right to health.'[37]

The conclusion of an agreement is as vital as its enforcement. As noted by a commentator, if countries with low technological development such as African countries 'want international intellectual property enforcement norms to be shaped in a way that takes their interests into account and that shows a greater appreciation of their significantly different socioeconomic conditions, they need to be more proactive'.[38] African countries may explore enforcement standards through their template that are cost-effective and socially optimal to their circumstances. Such standards should be ideal for a balance between the stimulation of innovation and creativity, and intellectual property protection. The absence of this balance may limit the scope of transfers.

(b) Stimulation of innovation and creativity

Technological development thrives through the stimulation of innovation and creativity. This is actualized based on policies that emphasize short-run and long-run feasibilities. Fundamentally, there should be a massive investment in education at all levels with emphasis on science and technological aspects of learning. Funding of education goes hand in hand with funding of R&D institutions. African countries must imbibe the culture of R&D rather than free riding on existing knowledge bases, or waiting for mere technological transfers. They must learn to originate

37 UN Human Rights Council, *Report of the Special Rapporteur on the Right of Everyone to the Enjoyment of the Highest Attainable Standard of Physical and Mental Health* 108.

38 See Peter K. Yu, 'TRIPS and Its Achilles' Heel' (2011) *Journal of Intellectual Property Law* 481, 527.

research in areas that particularly affect their lives and come out with fruitful results universally acknowledged as valid.

In the interim, however, African countries must strategize and optimize immediate technological transfer opportunities. This can be achieved through deliberate policies structured to make the best of international trade and investment flow. Investment inflow is determined by certain variables, including the size of markets, availability of natural resources, existence of viable infrastructure and institutions, political stability, quality of labour, and macroeconomic forces (such as exchange rate volatility, inconvertibility of currency, and economic growth).[39] Application of investment policies should be sensitive to the uniqueness of the country and responses to these variables. This means that a no 'one size fits all' recommendation is advised. Nevertheless, a country can structure trade and investment agreements to meet its technological goal, bearing in mind that foreign firms resist transfers in certain circumstances. For instance, some firms will be reluctant to undertake transfers if they are unsure of the final destination of the know-how, or if such know-how might get into the wrong hands. As pointed out in respect of licensing:

> [t]he essential challenge in licensing know-how is the double moral-hazard problem …: licensors may not fully reveal the tacit information without knowing local demand conditions and recipients may try to renege on a contract after learning the know-how. This uncertainty can deter licensing, particularly when there are high transactions costs in transferring know-how and limited enforcement capacities. Technology owners either would choose not to license to countries where such problems are severe, diminish the quality of the technologies offered, or keep their information in-house through FDI.[40]

This kind of challenge may be better managed by structuring market access against technological spillovers. In other words, the admission of investment into a host State should be hinged on, among other things, the capacity of the firm to transfer technology to the host State.

The transfer is one thing but absorptive capacity is another thing. Certainly, one of the greatest challenges faced in the technological transfer debate is the problem of absorptive capacity of the technological recipient.[41] Most developing countries, and preponderantly African countries, lack sufficient know-how and skill reservoirs to

39 UNCTAD, *Bilateral Investment Treaties* (UNCTAD, 1998) 141.

40 WIPO, *International Technology Transfer: an Analysis from the Perspective of Developing Countries* (2014) Committee on Development and Intellectual Property (CDIP), Fourteenth Session, Geneva 22.

41 UNCTAD, *Technology and Innovation Report 2012: Innovation, Technology and South-South Collaboration* 79.

absorb, utilize and adapt the technology for optimal performance.[42] Evidence indicates that the absorptive capacity of a host country is a crucial factor 'for obtaining significant spillover benefits from trade or FDI.'[43] Certainly, in the absence of 'adequate human capital or investments in R&D, spillovers may simply be infeasible … The implication is that liberalization of trade and open FDI policies need to be complemented by appropriate policies with respect to education, R&D, and human capital accumulation, if developing countries are to take full advantage of these channels of ITT.'[44] Where the absorptive capacities are readily available, the innovative capacity will crystallize. Innovation capabilities involve the ability to modify or change the existing knowledge base in the light of demanding and dynamic situations. Technological development thrives where both the absorptive capacity and innovation capabilities of countries are functionally optimal. African countries are mainly behind in these categories. They must therefore wake up from their state of inactivity and join the rest of the world in the march for technological development. As evidence indicates from a review of successful country experiences in technological development, the development of industrial competitiveness requires investments in capabilities of various kinds, such as design engineering, procurement, production, marketing and so on.[45] Moreover, the stimulation of industrial development is based on the improved exploitation of existing advantages (natural resources and unskilled or semi-skilled labour), while in part relying on the creation of new advantages (skills, technological capabilities, clusters and so on). Thus, some strategies (or parts of larger strategies) involved liberalizing export activity and attracting FDI to obtain existing advantages; others went beyond, to 'dynamize' existing advantages by intervening in factor and product markets. The basic choice was between the agents involved: local enterprises or TNCs. All countries used both, but with differing balance and emphasis, depending partly on the nature

42 Vinod Kumar, Uma Kumar and Aditha Persaud, 'Building Technological Capability through Importing Technology: The Case of Indonesian Manufacturing Industry' (1999) 24 *The Journal of Technology Transfer* 81 (noting that, in developing countries 'the cultivation of technological capability is affected by several factors such as a firm's technological absorption capacity in terms of R&D activities and availability of technical personnel; transfer channels; government's involvement; and a firm's learning culture').

43 WIPO, *International Technology Transfer: an Analysis From the Perspective of Developing Countries* 23.

44 *Ibid.* 23.

45 UNCTAD, *Investment and Technology Policies for Competitiveness: Review of Successful Country Experiences* (UNCTAD, 2003) 21.

of the technologies involved (local firms with simpler technologies) and partly on strategic objectives.[46]

(c) Financial incentives

Stimulation of innovation and creativity is intertwined with financial incentives, given that both require massive expense. Technological growth does not happen in a vacuum. Whether the transfer is accomplished through international means or indigenous growth, massive expense or funding underlines the policy of technological optimization and advancement. Therefore, a successful transfer is not merely dependent on the willingness of the transferor but, most importantly, the willingness of the recipient to properly fund the exercise. There should be a coordinated funding of human and technical capacities of the country. In other words, there should be a deliberate policy of funding education, research institutes, industrial capabilities and programmes tangential to technological advancement. As pointed out above, one of the greatest challenges in the discussion of technological transfer is the role of government funding in 'facilitating learning, technology acquisition, and dynamic comparative advantage that cannot be appropriated by private agents and hence will not be paid for by any individual firm'.[47] Government can deploy carefully targeted subsidies to stimulate key sectors, making them more efficient and competitive and providing positive spillovers to other sectors of the economy.[48] That is, through the foregoing a government can 'provide critical coordination of a sort not available through market-generated interactions'.[49] An efficient reliance on subsidy arrangements necessitates that the 'governments be effective at both identifying cases that justify subsidies and at implementing them appropriately',[50] without prejudice to obligations under the World Trade Organization (WTO) Agreement on Subsidies and Countervailing Measures.

Strictly speaking, government alone cannot fund such programmes. Corporate entities, profit-making institutions and individuals with financial capacity do contribute to funding R&D. Therefore, technological growth is properly aligned with

46 *Ibid.*

47 WIPO, '*International Technology Transfer: an Analysis From the Perspective of Developing Countries*', 23.

48 *Ibid.*

49 *Ibid.*

50 *Ibid.* 24.

proper funding from both the government and non-governmental bodies. It should be noted that in order to achieve such coordinated funding, the fund donated by non-governmental bodies must be utilized for the purpose for which it was donated, otherwise there will be disincentive for further funding. This is buttressed by the finding that:

> [a]mong the potential problems are that subsidies can serve to support inefficiency; that firms may behave strategically (by under-investing, for example) in order to win subsidies; and that subsidies can result in corruption, bad corporate governance and rent-seeking behavior. The biggest challenge of implementing subsidies is that they are difficult to control and that the government needs to establish an effective (credible) exit strategy that weeds out successful efforts from unsuccessful ones.[51]

(d) Scrutiny of bilateral agreement

Apart from financial incentives, African countries should be wary of TRIPS-Plus agreements. More often than not, African countries conclude trade and investment agreements that restrict their development aspirations. Such unbalanced agreements are sometimes caused by unequal bargaining power and the desire of the least powerful country for market access to an advanced economy. Unequal bargaining power ensures the imposition of these agreements on the weaker party in dire need of the investment.[52] Indeed, most developed countries have a template prepared on a 'take it or leave it' basis, knowing the desperation of capital importing countries to attract foreign capital. In effect, there is little or no room for equal bargaining, which may give room for the variation of the crystallized standard terms. However, the host country has the right to regulate the entry and establishment of foreign investment.[53] Such a right to determine admission should be exercised in a manner not inimical to the relevant country's trade and investment policy.

Moreover, African civil society and intellectuals should imbibe the culture of impact assessment of other countries' experiences in order to guide the government in determining the options to conclude, modify, or reject an agreement. It is understood that some of the agreements are concluded in an atmosphere of secrecy, but African civil society and intellectuals should be able to find ways of

51 *Ibid.*

52 Jose Luis Siqueiros, 'Bilateral Treaties on the Reciprocal Protection of Foreign Investment' (1994) 24 *California Western International Law Journal* 257.

53 K.J. Vandevelde, 'Investment Liberalisation and Economic Development: The Role of Bilateral Investment Treaties' (1998) 36 *Columbia Journal of Transnational Law* 514.

fostering greater transparency and openness. The willingness of government to listen is intertwined with the legitimacy of the election that brought the government to power. A democratic government will more likely listen than an authoritarian government. Be that as it may, African civil society and intellectuals owe it as a debt to find ways of obtaining important documents with broad technological policy implication. Increasingly, international investment agreements incorporate a provision on transparency that requires disclosure by the parties.[54] Although this applies mostly to laws, regulations and rulings emanating from the host State, it is considered that it could constitute a touchstone for greater openness and transparency in future negotiation and conclusion of agreements. The role of African civil society and intellectuals above goes hand in hand with constructive engagement.

(e) Constructive engagement

One of the main tools of modern governance is constructive criticism of the policy and direction of the government.[55] A responsive and responsible government relies on the strength of such criticism to correct and redirect itself. African civil society and intellectuals should consider the availability of this option to redirect government when derailment is imminent, particularly in the area of economic advancement (without prejudice to its application in other areas).[56] The process may start with constructive advice on the government pertaining to the direction of the economic policy thrust necessary for development, particularly international trade and investment agreements. This extends to the implications of the agreement to be entered into or already concluded by the government. Where the government is not heeding the advice, persuasion may be sought. If the aforementioned does not yield the required outcome, a more radical approach may be resorted to, such as whistle-blowing to galvanize others to join the clamour for the government to

54 UNCTAD, *Transparency* (UNCTAD, 2012) 16.

55 In the areas of trade and investment agreement, UNCTAD acknowledges the vital role of civil societies in fostering better policy, noting that they bring fresh information, ideas, and expertise, as well as information about what is happening on the ground, including playing a significant advocacy role. See UNCTAD, *A Compendium of UNCTAD Partnerships with Civil Society and the Private Sector* (UNCTAD, 2015) 2.

56 See Corporate Europe Observatory, *Civil Society call for full Transparency in EU-US Trade Negotiations* (2014) https://corporateeurope.org/international-trade/2014/05/civil-society-call-full-transparency-eu-us-trade-negotiations, accessed 4 July 2018.

change direction.[57] In fact, this approach seems controversial because of the potential brute force that may be resorted to, reminiscent of most governments of Africa. Nevertheless, a proper deployment of constructive engagement with government will foster an agreement favourable to the technological advancement of African countries, through public opinion sampling prior to the conclusion of trade and investment agreements.

Conclusion

The competition between the necessity to protect intellectual property rights and the availability of flexibilities to foster the technological development aspirations of developing countries continues to constitute a recurring conundrum. While the TRIPS Agreement has provided for some flexibilities to foster technological development essential to the developing countries, the effect in a practical sense has not been substantial. To make matters worse, the post-TRIPS regime characterized by TRIPS-Plus regimes are poised to embed even a stronger protection of intellectual property rights and standards. These will have far-reaching implications for the technological transfer options and opportunities for developing countries to catch up economically, particularly African countries. In effect, African countries ought to readjust their technological transfer and development policies in order to strengthen local capacities, internalize available transfer opportunities, as well as foster absorptive capacities and innovation capabilities of national recipients.

57 See Marika Armanovica and Roberto Bendini, *Civil Society's Concerns about the Transatlantic Trade and Investment Partnership* (2014) www.europarl.europa.eu/RegData/etudes/IDAN/2014/536404/EXPO_IDA(2014)536404-EN.pdf, accessed 4 July 2018.

6

Accountability of multinational corporations for human rights violations in investment regimes in Africa

Alain-Guy Sipowo

Introduction

When we speak of development and investment in Africa, it is primarily thought to be business opportunities, growth, and improvement of the economic conditions of people. The concept of development, which has led to intense debate, still continues to connote an idea of market, economy, wealth, production and consumption. We rarely question the dark side of it and when we do, we run the risk of attracting critiques and controversies. One of the rooted beliefs in people's imagination in Africa is that the continent has some catching up to do and must address its weaknesses at all costs. So, democracy, good governance, justice and the rule of law can wait. When it happens that governance or justice is invoked in connection with development and foreign direct investment (FDI), it is in the traditional sense, which refers to creating a social, political and legal environment conducive to the business climate.

Some authors consider that 'a favourable climate [for business] would include access to finance and imported inputs, enforcement of contracts, reliable regulatory standards, adequate power and other infrastructure support, and adequate competition in the domestic economy'.[1] In fact, social and political stability, as the favourable climate for business is sometimes called, is far from being the only determinant for attracting FDI. According to a 2014 World Bank report, one notes that some sub-Saharan African countries known for their instability have been major recipients of FDI. They are, for instance, the Democratic Republic of the Congo, Madagascar

1 Thomas Farole and Deborah Winkler (eds), *Making Foreign Direct Investment Work for Sub-Saharan Africa: Local Spillovers and Competitiveness in Global Value Chains* (The World Bank, 2014) 4.

or Sudan.[2] The presence of these countries in the list of top recipients of FDI is particularly worrisome. It indicates that instability can also be conducive to FDI. In other words, the favourable climate is FDI-biased, notwithstanding its negative social, political, economic or legal implications. It is in this context that the question of the role of the African human rights system with respect to the accountability of multinational corporations is posed.

While it is indisputable that Africa needs FDI to grow, the question as to whether this investment is sustainable, that is to say, whether it takes into account economic progress as much as social issues, is acute. If we had to put on a scale the contribution of FDI to development and its impact on the human rights of Africans, we would probably be facing a zero-sum equation, or simply a negative result. Indeed, more on that continent than elsewhere, multinational corporations, which are the core source of FDI, are associated with scourges like armed conflicts, corruption of governments, environmental destruction, exploitation of labour, and social upheaval. International institutions and economic organizations, such as the Organisation for Economic Co-operation and Development (OECD), have taken measures to regulate their behaviour in relation to the protection of human rights. This effort has given birth to a non-binding instrument whose purpose is to 'promote positive contributions by enterprises to economic, environmental and social progress worldwide'.[3] These guidelines are interesting, as they have been adopted by those very countries 'from which a large share of international direct investment originates and which are home to many of the largest multinational enterprises'.[4] The 2011 version of the guidelines has included a chapter on human rights thanks to a similar process within the United Nations (UN) to submit multinational corporations and other enterprises to international law, particularly international human rights norms.[5]

In fact, these guidelines have not delivered the awaited effects solely because they have lacked binding force or implementation mechanisms proportionate to

2 World Bank, *Foreign Direct Investment Flows into Sub-Saharan Africa. Science, Technology, and Skills for Africa's Development* (2014) http://documents.worldbank.org/curated/en/505071468203651135/Foreign-direct-investment-flows-into-Sub-Saharan-Africa, accessed 6 September 2016.

3 OECD, *OECD Guidelines for Multinational Enterprises* (2011 edition) 3.

4 *Ibid.*

5 United Nations Human Rights Office of the High Commissioner, *Guiding Principles on Business and Human Rights: Implementing the United Nations "Protect, Respect and Remedy" Framework* (New York and Geneva: United Nations, 2011).

the issues they are supposed to tackle. In Africa in particular, it appears that the international character of these guidelines diminishes their legal and political force.

With the OECD guidelines having been developed by the very countries exporting FDI, it is doubtful that the national focal points (NFPs) established to ensure compliance with the guidelines would mobilize the required energy to perform their function with independence and impartiality. In fact, even when these NFPs do take their work seriously, they are impeded from accomplishing meaningful surveillance over corporations because they lack the coercive or repressive power to render them accountable when they do not submit to the NFP's voluntary jurisdiction. In any event, if African countries were concerned by the submission of multinational corporations to international norms, it would not be advisable for them to rely on foreign mechanisms to act on their behalf. My conviction in this chapter is that Africa and Africans need to trace their own vision of what development is and, in that regard, set up the regulatory standards according to which they would measure economic and social progress. There are evident shortcomings in relying on foreign and external regulatory institutions and mechanisms to hold corporations accountable for their wrongdoings in Africa.

On the one hand, there is an argument of legitimacy and credibility to be made. It is difficult to contemplate the grounds on which foreigners should be concerned by the situation of human rights in Africa than African themselves. While public opinion in Western countries can be moved by ideas of 'global justice', the governments representing them do not generally share the same sympathy. Even if they do, it is hard to see this sympathy translated into bold actions that could lead to imposing constraints on their corporations in their operations abroad. In a global economic context of harsh competition, without an international system of accountability for multinational corporations, any OECD country would be reluctant to impose too many obligations on its multinationals for fear of side effects on its competitiveness. Therefore, asking NFPs to investigate multinationals' human rights records in foreign countries is asking those countries providing FDI in Africa to limit their economic expansion. Those countries find themselves in a clear dilemma where they have to choose between real enforcement of international norms and the risk of prejudicing their economic influence worldwide. For that reason, NFPs cannot be said to offer any guarantee of enforcement of corporate accountability for human rights abuse in foreign countries.

The legitimacy problem is not only posed as far as the independence and impartiality of foreign enforcement institutions are concerned. Even if foreign courts were able to hold corporations accountable in relation to human rights abuse in Africa, it might be seen in some African countries as interference in their domestic affairs and mostly as interference in their right to determine their economic policies. To say the least, making a determination as to the violation of human rights by a multinational, in particular when the violations are accompanied by corruption, is also making a judgment as to the manner with which African countries conduct their domestic affairs. Therefore, it would sometimes be the fear of being labelled 'neo-colonialists' more than a lack of independence and impartiality that would refrain Western regulatory mechanisms to investigate corporate wrongdoings in Africa.

On the other hand, passing the enforcement of human rights from multinational corporations to their countries of origin would convey the message of unwillingness or of inability of African countries to hold those corporations accountable. It would certainly strengthen the idea that those enterprises are more economically powerful than African states and are likely to influence their economic, political and social destiny. The truth is that African countries are in a better position than foreign institutions to inquire about human rights records of corporations on the continent.

First, since these corporations operate on their territories, for this sole reason, they have the necessary legitimacy and credibility to investigate the practice and behaviour of multinationals. It is the position most consonant with public international law that jurisdiction is above all territorial and that extraterritorial jurisdiction, as can be performed by foreign courts, is the exception.

Second, because of the consequences of enterprise accountability on economic development, African States are better placed to strike the proper balance between their quest for economic growth and the protection of human rights of individuals and and collective groups. It is of utmost importance that African countries affirm their model of development to the rest of the world. This can only be done through a proper assessment of the role of multinational corporations in their economy and society as a whole. To entrust Western countries with the task of holding their own corporations accountable while the latter operate on foreign soil would be seen as a surrender of their responsibility to people who might not take it seriously for one reason or another.

In terms of governance, and swapping the national level for the continental level, it is surprising to see that many Africans do not have confidence in their own human rights institutions. This has been visible through their eagerness to seize Western courts for their cases against multinational corporations in Europe, the United States of America and Canada. At first sight, seeing victims and groups of victims being obliged to cross the Atlantic to seek justice tells all about the state of human rights protection in Africa. Neither national institutions, nor the African human rights system, have been able to deliver the promise of justice on which they are founded. Henceforth, time should be considered ripe for African institutions to take stock of the failures of the past to build better societies for Africans. It is entirely imaginary to continue to believe that Africa's emergence depends solely on economic progress. The starting point of any vision for development should necessarily take into account human conditions. Furthermore, it is because multinational corporations often do not bear in mind such a precept that human rights institutions on the continent should pay attention to the way these entities conduct their business on the African continent.

In that respect, the role of the African human rights system is crucial for a few reasons. First, in a context where African States could be unwilling or unable to provide for an adequate response to human rights violations by corporations, the continental system can intervene as a last defence. Practical reasons militate for such an intervention. A State's shortage of financial resources and lack of expertise can be some of them, just to name a few. Most importantly, the political and social contexts in which violations take place make it unrealistic to expect national judiciaries to act independently and impartially against multinationals, which might have established close links with governmental institutions and officials. Secondly, after some years of promoting corporate social responsibility and other codes of conduct, corporations as well as States, have not shown that they can be trusted with the voluntary enforcement of their human rights obligations. Thirdly, cognizant of the potential impediments that victims of corporate wrongdoings could face, the UN Guiding Principles on Business and Human Rights (UNGP), which does not provide for a monitoring mechanism, calls on States to promote and facilitate access to reparation for victims, including through regional and international human rights organizations.

Starting from this recommendation, it is the ambition of this chapter to assess whether Africa is ready to seek corporate accountability for human rights violations, even in investment regimes. In Section 1, I will argue that investment law has developed in Africa not with the aim of helping Africans to develop their economy and improve their conditions of life, but rather as a means for foreign corporations to avoid accounting for their wrongdoings before African regulatory mechanisms. As in other areas where Africa has developed norms that distinguish themselves from those adopted internationally, it would be interesting to see whether with regard to the protection of human rights in general, there is a philosophical approach to corporate accountability in Africa that detracts itself from international guidelines and codes of conduct. How the African continent envisioned the role of corporations in its economy in particular and in societies in general while promoting and protecting FDI will be analysed. This is of paramount importance, since one would be tempted to believe that African countries concede more rights to corporations than impose obligations because of their unbridled pursuit of development.

In Section 2, I will analyse the new generation of investment treaties or codes, which tend to take into account public policy interests, such as human rights and the environment, in the context of investment promotion and protection. This analysis will help to ascertain whether the investment regime is capable of introspection to respond to one of its major critiques, this is that it only confers rights and do not impose obligations or responsibilities upon corporations.

Finally, I will provide some concluding remarks, in which I will try to ascertain whether there has been an evolution in investment regimes in Africa towards the protection of human rights and the accountability of multinational corporations thereof. Indeed, the overall assessment of the issue of business and human rights allows the conclusion to be drawn that the reason why recent African investment regimes tend more and more to impose obligations or responsibilities on corporations and they still fail to provide for strong enforcement mechanisms. The inter-State paradigm continues to be dominant, which prevents third party interests to be voiced efficiently in investment arbitration without the intermediary of States. Time appears not to be ripe for a system of accountability of multinational corporations for human rights abuses, at the top of which individual victims and indigenous communities would have a *locus standi*.

1 The investment regime and avoidance of accountability by multinational corporations in Africa

Avoidance of liability manifests itself in two ways: on the one hand, the investment regime reduces the regulatory capacity of African States, and thus their power to impose obligations and responsibilities on enterprises (Section 1(a)); On the other hand, the investment regime systematically refers to arbitration on the settlement of disputes that may arise between the host country and multinational companies (Section 1(b)).

(a) Constraining the regulatory power of host States

In recent years, international investment law has been at the centre of an intense debate and critique. At the heart of this debate is the concern of masses of populations worldwide regarding the inappropriate strike of balance between societal competing interests. The investment regime has tended to favor economic and investor 'rights' or 'interests' to the detriment of other public policies. While this issue has been put under the spotlight by scholars and non-governmental organizations more recently, it appears that this problem is not new at all, particularly with respect to the manner in which investment law has developed in the underdeveloped world in general and in Africa in particular. At a time where most people are concerned by global justice, investment law is far from being a legal regime capable of taking into account such a concern. This is because the foundational bases for the discipline take us back to a colonial era.

Indeed, the origin of the field is situated in the seventeenth century 'within the historical context of corporate law, diplomatic pressure, military intervention, and colonial annexation'.[6] In the colonial period, there was no need for investment law, since colonial empires had full rights to exploit and engage in trade with their colonies. When they had to employ the law, it was not always in the interest of all the parties engaged. This period is well known for unjust or unequal legal relationships as contained in friendship, commerce and navigation treaties, concessions and de jure or de facto domination of non-European peoples.[7] With the entry into the decolonization era, this harsh domination only changed for a softer one, notably through institutions and norms backed by the 'law'. Just as African countries did not have enough control over their economic relationships with Western countries during colonization, the bilateral investment treaties (BITs) they have entered into in great number from the aftermath of their independence through the 1990s to the time of writing, perpetuate this state of affairs.

No scholar would tell you what benefit host countries gain from investment treaties, apart from the idea that they would attract FDIs. Of course, by attracting such investments, they would pursue their development, create job opportunities for their populations and strengthen their economy. However, as a United Nations Economic Commission for Africa (UNECA) study has concluded, 'there is no conclusive evidence regarding the effect of these treaties on foreign investment'.[8] This is not to say that BITs cannot contribute to bringing FDI to Africa. UNECA's affirmation tends only to highlight that the benefits of those treaties might have been exaggerated.

6 Michael Fakhri, 'The Origins of International Investment Law: Empire, Environment, and the Safeguarding of Capital By Kate Miles' 18 (3) (2015) *Journal of International Economic Law* 697.

7 *Ibid.*

8 UNECA, *Investment Agreements Landscape in Africa* (Addis Ababa: UNECA, 2015) 1 para. 4.

In fact, and to do justice to history, the idea that host countries would receive more FDI by entering into BITs is nothing more than the guile that developed countries have used to secure the protection of their interests in distant countries. The objective assigned to BITs is often tersely summed up in the promotion and protection of investments, implying that they would take into account both the interests of the host countries (promotion) and the interests and rights of investors (protection). However, in the substantive content of the obligations defined by BITs, there is a place only for the protection of investments, as if this alone would catalyse their promotion, that is to say, for foreigners to decide to inject capital in the economy of host countries.

Efforts to improve the investment climate have brought African countries to enlarge the number of privileges and rights conferred to foreign corporations. This has been termed 'reduction of regulatory barriers to foreign investment',[9] meaning that African countries lower their legal standards to attract investments, something which is curiously encouraged in BITs as well as economic international institutions such as the International Monetary Fund (IMF) or the World Bank. In that regard, labor standards are weakened and some countries do not hesitate to offer 'tax rebates' and 'repatriation of capital from the proceeds of investment' to foreign companies.[10] This has only been possible when a particular standard or regulation could come in conflict with investors' interests or rights. Indeed, in some other areas, investors would call for stringent norms. This has been the case, for instance, with respect to intellectual property rights. Consequently, with demanding rules on intellectual property, Africa is unable to produce the most basic medicines to cure diseases that are only found on the continent and which eat up a significant part of the public health budget of African countries. Some investment treaties even include a provision prohibiting the receiving State to force the investor into technology, production process or other proprietary knowledge transfer.[11]

9 *Ibid.* para. 3.

10 *Ibid.* para. 18.

11 See, for instance, Canada–Cameroon BIT (2014) in Canada Treaty Series 2016/15, Article 9:

> [1. A Party may not impose the following requirements in connection with the establishment, acquisition, expansion, management, conduct or operation of an investment of an investor of a Party in its territory: … (f) to transfer technology, a production process or other proprietary knowledge to a person in its territory …].

(b) State-investors dispute settlement mechanisms as means of avoiding accountability for human rights abuses

One time back in history, the first-generation BITs only allowed for State-to-State dispute settlement. This was known as diplomatic protection. Nowadays, modern BITs exclusively incorporate investor-to-State arbitrations. This dispute settlement system is acclaimed by the International Centre for Settlement of Investment Disputes (ICSID) Tribunals as having contributed to lowering tensions between governments and reducing political discretion, which was the main feature of diplomatic protection.[12] However, this change of paradigm, while reinforcing private investors rights to have independent access to a dispute settlement mechanism, has neutralized the State capacity to stand against private actors' misbehaviours. Not only is the modern mechanism to settle investor-State disputes one-sided, it opens no way for the public to have their concerns voiced. This has left human rights and environmental issues out of the purview of arbitration tribunals.

From 1972 to 2014, the African continent participated in 111 investment arbitration cases, representing about one fifth of treaty-based arbitrations. In 2015, forty three of those cases were still pending despite having started, for some of them, as far back as 2004.[13] Many of them are ICSID arbitrations, while three are being conducted under United Nations Commission on International Trade Law (UNCITRAL) rules and a few under Southern African Development Community (SADC) or Arab State arbitration rules and panels.[14] In some high-profile cases, UNECA has assessed that 'the right of a government to regulate in the public interest appears to have taken second stage to private investor rights, in particular on issues relating to expropriation'.[15]

International legal personality has to do with the status of subjects of international law, as are natural persons with respect to national law. However, there

12 *Banro American Resources, Inc. and Société Aurifère du Kivu et du Maniema S.A.R.L.* v. *Democratic Republic of the Congo* (2002) 17 ICSID Rev. 8 FILJ 382, para. 15. See the Convention on the Settlement of Investment Disputes Between States and Nationals of other States (2006) https://icsid.worldbank.org/en/documents/icsiddocs/icsid%20convention%20english.pdf, accessed 29 June 2018, Article 27 (prohibiting the recourse to diplomatic protection by State Parties).

13 UNECA Report, *Investment Agreements Landscape in Africa*, para. 22.

14 *Ibid.* 23–4.

15 *Ibid.* 25.

seems to be no agreed definition of what international legal personality means.[16] For the purpose of this section, we are considering international legal personality according to an extensive approach, under which international legal personality means the capacity to be invested with rights and obligations by international law.[17] Investment treaties are among the first legal instruments to affirm the legal personality of legal entities, notably by providing for rights of 'investors', which most of the time and essentially are not natural persons but legal entities. Even with respect to the narrow conception of international legal personality, according to which subjects of international law should be capable of concluding agreements, bringing international claims and establishing diplomatic missions, investment treaties provide for the distinct feature of international legal personality, which is the capacity to bring international claims.[18] The intermediate approach to legal personality followed by the International Court of Justice (ICJ) in the *Reparation for Injuries Suffered in the Service of the United Nations* case is clearer. The Court considered in this case that an entity holds international legal personality if 'it is capable of possessing international rights and duties, and that it has capacity to maintain its rights by bringing international claims'.[19]

No one would contest that investment treaties, though not concluded by corporations but by States of origin and host States, invest these States with rights and with the procedural capacity to have those rights enforced through international arbitral tribunals. The problem, which has long been denounced, is the biased character of investment treaties, which, while recognizing plenty of rights attributed to (corporate) 'investors', have failed to impose legal duties on them. This has particularly been the case with respect to investment treaties involving African countries which 'confer more protection and rights on foreign investors, skewing conditions to the detriment of domestic or third party investors and reducing potential benefits for Africa, while also exposing host countries to the risk of legal disputes'.[20]

Indeed, traditionally, the purpose of investment treaties has been to promote and protect foreign investors in order to attract FDI. The consideration behind the

16 Vincent Chetail, 'The Legal Personality of Multinational Corporations, State Responsibility and Due Diligence: The Way Forward' (2013) in D. Alland *et al.* (eds) *Unity and Diversity of International Law. Essays in Honour of Prof. Pierre-Marie Dupuy*, 107. (Martinus Nijhoff, 2014) http://ssrn.com/abstract=2364450, accessed 6 July 2017.

17 *Ibid.* 107.

18 *Ibid.* 108.

19 International Court of Justice Reports, *Reparation for Injuries Suffered in the Service of the United Nations* (1949) Advisory Opinion, 174, 179.

20 UNECA Report, *Investment Agreements Landscape in Africa*, para. 4.

attraction of foreign investors is that their investment would contribute to the socio-economic development of the host country. However, beyond this general understanding of the aim of investment treaties, the intentions of parties are rarely the same. For foreigners, BITs serve to ensure that investment made in strategic sectors in former colonies are protected, whereas for African countries, entering into such treaties serve only as a means of asserting their international sovereignty.[21]

2 New generations of BITs and the protection of human rights against multinational corporations

A typical new-generation of BIT (NGBIT) is one that strikes a better balance between the private and public interests at stake.[22] To achieve this goal, NGBITs include some objectives which go beyond mere protection of investors. The main features of such NGBITs can be summarized as follows: (1) the counter-balance of investors' rights against those of the host State with extended obligations geared toward achieving sustainable development, including an obligation to uphold human rights; (2) the safeguard of the policy space of the host State and 3) the liability/accountability of corporations in case of wrongdoing. In the following developments, I will concentrate on the imposition of binding human rights obligations on corporations (Section 2(a)) and the means to hold them liable or accountable for breaching those obligations (Section 2(b)).

(a) Corporate obligations to uphold human rights in NGBITs

In the era before the NGBIT, corporate obligations to uphold human rights were only subsumed from the legal personality of multinational corporations. It has been argued that if corporations have rights, they also have duties. However, duties and obligations are not really the same. In any event, it was not clear, as far human rights obligations are concerned, what type of duties or obligations were bestowed on them. The UNGP is the most recent legal instrument that endeavours to sketch the human rights obligations of corporations. Just like the OECD guidelines, the guiding principles are not binding, which explains the UN's decision to set up a

21 *Ibid.* 15.

22 Tarcisio Gazzini, 'Nigeria and Morocco Move Towards a "New Generation" of Bilateral Investment Treaties' (2017) *EJIL: Talk!* www.ejiltalk.org/nigeria-and-morocco-move-towards-a-new-generation-of-bilateral-investment-treaties/, accessed 4 July 2017.

working group to draft an internationally binding instrument to regulate corporate behaviour with respect to human rights.

While this initiative is laudable, the general character of the instrument to be adopted could be its main weakness. A single 'one size fits all' convention might not necessarily be the best approach. Reaching a consensus on a general binding convention could be hard to achieve on the one hand and not the best option on the other because corporations are distinct from one sector of the economy to another. While it might be necessary in investment law to set out the human rights obligations of corporations, it is less sure that the same is desirable in other sectors. Also, a common understanding of the need for corporations to uphold human rights obligations in investment regimes might emerge more rapidly than in any other area.

NGBITs seem to have been built on the experience of State counterclaims in investor-State arbitrations to impose upon corporations an obligation to uphold human rights. In *Biloune* v. *Ghana* (1994), for instance, it was ruled that 'a ruling on human rights violations is outside the scope of [the tribunal] jurisdiction'.[23] Indeed, the Tribunal's jurisdiction is generally defined in the BIT and the relevant documents introducing the arbitration proceedings. The common understanding within the investor community is that in the absence of a sort of umbrella clause in a BIT providing for specific obligations, including human rights obligations, the respondent State cannot claim the breach of human rights obligations in an arbitration proceedings. Furthermore, since human rights obligations derive from rules of international law, these rules are 'directly binding on States but not on private parties',[24] such as multinational corporations. In a recent arbitral award, a tribunal held a nuance opinion about these arguments.

In *Urbaser* v. *Argentina*, the claimants sought payment of damages, arguing that the treatment of their investment in a concession for water and sewage services by Argentina violated their rights under the Spain–Argentina BIT. The respondent State, Argentina, raised a counterclaim in which it argued that the investors failed 'to provide the necessary investment into the Concession, thus violating its commitments and its obligations under international law based on the human right to

23 *Antoine Biloune and Marine Drive Complex Ltd* v. *Ghana Investments Centre and the Government of Ghana* (1994) *XIX Yearbook of Commercial Arbitration* 11.

24 *Urbaser S.A. and Consorcio de Aguas Bilbao Bizkaia Ur Partzuergoa* v. *The Argentine Republic* (8 December 2016) ICSID Case No. ARB/07/26, Award, para. 1129.

water'.[25] The Tribunal responded that though investors/companies can be subject of international law, there is no general obligation for companies to act in accordance with international human rights law (IHRL) unless it is provided for by a general rule of international law or a treaty.[26] Like the UNGP, the Tribunal found that just like a natural person, companies should not act in disregard of human rights,[27] meaning they should not 'engage in activity aimed at destroying such rights'.[28] For the Tribunal, BITs should not be interpreted in a vacuum. An investment treaty, according to the Tribunal, ' … has to be construed in harmony with other rules of international law of which it forms part, including those relating to human rights'.[29] However, this does not necessarily mean that companies are bound by international human rights norms. In the case considered, the respondent State could not argue that investors were bound by international law to provide for the human right to water only because there was an obligation under the concession to provide for water and sewage services.[30] It therefore appears that in the absence of express IHRL rules imposing positive obligations on business, their obligations under IHRL would be limited to negative obligations.[31]

It is the aim of NGBITs to explicitly provide for human rights obligations for corporations. In the Nigeria–Morocco BIT, signed in 2016, human rights obligations are explicitly placed on investors. Article 18(2) of the Treaty provides that 'investors and investment shall uphold human rights in the host State'. In paragraph 3 of the same Article 18, it is required from investors to 'act in accordance with core labour standards as required by the ILO [International Labour Organization] Declaration on Fundamental Principles and Rights of Work, 1998'. While this is certainly a step forward in terms of imposing human rights obligations on private parties, the content of the human rights obligations of corporations remains unresolved.[32] The Nigeria–Morocco 2016 BIT seems to have borrowed from the

25 *Ibid.* para. 36.
26 *Ibid.* para. 1207.
27 *Ibid.* para. 1196.
28 *Ibid.* para. 1199.
29 *Ibid.* para. 1200; *Tulip Real E and Development Netherlands B.V.* v. *Republic of Turkey* (30 December 2015) ICSID Case No. ARB/11/28, Decision on Annulment, paras 86–92 (referring to the principle of systemic integration).
30 *Urbaser* v. *Argentina* (8 December 2016), para. 1206.
31 *Ibid.* para. 1210.
32 Anil Yilmaz-Vastardis, 'Is International Investment Law Moving the Ball Forward on IHRL Obligations for Business Enterprises?' (2017) *EJIL: Talk!* www.ejiltalk.org/is-international-investment-law-moving-the-ball-forward-on-ihrl-obligations-for-business-enterprises/, accessed 5 July 2017.

Economic Community of West African States Treaty (ECOWAS) Supplementary Act on Investments, Article 14 of which states the following:

1. Investors or investments shall, in keeping with best practice requirements relating to their activities the size of their investments, strive to comply with on hygiene, security, health and social welfare rules in force in the host country.
2. Investors shall uphold human rights in the workplace and the community in which they are located. Investors shall not undertake or cause to be undertaken, acts that breach such human rights. Investors shall not manage or operate the investments in a manner that circumvents human rights obligations, labour standards as well as regional environmental and social obligations, to which the host State and/or home State are Parties.
3. Investors shall not by complicity with, or in assistance with others, including pubic authorities, violate human rights in times of peace or during socio-political upheavals.
4. Investors and investments shall act in accordance with fundamental labour standards as stipulated in the ILO Declaration on Fundamental Principles and Rights of Work, 1998.[33]

On close reading, nothing in these provisions mandate a corporation to undertake activities to fulfil the human rights of people. According to paragraph 1, investor or investment shall only '*strive* to comply with hygiene, security, health and social welfare rules in force in the host country'. It is questionable why the drafters of the Act did not require strict compliance with such basic rules. This reveals that the international community is far from being ready to impose positive legal human rights obligations on private parties. In this regard, one cannot say that NGBITs have made a breakthrough in international law in terms of human rights obligations of companies. While they provide in a binding instrument the obligation of corporations to respect and to do no harm to human rights, this was already a principle of general international law according to human rights instruments and the UNGP. The very novelty is probably the environmental assessment impact, which investors and investments 'shall conduct' prior to their establishment[34] and the provisions relating to the liability of investors for human rights violations.

33 ECOWAS, Supplementary Act A/SA.3/12/08 Adopting Community Rules on Investment and the Modalities for their Implementation with ECOWAS (19 December 2008) Article 12.

34 ECOWAS, Supplementary Act A/SA.3/12/08 Adopting Community Rules on Investment and the Modalities for their Implementation with ECOWAS Article 12.

(b) Liability of corporations for human rights violations in NGBITs

In NGBITs, the liability of investors or investments for human rights violations can be envisioned in two ways. On the one hand, there is liability outside an investment dispute, which would follow the traditional pathways of adjudication. The ECOWAS Supplementary Act for instance does not speak of liability for human rights violations per se, but it is difficult to dispute the fact that such a claim can still be brought under civil action, even if the standards of adjudication are not the same. Investors are thus subject to civil actions for liability in host States for any of their acts 'made in relation to the investment where such acts or decisions lead to significant damage, personal injuries or loss of life in the host State'.[35] The requirement that the acts or decisions causing significant damage, personal injuries or loss of life be made 'in relation to the investment' is questionable. It should not be read to mean that acts of investors outside their investment activities are immune from civil liability. In fact, investment-related acts and decisions, as well as those that do not have any link with investments, are just torts which entail civil liability without the need for it to be mentioned in a BIT. Indeed, it is only incantation to put in a treaty what is part of the right or power of a host State, that's regulating activities on its territory. The framing of the South African legislation is in that regard worth citing, as it reaffirms the right to regulate investor's activities, including by 'upholding the rights guaranteed in the Constitution'.[36]

The obligation upon home States to 'ensure that their legal systems and rules allow for, or do not prevent or unduly restrict, the bringing of court actions on their merits before domestic courts relating to the civil liability of investors …'[37] probably deserved to be put in a BIT rather than host States engaging the civil liability of investors in their legal systems. It has proven difficult in recent years for victims to bring civil claims against corporations in their home States when the host States failed as a result of corruption or any other lack of political will, to pursue the liability of investors. Those difficulties arise because of legal, political and economic obstacles that are sometimes dependent on home States. It is frustrating that the home State obligation to overcome obstacles for civil liability of investors does not entail a corresponding right for victims. Only the host State would be in a position

35 *Ibid.* Article 17.

36 Government of South Africa, Protection of Investment Act No. 22 of 2015, Vol 606 No. 39514 (2015) Official Gazette Article 12(1)(c)

37 ECOWAS, Supplementary Act A/SA.3/12/08, Article 29.

to demand the enforcement of the home State obligation to ensure its legal system and rules allow the bringing of court actions relating to the civil liability of investors.

NGBITs carry with them the ambition to go further than traditional and classical BITs. However, it is hard to say, in close reading of these NGBITs, that they are revolutionary, particularly with respect to liability outside the context of an investment dispute. Civil liability is just a classic tool to ensure liability and there is nothing new in reaffirming it in an international treaty. What would have been revolutionary is generally left out of the NGBITs. For instance, while some of the human rights violations are crimes and can even amount to international crimes, nothing is said of a possible criminal liability of investors, apart, as in the ECOWAS Supplementary Act, the rights of Member States to investigate, prosecute and punish corruption-related offences.[38]

Indeed, on the other hand, investment-related disputes could also be a forum for adjudication of human rights violations. At least, the philosophy underpinning NGBITs is that public policy interests of having human rights upheld should be balanced with investor's interests. As far as investment disputes are concerned, it means that the protection of human rights can be pursued in the context of State-investor arbitrations. How this should be achieved is a subject of divergent approaches, depending on the BIT. The dilemma has been whether the respondent State in an investment dispute or a non-disputing party, meaning a human rights victim for instance, should raise public policy interests or have a say or a standing in the arbitration proceedings. The SADC has admitted that in the SADC Model BIT the contracting parties could bring counterclaims against investors in order to have the obligations of investors relating to corruption, compliance with domestic law, environmental and social impact assessments and minimum standards for human rights and labour upheld.[39] This right to initiate a counterclaim against an investor is also provided for in the Indian Model BIT.[40]

38 *Ibid.* Article 30.

39 SADC, SADC Model Bilateral Investment Treaty Template with Commentary (2012) Article 39 www.iisd.org/itn/wp-content/uploads/2012/10/sadc-model-bit-template-final.pdf, accessed 6 July 2017; for general information, see Sean Woolfrey, 'The SADC Model Bilateral Investment Treaty Template: Towards a New Standard of Investor Protection in Southern Africa' (2014) *D14TB03 Tralac Trade Brief 10.*

40 Government of India, Model Text for the Indian Bilateral Investment Treaty (2015) Article 14(11) www.mygov.in/sites/default/files/master_image/Model%20Text%20for%20the%20Indian%20Bilateral%20Investment%20Treaty.pdf, accessed 6 July 2017; for a commentary, see: Grant Hanessian and Kabir Duggal, 'The Final 2015 Indian Model BIT: Is This the Change the World Wishes to See?' (2016) 32 (1) *ICSID Review* 216–26.

This is, however, not the case for the US–Rwandan BIT[41] and the Nigeria–Morocco BIT of 2016.[42] While the US–Rwandan BIT provides for the possibility for non-disputing parties to 'make oral and written submissions to the tribunal'[43] and the authority of the latter 'to accept and consider *amicus curiae* submissions from a person or entity that is not a disputing party',[44] the Nigeria–Morocco BIT remains dully silent on third party rights in investment arbitrations.[45]

The ECOWAS Supplementary Act appears to be the most advanced model BIT with regard to corporate liability in investment dispute arbitrations. It allows a host or home State to initiate proceedings before a tribunal established pursuant to the Supplementary Act if the investor or its investments breaches or fails to comply with its obligations under the Act, including therefore the obligation to uphold human rights.[46] This provision counters the traditional BIT paradigm, where only investors could initiate arbitration proceedings. Also, an 'intervener', a term not defined by the Act, may raise the persistent non-compliance with human rights obligations of an investor in a dispute settlement proceeding with the view that if the failure to comply is proven and relates to the issue before a tribunal, it could have an impact on the merits of a claim or on any damages awarded.[47] Finally, it is provided under the Act that 'a host Member State may initiate a counterclaim before any tribunal established pursuant to this Supplementary Act for damages resulting from an alleged breach of the Supplementary Act'.[48]

All the aforementioned provisions were adopted to counterbalance the dominant position of investors in investment regimes with respect to public policy issues. Though States are the very guardians of those interests in international law, one cannot ignore

41 Treaty Between the Government of the United States of America and the Government of the Republic of Rwanda concerning the Encouragement and Reciprocal Protection of Investment (19 February 2008).

42 Reciprocal Investment Promotion and Protection Agreement Between the Government of the Kingdom of Morocco and the Government of the Federal Republic of Nigeria https://investmentpolicy.unctad.org/international-investment-agreements/treaty-files/5409/download.

43 *Ibid.* Article 28(2).

44 *Ibid.* Article 28(3).

45 Gazzini, 'Nigeria and Morocco Move Towards a "New Generation" of Bilateral Investment Treaties'.

46 ECOWAS, Supplementary Act A/SA.3/12/08, Article 18(3).

47 *Ibid.* Article 18(4).

48 *Ibid.* Article 18(5).

that in some instances, they have blatantly abused them. This can be said of host States, as well as home States of investors. In NGBITs, most of the new rights and powers awarded to States would belong to them alone and non-disputing parties to investment arbitration would not be in a capacity to trigger them. The right to initiate a counterclaim remains a right of the State, even if it is done in the interest of human rights of individuals or an indigenous community. Consequently, if the counterclaim is successful, the State alone might be awarded the pecuniary compensation.

The sole power or right of third parties to provide the arbitral tribunal with written or oral submissions or for persons and entities to submit *amicus curiae* briefs is not enough, though the potential of this mechanism to draw the tribunal's attention to public policy interests cannot be underestimated.

Concluding remarks

The question of whether human rights are protected in investment regimes and whether the liability of multinational corporations, which are most often investors, can be established in this respect, can no longer receive only a negative response. There has been a notable trend to restrict the self-contained nature of investment treaties. They are now permeable to objectives broader than the protection and promotion of investors and their investments. On the African continent, such a development, even though it appears slow and incoherent, is still to be welcomed. It comes mainly from the most important economies such as South Africa, Nigeria and Morocco, but it should be followed by all African States.

In investment treaties the inclusion of human rights obligations and rules on investors and investments' liability in the event of infringement of these rights may appear, so to speak, like an incantation. Such a conclusion would ignore the fact that African countries are emerging from a system of BITs that 'primarily intended to protect the vested interests of developed country partners already present in the region'.[49] Under such regimes, the power to regulate the activities of investors was locked in arrangements beneficial to foreigners, thereby neutralizing or inhibiting the ability of African countries to adequately play their role as guardians of collective interests. The new generations of investment treaties can be criticized for recalling the obvious, namely: investors must respect human rights; public authorities have the power to

49 UNECA, *Investment Policies and Bilateral Investment Treaties in Africa: Implications for Regional Integration* (2016) 17 www.uneca.org/sites/default/files/PublicationFiles/eng_investment_landscaping_study.pdf, accessed 20 July 2017.

regulate investors' activities in the light of social interests in the areas of the environment, human rights and workers' rights; that host or home States, as well as private persons, may exercise civil remedies in the event of default by investors in their obligations. These obvious principles are worth reiterating, precisely because most African States do not always implement their international treaty obligations.

These principles are reinstated in NGBITs, alongside some novelties, particularly with regard to the investment dispute settlement system. Some of these NGBITs reaffirm the central role of national courts in adjudicating investment-related disputes instead of referring them to arbitral tribunals. The consequences for human rights are undeniable, since ordinary courts have a constitutional obligation to guarantee fundamental rights, which arbitral tribunals could easily lose sight of because of the specific nature of their constitutional and procedural rules. In this respect, South Africa has made the most radical choice by terminating its BITs, which it has replaced by a single piece of national legislation. Other less radical solutions pose the problem of their ineffectiveness. This is the case of the right of African States to initiate counterclaims in arbitration and the right of third parties to submit written or oral submissions on the obligations of investors and their investments to safeguard, in their activities, the public interests of protecting the environment, human rights and workers' rights or fighting corruption.

For me, these few measures to offset the rights of investors are certainly encouraging, but insufficient. They essentially reaffirm the tutelary figure of the State, which alone carries the interests of its nationals in the international arena. From an investment law perspective, this might be the most appropriate approach because a multiple party arbitration would be counterproductive to the economic interests of investors and States. After all, arbitration tribunals should not become human rights courts. Therefore, human rights activists and civil society actors should bear in mind that the liability of corporations for human rights violations can be sought somewhere other than in investment regimes or before investment tribunals. There is certainly the possibility for victims of corporate wrongdoing to bring their case to national courts or host States and home States of investors. However, other international mechanisms can be triggered when a State fails to guarantee that the harm suffered by victims because of investors is properly addressed.

On the one hand, the human rights system of the African Union has the capacity to ensure the compliance of corporations with their international obligation to respect human rights. The African Commission on Human and Peoples' Rights (known as 'the Commission') and its Court do not have direct enforcement jurisdiction against corporations certainly, but they can use their supervisory and monitoring function, as well as their adjudicatory power, against States to inquire about the human rights performance of private persons. The African Charter on Human and Peoples' Rights provides that every individual shall have duties.[50] A teleological interpretation of the notion 'individual' should allow this term to be read as 'private persons' and to include corporations and thus investors. The duties of the individual are owed to other individuals, to the family, to the community and to the State[51] and comprise the duty of mutual respect and tolerance, to pay taxes, to contribute to the moral well-being of society, and to preserve and strengthen social and national solidarity. Most of these duties are consonant with the sustainable development objectives, to which corporations should contribute.[52]

According to the African Court on Human and Peoples' Rights, the State has the duty to enforce on an individual the obligation under Article 27(2) of the Charter to exercise its rights with due regard to common interest.[53] It is in line with this that Nigerian plaintiffs filed a complaint with the Commission in 2005 alleging violation of Articles 27 and 29 of the Charter by companies involved in smuggling activities in Nigeria. They argued that, by engaging in the smuggling of narcotics and their modified forms, minerals, illegal arms, and pharmaceutical products, the smugglers deprived Nigeria of 101 trillion naira annually, causing the impoverishment and even murders of many people. Though the Commission declared the case inadmissible for non-exhaustion of local remedies,[54] this case is proof that corporate activities can be assessed in settings other than investment arbitration.

50 African Charter on Human and Peoples' Rights (27 June 1981) Article 27. See also *Lohé Issa Konaté* v. *The Republic of Burkina Faso* (16 February 2016) No. 004/2013, Separate Opinion of Judges Elsie N. Thompson, A.B. Akuffo, Bernard Ngoppe and Duncan Tambala, para. 134.

51 African Charter on Human and Peoples' Rights, Article 29.

52 See Johannesburg Declaration on Sustainable Development annex to the Report of the World Summit on Sustainable Development, Johannesburg, South Africa, 26 August–4 September 2002 (A/CONF.199/20) (New York: United Nations, 2002) 4, para. 27:

> 'We agree that in pursuit of its legitimate activities the private sector, including both large and small companies, has a duty to contribute to the evolution of equitable and sustainable communities and societies'.

See also para. 29:

> 'We agree that there is a need for private sector corporations to enforce corporate accountability, which should take place within a transparent and stable regulatory environment'.

53 *Lohé Issa Konaté* v. *The Republic of Burkina Faso*, para. 4.

54 *Ilesanmi* v. *Nigeria* (11 May 2005) 18th Activity Report, Tripoli: January 2005–July 2005.

On the other hand, the possibility that a corporation, hence an investor, could be held accountable for human rights abuses directly before an international tribunal should become a reality when the Amended Protocol to the African Court of Human and Peoples' Rights comes into force. The 2014 version of the Protocol adds an international criminal law section to the African Court of Justice and Human Rights, complementing other sections, namely the general section and the human and peoples' rights sections.[55] The jurisdiction of the international criminal law section extends to crimes under the Rome Statute of the International Criminal Court, but also to such crimes as unconstitutional change of government, piracy, terrorism, mercenarism, corruption, money laundering, people trafficking, drug trafficking, hazardous waste trafficking and illicit exploitation of natural resources. Some of these crimes come in enforcement of known African treaties, which do not necessarily provide for obligations of legal persons. While some of the crimes do not entertain clear links with the protection of human rights, they are, nevertheless, conducive to situations of ill governance or to social and political instability detrimental to human rights protection. Most of them can, however, be committed by natural persons, as well as legal ones. Therefore, it is quite right that the Protocol provide for corporate criminal liability.[56]

The Protocol is not yet in force, as the deposit of instruments of ratification by fifteen Member States is required according to Article 11. When it comes into force, the Protocol will be the first internationally binding instrument to provide for corporate criminal liability under international law. This is quite a breakthrough. It was not accepted in the drafting process of the Rome Statute of the International Criminal Court because corporate criminal liability was not widespread in the legal traditions of the world. However, the African Union seems not to have been discouraged by such a state of the law in Africa. The complementarity principle that the Protocol enshrines would certainly allow for rapid growth of corporate criminal liability when the Protocol comes into force. Indeed, it is likely that a State, which would not prosecute a crime under the Protocol for lack of legal basis under its national law, would be seen as unwilling or unable to do.[57]

In a nutshell, as an arbitration tribunal pointed out, BITs should not be read in isolation from other rules of international law, including international human rights

55 African Union, Protocol on Amendments to the Protocol on the Statute of the African Court of Justice and Human Rights (adopted by the twenty-third Ordinary Session of the Assembly, held in Malabo, Equatorial Guinea, 27 June 2014), Annex, Article 7.

56 *Ibid.* Article 46C.

57 *Ibid.* Article 46H.

law.[58] This is true for classic BITs and is even more true for NGBITs, which specifically provide for human rights obligations of investors, and provide means and ways for ensuring their liability. However, it is hoped that the use of these remedies will not be thwarted by such corrupt practices as those that have long impeded African States to make full use of their regulatory powers against multinational corporations.

58 World Trade Organization, United States — Standards for Reformulated and Conventional Gasoline (1996) Appellate Body.

Part II

Experiences of selected African countries with international investment law

7

The constitutional limitations on enforcement of arbitral awards in Ghana

Dominic Npoanlari Dagbanja

Introduction

States and their governments enter into various forms of contracts with multinational business entities and other legal persons of foreign nationality. Such agreements may be for loans, supplies and services, construction and operation of transport, exploit natural resources, energy, and network and telephone systems and so on.[1] States also enter into international investment agreements (IIAs) to protect foreign investment. These agreements may be required to be made in accordance with relevant rules of contract law, public international law and private international law. Municipal law may equally place significant requirements on the conclusion of such agreements, the object of which may be to protect the public purse or the public interest broadly. Indeed, it is commonly the case that constitutions and municipal law generally require international business transaction and IIAs involving the State to be concluded in certain ways. In this chapter, I will assess the implications of the doctrine of constitutional supremacy on the enforceability of arbitral awards in a situation in which a constitution regulates the conclusion of international business transactions or IIAs. The particular focus is on international business transactions involving the State and IIAs that have not been reached or concluded in accordance with the terms of the Constitution of the Republic of Ghana 1992 (the Constitution). The question is: is an arbitral award that is founded on an unconstitutional international business transaction or IIA enforceable in Ghana?

Underpinning the doctrine of constitutional supremacy is the idea that the State and its institutions are creatures of the constitution and that the exercise of the powers of the State must be done within the confines of the legal source of those

1 Ian Brownlie, *Principles of Public International Law (7th ed)*, (Oxford University Press, 2008) 546.

powers. Thus, at its most basic level, Albert Dicey defines a 'constitution' as comprising 'rules which directly or indirectly affect the distribution of or the exercise of the sovereign power in the state'.[2] According to Dicey, constitutions define the holders of sovereign power, regulate the relations among institutions of the State, and determine the manner in which sovereign power shall be exercised.[3] Kelsen describes a constitution as 'the positive norm or norms which regulate the creation of general legal norms' and 'represents the highest level of positive law'.[4] Leslie Rubin and Pauli Murray state that constitutional supremacy 'is the doctrine applied to written constitutions which create the various organs of government and mark out the limits of their respective powers'.[5] In Kelsen's language, a norm, such as a constitution, which is the reason for the validity of another norm, is called a *'basic norm (Grundnorm)'*[6] or 'higher norm'.[7]

In *Marbury* v. *Madison*,[8] the Supreme Court of the United States of America held that it is the people who have the original right to establish for government the principles that are most conducive to their own happiness. The principles so established by the people are fundamental. Where the powers of government are limited, the limitations so imposed will not serve their purposes for the people.[9] The theory underlying the supremacy of the constitution is 'constitutionalism'. According to Professor Stanley de Smith, constitutionalism is the principle that exercising of political power is to be done within rules that determine the validity of legislative and executive actions by 'prescribing the procedure according to which it must be performed or by delimiting its permissible content'.[10]

For Ghana, the principles of constitutional supremacy and constitutionalism are entrenched in the Constitution. Article 1(1) states that the Constitution is 'the supreme law of Ghana and any other law found to be inconsistent with any

2 A.V. Dicey, *Introduction to the Study of the Law of the Constitution* (10th ed), (Palgrave Macmillan UK, 1959) 23.

3 *Ibid.*

4 Hans Kelsen, *Pure Theory of Law*, trans. M. Knight (Berkeley: University of California Press, 1967) 222.

5 Leslie Rubin and Pauli Murray, *The Constitution and Government of Ghana (2nd ed)* (London: Sweet and Maxwell, 1961) 52.

6 Hans Kelsen, *Pure Theory of Law* 8.

7 *Ibid.* 193.

8 *Marbury* v. *Madison* 1 Cranch (US) 137, 176–7 (1803).

9 *Ibid.* 177.

10 S.A. de Smith, 'Constitutionalism in the Commonwealth Today' (1962) 4 (2) *Malaya Law Review* 205.

provision of this Constitution shall, to the extent of the inconsistency, be void'. The preamble shows that the Constitution was enacted by the people of Ghana in the exercise of their 'natural and inalienable right to establish a framework of government which shall secure for [themselves] and posterity the blessings of liberty, equality of opportunity and prosperity'. The people, then, are the source of the legal validity of the Constitution and governments created under the Constitution must work to advance the interests of the people and act within the limits laid down in the Constitution. In the celebrated case of *Tuffuor* v. *Attorney-General*, the Supreme Court of Ghana, per Justice Sowah, underscored the supremacy and importance of the Constitution, stating that:[11]

> A written Constitution ... is not an ordinary Act of Parliament. It embodies the will of a people. It also mirrors their history. Account, therefore, needs to be taken of it as a landmark in a people's search for progress. It contains within it their aspirations and their hopes for a better and fuller life ... It is the fountainhead for the authority which each of the three arms of government possesses and exercises. It is a source of strength. It is a source of power. The executive, the legislature and the judiciary are created by the Constitution. Their authority is derived from the Constitution. Their sustenance is derived from the Constitution.

In *New Patriotic Party* v. *Attorney-General*,[12] the Supreme Court stated that the Constitution is the supreme law of Ghana and therefore 'laws, *municipal or otherwise*, which are found to be inconsistent with the Constitution, cannot be binding on the State whatever their nature. International laws ... are not binding on Ghana until such laws have been adopted or ratified by the municipal laws'.[13] It follows that, as a matter of municipal law, all laws made in Ghana, including treaties, must comply with the Constitution, both procedurally and substantively. On the supremacy of the Constitution, Justice Date-Bah, delivering a unanimous decision of the Supreme Court, stated in *Adofo* v. *Attorney-General*:[14]

> The power to strike down legislation in conflict with any provision of the Constitution ... is one of the most important powers of this court. It is a power to safeguard liberty from encroachment by the legislature ... It is a power accorded this court by clear provisions in the Constitution ... whose exercise is ... mandated by binding precedent from this court. That binding precedent includes ... article 1(2) of the Constitution ... which provides as follows: 'This Constitution shall be the supreme law of Ghana and any other law found to be inconsistent with any provision of this Constitution shall,

11 *Tuffuor* v. *Attorney-General* (1980) GLR 637, 647–8.

12 *New Patriotic Party* v. *Attorney-General* (1997–8) 1 GLR 378 (SC).

13 *Ibid*. 412–3 (emphasis added).

14 *Adofo* v. *Attorney-General* (2003–5) 1 GLR 239, 245–6.

> to the extent of the inconsistency, be void.' This constitutional provision unequivocally and authoritatively establishes a doctrine of supremacy of the Constitution … in the Ghanaian jurisdiction. This doctrine implies that … Parliament's enactments and those of previous legislatures are subject to the supremacy of the Constitution.
>
> The doctrine of the supremacy of the Constitution … should logically imply the power of judicial review of the constitutionality of legislation in order to enforce that supremacy … The power of judicial review of the constitutionality of legislation, which is explicitly conferred on this court by articles 2(1) and 130(1) of the Constitution … is one that should be vigilantly deployed by this court in discharge of the obligation of this court to uphold the Constitution.[15]

The principle of constitutional supremacy is therefore entrenched in Ghana. The courts have, in the light of their abiding faith in this doctrine, held as unconstitutional, international business agreements with the State that have not been made in accordance with constitutional requirements. Accordingly, the courts have held as a result that remedies are not available to foreign legal persons under unconstitutional international agreements. This matter has been considered in particular in relation to international business and economic transactions, and not necessarily under IIAs. However, these decisions have application in relation to IIAs and other treaties because the Constitution specifies requirements and procedures for the execution of agreements and treaties. Thus, to the extent that a particular IIA was not made within the terms of the Constitution, it would be unconstitutional and the courts would not enforce an award made under such an IIA. However, the issue with strict adherence to the doctrine of constitutional supremacy in relation to IIAs is that it stands to conflict with the principle that in the event of conflict between municipal law and international law, the latter shall prevail.[16] The courts in Ghana do not seem to have given particular regard to this superiority of international law principle when it comes to the enforcement of unconstitutional international business transactions. The broader issue of the nature of the relationship between international law and municipal law in Ghana needs consideration in a separate essay. Such an analysis is important because the issue of how the courts will resolve the conflict of Ghana's obligations to act within the terms of the Constitution and treaties that the country is a party has not been resolved. This current chapter establishes that the doctrine of constitutional supremacy places limitations on the enforcement of constitutionally illegal international business transactions and IIAs

15 *Ibid.* 245.

16 For the relation between municipal law and international law, see Brownlie, *Principles of Public International Law* 31–67.

in Ghana. It also points out the potential conflict between municipal law and international legal obligations in Ghana.

1 Constitutional supremacy and the status of treaties and customary international law in Ghana

A discussion on the enforceability of arbitral awards needs to follow an analysis of the legal status of international legal instruments which are the foundation of those agreements. Article 11 of the Constitution which deals with sources of law does not include treaties as part of the laws of Ghana. Under Article 75, treaties can be executed by the President but they must be ratified by Parliament to have legal effect. In *The Republic* v. *High Court: Ex Parte Attorney-General,*[17] the Supreme Court of Ghana held that even ratified treaties do not alter domestic law until they are incorporated into Ghanaian law by legislation. According to the Court, customary international law is part of Ghanaian law, being incorporated by common law case law provided the customary international law is not inconsistent with statutes or rules finally declared by municipal courts.[18] With respect to treaties, the Court said if the performance of a treaty's obligations entails alteration of existing domestic law rights and obligations, then there is the need for legislative incorporation of the treaty before it can have legal effect.[19] The Supreme Court held that even Articles 40 and 73 of the Constitution, which require the Government of Ghana to promote respect for international law and treaty obligations and to conduct its international affairs in consonance with accepted principles of public international law, do not alter the dualist position of Ghana. These provisions also do not 'authorize the courts to enforce treaty provisions that change rights and obligations in the municipal law of Ghana without legislative backing. If the law were otherwise, it would give the Executive an opportunity to bypass Parliament in changing rights and obligations of citizens and residents of Ghana.'[20] In this regard, Ghana follows the constitutionalist approach to the question of whether the Constitution or international law limits a State's legal authority in making treaties and entering into other international transactions. The constitutionalists 'hold that under international law, internal law governs the authority, the procedures and conditions under which a

17 *The Republic* v. *High Court* Ex Parte *Attorney-General*, Ruling, Civil Motion (20 June 2013) No. J5/10/2013, ILDC 2547 (GH 2013).

18 *Ibid.* 2.

19 *Ibid.* 5.

20 *Ibid.* 6.

state may be bound by a treaty. Violations of those internal law provisions may make the treaty void or voidable.'[21]

From an international law perspective, whether a treaty cannot be binding on a State because the expression of that State's consent to be bound by the treaty was expressed in violation of internal law depends, in part, on the interpretation of the Vienna Convention on the Law of Treaties (VCLT).[22] Article 26 of the VCLT gives effect to the *pacta sunt servanda* principle in international law, namely that every treaty 'in force is binding upon the parties to it and must be performed by them in good faith'.[23] The principle of the law of treaties as reflected in Article 27 of the VCLT is also that a 'party may not invoke the provisions of its internal law as justification for its failure to perform a treaty'.[24] This principle is premised on the treaty in question having been validly made in the first place. Thus, the VCLT recognizes that an expression of consent to be bound may be expressed in violation of internal law and that in such a case a State may not be bound by the treaty concerned. According to Article 46:

> A State may not invoke the fact that its consent to be bound by a treaty has been expressed *in violation of a provision of its internal law* regarding competence to conclude treaties as invalidating its consent unless *that violation was manifest* and concerned a rule of its internal law *of fundamental importance.*
>
> A *violation is manifest* if it would be objectively evident to any State conducting itself in the matter in accordance with normal practice and in good faith [emphasis added].[25]

A constitution is an 'internal law of fundamental importance' because it is the supreme law of the land. It creates rights and governance institutions, defines the powers of governments and the limits to those powers, and protects fundamental rights of human beings. In this regard, constitutions give expression to fundamental

21 Kojo Yelpaala, 'Fundamentalism in Public Health and Safety in Bilateral Investment Treaties Part II' (2008) 3 (2) *Asian Journal of WTO & International Health Law and Policy* 465, 480.

22 Anthony Aust, *Modern Treaty Law and Practice* (Cambridge University Press, 2007) 312.

23 United Nations, Vienna on the Law of Treaties (with Annex). Concluded at Vienna on 23 May 1969 https://treaties.un.org/doc/publication/unts/volume%201155/volume-1155-i-18232-english.pdf.

24 *Ibid.*

25 *Ibid.*

values of society and polity, and reflect the collective identity and values of the people.[26]

Accordingly, where an expression of consent to be bound by a treaty is made contrary to substantive provisions of a constitution or its procedural requirements, a State may subsequently argue that its consent to the treaty was expressed in violation of its supreme law and is, therefore, not binding on it. In *Land and Maritime Boundary between Cameroon and Nigeria*,[27] Nigeria argued that its constitutional rules regarding the ratification of treaties were not complied with in respect of a declaration entered into between it and Cameroon, and that the declaration was invalid.[28] Nigeria further argued that Cameroon knew, or ought to have known, that the Head of State of Nigeria had no power legally to bind Nigeria without consulting the Nigerian Government.[29] The International Court of Justice (ICJ) rejected these arguments on the basis that the signatures of the Heads of State of Cameroon and Nigeria were sufficient to make the declaration binding without the need for ratification.[30] Accordingly, the ICJ held that the declaration was 'binding and as establishing a legal obligation on Nigeria'.[31] The Court reasoned further that:

> The rules concerning the authority to sign treaties for a State are constitutional rules of fundamental importance. However, *a limitation of* a Head of State's *capacity* in this respect is not manifest in the sense of Article 46, paragraph 2 [of the VCLT], unless at least properly publicized. This is particularly so because Heads of State belong to the group of persons who, in accordance with Article 7, paragraph 2, of the Convention '[i]n virtue of their functions and without having to produce full powers' are considered as representing their State.
>
> [T]here is no general legal obligation for States to keep themselves informed of legislative and constitutional developments in other States which are or may become important for the international relations of these States. [32]

26 J.H.H. Weiler, 'In Defence of the Status Quo: Europe's Constitutional *Sonderweg*' in J.H.H.Weiler and Marlene Wind (eds), *European Constitutionalism Beyond the State* (Cambridge University Press, 2003) 7, 15.

27 *Land and Maritime Boundary between Cameroon and Nigeria (Cameroon* v. *Nigeria: Equatorial Guinea intervening)*, (10 October 2002), *ICJ Reports*, Judgment 303.

28 *Ibid*, paras 258–9 and 265.

29 *Ibid*.

30 *Ibid*, para. 264.

31 *Ibid*, para. 268.

32 *Ibid*, paras 265 and 266 (emphasis added).

Under Article 7(1), a person is considered as 'representing a State for the purpose of adopting or authenticating the text of a treaty or for the purpose of expressing the consent of the State to be bound by a treaty if' the person 'produces appropriate full powers'.[33] The production of full powers makes manifest the authority to adopt the text of the treaty or expression of consent to be bound. By Article 7(2), heads of State, heads of government, ministers for foreign affairs and heads of diplomatic missions are, by virtue of their functions, considered as representing the State in treaty making. They may, therefore, perform all acts relating to the conclusion of a treaty or can adopt the text of a treaty without having to produce full powers.

Article 7 is about *establishing* the *authority or capacity* to represent the State in the making of a treaty[34] and the legal limitations on how the person so empowered to represent the State *should express a State's consent to be bound*. The fact that a person has full powers to represent a State in the making of a treaty is not conclusive that the person has authority to agree to every term of the treaty or that the person will express a State's consent to be bound by the treaty in accordance with internal law of fundamental importance. Although persons such the heads of State, heads of government and ministers for foreign affairs are not required to produce appropriate full powers when performing acts relating to the conclusion of a treaty, it is still open and possible that they may perform the acts in question either in accordance with or against the dictates of internal law. Everybody within a constitutional form of government, irrespective of their position or functions is, supposed to exercise their powers within the confines of the law. International law must not authorize people to do that which is expressly forbidden by municipal law. Therefore, the authority of a head of State and other specified persons to conclude treaties without the need to produce full powers should be treated as a rebuttable presumption, so that the functions of the person cannot override express and unambiguous internal law governing the exercise of that authority. The functions of a person should not be treated as more conclusive than the need to actually establish the competence to conclude a treaty. There is the risk of a narrow interpretation of Article 7(2) of the VCLT focusing solely on the functions of the person expressing the consent leading to that conclusion.

33 *Ibid.*

34 On competence to conclude treaties, see: *Application of the on the Prevention and Punishment of the Crime of Genocide (Bosnia and Herzegovina* v. *Serbia and Montenegro)* (13 September 1993) Provisional Measures (Separate Opinion of Judge ad hoc Lauterpach), *ICJ Reports* (1993), para. 102.

It is questionable whether the ICJ was legally right when it held that 'a limitation of a Head of State's capacity … is not manifest' unless the limitation is published because heads of State belong to the group of persons who can perform treaty conclusion acts without having to produce full powers. There is nothing in Articles 7 and 46 of the VCLT that suggests that the basis for determining whether an expression of consent to be bound by a treaty was expressed in violation of internal law is to be limited to the instrument authoring the expressing of consent or publication.

The instrument authorizing the expression of consent to be bound by a treaty may not exhaust all factors that a person must take into consideration before expressing the consent to be bound. The instrument may only authorize the person to go and negotiate, and agree to the terms of the treaty and may not contain the specifics of what terms to agree or not to agree to. In other words, while the instrument giving authorization to express consent may deal with both the capacity to express consent and the extent of the person's powers in relation to the performance of this function, the instrument may be of limited scope in terms of the extent of that person's powers in the exercise of that representative function. If the instrument simply gives the person the capacity to conclude a treaty without specifying what the person may or may not agree to, which in practice seems to be the case, it will be out of context to argue that the person is thereby seized of the power to agree to any and every term, irrespective of its objective illegality under existing law, whether or not obvious at the time of concluding the treaty. If limitations on the expression of consent to be bound are to be judged solely on the basis of the instrument showing the full powers of the person to represent the State in the making of the treaty or on publication, then those who are not required to produce full powers could always make any and every type of treaty, in spite of any fundamental limitations in internal law which may not have been obvious at the time of concluding the treaty. In a situation where the instrument authorizing a person to adopt the text of a treaty does nothing beyond simply authorizing the person to express consent to be bound, the person's position will not be different from those who are not required to produce full powers.

The objectives of Article 46 are twofold: (1) to ensure that a State simply does not invoke non-compliance with internal law to avoid treaty obligations and thereby preserve the rights of the other contracting party that says the treaty is binding; and (2) to remedy violations of fundamental internal law in the making of a treaty in favour of the State that says its internal law has been violated in the making of the treaty. The right to say a violation of internal was not manifest is to protect the rights of the State that says the treaty is binding. The right to say the treaty is not binding is for the other State to secure compliance with its internal law of fundamental importance. So, there has to be a balance between these competing objectives in interpreting Article 46. It would be lopsided to interpret Article 46 based on a predisposition to make a treaty binding.

Violation of internal law has to be manifest for Article 46 to apply. For example, violation of a constitution would be manifestly evident to a State signing investment treaties with another if the treaties were to expressly prohibit the courts from entertaining suits brought against foreign investors for violation of human rights in the host State. A breach of a constitution is more likely to be manifest to another State when the breach would also amount to a breach of general international law obligations – in particular, when both parties to the investment treaty are also parties to another treaty that imposes specific human rights or environmental obligations on the parties. In this regard, it is significant to note that most States that are parties to investment treaties are also members of the United Nations (UN) and signatories or parties to the UN covenants on civil, political, economic, social and cultural rights.

The objective to cure violations of internal law would be defeated if it were held that in each and every case compliance with internal law was conclusive if the other State party had no reason to doubt it or if a treaty that did not comply with internal law anyway could nevertheless be valid and have legal effect because of the functions of the person who concluded the treaty. The objective of Article 46 will also be defeated if it is interpreted in such a manner that it becomes an instrument for violation or non-compliance with internal law by relevant persons in concluding international agreements. So it may be treated as conclusive if a State party has no reason to doubt compliance with internal law and capacity to make a treaty can be presumed in order to protect the State that has no manifest reason to believe the internal law of its contracting party had not been complied with. This must not, however, lead to a situation where the objective purpose of Article 46 for a State to excuse itself from the binding effect of a treaty for non-compliance with its internal law to be defeated. Accordingly, it is proposed that violations of internal law should be treated as manifest if it would be objectively manifest to the parties conducting themselves at the time of concluding a treaty that one contracting party could not ordinarily have entered into the treaty or agreed to a particular treaty term, for example, because the treaty would undermine the protection of fundamental human rights in the territory of that party.

It is proposed that the nature of the obligations under the treaty, and the basis of a claim of invalidity or non-binding nature of a treaty or its provision, should also help determine whether expression of consent was expressed in violation of internal law. If, in substance, the obligation is one that a State could not have assumed in the first place, then a State should not be bound by such an obligation, irrespective of the status of the person who purportedly expressed the consent of the State to be bound. Determining whether an expression of consent to be bound by a treaty was expressed in violation of internal law should not be based solely on the instrument authorizing the expression of consent or publication. The language in Articles 7 and 46 does not seem to establish a rigid standard.

Violation of internal law may be manifest depending on the nature of the terms of the treaty. Therefore, the means for determining whether an expression of consent to be bound by a treaty should include the instrument authorizing the expression of consent, internal law and the terms of the treaty in question (whether those terms could objectively have been agreed to). It is on this basis that a State may claim the binding effect of a treaty on the parties. It is the ICJ's position that a State does not have a general legal obligation to keep itself informed of legislative and constitutional developments in other States. However, since each State entering into a treaty is aware, or ought to be aware, that under Article 46 a contracting State may not be bound by a treaty if the expression of consent is made in manifest violation of internal law. A contracting party should not only comply with its internal law but also should at least in good faith and out of abundance of caution verify or seek confirmation (at least in its own interest) if the other party has complied with internal law. This is one way a State can act to meet the requirement in Article 46 that States conduct themselves in good faith in concluding a treaty. The good faith obligation does not require a State to monitor another contracting party to ensure the latter complies with its internal law. However, it should be treated as requiring each contracting party to take prudent steps that protect its interests. That way, either State may be estopped from arguing that a violation of internal law is or is not manifest as the case may be. The precautionary principle in international environmental law and international law generally reflects the value of risk avoidance.[35] Verification by a contracting State can help its contracting partner to discover violations of its internal law that are not obvious but are fundamental, and will be in the mutual benefit of both parties.

The position outlined above is espoused on the basis that each State must act to protect its interests in treaty making. If a State's representatives enter into a treaty in disregard of the legal consequences attached to non-compliance with its internal

35 Andrew Jordan and Timothy O'Riordan, 'The Precautionary Principle: A Legal and Policy History' in Marco Martuzzi and Joel Tickner (eds), *The Precautionary Principle: Protecting Public Health, the Environment and the Future of our Children* (Copenhagen: World Health Organization Europe, 2004) 31.

law or non-compliance with the internal law of its treaty partner, then the State failing to take such consequences into account should hardly be able to say it was or was not manifest that internal law had not been complied with. Given the two objectives of Article 46 as set out this subsection, the burden should be on both States to act prudently in concluding a treaty. This is necessary to ensure that each of the contracting parties acts fairly, honestly and in good faith towards each other in treaty making. More importantly, Article 46 requires to be 'manifest' for an expression of consent to not bind a State is a 'violation of … internal law' resulting from the expression of consent, not the 'limitation of … capacity' to express the consent, as the ICJ suggests. Thus, if in practice and in good faith, a treaty's terms will have a telling and obvious limiting effect on the right to regulate in the public interest under an internal law such as a constitution, the expression of consent to be bound would have been expressed in violation of internal law of fundamental importance and the State should not be bound by the treaty. Thus, by virtue of Article 46 of the VCLT, it is not necessarily against the rules of international law to hold as unconstitutional and enforceable a treaty that is violates internal law of fundamental importance.

2 Constitutional supremacy and international business and economic transactions in Ghana

The issue of the constitutionality of international business transactions and the enforceability of arbitral awards founded on them also came for consideration before the Supreme Court of Ghana. Under Article 181(5) of the Constitution, an 'international business or economic transaction' to which the Government of Ghana is a party must be laid before and approved by Parliament. Unless this is done, it cannot come into operation. The Supreme Court has upheld that an international business or economic transaction that has not received parliamentary approval is not binding on the State and no remedies can be claimed under such an agreement. A case in point where this provision was interpreted is *The Attorney-General* v. *Faroe Atlantic Co. Ltd.*[36] Faroe Atlantic Co. Ltd., a United Kingdom company, entered into a Power Purchase Agreement (PPA) with the Government of Ghana for the sale and purchase of electric power. The company alleged that the Government breached the PPA and brought action for specific performance of the agreement or in the alternative damages for the breach. The High Court gave judgment in favor of Faroe Atlantic Co. Ltd. and, upon hearing further evidence, ruled that the Government should pay Faroe Atlantic Co. Ltd. USD 6,298,354. The Court also ordered Faroe

36 *The Attorney-General* v. *Faroe Atlantic Co. Ltd* [2005–2006] SCGLR 271 (SC).

Atlantic Co. Ltd. to refund certain advance payments the Government had made to the company. The Government appealed to the Court of Appeal, arguing that the trial court erred by awarding the damages and interest to the company. The Court of Appeal dismissed the appeal and affirmed the decision of the trial High Court. The Government appealed to the Supreme Court, being dissatisfied with the award of damages. The Government argued for the first time before the Supreme Court that the PPA was an international business transaction and that since it was not approved by Parliament as required by Article 181(5) of the Constitution, it conflicted with the Constitution and therefore was null and void. The Government argued that damages could not arise out of an unconstitutional agreement. The issues the Court had decided on were: (1) whether or not the State could be bound by a PPA between the Government of Ghana and a foreign company for the sale and purchase of electric power which had not received parliamentary ratification; and (2) whether damages were available for an international business or economic transaction that had not received parliamentary approval.

The Supreme Court held that the claim against the State must be dismissed and Faroe Atlantic Co. Ltd. must pay back an advance payment made to it by the Government. The Court reasoned that an international economic or business transaction between the Government of Ghana and a foreign registered and resident company was an international business transaction within the meaning of Article 181(5) of the Constitution. Such a transaction has to be laid before Parliament for approval before it can come into operation. Failure to secure such Parliamentary approval would result in the nullity of the relevant agreement.[37] The Court said the PPA was an international business or economic transaction (given the company was incorporated in the United Kingdom and the sale and purchase of electricity under the agreement) and therefore needed parliamentary approval in terms of Article 181(5) of the Constitution.[38] The PPA was an international business transaction, since it involved a foreign company engaged in the business of energy generation and supply, and the Government of Ghana.[39] When one contracting party agreed to supply and another contracting party agreed to purchase and pay for the supply, a business transaction was thereby created. If one of the parties was a non-Ghanaian entity and the other party was the Government of Ghana, then the business transaction was international. In such a case, Article 181(5) of the Constitution became applicable.

37 *Ibid.* 294, 295.
38 *Ibid.* 297.
39 *Ibid.* 297.

In the opinion of the Court, Article 1(2) of the Constitution which deals with constitutional supremacy, is a peremptory norm. It was analogous to *ius cogens* whose enforcement cannot be impeded by the normal rules. Therefore, an award of damages for the breach of what was an unconstitutional contract must be refused.[40] The powers of government must be exercised within constitutional limits. As the supreme law of the land, the Constitution was applicable at all times and to all acts and things. In particular, acts and things done for and on behalf of Ghana must always be tested against constitutional provisions. In the course of judicial proceedings, it was incumbent upon every judge to keep constitutional provisions in mind to assure compliance, not only by parties but also by the court itself.[41] It means that where the Constitution stipulated that parliamentary authorization was required for certain transactions, any transaction to which the provisions were applicable that was concluded without the authorization of Parliament could not take effect without such authorization.[42] Where the Government entered into an international business or economic transaction, it must comply with constitutional requirements *mutatis mutandis*, namely the agreement must be laid before and be approved by a parliamentary resolution before such an agreement or transaction can come into force. The purpose of the constitutional requirement for parliamentary approval of an international business or economic transaction and loan agreements was to ensure transparency, openness and parliamentary consent in relation to international contracts and debts contracted by the State.[43] Since the PPA was concluded without complying with a mandatory clause of the Constitution, it would not bind the State. Restitution of money paid under such an agreement should not be allowed and any advance payment made under the agreement must be refunded to the State.[44]

This case raises the important issue of the relationship between international law and municipal law in Ghana: the extent to which the principle of constitutional supremacy may lead to the voiding of an international business or economic transaction. As the Supreme Court itself held, the PPA that gave rise to the legal conflict in this case was an international business or economic transaction.[45] Its international nature meant that it required parliamentary approval, a lack of which meant it was constitutionally void and could not give rise to damages in domestic law. However,

40 *Ibid.* 298.
41 *Ibid.* 304.
42 *Ibid.* 305.
43 *Ibid.* 295, 296.
44 *Ibid.* 302.
45 *Ibid.* 306.

the fact that the PPA was held to be an international business or economic transaction meant that it could be governed by international law. Faroe Atlantic Co. Ltd. could argue that it was entitled to compensation because of misrepresentation and not necessarily on the basis of the PPA. It is the State and its officials who are under a duty to comply with the Constitution when entering into international agreements. If a private party enters into a transaction on the basis that the Constitution had been complied with, then a private party should be entitled to compensation for being misled into an unconstitutional agreement. Such a remedy would be founded on misrepresentation in contract law and not necessarily reliance on the unconstitutional agreement. This appears to be the only way to do justice to the private party who has no say in what State officials decide to do in terms of following the requirements of their national constitutions.

3 The enforceability of arbitral awards in Ghana

In *Balkan Energy Limited* v. *Ghana*,[46] Balkan Energy Ltd. (Ghana) (BELG) entered into a PPA with Ghana in 2007 for the refurbishment and commissioning of dual-fired (diesel and gas) barges and associated facilities. The PPA provided that if any disputes arose out of or in relation to PPA and could not be settled through direct discussion of the parties, the matter would be referred to binding arbitration. The arbitration was to be governed by and conducted in accordance with United Nations Commission on International Trade Law Rules of Arbitration of 1976 (the UNCITRAL Rules).[47] The terms of appointment of arbitrators specified the UNCITRAL Rules as the governing rules of the arbitration and the laws of Ghana as the governing law of the PPA.[48] Balkan Energy Limited (BELG) alleged breach of the PPA and commenced arbitration proceedings against Ghana.[49] Ghana objected to the jurisdiction of the Interim Tribunal, arguing that both the PPA and the arbitration clause were void because the PPA did not receive parliamentary approval as required by Article 181(5) of the Constitution.[50] Ghana maintained that both the PPA and the arbitration clause were an 'international business or economic transaction', and were therefore void and unenforceable for lack of prior parliamentary

46 *Balkan Energy (Ghana) Limited* v. *The Republic of Ghana* (22 December 2010), PCA Case No. 2010-7, Interim Award.

47 *Ibid.* para. 43.

48 *Ibid.* para. 17.

49 *Ibid.* paras 4 and 6–7.

50 *Ibid.* para. 9.

approval.[51] Ghana argued that the determination of the validity of either the PPA or the arbitration clause involved questions of interpretation of the Constitution and was, therefore, non-arbitrable.[52]

The Tribunal held that it was competent to decide on the validity of the arbitration agreement and had jurisdiction to entertain the substantive suit under the competence-competence and separability principles in international arbitration, which allow tribunals to determine questions concerning their jurisdiction and the substantive validity of the arbitration clause, respectively.[53] The Tribunal held that there were strong arguments to be made 'in favour of defining the scope of arbitrable matters in accordance with the *lex loci arbitri* … [T]he Parties' agreement to dispute settlement before the PCA [Permanent Court of Arbitration] is an indicator that the Parties intended to remove questions relating to dispute resolution – as opposed to the substantive performance of the contract – from the place of either Party, to a neutral forum.'[54] The Tribunal ultimately concluded that the proper law governing the validity of the arbitration agreement was Dutch law and therefore Article 181(5) of the Constitution of Ghana did not in any way affect the validity of the arbitration agreement.[55]

In the Interim Award on jurisdiction, the Tribunal left the question of the substantive validity of the PPA to be decided on the merits.[56] So in the Award on the Merits, the Tribunal, composed of the same panel as in the Interim Award, considered whether the PPA was valid and enforceable.[57] Before this suit was instituted, the Supreme Court had already heard arguments in *The Attorney-General* v. *Balkan Energy Limited (Ghana)*[58] on whether the same PPA and the agreement to arbitrate each constituted an international business or economic transaction within the meaning of Article 181(5) of the Constitution. The Supreme Court held that a business or economic transaction is international if it is 'major' with a 'significant' foreign element or the parties to the transaction have a foreign nationality or reside in different countries or, in the case of companies, the place of their central

51 *Ibid.* paras 117–9.
52 *Ibid.* para. 64.
53 *Ibid.* paras 100, 115, 152–3, 167 and 99.
54 *Ibid.* para. 142.
55 *Ibid.* para. 154.
56 *Ibid.* para. 138.
57 *Balkan Energy Limited (Ghana)* v. *The Republic of Ghana* (1 April 2014) PCA Case No. 2010–7.
58 *The Attorney-General* v. *Balkan Energy Limited (Ghana)* (16 May 2012) Writ No. J6/1/2012.

management and control is outside Ghana.[59] The Court held that the analysis of Article 181(5) should focus on the substance of the transaction over its form.[60] In relation to the PPA, the Court observed that the transaction for the refurbishment of the barge involved a foreign investment by a United States (US) company in a power generation project for the supply of energy to Ghana that involved negotiations with the Government of Ghana. Although BELG was incorporated under the laws of Ghana, it was wholly owned by a US company. The directors were foreign, and the control and central management of the company were in foreign hands. The PPA not only provided for investor-State dispute settlement (ISDS), but some of its clauses, such as the waiver of sovereign immunity, are usually contained in foreign investment transactions.[61] Based on these findings, the Supreme Court held that the PPA constituted 'an international business transaction within the meaning of Article 181(5) of the Constitution'.[62]

The Tribunal held a view to the contrary. According to Tribunal's the Supreme Court's interpretation of Article 181(5) of the Constitution 'was plausible but it is only one possible alternative'.[63] The Tribunal admitted that the Court had made an affirmative finding that the PPA constituted an international business transaction under Article 181(5).[64] It agreed with the reasoning of the Court that the PPA embodied the existence of significant foreign components and contained several international components, such as the nature of the business and the related investments made, and the waiver of sovereign immunity.[65] The Tribunal also admitted that the Court 'rightly considered' Article 181(5) 'as a whole, the main concern of which … is that an agreement entered into by the Government for the granting of a loan out of public funds or public accounts must be authorized by Parliament'.[66] Yet, when confronted with whether the PPA constituted an international business transaction within the meaning of Article 181(5) of the Constitution, the Tribunal determined that it was not. In *Attorney-General* v. *Balkan Energy Limited (Ghana)*, the Supreme Court had emphasized substance over form in determining whether a transaction was international and needed parliamentary approval. The Tribunal insisted on form over substance, holding that, although the PPA involved foreign

59 *Ibid.* 34, 37.
60 *Ibid.* 31.
61 *Ibid.* 38, 39.
62 *Ibid.* 40, 41.
63 *Balkan Energy Limited (Ghana)* v. *The Republic of Ghana* para. 387.
64 *Ibid.* para. 376.
65 *Ibid.* para. 380.
66 *Ibid.* para. 380.

components as found by the Court, it was entered into by a company registered in Ghana and which had its principal place of business in Ghana. Further, it held that the production envisaged under the PPA was to supply the domestic electricity market and payments were to be made in Ghana, which suggested that 'performance under the PPA was entirely a domestic business'.[67] Disregarding the criteria specified by the Supreme Court, the Tribunal upheld BELG's arguments that it 'was organized as a Ghanaian company in compliance with the applicable legislation' and thus 'the foreign ownership of the company or the foreign nationality of its executives should not necessarily be an obstacle to concluding' that it is not an international business transaction.[68] According to the Tribunal, the identification of a number of internationally-related components of the PPA made by the Attorney-General and accepted by the Supreme Court 'do not alter the fact that the company was incorporated in Ghana as required by the Ghanaian legislation and regulations'.[69] It distinguished the case from 'a situation in which a foreign company or an agency … operates in a certain country without a proper legal registration therein'.[70]

The State was ordered to pay BELG USD 12 million and interest thereon in consideration of works BELG commissioned at the power station and USD 50,000 in respect of the arrest of one of BELG's officers. The investor was ordered to pay the amount of USD 300,000 for its own breach of contract. Each party was to pay half of the costs of arbitration which totalled USD1 million.[71] The question is whether this award is enforceable, given that the decision of the Tribunal conflicts with that of the Supreme Court, the decisions of which must be followed.

The positions arrived at by the various tribunals are contrary to or different from the decisions arrived at by the Supreme Court. This was not the case of a national court being legally wrong, biased, incompetent or unjust. In making these interpretive decisions, the tribunals in the two BELG cases were usurping the powers of the Supreme Court, which, under Article 130 of Constitution, has exclusive original jurisdiction in matters relating to the enforcement or interpretation of the Constitution. For example, although the Tribunal held that the Court's interpretation of Article 181(5) of the Constitution was a 'plausible … alternative',[72] the Tribunal failed to establish why (whether under municipal law or general international law)

67 *Ibid.* para. 388.
68 *Ibid.* para. 380.
69 *Ibid.* para. 383.
70 *Ibid.*
71 *Ibid.* para. 642.
72 *Ibid.* para. 387.

its approach to the interpretation of the constitutional provision (which is also an alternative) should prevail over that of the Supreme Court.

The Tribunal stated that it 'could not presume to decide an issue of constitutional interpretation in Ghana when the highest courts of the country have considered the matter under their respective jurisdictions'. Yet, this is exactly what the Tribunal did when it made a determination on the validity of the PPA under the Constitution. The issue there was not whether the Tribunal was entitled to exercise jurisdiction on the merits of the claim under arbitration agreement, but whether it had the competence to interpret the constitutionality of the PPA against the background of the Supreme Court's decision on the matter. The refusal to follow the decision of the Supreme Court in spite of the parties' choice of Ghanaian law is an example of investment tribunals using their powers to protect foreign investment at the expense of the jurisdiction of municipal courts and the interest pursued by the State. As the tribunals did not find that the Supreme Court was legally wrong (a determination they could not make under the Constitution anyway), there is no reason for their opposing positions to command more obedience and observance. Therefore, the decisions of the tribunals, which are parallel to those of the Supreme Court, should be treated as not having the legal effect of overruling or quashing the decision of the Court and they should not be recognized in Ghana. This is particularly the case when the parties had chosen Ghanaian law as the governing law to the PPA. The laws of Ghana include decisions of the courts of Ghana. The application of the laws of the Netherlands (seat of arbitration) was intended to allow the Tribunal to evade the effect of applying the choice of law made by the parties. In making the choice of applicable law, the parties intended to exclude every other law that could possibly be connected to their dispute. If that choice of law was not made in favour of the law of the seat of arbitration, the law of the seat of arbitration should have nothing to do with the dispute.

Under Articles 129 and 133 of the Constitution, the Supreme Court is the final court of appeal but the Court may review its decisions in the interest of the administration of justice. As BELG did not exercise this constitutional right of review, it would be legally impossible for the arbitral award in its favour to be enforced in Ghana. Moreover, in *Amidu* v. *The Attorney-General* et al.,[73] the Supreme Court held that:[74]

73 *Amidu* et al. v. *The Attorney-General* et al. (21 June 2013) Writ No. JI/15/2012, Judgment.
74 *Ibid.* 24.

> there should be less room to award a restitutionary remedy where … breach is of a constitutional provision. A contract which breaches article 181(5) of the Constitution is null and void and therefore creates no rights. It should not be legitimate to evade this nullity by the grant of a restitutionary remedy. Although one accepts the cogency of the argument that there is need to avoid unjust enrichment to the State through its receipt of benefits it has not paid for, there is the higher order countervailing argument that the enforcement of the Constitution should not be undermined by allowing the State and its partners an avenue or opportunity for doing indirectly what it is constitutionally prohibited from doing directly. The supremacy of the Constitution in the hierarchy of legal norms in the legal system has to be preserved and jealously guarded.

So unless it is shown that the PPA did not need parliamentary approval, even though it was international business or an economic transaction within the meaning of Article 181(5) of the Constitution, the award would be legally unenforceable in Ghana. Constitutionally, enforcement cannot be made without the Supreme Court having reviewed and departed from its previous decisions on the constitutional effect of a transaction that has not received parliamentary approval or its position on damages not being available in respect of unconstitutional agreements or contract.

Under Articles 26 and 27 of the VCLT, a State is under obligation to perform a treaty it has entered into and it may not invoke the provisions of its internal law as justification for its failure to perform the treaty. However, under Article V(2)(b) of the United Nations Convention on the Recognition and Enforcement of Foreign Arbitral Awards (the New York Convention),[75] which entered into force on 7 June 1958, the recognition and enforcement of an arbitral award may be refused if the competent authority in the country where recognition and enforcement is sought, finds that the subject matter of the legal dispute is not capable of settlement by arbitration under the law of that country, or recognition or enforcement of the award would be contrary to the public policy of that country. The New York Convention also recognizes in Article II(3) that the courts of a State which has agreed to ISDS have the competence to make a finding that an agreement to arbitrate 'is null and void, inoperative or incapable of being performed'. International public policy estoppel (whatever its content) cannot operate to prevent a State from invoking internal law as an excuse to not perform an international obligation because the VCLT expressly gives States this right. Policy cannot prevail over explicit statement

75 United Nations, Convention on the Recognition and Enforcement of Foreign Arbitral Awards (New York, 1958) https://www.uncitral.org/pdf/english/texts/arbitration/NY-conv/New-York--E.pdf.

of the law. Moreover, in *The Republic* v. *High Court Accra, Ex Parte Attorney-General,*[76] the Supreme Court held that 'there is no obligation to enforce a foreign judgment which offends the local public policy of the forum state.'[77] These are legal grounds in international investment law on which the enforceability of the tribunals' awards in favor of the companies can be impeached in Ghana. These policy grounds can be used to challenge any effort to enforce the decisions from any forum outside Ghana.

The investor would have a case arguing under Article 46 of the VCLT that violation of the Constitution was not manifest. However, the discretion under the New York Convention[78] for a State to not recognize or enforce an award if the subject matter is not capable of arbitration or is contrary to public policy is not predicated on whether the basis of the violation of internal law of fundamental importance or public policy was manifest. The Supreme Court has held in *The Republic* v. *High Court: Ex Parte; Attorney-General* that 'the independence of Ghanaian courts is subject to the received common law rules on conflict of laws relating to foreign judgments'.[79] Those rules in addition to statute require recognition of foreign judgments and thus 'allow for the application of principle of *res judicata* for the purpose of proceedings properly brought in a Ghanaian court in which issues determined in a foreign court arise'.[80] Therefore, the investors could also argue that the State is estopped from litigating again the constitutionality of the various agreements in Ghanaian courts. However, one of the requirements of issue estoppel is that 'the foreign court must be a court of competent jurisdiction; and its decision must have been final and conclusive'.[81] As the issue of the constitutionality of the agreements is not within the jurisdiction of the arbitral tribunals, they were not competent to make decisions on it and their decisions made thereof are not final and conclusive. Consequently, the State is still entitled to raise the issue of constitutionality of the agreements and their enforceability within the domestic context in the light of public policy, the Constitution and the New York Convention.

76 *The Republic* v. *High Court Accra, Ex Parte Attorney-General* (20 June 2013) Case No. J5/10/2013.

77 *Ibid.* 23.

78 United Nations, Convention on the Recognition and Enforcement of Foreign Arbitral Awards V(2)(b).

79 *The Republic* v. *High Court Accra, Ex Parte Attorney-General* 15.

80 *Ibid.*

81 *Ibid.* 18.

The Convention on the Settlement of Investment Disputes between States and Nationals of Other States (the ICSID Convention),[82] which entered into force on 14 October 1966, also makes the execution of arbitral awards subject to the law of the place where execution is sought. Under Article 54(1) of the ICSID Convention, an arbitration award is binding. However, by Article 54(3) of the Convention, '[e]xecution of the award shall be governed by the laws concerning the execution of judgments in force in the State in whose territories such execution is sought'. According to the *Black's Law Dictionary*, 'execution' means 'the legal process of enforcing the judgment',[83] that is, to cause the judgment to take effect. By this provision, if the law governing the execution of judgments in the country in which enforcement is sought does not permit particular judgments, whether local judgments or foreign judgments, to be enforced or to take effect, they cannot be executed in that country. The effect of Article 54(3) of the ICSID Convention then is that an arbitral award is binding subject to whether it can be executed in accordance with the law governing the execution of judgments in the territory it is sought to be enforced. In effect, it is not every binding award or judgment that can be executed depending on the law governing the execution of judgments. Thus, laws in Ghana, including judicial decisions governing the enforcement of judgments, such as foreign judgments and awards, shall determine the enforceability of arbitral awards in Ghana, whether investment treaty arbitration awards or international commercial arbitration awards.

The State must not benefit from wrongs carried out by its officials and innocent private parties must not be made to suffer for the failures of State officials to duly perform their functions. Therefore, mechanisms have to be put in place within the domestic context to protect innocent parties who reasonably rely on the decisions of competent State officials to their detriment, especially if the matter on which advice is given is not manifestly contrary to the public policy of the State. This position needs to be qualified by the point that each foreign party to a transaction with the State is at liberty to engage lawyers to advise them on particular legal positions arrived at by government officials. If they fail to do so, any remedies that may be available to them for relying on wrong or misleading legal positions of government officials should either be nil or qualified or mitigated by their failure to take action to protect their own interest.

82 ICSID/15/Rev.1.

83 Henry Black, *Black's Law Dictionary (5th ed.)* (West Publishing Company, 1979) 510.

Conclusion

Treaties and international business and economic transactions presuppose norms necessary for their coming into existence.[84] These norms determine the capacity to act in international law, the conditions that must be fulfilled for an international treaty or transaction to come into existence and the juridical consequences to be attached to the conclusion of an international treaty or international business transaction.[85] To this effect, if a treaty or international business and economic transaction that does not comply with constitutional conditions comes into force it should be held invalid or unenforceable. Where it is manifest that conditions that must be fulfilled for a treaty or international agreement to come into existence have not been fulfilled, neither party should be entitled to rely on such a treaty or agreement to claim rights. Again, parties to treaties and international agreements should have an obligation to verify if domestic norms have been complied with in the conclusion of such agreements. Where they fail to do so, they should not be entitled to rely on those agreements.

The analysis of the situation in Ghana shows that the courts are willing to uphold constitutional principles and that arbitral awards would not be enforced in Ghana if the international agreements on which they are founded are unconstitutional. International law and international investment law intended for the protection of foreign investors also require that international treaties and other agreements and awards made under them should not be enforceable if they violate internal law of fundamental importance and the public policy of the host State. Municipal law, international law and international investment law should be respected and upheld by arbitral tribunals, not only when they work in the interest of the investor but also when they work in the interest of the State to the detriment of the investors. Fairness in the interpretation and enforcement of the legal regime for the protection of foreign investors cannot be achieved otherwise. There is particular case to hold an IIA or international business transaction as unconstitutional and unenforceable when the parties, well aware of their rights under the IIA or other international agreements and laws, proceeded to make a choice of particular municipal law. By choosing that law, the parties mean to make only the chosen law applicable and to exclude the laws not chosen. The chosen law might not be followed, only if there is a manifest case of both parties colluding to avoid the application of a particular

84 Alfred von Verdross, 'Forbidden Treaties in International Law: Comments on Professor Garner's Report on "The Law of Treaties"' (1937) 31 (4) *American Journal of International Law* 571–2.

85 *Ibid.*

mandatory law that they could manifestly and objectively not avoid. The chosen law must not be avoided simply because a tribunal does not like the consequences of applying it. In this regard, since in the PPA the parties had chosen under Ghanaian law, the Tribunal in the case of *Balkan Energy Limited (Ghana)* v. *The Republic of Ghana* was wrong in refusing to apply Ghanaian law if its application would have invalidated the PPA.

8

Rethinking the promotion and protection of foreign investments: South Africa's Protection of Investment Act 22 of 2015

Tarcisio Gazzini

Introduction

After many years of popularity, investment treaties have recently caused increasing concern among States, most prominently for the imbalance of their content, the often inadequate safeguard to the regulatory powers of the host State and the shortcomings of international investment arbitration. Some States have upgraded their investment treaties, others have revised their investment treaty model, and others have opted for facilitation agreements. South Africa has taken a different route: it has terminated several investment treaties and adopted a piece of domestic legislation specifically on the protection of investment. South Africa's Protection of Investment Act 22 of 2015,[1] is largely pegged to the Constitution and based on the extension to foreign investors of the protection granted to nationals, including the provisions on expropriation and regulatory powers. This chapter attempts to discuss and compare the protection foreign investors may expect to enjoy under the Act. It argues that the Act offers a level of protection definitely lower than that normally provided by international investment treaties from both substantive and procedural standpoints. It remains to be seen whether such a rather drastic departure from treaty standards was appropriate and, what the consequences of the replacement of investment treaties with the Act will have, keeping in mind the still unproven causal relationship between investment treaties and the flow of foreign investment.

1 See www.gov.za/sites/default/files/gcis_document/201512/39514act22of2015protectionofinvestmentact.pdf, accessed 21 September 2020.

1 Growing unpopularity of bilateral investment treaties

At the end of June 2018, 868 bilateral investment treaties (BITs) had been concluded among African States or between them and non-African States.[2] Only 515 of them (or 59.33%), however, are currently in force. Yet, the bilateral network remains underdeveloped, as these treaties correspond roughly to 5.76% of the treaty network necessary to cover all bilateral relationships among African States and between them and the rest of the world.[3] Furthermore, the number of BITs concluded by African States varies remarkably. Suffice it to say, the aggregate number of BITs applicable to Algeria, Egypt, Libya, Morocco and Tunisia amount to 206 (out of 301 signed), or the equivalent of 40% of the BITs in force in the entire continent.

While regionalism is clearly on the rise in the continent[4] and several African subregional organizations have concluded important and often innovative investment agreements,[5] BITs have lost their appeal and are not as popular as they used to be in the 1990s and 2000s. They have been increasingly perceived as inconvenient for the host State for several reasons,[6] including their unbalanced content,

2 United Nations Conference on Trade and Development (UNCTAD) Investment Policy Hub International Investment Agreements Navigator http://investmentpolicyhub.unctad.org/IIA, accessed 30 June 2018.

3 To cover the totality of bilateral relationships between the fifty four African States, it is necessary to conclude a number of BITs equivalent to: 54 (54–1) / 2 or 1 431 BITs. See Emile Giraud, 'Modification et terminaison des traités collectifs' (1961) 49 *Annuaire de l'Institut de droit international* 1, 16 ff. To cover the bilateral relationships between the fifty four African States and the remaining States in the world – using the 193 current Member States of the United Nations (UN) as benchmark – it is necessary to conclude 54 x (193–54) = 7 506 BITs. The grand total is 8 937 BITs.

4 UNCTAD, *The Rise of Regionalism in International Investment Policymaking: Consolidation or Complexity?* (IIA Issues Note No. 3 June 2013) http://unctad.org/en/pages/newsdetails.aspx?OriginalVersionID=532, accessed 30 June 2018.

5 See Tarcisio Gazzini and Erik Denters, 'The Role of African Regional Organizations in the Promotion and Protection of Foreign Investment' (2017) 18 (3) *The Journal of World Investment & Trade* 449. On regionalism in general, see Leon Trakman and Nicola Ranieri (eds), *Regionalism in International Investment Law* (Oxford University Press 2013); Wolfgang Alschner, 'Regionalism and Overlap in Investment Treaty Law – Towards Consolidation or Contradiction?' (2014) 17 (2) *Journal of International Economic Law* 271.

6 For a balanced assessment of these treaties, see Gus Van Harten, 'Five Justifications for Investment Treaties: A Critical Discussion' (2010) 2 (1) *Trade, Law & Development* 1. For a critical look at the BIT between China and African States, see Uche Ewelukwa Ofodile, 'Africa-China Bilateral Investment Treaties: A Critique' (2013) 35 *Michigan Journal of International Law* 131.

the undue restrictions on the regulatory powers of the host State, the lack of transparency and public scrutiny, and the exposure to arbitral claims which may trigger large compensation.[7] Moreover, there is no clear evidence yet that investment treaties are necessary to attract foreign investments and stimulate economic growth.[8] With regard to Africa, it has been observed that '[t]he impact of bilateral investment treaties on economic and social development in Africa remains debatable. There is no conclusive evidence regarding the effect of these treaties on foreign investment.'[9]

Dissatisfaction with traditional BITs has generated four main types of reaction. The first reaction is rather generalized and relates to the deceleration which has recently characterized the entry into force of BITs. In Africa, in particular, only twenty-three BITs – including 3 between African countries – have entered into force since January 2014. The second reaction is less evident and concerns the attempts to upgrade these treaties, strike a better balance between the private and public interests at stake, and ultimately bring them in line with the evolution of international law. In this regard, the BIT concluded – but not entered into force yet – between Morocco and Nigeria is remarkably innovative. While granting foreign investors an adequate substantive and procedural protection, the treaty imposes several obligations on the foreign investors (including the obligation to carry out an environmental and social impact assessment, apply the precautionary principle, ensure an appropriate protection of labour and human rights, and comply with international accepted standards of corporate

7 See Xavier Carim, 'Lessons from South Africa's BITs Review' (25 November 2013) 109 *Columbia FDI Perspectives* http://ccsi.columbia.edu/files/2013/10/No_109_-_Carim_-_FINAL.pdf, accessed 30 June 2018. See also R. Davies, Minister of Trade and Industry of South Africa, *2007 UNCTAD's Investment Policy Framework for Sustainable Development, Geneva*, www.dti.gov.za/delegationspeechdetail.jsp?id=2506, accessed 30 June 2018.

8 UNCTAD, *The Impact of International Investment Agreements on Foreign Direct Investment: An Overview of Empirical Studies 1998–2014* (IIA Issues Note, Working Draft, September 2014) http://investmentpolicyhub.unctad.org/Upload/Documents/unctad-web-diae-pcb-2014-Sep%2024.pdf, accessed 30 June 2018.

9 UN Economic Commission for Africa (UNECA), Committee on Regional Cooperation and Integration, *Investment Agreements Landscape in Africa* (E/ECA/CRCI/9/5) (21 October 2015) www.uneca.org/sites/default/files/uploaded-documents/RITD/2015/CRCI-Oct2015/report-on-investment-agreements.pdf, accessed 30 June 2018.

governance and corporate social responsibility).[10] Pursuing similar objectives, other States have substantially amended their models for the conclusion of BITs.[11] The third reaction has led to the conclusion of so-called 'facilitation agreements', which radically downgrade the substantive protection of foreign investment and do not provide for judicial or arbitral proceedings against the host State.[12] The fourth reaction, of which South Africa is the main proponent, is the termination of BITs and the adoption of a piece of domestic legislation on the protection of investment.[13]

2 Adoption and content of the Act

In 2007, South Africa undertook a thorough review of its BITs with a view to assessing their impact on both the economic growth of the country and the exercise by the Government of its regulatory powers.[14] The results of the review were

10 Signed on 3 December 2016. See also BITs between Japan and Mozambique (2013); the BITs concluded by Canada with Benin (2013), Côte d'Ivoire (2014), Mali (2014), Senegal (2014) and the United Republic of Tanzania (2013); the BIT between the United States of America and Rwanda (2008). See also the South African Development Community (SADC) Model Bilateral Investment Treaty Template with Commentary (2012) www.iisd.org/itn/wp-content/uploads/2012/10/sadc-model-bit-template-final.pdf, accessed 30 June 2018.

11 See, most notably, the new Indian model BIT: Government of India, Model Text for the Indian Bilateral Investment Treaty (2015) www.mygov.in/sites/default/files/master_image/Model%20Text%20for%20the%20Indian%20Bilateral%20Investment%20Treaty.pdf, accessed 30 June 2018.

12 See the Cooperation and Investment Facilitation Treaty (CFIT) recently concluded between Brazil and Mozambique www.itamaraty.gov.br/index.%20php?option=com_content&view=article&id=8511&catid=42&Itemid=280&lang=pt-BR, accessed 30 June 2018.

13 On South African investment treaty practice and policy, see Engela C. Schlemmer, 'An Overview of South Africa's Bilateral Investment Treaties and Investment Policy' (2016) 31 (1) *ICSID Review* 167.

14 Several authors, including Lorenzo Cotula, Xiaoxue Weng, Qianru Ma and Peng Ren, have argued that 'there is a strong case for African governments to conduct rigorous reviews of the performance of their investment treaties, including both costs and benefits' (Lorenzo Cotula *et al.*, *China-Africa Investment Treaties: Do they Work?* (London: International Institute for Environment and Development, 2016) 51 http://pubs.iied.org/pdfs/17588IIED.pdf, accessed 30 June 2018).

published in 2009[15] and revealed that 'the current system [had] open[ed] the door for narrow commercial interests to subject matters of vital national interest to unpredictable international arbitration that may constitute direct challenges to legitimate, constitutional and democratic policy-making'.[16] On the basis of the findings of the review, the Government of South Africa decided to terminated ten BITs (with Argentina, Austria, Belgium–Luxembourg Economic Union, Denmark, France, Germany, the Netherlands, Spain, Switzerland, the United Kingdom), thus reducing the number of BITs in force to 12, according to the UNCTAD International Investment Agreements Navigator.[17]

At the domestic level, the Government prepared draft legislation on the protection of investment. Published in October 2013, the draft was open to public comment and it triggered the reaction of several stakeholders.[18] The bill was then formally introduced in the National Assembly on 22 July 2015 under the title 'Promotion and Protection of Investment Bill' and eventually promulgated in the final form on 15 December under the new title, which dropped the reference to 'promotion'.

The Act consists of 16 articles (including the last three on practical matters and transitional arrangements). Its structure is broadly modelled on traditional BITs, although it presents macroscopic differences, both substantially and procedurally. Similar to traditional BITs, the Act contains a rather sophisticated definition of investment composed of three categories. Under Section 2.1, an investment is:

(a) any lawful enterprise established, acquired or expanded by an investor in accordance with the laws of the Republic, committing resources of economic value over a reasonable period of time, in anticipation of profit
(b) the holding or acquisition of shares, debentures or other ownership instruments of such an enterprise

15 Department of Trade and Industry of South Africa, *Bilateral Investment Policy Framework Review* (General Notice 961, Government Gazette 32386, 7 July 2009).

16 Xavier Carim, 'Lessons from South Africa's BITs Review'. See also R. Davies, Minister of Trade and Industry of South Africa, *2007 UNCTAD's Investment Policy Framework for Sustainable Development, Geneva.*

17 The remaining BITs in force are with the Russian Federation, Nigeria, South Korea, Cuba, China, Mauritius, Greece, Sweden, Senegal, Finland, Zimbabwe and Italy http://investmentpolicyhub.unctad.org, accessed 30 June 2018.

18 Among the numerous reactions, see European Union Chamber of Commerce and Industry in Southern Africa, 'The Promotion and Protection of Investment Bill 2013' (August 2015) www.politicsweb.co.za/documents/this-bill-wont-protect-or-promote-investment--eu-c, accessed 31 January 2019.

(c) the holding, acquisition or merger by such an enterprise with another enterprise outside the Republic to the extent that such holding, acquisition or merger with another enterprise outside the Republic, has an effect on an investment contemplated by paragraphs (a) and (b) in the Republic.

Category (a) is reminiscent of the so-called '*Salini* test', based on three elements of the notion of investment, namely 'contributions, certain duration of performance of the contract and a participation in the risks of the transaction'.[19] Interestingly, no mention is made of the contribution to the economic development of the host State, which has been referred to in the preamble of the Act and that some arbitral tribunals have considered as an additional requirement for the purpose of the definition of 'investment'.[20]

Section 2.2 further provides a comprehensive but non-exhaustive list of assets. The term 'assets', which is presumably used here as synonymous with 'resources' under Section 2.1, includes (a) shares, stocks, debentures, securities, or other equity instruments of the enterprise or another enterprise; (b) a debt security of another enterprise; (c) loans to an enterprise; (d) movable or immovable property or other property rights such as mortgages, liens or pledges; (e) claims to money or to any performance under contract having a financial value; (f) copyrights,

19 *Salini Costruttori S.p.A. and Italstrade S.p.A.* v. *Kingdom of Morocco [I]* (31 July 2001) ICSID Case No. ARB/00/4, para. 52 *in fine*. On the definition of investment, see in particular: Noah Rubins, 'The Notion of "Investment" in International Investment Arbitration' in Norbert Horn and Stefan Kröll (eds), *Arbitrating Foreign Investment Disputes: Procedural and Substantive Legal Aspects* (Kluwer Law International, 2004) 283; Sebastien Manciaux, 'The Notion of Investment: New Controversies' (2008) 9 (6) *The Journal of World Investment & Trade* 443; Paolo Vargiu, 'Beyond Hallmarks and Formal Requirements: a "Jurisprudence Constante" on the Notion of Investment in the ICSID' (2009) 10 (5) *The Journal of World Investment & Trade* 754; Emmanuel Gaillard, 'Identify or Define? Reflections on the Evolution of the Concept of Investment in ICSID Practice' in Christina Binder, *et al.* (eds), *International Investment Law for the 21th Century. Essays in Honour of Christoph Schreuer* (Oxford University Press 2009) 403; Katia Yannaca-Small, *Arbitration under International Investment Agreements. A Guide to the Key Issues* (Oxford University Press, 2010) 243; Céline Lévesque, '*Abaclat and Others* v *Argentine Republic*: The Definition of Investment' (2012) 27 (2) *ICSID Review*.

20 See, for instance, *Helnan International Hotels A/S* v. *Arab Republic of Egypt* (17 October 2006) ICSID Case No. ARB/05/19, Jurisdiction, para. 77. *Contra*, see *Victor Pey Casado and President Allende Foundation* v. *Republic of Chile* (8 May 2008) ICSID Case No. ARB/98/2, Award, para. 232.

know-how, goodwill, or intellectual property rights such as patents, trademarks, industrial designs and trade names; (g) returns such as profits, dividends, royalties or income yielded by an investment; or (h) rights or concessions conferred by law or under contract, including licenses to cultivate, extract or exploit natural resources.

The Act does not contain any detailed definition of 'investor'. Instead, Section 1 laconically defines in a rather circular manner 'investor' as an enterprise making an investment. The definition of 'investor' is completed by that of 'enterprise', which clarifies that the Act protects both natural and legal persons, regardless as to whether the enterprise is incorporated in South Africa. Since nationality is irrelevant for the purpose of the substantive protection granted under the Act, there seems to be no need for a definition of 'investor' similar to those that can be found in investment treaties. Nonetheless, the nationality of foreign investors is relevant for the purpose of international arbitration between South Africa and the home State, even if such a mechanism – whose recourse has been rather exceptional in State practice – is not mandatory under Section 13(5) of the Act.

The Act's aims are threefold as enunciated in Section 4. First, it purports to protect investment in accordance with and subject to the Constitution, with a view to striking a balance between the public interest, and the rights and interests of investors. Second, it affirms and safeguards the sovereign rights of South Africa to regulate investments in the public interest. Third, it confirms the application of the Bill of Rights in the Constitution, as well as of all relevant laws, to all investments made in South Africa.

Section 3 of the Act, which is entirely consecrated to interpretation, is an intriguing provision. It provides that the Act must be interpreted and applied in accordance with its purposes, the Constitution – including the *interpretation* of the Bill of Rights, customary international law and international law, disciplined in Sections 39, 232 and 233 of the Constitution, respectively – as well as relevant international treaties to which South Africa is or becomes a party.

Section 39 (Interpretation of Bill of Rights) reads:

1. When interpreting the Bill of Rights, a court, tribunal or forum (a) *must* promote the values that underlie an open and democratic society based on human dignity, equality and freedom; (b) *must* consider international law; and (c) *may* consider foreign law.
2. When interpreting any legislation, and when developing the common law or customary law, every court, tribunal or forum must promote the spirit, purport and objects of the Bill of Rights.

3. The Bill of Rights does not deny the existence of any other rights or freedoms that are recognised or conferred by common law, customary law or legislation, to the extent that they are consistent with the Bill. [21]

Section 232 deals with the legal status of customary international law in the South African legal system and establishes that customary international law is law in the Republic unless it is inconsistent with the Constitution or an Act of Parliament.

Interestingly, Section 3 of the Act does not contain any reference to Section 231.4 of the Constitution, the equivalent of Section 232 for international treaties. Section 231.4 states that international treaties become law in the Republic when enacted into law by national legislation, whereas self-executing provisions contained in international treaties approved by the Parliament is law of the Republic, provided they are not inconsistent with the Constitution or an Act of the Parliament.

According to Section 233, finally, when interpreting any legislation, courts in South Africa must prefer any reasonable interpretation of the legislation that is consistent with international law over any alternative interpretation that is inconsistent with international law.

The Act applies to all investments falling within the definition of Section 2, or, using the terminology of Section 5 of the Act, 'to all investments made in accordance with the requirements set out in Section 2'. It also provides that all investments must be established in accordance with domestic law (Section 7.1) and clearly excludes any pre-establishment rights (Section 7.2).

The catalogue of provisions on investment protection of the Act is limited to five provisions. Under Section 6, the Government must ensure that 'administrative, legislative and judicial processes' do not operate in a manner that is arbitrary or that denies administrative and procedural justice to investors in accordance with the Constitution and relevant legislation. In spite of the absence of any reference to fairness, apart from fair public hearing before a court, the section is titled 'Fair administrative treatment' (without any mention of administrative and judicial treatment).

The standard embodied in Section 6, which did not appear in the draft submitted in July 2009, is essentially national and based on the prohibition of arbitrary treatment and on denial of administrative and procedural justice as provided in domestic legislation. It is then further substantiated by three *renvois* to Articles 32–34 of the Constitution, concerning, the right to be given written reasons and administrative review, the right to access government-held information, and right

21 Emphasis added.

to a fair public hearing before a court or another independent and partial tribunal or forum, respectively.[22]

Reminiscent of the so-called Calvo Doctrine,[23] Section 8.1 (National treatment) provides that foreign investors cannot be treated less favourably than domestic investors in like circumstances. Section 8.2 offers a non-exhaustive list of elements that have to be taken into account in order to establish the existence of 'like circumstances', such as (a) the effect of the foreign investment on the Republic, and the cumulative effects of all investments; (b) the sector that the foreign investments are in; (c) the aim of any measure relating to foreign investments; (d) factors relating to the foreign investor or the foreign investment in relation to the measure concerned; (e) the effect on third persons and the local community; (f) the effect on employment; and (g) the direct and indirect effect on the environment.

Yet, the scope of application of the national treatment is significantly reduced by the express exclusion of the extension to foreign investors of preferences or privileges resulting from, *inter alia*: (a) government procurement processes; (b) public subsidies and grants; (c) promotion of equality or protection of historically disadvantaged persons, promotion of cultural heritage, indigenous knowledge and related biological resources, or national heritage; and (d) assistance or development of small- and medium-sized businesses or new industries (Section 8.4).

Under Section 9, South Africa must ensure the physical security of foreign investors 'as may be generally provided to domestic investors in accordance with minimum standard of treatment of customary international law (MSCIL) and subject to available resources and capacity'.

The Act contains a section reminiscent of, yet significantly different from, the other key provision normally found in investment treaties, namely expropriation. Section 10 of the Act confines itself to only extending to foreign investors the right to property protected under Section 25 of the Constitution, a rather complex provision

22 See Department of Trade and Industry of South Africa, *Bilateral Investment Policy Framework Review* (General Notice 961, Government Gazette 32386 (7 July 2009) Sections 32–4.

23 On the clause, see, in particular, Amos S. Hershey, 'The Calvo and Drago Doctrines' (1907) *American Journal of International Law* 26; K. Lipstein, 'The Place of the Calvo Clause in International Law' (1945) 22 *British Yearbook of International Law* 130; and, more recently, Christoph Schreuer, 'Calvo's Grandchildren: The Return of Local Remedies in Investment Arbitration' (2005) 4 *Law and Practice International Courts and Tribunals* 1.

of more than 350 words.[24] Section 25 indicates, *inter alia*, the requirements that are to be satisfied in case of expropriation. First, no one may be deprived of property except in terms of law of general application. Second, no law may permit arbitrary deprivation of property. Third, property may be expropriated only for a public purpose or in the public interest, which includes land reform and equitable access to all of South Africa's natural resources. Fourth, expropriation entails the obligation to pay just and equitable compensation fixed, in case of disagreement, by a domestic court and reflecting an equitable balance between the public interest and the interests of those affected, having regard to all relevant circumstances.

Section 25 of the Constitution further clarifies, *inter alia*, that the State *must* take reasonable legislative and other measures, within its available resources, to foster conditions which enable citizens to gain access to land on an equitable basis and that nothing in Section 9 prevents the State from taking legislative and other

24 Section 25 (Property) reads: '1. No one may be deprived of property except in terms of law of general application, and no law may permit arbitrary deprivation of property. 2. Property may be expropriated only in terms of law of general application (a) for a public purpose or in the public interest; and (b) subject to compensation, the amount of which and the time and manner of payment of which have either been agreed to by those affected or decided or approved by a court. 3. The amount of the compensation and the time and manner of payment must be just and equitable, reflecting an equitable balance between the public interest and the interests of those affected, having regard to all relevant circumstances, including (a) the current use of the property; (b) the history of the acquisition and use of the property; (c) the market value of the property; (d) the extent of direct investment and subsidy in the acquisition and beneficial capital improvement of the property; and (e) the purpose of the expropriation. 4. For the purposes of this section (a) the public interest includes the nation's commitment to land reform, and to reforms to bring about equitable access to all South Africa's natural resources; and (b) property is not limited to land. 5. The must take reasonable legislative and other measures, within its available resources, to foster conditions which enable citizens to gain access to land on an equitable basis. 6. A person or community whose tenure of land is legally insecure as a result of past racially discriminatory laws or practices is entitled, to the extent provided by an Act of Parliament, either to tenure which is legally secure or to comparable redress. 7. A person or community dispossessed of property after 19 June 1913 as a result of past racially discriminatory laws or practices is entitled, to the extent provided by an Act of Parliament, either to restitution of that property or to equitable redress. 8. No provision of this section may impede the from taking legislative and other measures to achieve land, water and related reform, in order to redress the results of past racial discrimination, provided that any departure from the provisions of this section is in accordance with the provisions of section 36(1). 9. Parliament must enact the legislation referred to in subsection (6).'

measures to achieve land, water and related reform, in order to redress the results of past racial discrimination.

The final substantive provision relates to the right of foreign investors to repatriate funds, subject to taxation and other applicable legislation (Section 11).

A key provision of the Act is Section 12 (Right to regulate) providing in paragraph 1 that nothing in the Act precludes the adoption by the Government, in accordance with the Constitution and applicable legislation, of measures concerning, *inter alia*: (a) redressing historical, social and economic inequalities and injustices; (b) upholding the basic values and principles governing the public administration; (c) upholding the rights guaranteed in the Constitution; (d) promoting and preserving cultural heritage and practices, indigenous knowledge and biological resources related thereto, or national heritage; (e) fostering economic development, industrialization and beneficiation; (f) achieving the progressive realisation of socioeconomic rights; or (g) protecting the environment and the conservation, and sustainable use of natural resources.

Furthermore, under paragraph 2 of Section 12, the Government or any organ of the State may take measures that are necessary to comply with international obligations related to international peace and security, or the protection of the security interests, including the financial stability of the Republic.

With regard to the settlement of disputes between the investor and the Government, the Act makes available to the former two types of domestic remedies. Within six months of 'becoming aware of the dispute', the investor may request the Department of Trade and Industry (TDI) 'to facilitate the resolution of such dispute by appointing a mediator' (Section 13.1). Under Section 13.2, the mediator is appointed by the Government and the investor from a list maintained by the DTI or, in the absence of such list, from an individual proposed by either party. If the DTI is party to the dispute, the parties *may* jointly request the Judge President of one of the divisions of the High Court to appoint a mediator.

Alternatively, under Section 13.4 and subject to applicable legislation, an investor, upon becoming aware of a dispute, 'is not precluded from approaching any competent court, independent tribunal or statutory body within the Republic for the resolution of a dispute relating to an investment'.

The Act also foresees the possibility of arbitration between South Africa and the national State of the investor in respect of investments covered by this Act. In this case, the Government *may* consent to international arbitration, subject to the exhaustion of domestic remedies. In considering such a request, the Government must respect the administrative processes set out in Section 6 of the Act (Fair and administrative treatment).

3 Preliminary assessment of the Act

The Act is a strong response to the perceived inadequacy of investment treaties, which are facing growing criticism for three main reasons. First and in spite of some recent interesting developments and with significant exceptions,[25] these treaties remain manifestly unbalanced in favour of the investor, to the point that in *Spyridon Roussalis* v. *Romania*, the Tribunal candidly admitted that the BIT between Greece and Romania 'imposes no obligation on investors, only on contracting States'.[26] Second, investment treaties are often perceived by the host State as unduly restricting its regulatory powers and its capacity to protect collective interests and pursue its social and economic policies.[27] Third, investment arbitration is not considered as offering adequate guarantees in terms of legitimacy, transparency and coherence.[28]

The disaffection for investment treaties, combined with the lack of clear evidence that investment treaties are necessary to attract foreign investments and stimulate economic growth,[29] has pushed several States to reconsider their approach to the legal protection of such investments. In recent years, States have demonstrated a good deal of reluctance to ratify BITs, upgraded their BITs, revised their BIT models, or opted for much less facilitation treaties.[30] The South African Government has

25 For two examples of quite innovative investment treaties, see the BIT between Morocco and Nigeria (not in force at time of writing); see Supplementary Act A/SA.3/12/08 Adopting Community Rules on Investment and the Modalities for its Implementation within ECOWAS (19 December 2008) www.privatesector.ecowas.int/en/III/Supplementary_Act_Investment.pdf, accessed 30 June 2018.

26 *Spyridon Roussalis* v. *Romania* (7 December 2011), ICSID Case No. ARB/06/1, Award, para. 871.

27 It has been declared recently that '[o]ne common issue is the need to clarify the interaction between international investment instruments and domestic investment policy as well as policy in other areas – for e.g., sustainable development and environmental regulation. Governments must always be concerned about ensuring that there is sufficient policy space for them to engage in reconciling competing interests.' (Commonwealth Investment Experts Group Meeting for the African Region (Kampala, Uganda, 20–21 October 2011), on file with author.)

28 See, in particular, Michael Waibel, *et al.* (eds), *The Backlash Against Investment Arbitration* (Kluwer Law International, 2010); Jean E. Kalicki, Anna Joubin-Bret (eds), *Reshaping the Investor-State Dispute Settlement System* (Leiden: Brill-Nijhoff, 2015).

29 UNCTAD, *The Impact of International Investment Agreements on Foreign Direct Investment: An Overview of Empirical Studies 1998–2014*.

30 See Section 1 of this chapter.

opted for a different route based on the assumption that domestic legislation is more appropriate than international legal instruments to regulate foreign investment.

The Act is firmly anchored to the Constitution, as is evident first in Sections 3 and 4. Section 3 indicates that it must be interpreted, *inter alia*, in accordance with the Constitution. Section 4 enunciates its objectives and subsection (a) eloquently provides that foreign investments are to be protected 'in accordance with and subject to the Constitution'. The Act also contains several references and *renvois* to the Constitution, most prominently with regard to Section 6 (Fair administrative treatment), Section 9 (Legal protection of investment) and Section 12 (Right to regulate).

The choice to move away from international treaties in favour of a domestic piece of legislation solidly pegged to the Constitution is an interesting compromise. Domestic legislation unavoidably exposes foreign investors to greater risks and instability, as the legislator may at any time amend the legal rules, whereas modifying a treaty requires the agreement of all parties. Pegging the Act to the Constitution, however, significantly mitigates such exposure due to the rigidity of the Constitution, which can be modified only in accordance with a more complex procedure.[31] Yet, the Acts and the Constitution itself make several references to other pieces of domestic legislation, thus paving the way for the 'ordinary' legislative intervention to complete and elaborate on the rules contained in the Act and the Constitution. Here, the risks foreign investors are exposed to become more significant.

With regard to the substantive provisions, the Act does not impose any new obligations on the investor. The only obligation expressly mentioned in the Act is the obligation to comply with domestic law, which, needless to say, exists regardless of any express provision.[32] From this perspective, the legislator has preferred to include in the Act several references to domestic legislation rather than to insert in the Act any obligations for the investors like those that have slowly found their way into investment treaties, such as obligations on transparency, access to documents,

31 See Section 74 (Bills amending the Constitution).

32 In *Parkerings-Compagniet AS* v. *Republic of Lithuania* (11 September 2007) ICSID Case No. ARB/05/8, Award, para. 332, for instance, the Tribunal pointed out that '[i]t is each State's undeniable right and privilege to exercise its sovereign legislative power. A State has the right to enact, modify or cancel a law at its own discretion'.

consultation, corporate social responsibility, corruption, or social and environmental impact assessment.[33]

Moving to the catalogue of provisions on the protection of investments contained in the Act, the key provision on fair administrative treatment (Section 6) is completely different from the fair and equitable treatment (FET) normally found in investment treaties.[34] FET is a rather vague international standard that investment tribunals have progressively shaped through a largely consistent body of decisions.[35] As pointed out by a tribunal, the standard:

> 'encompasses *inter alia* the following concrete principles: the State must act in a transparent manner; the State is obliged to act in good faith; the State's conduct cannot be arbitrary, grossly unfair, unjust, idiosyncratic, discriminatory, or lacking in due process; the State must respect procedural propriety and due process. The case law also confirms that to comply with the standard, the State must respect the investor's reasonable and legitimate expectations'.[36]

Such concrete principles are regularly recognized and applied by the generality of States within their respective jurisdictions, as well as by international arbitral tribunals.

The standard contained in Section 6 of the Act, on the contrary, does not go much further than confirming the protection granted to investment in the Constitution. Significantly, it does not make any express reference to non-discriminatory measures

33 See, for instance, Chapter III of the Supplementary Act A/SA.3/12/08 Adopting Community Rules on Investment and the Modalities for its Implementation within ECOWAS, which contains a comprehensive catalogue of foreign investors' obligations and duties. Among them, Article 12 imposes on foreign investors the obligation to conduct an environmental and social impact assessment of the potential investment, to duly apply the precautionary principle, and to make the documents related to the investment available to the local community.

34 See, for instance, Article 3.1 of the BIT between South Africa and China, according to which, '[i]nvestments and activities associated with investments of investors of either Contracting Party shall be accorded fair and equitable treatment and shall enjoy protection in the territory of the other Contracting Party. Neither Contracting Party shall in any way impair by unreasonable or discriminatory measures the management, maintenance, use, enjoyment or disposal of investments in its territory of investors of the other Contracting Party'.

35 As pointed out in *Total S.A.* v. *The Argentine Republic* (27 December 2010) ICSID Case No. ARB/04/01, Liability, para. 109, 'tribunals have endeavoured to pinpoint some typical obligations that may be included in the standard, as well as types of conduct that would breach the standard, in order to be guided in their analysis of the issue before them'.

36 *Rumeli Telekom A.S. and Telsim Mobil Telekomunikasyon Hizmetleri A.S.* v. *Republic of Kazakhstan* (29 July 2008) ICSID Case No. ARB/05/16, Award, para. 609.

lest restricting the regulatory powers of South Africa, especially with regard to the implementation of policies aimed at correcting past discriminatory measures.[37]

The distinction between arbitrary measures (or 'arbitrary deprivation of property' using the wording of Article 25 of the Constitution) and discriminatory measures has emerged sufficiently clearly in international law and in foreign investment law in particular.[38] The former category possesses a manifestly negative connotation since arbitrary measures inflict damage on the foreign investor without serving a legitimate purpose,[39] or bear 'no rational relationship ... between a measure adopted by the government and the alleged purpose or goal of that measure'.[40] Relying on both International Court of Justice jurisprudence[41] and dictionaries, several investment tribunals have described arbitrary measures or means as 'derived from mere opinion', 'capricious', 'unrestrained', 'despotic', 'founded on prejudice or preference rather than on reason or fact'[42] 'fixed or done capriciously or at pleasure', 'without adequate determining principle', 'depending on the will alone', 'without cause based upon the law'.[43] In a similar vein, the South Africa Constitutional Court has held

37 It is worth noting that BITs concluded by South Africa normally prohibit unreasonable or discriminatory measures, see, for instance, Article 41.1 of the BIT with China, Article 4.1 of the BIT with Nigeria and Article 3.1 of the BIT with Argentina.

38 Christoph Schreuer, 'Protection Against Arbitrary or Discriminatory Measures' in Roger P. Alford and Catherine A. Rogers (eds) *The Future of Investment Arbitration* (New York: Oxford University Press, 2009) 183, with reference to some arbitral decisions in footnote 60.

39 *Ibid.*, especially 198.

40 Patrick Dumberry, 'The Prohibition Against Arbitrary Conduct and the Fair and Equitable Treatment Standard under NAFTA Article 1105' (2014) 15 *The Journal of World Investment & Trade* 117, 122–3.

41 In *Elettronica Sicula S.p.A. (ELSI)* (1989) Judgment, *ICJ Reports*, 15, on p. 76, the Court described an arbitrary conduct as 'wilful disregard of due process of law, an act which shocks, or at least surprises, a sense of juridical propriety', in the *Colombian-Peruvian Asylum Case* (1950), Judgment, *ICJ Reports*, 266, on p. 284, it held that 'arbitrary action is substituted for the rule of law. Such would be the case if the administration of justice were corrupted by measures clearly prompted by political aims'.

42 UNCTAD, *Fair and Equitable Treatment*, UNCTAD Series on Issues in International Investment Agreements II (New York and Geneva: United Nations, 2012) 78.

43 See, for instance, *Siemens A.G.* v. *The Argentine Republic* (17 January 2007) ICSID Case No. ARB/02/8, Award, para. 318, in *Methanex Corporation* v. *United States* of America (3 August 2005) Award, Part IV, Chapter B, para. 1, the Tribunal referred to 'malign intent'. On the application of the notion of arbitrariness, see, in particular, Veijo Heiskanen, 'Arbitrary and Unreasonable Measures', in August Reinisch (ed), *Standards of Investment Protection* (Oxford University Press, 2008) 87; Jacob Stone, 'Arbitrariness, the Fair and Equitable Treatment Standard and the International Law of Investment' (2012) 25 (1) *Leiden Journal of International Law* 77.

that a conduct is arbitrary when 'capricious or proceeding merely from the will and not based on reason or principle'.[44]

The choice made in Section 6 not to expressly refer to discriminatory conduct is of great importance from the standpoint of the exercise of regulatory powers by South Africa. South African authorities may adopt measures having a, probably de facto, discriminatory nature, but not amounting to arbitrariness, in pursuing their public policies. These policies include those intended to redress the consequences of past discriminatory measures, to promote the well-being of historically disadvantaged categories, or to implement land reform. From this perspective, Section 6 must be read together not only with the relevant parts of the Constitution it refers to, but also with Section 9 of the Constitution and Section 12 of the Act on the power to regulate.

It is true that Section 6 requires South Africa to ensure administrative and procedural justice. Such a requirement, however, relates to access to the competent tribunals or other bodies, as well as property of the administration of justice. It is argued that such a requirement does not undermine measures adopted by public authorities to pursue public policies, even if they may be discriminatory against foreign investors, provided that the latter have access to justice and justice is properly administered.

The national treatment standard contained in Section 8 is in principle comparable with that guaranteed by investment treaties, if not for its source.[45] The innovative element is the detailed yet non-exhaustive list of elements to be taken into account to determine the existence of 'like circumstances', which appears to be well articulated and may be expected not only to facilitate the application of the Act, but also to enhance the predictability and consistency of the related judicial and arbitral decisions.

The specifications in Section 8.4, however, water down the standard rather drastically by carving out important and broadly worded exceptions to the extension to foreign investors of the treatment reserved to domestic investors. In spite of the apparent close character of the list of exceptions, Section 8.4 leaves the Government

44 *Beckingham* v. *Boksburg Liquor Licencing Board* (1931) TPD 280, 282, and *Johannesburg Liquor Licencing Board* v. *Kuhn* (1963) (4) SA 666 (A) at 671C.

45 Article 10(1) of the BIT with China, for instance, provides that '[i]f the treatment to be accorded by one Contracting Party in accordance with its laws and regulations to investments or activities associated with such investments of investors of the other Contracting Party is more favourable than the treatment provided for in this Agreement, the more favourable treatment shall be applicable'.

great room for manoeuvre, especially when it comes to promoting the achievement of equality, cultural heritage and practices, or developing small, medium or new industries.

The policy space of the government is further safeguarded by Section 12 on the right to regulate, this time with a non-comprehensive list of categories of measures. It must be noted that these measures do not need to be *necessary* to protect certain social interests, such as the environment or public health. They allow a proactive role of South Africa and their general nature makes hardly feasible any administrative or judicial control beyond compliance with the procedural guarantees contained in Section 6 of the Act, as well as the principles of good faith, proportionality and reasonableness.

While it is certainly legitimate to ensure that the host State is able to exercise its rights and fulfil its duties,[46] the combination of Section 8.4 and Section 12 substantially weakens the protection of foreign investments. One may wonder whether a more balanced approach could be inspired by provisions contained in existing BITs, such as Article 3(3)(c) of the BIT between South Africa and the Czech Republic, which excludes foreign investors from the enjoyment of any treatment preference or privilege which may be granted by the host State in relation to 'any law or other measure the purpose of which is to promote the achievement of equality in its territory, or designed to protect or advance persons, or categories of persons, previously disadvantaged by unfair discrimination'.[47]

Section 9 on the legal protection of property is not particularly well drafted, as MSCIL by definition applies only to foreign investors, while the use of the modal 'may' with reference to the protection accorded to domestic investors seems rather ambiguous. More importantly, it limits the protection to physical security and introduces a limitation to the related obligation to the available resources. Both treaty practice and arbitral awards vary significantly with regard to whether the obligation

46 In the preamble of the Pan-African Investment Code (PAIC), for instance, the Parties recognized 'their right to regulate all the aspects relating to investments within their territories with a view to meeting national policy objectives and to promoting sustainable development objectives' (https://au.int/en/documents/20161231/pan-african-investment-code-paic, accessed 31 January 2019).

47 Article 4 *bis* of the Protocol to the BIT with the Islamic Republic of Iran, likewise, excludes the extension to investors of the benefit of any treatment, preference or privilege resulting from, *inter alia*, 'any law or other measure taken, pursuant to Article (9) of the Constitution of the Republic of South Africa, 1996 (Act 108, 1996) the purpose of which is to promote the achievement of equality in its territory, or designed to protect or advance persons, or categories of persons, disadvantaged by unfair discrimination'.

to ensure full protection goes beyond physical security.[48] The standard protected under Section 9 therefore cannot be considered as a departure from current practice, but rather a confirmation of a tendency to reduce it to physical security.[49]

Section 10 of the Act (Protection of property) – which is essentially a *renvoi* to Section 25 of the Constitution – does not reassure foreign investors in the event of expropriation. First of all, it deals only with direct expropriation, i.e. transfer of the title to property, and not also to indirect expropriation, which today is by far the most frequent form of deprivation of property.[50] Second, it imposes expressly only three of the four requirements imposed by international law to lawfully expropriate foreign investment, namely public interest, respect of procedural rules and compensation. In line with the approach taken with regard to national treatment standards and the right to regulate, mention is made to arbitrary measures, but not to discriminatory measures. Quite the contrary, foreign investors may suffer the consequence of measures aimed at redressing past racial discrimination, undertaking land reform, and promoting equitable access to all of South Africa's natural resources.

These measures can be described as 'positive discrimination' and are certainly legitimate from a social and political standpoint. From a strictly legal perspective, however, Section 10 hardly reassures foreign investors due to the vagueness and subjectivity of the just and equitable level of compensation, which reflects an equitable balance between the public interest and the interests of those affected. This is definitely much less satisfactory, from the foreign investor's standpoint, than the 'prompt, full and adequate' formula that can be found, in different variants, in the overwhelming majority of investment treaties.[51]

If the substantive provisions of the Act can scarcely meet the level of protection normally offered by investment treaties, the settlement of dispute mechanism appears to be hardly satisfactory. Mediation is certainly to be encouraged for several

48 See, in particular, George K. Foster, 'Recovering "Protection and Security": The Treaty Standard's Obscure Origins, Forgotten Meaning, and Key Current Significance' (2012) 45 *Vanderbilt Journal of Transnational Law* 1095.

49 See, for instance, Article 3.2 of the Indian Model BIT (Government of India, Model Text for the Indian Bilateral Investment Treaty (2015)), according to which 'full protection and security' only refers to a Party's obligations relating to physical security of investors and to investments made by the investors of the other Party and not to any other obligation whatsoever.

50 See, for instance, Article 4.1 of the BIT between South Africa and China.

51 See, for example, Article 6.1 of the BIT between South Africa and Argentina (terminated).

reasons, including the higher probability to continue – if not to strengthen – the underlying business partnership, as well as the flexibility it offers – especially with regard to expropriation by allowing the parties to avoid the gamble of either full compensation or no compensation at all.[52] By definition, however, its effectiveness depends on the concerned parties' commitment and willingness to settle the dispute in a friendly manner. The exercise may be frustrated by financial implications, political considerations or public pressure, especially when the dispute relates to investments in sensitive sectors.

Leaving aside diplomatic protection, in the absence of an applicable treaty providing for international arbitration, foreign investors in South Africa may only have recourse to domestic adjudicatory bodies, which are not necessarily courts. The settlement of the dispute before domestic courts, tribunals or statutory bodies provided for in Section 13.4 calls for several comments. To start with, the remedy in Section 13.4 is independent from any attempt to settle the dispute through mediation. Besides, the verb 'to approach' used to describe the initiation of the proceeding under Section 13.4 is not particularly felicitous. Perhaps more importantly, Section 13.4 must be read in conjunction with Section 6.4 (a fortiori considering that under Section 6.4 the latter is 'subject' to the former). However, it remains unclear what the effects of the *renvoi* operated by Section 6.4 to Article 34 of the Constitution are, according to which the dispute could be settled by a court or, where appropriate, another independent and impartial tribunal or forum.

Moreover, the reference in Section 6.4 to disputes 'that can be resolved by the application of law', , remains rather cryptic and apparently assumes the existence of disputes that *cannot* be resolved by the application of law. This begs the questions: on what are the criteria to establish whether a dispute is susceptible to be settled by the application of law?; who will make the related determination?; and what happens to disputes that cannot be settled by the application of the law?

52 See the symposium on alternative dispute resolution in investment disputes (2014) 29 (1) *ICSID Review* 1. See also N.D. Rubins, 'Use of Mediation for Investment Disputes' (2004) 1 *Transnational Dispute Settlement* 1; J.J. Coe, Jnr, 'Toward a Complementary Use of Conciliation in Investor-State Disputes – A Preliminary Sketch' (2007) 12 (7) *UC Davis Journal of International Law & Policy* 7; Thomas W. Wälde, 'Efficient Management of Transnational Disputes: Mutual Gain by Mediation or Joint Loss in Litigation' (2006) 22 (2) *Arbitration International* 205; Stephen M. Schwebel, 'Is Mediation of Foreign Investment Dispute Plausible?' (2007) 22 (2) *ICSID Review – Foreign Investment Law Journal*237; Tarcisio Gazzini, 'Mediation in the Settlement of Disputes between Foreign Investors and States' in Bernardo Cortese (ed), *Liber Amicorum M.L. Picchio Forlati* (Cedam, 2014) 395.

Furthermore, the abandonment of investor-State arbitration is a rather drastic measure. Investment arbitration has been celebrated by numerous tribunals and in literature as a remarkable development, bringing the dispute outside the reach of politics with a view to ensuring equality of the parties in efficient proceedings conducted by independent tribunals.[53] While there is no doubt that investment arbitration presents several problems, it remains to be seen whether the bold move backward made by the Act was indispensable or whether South Africa could have better calibrated the exposure of the host State (for instance, by restricting or conditioning access to arbitration, or by expressly introducing counter-claims), in order to enhance transparency, participation and public scrutiny.

The settlement of disputes through State-State arbitration, which completes Section 13, can hardly be expected to improve much the procedural protection of foreign investors, not only due to its entirely voluntary character, but also because States are traditionally rather reluctant to resort to this kind of arbitration.[54] Equally important, even assuming arbitration under Section 13 is possible, the entire proceedings and all decisions related to the dispute (including a possible friendly settlement or an agreement on compensation) will be firmly in the hands of the home State, with all associated shortcomings and implications. Furthermore, with regard to the proceedings, the silence of the Act on the determination of the nationality of foreign investors unavoidably adds further uncertainty on the entire procedure.

In conclusion, one may even wonder what is the added value of the procedural rules of the Act given that that they hardly offer foreign investors anything more that the remedies already available under the Constitution and confine international arbitration to State-State voluntary arbitration.

53 As pointed out in *Gas Natural SDG, S.A.* v. *The Argentine Republic* (17 June 2005) ICSID Case No. ARB/03/10, Jurisdiction, paras 29 ff (notes omitted), '[t]he creation of ICSID and the adoption of bilateral investment treaties offered to investors assurances that disputes that might flow from their investments would not be subject to the perceived hazards of delays and political pressures of adjudication in national courts. Correspondingly, the prospect of international arbitration was designed to offer to hosts freedom from political pressures by governments of the of which the investor is a national'.

54 See Michele Potestà, 'State-to-State Dispute Settlement Pursuant to Bilateral Investment Treaties: Is there Potential?' in N. Boschiero *et al.* (eds), *International Courts and the Development of International Law. Essays in Honour of T. Treves* (Springer, 2013) 753.

Conclusions

The Protection of Investment Act 22 of 2015 has resolutely rebalanced in favour of the State the private and public rights related to foreign investment in South Africa. While it is undisputed that States can and should review their investment treaty policy, and, if appropriate, switch from international treaties to domestic legislation, the drastic reduction of the protection of foreign investors, both in terms of substantive and procedural provisions, is not entirely convincing. It is argued that a better equilibrium could have been achieved by adjusting the existing level of legal protection for foreign investors. This could have been achieved either through the renegotiation of existing investment treaties or the adoption of domestic legislation, striking an even-handed balance between the need to reassure foreign investors and that of preserving the capacity of South Africa to fully exercise its sovereign prerogatives and meet its responsibilities.

The host State could have reconsidered, and possibly limited, the rights of foreign investors, as well as introduced obligations on them, including social and environmental impact assessment, corporate social responsibility, consultation, transparency, fight against corruption, access to information and documents, and so on. In this regard, the SADC model BIT[55] and the recent Indian model BIT,[56] as well as some modern investment treaties, such as the 2016 BIT between Morocco and Nigeria[57] or ECOWAS Supplementary Act,[58] could have been useful sources of inspiration.

Furthermore, the right to regulate certainly deserves to be adequately safeguarded, with carefully drafted specific or general exceptions, possibly modelled after General Agreement on Tariffs and Trade Article XX, rather than vague and politically charged provisions such as those that appear in the Act. Furthermore, provisions especially designed to allow the adoption by South Africa of the measures necessary to redress past discrimination and injustices, such as Article 3(3)(c) of the current BIT with the Czech Republic,[59] could have been further developed.

55 See SADC, Model Bilateral Investment Treaty Template with Commentary.

56 See Government of India, Model Text for the Indian Bilateral Investment Treaty.

57 See Morocco–Nigeria BIT (2016) https://investmentpolicy.unctad.org/international-investment-agreements/treaties/bilateral-investment-treaties/3711/morocco--nigeria-bit-2016.

58 See ECOWAS, Supplementary Act A/SA.3/12/08 Adopting Community Rules on Investment and the Modalities for its Implementation within ECOWAS.

59 See South Africa–Czech Republic BIT.

Finally, wiping out investor-State arbitration may prove unnecessary, if not counterproductive. A variety of options are available between keeping the existing – admittedly unsatisfactory – regime and a flat rejection of the said regime. The current concerns on the legal protection of foreign investment could indeed be addressed by introducing appropriate provisions on the exhaustion of domestic remedies, fork-in-the-road clauses, provisions on counterclaims – if not even claims – put forward by the State, and so on.

Now it remains to be seen what impact the Act will have on the flow of foreign investment to South Africa. Such assessment is particularly arduous for several reasons, including the difficulties to establish a link between the Act and the evolution of the flow of foreign investment and to ensure that such flow responds to the objective of foreign investment.[60]

60 According to UNCTAD, foreign direct investment to South Africa has declined by 41% to USD 1.3 billion 'as the country was beset by an underperforming commodity sector and political uncertainty' (UNCTAD, *World Investment Report 2018* http://unctad.org/en/PublicationsLibrary/wir2018_en.pdf, accessed 30 June 2018).

9

Electoral democracy, foreign capital flows and the human rights infrastructure in Nigeria

Victor Adetula and Olugbemi Jaiyebo

Introduction

Significant changes have been witnessed across the globe since the end of the Cold War. For instance, the neoliberal global order under the influence of the United States of America (USA) created a favourable environment for the spread of Western liberal democracy to other parts of the world. In Africa, it exerted significant pressures on authoritarian governments and set them on the path of reform that culminated in different forms of liberal democratic transition.[1] There is also a growing global consensus on the legitimacy of such Western values as individualism, liberty, human rights, equality before the law, free markets, the rule of law and, most significantly, liberal democracy.[2]

The experiences recorded in Africa have emphasized elections to help citizens determine occupants of State power without consideration for the nature and character of the State. The consequence has been the survival of a State that lacks autonomy to inaugurate, influence and supervize political transitions and other auxiliary programmes including economic reforms. In this chapter, we employ the term 'electoral democracy' to reflect the phenomenon of periodic voting, which may not necessarily embody the culture of democracy.

1 Michael Bratton and Nicholas Van de Walle, *Democratic Experiments in Africa: Regime Transitions in Comparative Perspective* (Cambridge University Press, 1997).

2 Victor A.O Adetula, 'Measuring democracy and "good governance" in Africa: A critique of assumptions and methods' in Kwandiwe Kondlo and Chinenyengozi Ejiogu (eds), *Africa in Focus Governance in the 21st Century* (Human Science Research Council, HSRC, 2011).

Nigeria successfully implemented a military to civilian transition programme in May 1999 and conducted five general elections between 1999 and 2015. We note Nigeria's democratic experiment since 1999 as consisting essentially of a measure of political rights and civil liberties of citizens, but not a good measure of economic freedoms.[3] Successive administrations in the country have inaugurated economic reform programmes, which are markedly sensitive to the demands and requirements of the international community. It should be recalled that in the 1990s the interpretation of human rights and the priority accorded to its different facets by successive governments made a conflictual panorama between the State and civil society imminent.

Since the reintroduction of electoral democracy in Nigeria in 1999, there has been to some extent, respect for the rule of law, legal protection for agreements freely entered, a functional judicial system and a system of checks and balances between arms of government. Nigeria's economic strategy has focused on macroeconomic stabilization and structural reforms. The nation offers investors a low-cost labor pool, abundant natural resources, and potentially the largest domestic market in sub-Saharan Africa. Returns on investments in Nigeria are among the highest in the world. While the risk levels may be considered high, the returns on investment are even higher.

The political reform programmes witnessed in Africa in the course of the 'wave of democratization' were expected in part to create a conducive environment for foreign investment and capital flow. There is, however, concern that weak national legislation and implementation cannot effectively mitigate the negative impact of contemporary globalization on vulnerable economies. Arguably, the pervasiveness of weak national legislation and implementation are in part linked to the 'unholy alliance' between foreign capital and the State. Other factors, such as the lack of necessary technical expertise and the unfavourable international environment, constitute risk factors for sustainable development.

Against the background that acknowledges effective and functional human rights infrastructure as a 'sine qua non' to the prevention of a re-colonization of a country through foreign flows of capital, this chapter probes the interface of foreign capital with human rights in Nigeria. It examines the extent to which the human rights system in Nigeria is being repositioned to engage the increasing influx of international economic players and to bring transnational economic entities in compliance with local and international human rights standards.

3 Aparna Mathur and Kartikeya Singh, 'Foreign Direct Investment, Corruption and Democracy' (2013) 45 (8) *Applied Economics* 991.

We examine the shift from litigating human rights violations in foreign courts to seeking remedies in Africa and further to communities engaging in self-help for redress of perceived human rights abuses. The chapter projects the confluence of business with human rights as the platform for sustainable investment and development in Nigeria. We demonstrate the commitment of the business community to human rights values and informed local communities as cornerstones of a redefined human rights community.

1 Reforms and investment environment

In the 1970s and 1980s Nigeria reaped increased revenues from the expansion of oil production and oil prices. The average prices of crude oil rose from USD 2.4 per barrel in 1970 to USD 14.6 in 1975. These revenues paved the way for the adoption of a State-led development strategy that ascribes economic growth to economic nationalism and interventionism.[4] The State participated directly in economic activities through State-owned corporations and much of the social services were subsidized. Also, the participation of foreigners in the economy was legally restricted to specified sectors. There has since been a shift towards greater openness in the national economy within the framework of neo-liberal reform. The Federal Government of Nigeria implemented an elaborate privatization plan geared towards making the private sector the nation's development engine. Foreign exchange and other commercial-related laws were amended and/or promulgated to establish a more conducive and favorable environment for foreign investors.

Prior to 1999, foreign capital flows, such as lending by governments and international organizations, bank lending, short- and long-term investment in private and public bonds, investments in equities and direct investment in productive capacity, were reportedly constrained in Nigeria in part due to the unfavorable political environment and the restrictions imposed on the economy. These restraints resulted in foreign direct investment (FDI) averaging only USD 1.1 billion between 1983 and 1999, with intra-company loans accounting for about 71%. In 1999, the Nigerian national economy was reportedly worth USD 36 billion, ranking fifth in Africa. During the same period the net official development assistance received by Nigeria was put at USD 151,800,000 by the Organisation for Economic Co-operation and Development (OECD). By the mid-2000s, foreign capital inflows

4 Coronation Capital, *Nigeria's Fourth Republic. Economy and Opportunities Beyond Politics* http://coronationcapital.com.ng/ccMedia/CoronationCapital/images/PDF's/economic_report_new.pdf?ext=.pdf, accessed 21 February 2019.

increased significantly, with FDI averaging USD 6.3 billion annually since 2004, and peaking at USD 8.9 billion in 2011. In 2013 Nigeria's economy expanded further and came out top of Africa's GDP table with USD 522 billion. The net official development assistance to Nigeria had risen to USD 2,476,180,000 in 2014.[5]

Nigeria's return to civil rule, coupled with capital control relaxations, may have contributed to its profile in the 'Africa rising' discourse. Nigeria's economic profile earned its consideration for inclusion in the Next 11 (or N-11) emerging countries identified by Goldman Sachs to have the potential for attaining global competitiveness based on their economic and demographic settings, and the foundation for reforms already laid. In conjunction with the New Partnership for Africa's Development (NEPAD), the Federal Government of Nigeria engaged in an investment policy review exercise to align investment laws, policies and strategies with the OECD Policy Framework for Investment, a tool to mobilize investment in support of economic growth and sustainable development. It has been observed that the need to attract FDI usually puts governments under pressure to alter patterns of domestic economic policy, and possibly even challenge the de facto sovereignty of the nation-State and the capacity for democratic governance.[6]

In the vast majority of cases, investors care more about how their rights and how their investments can be best secured and not so much about the rights of the citizens or the human rights situation in the host country. While companies have delivered innovations and efficiencies that have dramatically raised standards of living and lifted millions of people out of poverty, they have also caused and contributed to human rights abuses around the world.[7] The perception of transnational corporations as human rights abusers is dominant in Nigeria on the evidence of the oil companies in the Niger Delta, the mining companies in Enugu and the Jos Plateau, and the experimentation of uncertified drugs in Kano. The pervasiveness of human rights violations that are associated with the operations of some foreign-owned businesses in Nigeria require an examination of the human rights infrastructure and a probe of the relationship between the Nigerian State and foreign capital.

5 www.indexmundi.com, accessed 22 October 2016.

6 Nathan Jensen, 'Democratic Governance and Multinational Corporations: Political Regimes and Inflows of Foreign Direct Investment' (Summer, 2003) 57 (3) *International Organisation* 587.

7 The Kenan Institute for Ethics, Duke University, *The U.N. Guiding Principles on Business and Human Rights Analysis and Implementation* (2012) https://kenan.ethics.duke.edu/new-report-on-the-u-n-guiding-principles-on-business-and-human-rights-released-2/, accessed 21 February 2019.

Globalization comes with challenges for governance and the management of global public goods (such as health, education, human security, etc.). The adoption and implementation of economic liberalization policies and programmes in many countries has not only deregulated the economy but also whittled away the power of the State to regulate the activities of foreign firms. This is even more the case, as governments are constantly subjected to the need to compete with other governments to retain the favour of the big companies that drive their economies.[8] Much of the critique of privatization hovers around the power now wielded by private actors with respect to traditional public functions such as providing water, gas and electricity, telecommunication, public transportation, or even welfare services. On the part of the State, the management styles of new 'democratic' governments have alienated the majority of citizens, whose living conditions have not directly benefited from reform programmes. As access to goods and jobs deteriorated, citizens became less supportive of the State. The non-performance in the delivery of public goods and the prevalence of abject poverty are major risk factors for violent conflicts in many African countries.

2 Human rights and human rights infrastructure

Western ideas and thoughts have significantly influenced the human rights practice of most of the former colonies like Nigeria. That is the universal human rights discourse that sees the society as autonomized and individualistic. This conception is based on the assumption that society is made up of legal subjects that are conscious of their separateness and their particular interests, and are anxious to protect them. In this regard, legal rights is a claim which the individual may make against other members of society and simultaneously there is an obligation on the part of society to uphold this claim.[9] This conception is rather restrictive and of course is based on certain historical conditions that are specific to liberal democracy, such as the generalization of commodity production and exchange, a market society, social atomization and organic solidarity, and a developed system of capitalist production. However, the constitution of African societies as liberal

8 Johan van der Walt, 'Blixen's Difference: Horizontal Application of Fundamental Rights and the Resistance to Neocolonialism' (2003) 1 *Law Social Justice & Global Development*.

9 Julius O. Ihonvbere (ed.), *The Political Economy of Crisis and Underdevelopment in Africa: Selected Works of Claude Ake* (JAD Publishers, 1989).

democracies to date has been very difficult because the development of the above societal characteristics has remained at a very rudimentary level.[10]

Our perspective in this chapter identifies with the discourse on human rights in Africa which transcends the techno-juristic characterization of human rights to incorporate the details of the collective struggles of the people for the right to development, including the discussion of human rights in the context of overall imperialist domination. Furthermore, in order for the discourse on human rights in Africa to be relevant to African development, it is necessary for human rights to be conceptualized within the history of Africa that appreciates, for example, the status and roles of the different phases of imperialism. It is only within this context that human rights can be appreciated as products of certain historical developments. Further clarification is required here to put our discussion in proper perspective. First, State repression and human rights abuse in Africa have been part of the African social condition just like imperialism, foreign domination and exploitation. Yet, the copious documentation and incantation of violations of human rights in Africa by international human rights non-governmental organizations (NGOs) and their home governments have chosen to leave the latter category out of their records of human rights abuses. Secondly, human rights violations in Africa cannot be divorced from the deepening crisis of State and society in Africa. Thirdly, these conditions limit democratic possibility in Africa and the consequences of this is the retreat of democracy and authoritarian reversal.

Chapter IV of the 1999 Nigerian Constitution is the cornerstone of Nigeria's human rights infrastructure. The Constitution guarantees the right to life, dignity of the human person, personal liberty, fair hearing, private and family life, freedom of thought, conscience and religion, freedom of expression and the press, peaceful assembly and association, freedom of movement, freedom from discrimination, freedom to acquire immovable property, and protection from compulsory acquisition of property. Section 46 of the Constitution provides for access to remedies. In this regard the Chief Justice of Nigeria promulgated the Fundamental Rights (Enforcement Procedure) Rules 2009 under Chapter IV of the Constitution to ensure speedy disposition of matters pertaining to the enforcement of fundamental human rights. Order IV of the Fundamental Rights Rules provides that an application for the enforcement of fundamental rights shall be fixed for hearing within seven days from the date the application was filed.[11] The hearing of the application may from

10 *Ibid.*

11 See The Constitution of the Federal Republic of Nigeria (1999) Fundamental Rights (Enforcement Procedure) Rules under Chapter IV of the Constitution Arrangement of Orders.

time to time be adjourned, where extremely expedient, provided the court is always guided by the urgent nature of applications under the Rules. Aside from litigating for the enforcement of fundamental human rights, the Nigerian human rights infrastructure enables aggrieved persons to petition the National Human Rights Commission[12] on alleged violations of human rights. The Commission is an extra-judicial mechanism for enhancement of the enjoyment of human rights in Nigeria. In situations where the alleged violator is the Nigerian Government there is the additional option of seeking redress through the Public Complaints Commission.[13]

Apart from domestic courts, Nigerians have access to remedies in several international fora. There is access to the Court of Justice of the Economic Community of West African States (ECOWAS) and the human rights institutions established by the African Union. Nigeria is a State party to the core international human rights treaties, including the International Covenant on Civil and Political Rights; the International Covenant on Economic, Social and Cultural Rights; and the International Convention on the Elimination of All Forms of Racial Discrimination. The Federal Government submits periodic reports to human rights protection bodies and has hosted several of their fact-finding and investigation teams. It is, however, worrisome that Nigeria's adhesion to international treaties has not been fully translated into compliance and commitment in the domestic sphere. For example, while the category of rights in the United Nations (UN) International Covenant for Social and Economic Rights are acknowledged in the Nigerian Constitution as ideals and aspirations that the State must seek to attain, operationally they are matters outside the scope of judicial enforcement.

With respect to multinational businesses, there are several voluntary and model codes of conduct that could serve as tools of accountability. Prominent among such initiatives are the OECD's Guidelines for Multinational Enterprises,[14] the Fair Labor Association's working conditions in factories, the Voluntary Principles on Security and Human Rights of 2000 for extractive companies[15] and the Extractive Industries Transparency Initiative (EITI).

12 Established by the Nigerian Human Rights Commission Act 1995 as amended in 2010.

13 Established by the Public Complaints Commission Act Chapter P37 Laws of Federation of Nigeria 2004.

14 OECD, *Guidelines for Multinational Enterprises* (2011) OECD Publishing.

15 The Kenan Institute for Ethics, Duke University, *The U.N. Guiding Principles on Business and Human Rights Analysis and Implementation.*

The UN Global Compact (the Compact) enjoins companies to align strategies and operations with universal principles on human rights, labor rights, the environment and anti-corruption measures, and take actions that advance societal goals. The Global Compact Network Nigeria (the Network), launched in 2006, is housed in the Nigerian Economic Summit Group and had 121 members as at January 2017. The Network is a platform for companies and non-business stakeholders to bring the Compact within national contexts and advance local priorities and needs.

In 2011, the UN Human Rights Council unanimously endorsed the UN Guiding Principles on Business and Human Rights, a set of guidelines for States and companies to prevent and address human rights abuses committed in the course of business operations. The UN Working Group on Business and Human Rights was established to aid in the implementation of the guidelines. The Guiding Principles affirm that under existing international human rights law, States have the duty to protect against human rights abuses by all actors in society, including businesses. States must prevent, investigate, punish and redress human rights abuses that take place in domestic business operations. This includes enacting and enforcing laws that require businesses to respect human rights; creating a regulatory environment that facilitates business respect for human rights; and providing guidance to companies on their responsibilities. The human rights obligations of States, from providing security to delivering utilities, are not voided when such functions are carried out by State-owned or private business enterprises.

Aside from the duty of the State to protect, there is a responsibility imposed on corporations to respect human rights in the conducting of their commercial and other activities. The Guiding Principles affirm that business enterprises must prevent, mitigate and, where appropriate, remedy human rights abuses that they cause or contribute to, even if these impacts have been carried out by suppliers or business partners. To meet the responsibility of respecting human rights, business enterprises must have the necessary policies and processes in place. The Guiding Principles identify three components of this responsibility. First, companies must institute a policy commitment to meet the responsibility to respect human rights. Second, they must undertake ongoing human rights due diligence to identify, prevent, mitigate and account for their human rights impacts. Finally, they must have processes in place to enable remediation for any adverse human rights impacts they cause or to which they contribute.

One of the fundamental principles of the international human rights system is that when a right is violated, victims must have access to an effective remedy. The Guiding Principles affirm that the State duty to protect rights includes ensuring that when human rights are violated by companies within their territory and/or jurisdiction, the State must ensure access to an effective remedy for those affected. The

State duty to provide access to effective remedy includes taking appropriate steps to ensure that State-based domestic judicial mechanisms are able to effectively address business-related human rights abuses. In addition to court systems, States should provide effective and appropriate non-judicial grievance mechanisms with the capacity to hear and adjudicate business-related human rights complaints as part of a comprehensive State-based system for remedy. The access to remedy principles also stipulate that business enterprises should provide for, or participate in, effective mechanisms for fielding and addressing grievances from individuals and communities who may be adversely impacted by the company's operations.

The World Bank, and its private-sector lending arm, the International Finance Corporation (IFC), provide other important avenues for advancing the business and human rights agenda. The IFC has already incorporated elements of the Guiding Principles into its Environmental and Social Framework for sustainable development. The current review of the World Bank's social safeguard policies offers an opportunity for integrating key elements of the Guiding Principles to prevent and mitigate the risk of negative human rights impacts in relation to the Bank's lending activities.[16] Significant progress will be achieved in bringing more multinational corporations in line with human rights values if the World Bank and the IFC follow through with this agenda of mainstreaming human rights.

The human rights infrastructure of Nigeria is significantly impacted, for better or for worse, by governance. Quality of governance can be measured by citizens' satisfaction with access to good life and improvement in the service delivery to the people. The UN Country Team (UNCT) while developing the third UN Development Assistance Framework (UNDAF III) 2014–2017, identified nine broad governance challenges, including poor public service delivery, inadequate mechanisms for involvement of people in governance and poor accountability on the part of government, and inadequate or partial enforcement of rules and regulations and an inconsistent justice system, among others. These challenges speak not only to the depth of democratic culture in the country but also to the capability of the governance structure to effectively hold powerful and non-compliant multinational enterprises in check. An analysis of the governance characteristics of Nigeria since the return to civil rule show improvement in the entrenchment of rule of law and civil

16 UN General Assembly, *Report of the Secretary-General on the Challenges, Strategies and Developments with regard to the Implementation of the Resolution 21/5 by the United Nations System, including Programs, Funds and Agencies. Report of the Secretary-General* (Human Rights Council, twenty-sixth session, A/HRC/26/20, 1 April 2014).

liberty. However, good governance defined in terms of ensuring citizens' access to basic needs has not recorded progress. Using the human development index (HDI) as a measuring framework, Nigeria's HDI value for 2014 and 2015 puts the country in the low human development category, positioning it at 152 out of 188 countries in 2014.

There is close association between bad governance and corruption. The Nigerian Government was characterized by corruption, lack of accountability and financial recklessness. These in turn promoted social injustice and political instability. Lack of transparency and accountability in government processes and procedures made the delivery of social services almost impossible. The perception of corruption index averages (on the scale 0–4) for Nigeria for 2011–2013 period was 2.22, and it was the highest among the 34 countries that were surveyed by Afrobarometer.[17] Until recently, Nigeria has consistently fared poorly in the annual Ease of Doing Business ranking list in the Global Competitive Index published by the World Economic Forum. According to Afrobarometer surveys conducted in 34 African countries between October 2011 and June 2013, 82% of respondents from Nigeria recorded low rating for government efforts to fight corruption. Theft of oil revenues such as the one announced by the former Nigerian Minister of Finance, Ngozi Okonjo-Iweala, was rampant during the Jonathan administration. On 20 January 2014, she announced that nearly USD 11 billion earned from the sale of crude oil between January 2012 and July 2013 was missing from the Federation account.[18] Former Governor of the Nigerian Central Bank Sanusi Lamido Sanusi, who showed keen interest in the missing funds from the Nigerian National Petroleum Corporation (NNPC), later appeared before the National Assembly Committee on the NNPC, during which he estimated the missing fund to be closer to USD 20 billion.[19] Leakage of national wealth through inflated contracts, over invoicing, rackets in fuel imports, and embezzlement of public funds by public officials has severe consequences for the delivery of public services to the people. The Nigerian economy is the second largest in Africa but there is increasing poverty, inequality and exclusion.

17 Afrobarometer Online Data Analysis www.afrobarometer.org, accessed 20 September 2016.

18 Platts, 'Nigeria's NNPC Must Account for $10.8 billion Oil Revenue: Finance Minister' www.platts.com/latest-news/oil/lagos/nigerias-nnpc-must-account-for-108-billion-oil-26632828, accessed 12 February 2016.

19 Adam Nossiter, 'Nigerians Ask Why Oil Funds Are Missing', *The New York Times* (10 March 2014). In February 2014 the Governor of the Central Bank Sanusi Lamido Sanusi was suspended from office under circumstances that remains unclear to date.

There is concern that the prosperity of Nigeria is not reflected in the daily life of majority of the population.

3 Business interests, the State and human rights violation

Oil exploration in the Niger Delta region of Nigeria has brought unknowable wealth to some foreign companies and untold hardships to several host communities. Agitation and discontent with the conduct of multinational oil companies and unresponsiveness of the Nigerian State simmered in the Niger Delta region for decades. The initial response of the Nigerian State was the use of force to subdue the agitations and protests. The Federal Government scaled up propaganda to give the impression that it was indeed in a position to guarantee an environment conducive for oil exploration in the region. The execution of Ken Saro-Wiwa and eight other activists (known as 'the Ogoni nine') brought the agitations of the oil-producing communities into the limelight internationally. Arguably, the pressure on the oil companies' operation in the Niger Delta, due in part to the community protests, calls for reparations and environmental remediation in the 1990s, generated responses, most of which were hastily conceived and poorly executed. For example, the Shell Petroleum Development Company of Nigeria, on behalf of its joint venture partners, commissioned the Niger Delta Environmental Survey. However, as the protests reduced in intensity so did the commitment to full implementation of the project. It was only on very few occasions that the oil corporations assumed responsibilities outside of a legal framework. On those occasions it had either been because of social pressure or in reaction to errors, scandals or accidents involving the corporation concerned. These reactive responses were generally transient and not particularly rigorous in character.[20] The modus operandi of multinational corporations played out very well as the Niger Delta Environmental Survey went comatose. For the peoples of the Niger Delta, the struggle continued.

The Federal Government in its submission to the African Commission on Human and Peoples' Rights in *Communication 155/96*[21] conceded that there is no denying the fact that a lot of atrocities were and are still being committed by the oil companies in the Niger Delta area. Thereupon the Commission found the Federal Republic of

20 Douglass Cassel, 'Corporate Initiatives: A Second Human Rights Revolution' (1995) 19 *Fordham International Law Journal* 1963.

21 *The Social and Economic Rights Action Center and the Center for Economic and Social Rights* v. *Nigeria (Communication 155/96)* ACHPR/COMM/A044/1 (27 May 2002), submitted at the thirtieth ordinary session, held in Banjul, the Gambia, from 13–27 October 2001.

Nigeria in violation of Articles 2, 4, 14, 16, 18(1), 21 and 24 of the African Charter on Human and Peoples' Rights. At the request of the Federal Government of Nigeria, in July 2006 the UN Environment Programme (UNEP) conducted an independent, comprehensive assessment of the environmental and health impacts of oil contamination in Ogoniland with options for remediation. The assessors concluded that the environmental restoration of Ogoniland is possible but may take twenty to thirty years. It recommended that an Environmental Restoration Fund for Ogoniland be set up with an initial capital injection of one billion dollars contributed by the oil industry and the Government.[22] Activists have demanded that oil companies in Nigeria be held to the same standard as elsewhere in the world.[23]

The trends and patterns in the relationship between the Nigerian State and the oil companies is better understood within the context of the discourse on business-State alliance in societies that are characterized by bad governance, corruption and lack of transparency. This is further complicated by a global order that is dominated by neoliberalism and the unbridled influence of international capital and market forces. In this context, capitalism thrives as the economic system with the highest utilitarian value. Within this framework, capital is in lockstep with capitalists[24] and business and State are deeply intertwined. Business interests dominate the halls of the US Capitol, and the reality of corporate capture is even more pronounced in less developed countries where government officials are also beneficiaries of government concessions. These developments have grave consequences for citizens whose rights are most likely to be tampered with, including their rights to be protected and to hold corporations and governments accountable. These issues raise questions about the social and political role of economic actors. To what extent should

22 UNEP, *Environmental Assessment of Ogoniland* http://web.unep.org/disastersandconflicts/where-we-work/nigeria/what-we-do/environmental-assessment-ogoniland-report, accessed 2 February 2017.

23 Ivana Sekularac and Anthony Deutsch, 'Dutch Court Says Shell Partly Responsible for Nigeria Spills, *Business & Human Rights Resource Centre* https://business-humanrights.org/en/dutch-court-says-shell-partly-responsible-for-nigeria-spills, accessed 22 October 2016.

24 Puvan Selvanathan, 'Open Letter from Puvan Selvanathan to President of the UN Human Rights Council', *Business & Human Rights Resource Centre* (2016) www.business-humanrights.org/sites/default/files/documents/Letter%20to%20the%20President%20HRC.pdf, accessed 21 February 2019.

the regulation of corporations be left to the market forces, contract law among corporate stakeholders, or to public regulation by the State?[25]

Holding transnational corporations accountable for human rights violations has been 'hit-and-miss' for the past four decades. Claims and counter-claims proliferate, initiatives abound, and yet no effort reaches significant scale. Amid this confusing mix, States as well as companies, continue to fly below the radar.[26]

Human rights advocates favour binding standards imposed on companies directly under international law. Business traditionally has favoured voluntary initiatives coupled with the identification of best practices and the development of management tools, arguing that the market itself will drive the process of change. The cardinal shortcoming of both approaches is that neither can tell a compelling story about how to get from here to there, or what the 'there' would look like.[27] Transnational corporations have consistently insisted on voluntary codes of conduct as the way forward, but there are reasons for reservations about their efficacy.[28] The primary concern of corporations as private amalgamations of capital is maximizing the value of the capital so amalgamated to serve the interest of the holders of capital. In this context, corporations could serve others only by default, and to the extent that such a service does not fundamentally shift attention and focus from their primary mission. Although these assumptions are grounded in principles of domestic corporate law, it is of importance to note that attacks on these assumptions

25 Larry Backer, 'Multinational Corporations, Transnational Law: The United Nations' Norms on the Responsibilities of Transnational Corporations as a Harbinger of Corporate Social Responsibility in International Law' (2005) 37 *Columbia Human Rights Law Review* 101.

26 John Ruggie, *Promotion and Protection of all Human Rights, Civil, Political, Economic, Social and Cultural Rights, including the Right to Development. Protect, Respect and Remedy: a Framework for Business and Human Rights. Report of the Special Representative of the Secretary-General on the issue of Human Rights and Transnational Corporations and Other Business Enterprises* A/HRC/8/5 (7 April 2008), submitted to the eighth session of the Human Rights Council.

27 *Ibid.*

28 Sarah Joseph, *Corporations and Transnational Human Rights Litigation* (Hart Publishing, 2004) 8; Philip Alston 'Ships Passing in the Night: The Current State of the Human Rights and Development Debate Seen through the Lens of the Millennium Development Goals' (2005) 27 (3) *Human Rights Quarterly* 755, 829.

that regard profit as the 'raison d'être'[29] of corporations have been strengthened by international law and human rights.[30]

Another concern is whether the governments of developing countries have the capacity to meet their human rights obligations to their citizens, including enforcing regulations and demanding accountability of transnational corporations. Many of these governments have a history of 'dialogue' and 'cooperation' with the corporations in terms of their acceptance of human rights as the business of business. The main defect of the 'dialogue-cooperation strategy' is surrendering human rights to the power of global business. The approach elevates business and presents human rights as a subject matter of negotiations and bargaining.[31] This approach prioritizes voluntary standards which equals to no controls. We, the authors of this chapter, share the opinion that human rights are beyond profit and business corporations need to follow human rights as part of their license to operate. Any legal regime of corporate responsibility should keep in mind the preemptory nature of human rights.

Several attempts have been made in foreign and national courts to hold international businesses accountable for human rights violations committed in Nigeria. A discussion of selected court cases is undertaken to demonstrate not only the emerging trends in the business-human rights relationship but also the uncertainties and lack of clarity that surround the relationship. A year after the execution of Ken Saro-Wiwa and eight others, their families brought suit in the USA against Royal Dutch Shell, Shell Nigeria and Brian Anderson, then Head of Shell Nigeria, for compensation and damages for their complicity in the State-sponsored murder of the Ogoni nine.[32] The case was brought under the 1789 Alien Tort Claims Act (ACTA) as supplemented by the 1991 Torture Victim Protection Act (TVPA), which allow foreign nationals to sue in the US Federal Court for a tort committed in violation of international law or US treaties.

29 The most important reason or purpose for existence.

30 Larry Backer, 'Multinational Corporations, Transnational Law: The United Nations' Norms on the Responsibilities of Transnational Corporations as a Harbinger of Corporate Social Responsibility in International Law'.

31 Surya Deva, 'Human Rights Violations by Multinational Corporations and International Law: Where from Here?' (2003) 19 *Connecticut Journal of International Law* 1; Backer, 'Multinational Corporations, Transnational Law: The United Nations' Norms on the Responsibilities of Transnational Corporations as a Harbinger of Corporate Social Responsibility in International Law'.

32 *Wiwa* v. *Royal Dutch Petroleum Company* (2001) 226 F. 3d 88 (Second circuit, 2000) Cert. denied 532 U.S. 941.

On the eve of the trial, the parties agreed to a settlement for all three lawsuits. Without admitting any guilt or wrongdoing, the settlement provided a total of USD 15.5 million to compensate the plaintiffs, establish a trust for the benefit of the Ogoni people, and cover some of the legal costs associated with the case. The Wiwa *et al.* settlement was a major victory in the long-drawn-out battle to hold multinational corporations liable for complicity in human rights violations. The human rights community was energized and the multinational corporations embraced the high probability of a deluge of litigation in the horizon.

Three American-based Chevron companies ('Chevron') were sued in the California District Court in *Bowoto* v. *Chevron Texaco Corporation*.[33] The case arose from a violent episode that occurred on the Parabe oil platform operated by Chevron Nigeria Limited (CNL), nine miles off the coast of Nigeria in 1998. On 25 May 1998, over 100 Nigerians took over the Parabe platform to protest CNL's destruction of the environment and refusal to provide jobs to the local population. The parties dispute the peacefulness of the protest. There is, however, no dispute that on the fourth day of the protest, CNL sought the assistance of the Nigerian Government security forces to end the protest. When the soldiers arrived on the platform, they shot a number of the protestors, resulting in two fatalities. In 1999, the injured protestors and the family of a deceased protestor filed a lawsuit in the Northern District of California against Chevron, raising a number of claims related to the military raid of the Parabe platform under the Alien Tort Statute (ATS), Nigerian law, and Californian law. After ten years of pretrial litigation and discovery, the jury rendered a verdict in favor of Chevron on all claims. The plaintiffs appealed.[34] The US Court of Appeals for the Ninth Circuit affirmed the dismissal of the ATS wrongful death and survival claims, and agreed with the District Court that Congress did not intend the TVPA to apply to corporations. In late April 2012 the Supreme Court declined to hear the appeal.[35]

The Movement for the Survival of the Ogoni People (MOSOP) campaigned against the environmental damage caused by oil exploration in the Ogoni region of Nigeria. Barinem Kiobel and other members of MOSOP were executed in furtherance of a murder conviction by a special court established by the military government using procedures not compliant with international fair trial standards.

33 312 F. Supp. 2d 1229 (2004) Dist. Court ND California.

34 *Larry Bowoto* et al. v. *Chevron Corporation* et al. (2010) 621 F.3d 1116, United States Court of Appeals, Ninth Circuit.

35 132 Second Circuit. 1968 Supreme Court 2012.

Royal Dutch/Shell was sued again in the United States federal court.[36] In *Kiobel* et al. v. *Royal Dutch Petroleum Co.* et al. a suit filed under the ATS, the respondents – Dutch, British and Nigerian corporations – were alleged to have aided and abetted the Nigerian Government in committing violations of international law in Nigeria. The District Court dismissed several of the petitioners' claims, but on interlocutory appeal, the Second Circuit dismissed the entire complaint,[37] reasoning that the law of nations does not recognize corporate liability.

On 17 April 2013 the Supreme Court held that the presumption against extraterritoriality applies to claims under the ATS, and nothing in the statute rebuts that presumption. Passed as part of the Judiciary Act of 1789, the ATS is a jurisdictional statute that creates no causes of action. It permits federal courts to recognize private claims for a modest number of international law violations under federal common law. The court relied on *Sosa* v. *Alvarez-Machain*[38] and held that a claim under the ATS does not reach conduct occurring in a foreign sovereign's territory. The Supreme Court concluded that there is no indication that the ATS was passed to make the USA a uniquely hospitable forum for the enforcement of international norms.

In the *Bodo Community* et al. v. *Shell Petroleum Development Company of Nigeria Ltd*,[39] the claimants sought damages at common law and statutory compensation under the law of Nigeria in relation to oil spills from pipelines said to have been caused by Shell Petroleum Development Company of Nigeria (known as Shell or SPDC) in the Niger Delta. The claims relate to two crude oil spills from a 24-inch pipeline in the Bodo area, said to have occurred between 28 August and 7 November 2008, and 7 December 2008 and 19 February 2009. The full extent of the spillages and their timing was disputed. Subject to such disputes, Shell admitted liability under Nigeria's Oil Pipelines Act for these spillages. In January 2015 the claims settled for a total of GBP 55 million, plus costs prior to the substantive trial, which was to have taken place in May 2015.

Several attempts have been made in the Netherlands to hold Shell and its parent company liable for wrongful acts done in Nigeria. In *Barizaa Manson Tete Dooh* et al. v. *Royal Dutch Shell Plc.* et al.[40] and *Fidelis Ayoro Oguru* et al. v. *Royal Dutch Shell Plc.* et al.,[41] the District Court dismissed all the claims initiated by the plaintiffs.

36 *Kiobel* et al. v. *Royal Dutch Petroleum Co.* et al. (2013) 133 Second Circuit 1659.

37 621 F.3d 111 Court of Appeals (Second circuit, 2010).

38 542 U.S. 692.

39 (2014) EWHC 1973 (TCC).

40 C/09/337058 / HA ZA 09–1581 and C/09/365482 HA ZA 10–1665.

41 C/09/337050 / HA ZA 09–1580.

In December 2015, a Dutch appeals court reversed the dismissal and permitted the balance of the claims to go forward. The Appeals Court also ruled that Shell must grant the claimants access to certain internal company documents essential to the case. However, in *Friday Alfred Akpan* v. *Royal Dutch Shell Plc.* et al.,[42] the District Court rendered a declaratory judgment to the effect that under Nigerian law, the SPDC committed a specific tort of negligence against Akpan by insufficiently securing the well head of the IBIBIO-I well against sabotage that was easily committed at that time, prior to the two oil spills in 2006 and 2007 near Ikot Ada Udo. It ordered the SPDC to compensate Akpan for the damage he suffered as a result. The decision to take jurisdiction on an international claim was a novel one in Dutch jurisprudence.

The January 2017 judgment in the United Kingdom (UK) in *His Royal Highness Emere Godwin Bebe Okpabi* et al. v. *Royal Dutch Shell Plc and Shell P.D.C. of Nigeria Ltd*[43] arose from two sets of proceedings relating to oil operations in Nigeria, that were heard together, and in those sets of proceedings there were four applications. The first defendant in each action was Royal Dutch Shell Plc. (RDS), the ultimate holding company of the worldwide Shell Group and the second defendant was the SPDC, the Nigerian company that is responsible for Shell onshore oil operations in Nigeria. The precise corporate relationship between SPDC and RDS is directly relevant to the issues on this application. The first set of proceedings were brought by twenty named claimants for themselves and on behalf of the people of the Ogale community in Nigeria, comprising approximately 40 000 individuals seeking damages arising as a result of serious and ongoing pollution and environmental damage caused by oil spills emanating from the Defendants' oil pipelines and associated infrastructure in and around the Ogale community. The second set of proceedings, with 2 335 different claimants, were claims for damages arising as a result of serious and ongoing pollution and environmental damage caused by oil spills emanating from the Defendants' oil pipelines and associated infrastructure in and around Bille Kingdom in Nigeria.

The claims against RDS were based on the tort of negligence under the common law, while the claims against SPDC were based on relevant causes of action under Nigerian statute and common law. The claimants in both sets of proceedings were all Nigerian citizens resident in Nigeria. RDS was a UK corporation with a registered office in the UK. The claimants argued that both defendants were legally responsible for the oil pollution that has seriously affected huge areas of land, and the health and

42 C/09/337058 / HA ZA 09-1581.

43 2017 EWHC 89 (TCC).

livelihood of many thousands of people, whose chances of redress rest substantially (or even entirely) on the ability to bring proceedings in jurisdiction. The defendants, on the other hand, took the position that these claims have nothing whatsoever to do with the UK and should proceed in Nigeria.

The court held that there is simply no connection whatsoever between the jurisdiction and the claims brought by the claimants, who are Nigerian citizens, for breaches of statutory duty and/or in common law for acts and omissions in Nigeria, by a Nigerian company. Accordingly, the findings on the issue of a duty of care on the part of RDS are effectively dispositive of both applications in both sets of proceedings.

The lawsuits against the multinational oil companies in foreign courts have mixed results. The chances of success in the USA are almost nil and with the January 2017 decision, there are virtually no chances of reprieve in the UK. The courts in the Netherlands are breaking new ground to accommodate human rights and environmental law claims against multinationals for acts committed abroad.

Aside from multinational oil corporations, claims have been made against other major transnational economic entities operating in Nigeria. Pfizer was the defendant in a series of litigation in Nigeria and the USA. *Rabi Abdullahi* et al. v. *Pfizer, Inc.*[44] was a consolidated appeal from the judgments of the US District Court for the Southern District of New York, dismissing two complaints for lack of subject matter jurisdiction under the ATS, and on the grounds of *forum non conveniens*. The Plaintiffs-Appellants alleged that Pfizer violated a customary international law norm prohibiting involuntary medical experimentation on humans when it tested an experimental antibiotic on children and the plaintiffs in Nigeria, without their consent or knowledge. Some other children and their guardians who were part of Pfizer's Nigerian drug experiment, brought a similar action against Pfizer, alleging violations of the ATS, the Connecticut Unfair Trade Practices Act, and the Connecticut Product Liability Act. Pfizer moved to dismiss both actions for lack of subject matter jurisdiction and on the basis of *forum non coveniens*. The District Court granted the motions and both sets of plaintiffs have appealed. The Court of Appeals, Second Circuit, held that the District Court incorrectly determined that the prohibition in customary international law against nonconsensual human medical experimentation cannot be enforced through the ATS, and that the District Court incorrectly applied Connecticut's choice of law rules in the Adamu action. Consequently, it reversed and remanded the cases to the District Court for further proceedings. In 2011 Pfizer entered into a confidential settlement with the

44 562 F 3d 16 (2009) Second Circuit.

plaintiffs. Pfizer also entered into settlement with the Kano State Government and the Federal Government on the litigations initiated by the respective governments in Nigeria.[45]

The Nigerian human rights infrastructure provides adequate access to domestic courts. In this regard, the courts provide the platform for the citizens to hold international businesses accountable for human rights violations. With respect to the oil and gas industry where there are substantial human rights problems, the question gets compounded by the fact that the Nigerian State is intimately linked to the logic and interests of the capital holders in the industry. The case involving Pfizer in Kano State may not have brought out clearly the complicity of the Nigerian State. However, it confirms the point we made earlier concerning the preference of international business for the 'dialogue-cooperation strategy', which at best merely begs the human rights question instead of addressing it. Disappointedly, the experiment with electoral democracy since 1999 has not fundamentally changed the relationship between business and human rights in favor of the citizens. It is worth mentioning that in *SERAP* v. *Federal Republic of Nigeria*[46] the ECOWAS Community Court of Justice held that the Federal Republic of Nigeria cannot invoke the non-justiciability or enforceability of the International Covenant on Economic, Social and Cultural Rights as a means for shirking its responsibility in ensuring the protection and guarantee for its citizens within the framework of commitments it has made vis-à-vis the Economic Community of West African States and the Charter.

Conclusion

A functional human rights infrastructure that acknowledges the interests of a broad spectrum of stakeholders is conditional for peace and sustainable development in Nigeria. Citizens need to be active participants rather than spectators in a drama that is played out by others. Respect for human rights is most realizable when the mechanism for its enforcement is closest to the people. In a country like Nigeria, an examination of the human rights infrastructure at the local government level might be the true measure of the potency of the human rights system. Building the legal and physical infrastructure to protect human rights and to punish violations is a costly process that requires not only conviction on behalf of a government, but

45 Pfizer lawsuit (re Nigeria). *Business & Human Rights Resource Centre* https://business-humanrights.org/en/pfizer-lawsuit-re-nigeria, accessed 22 October 2016.

46 Judgment No. ECW/CCJ/JUD/18/12, delivered on 14 December 2012.

also substantial resources and expertise that are often lacking in States that violate human rights and are suffering from legacies of repression.

What is required is a human rights infrastructure that is composed of laws, institutions, policy instruments and policy strategies. An inter-linked framework of different elements to promote equality, eliminate poverty and defend human rights holds the potential to achieve the necessary progress.[47] Significant progress has been made by the UN Guiding Principles, but the international community must take a step further to muster the political will to recognize corporations as legal persons in international law and make them accountable for human rights violations.

International businesses operating in Nigeria need more than a license from the Federal Government to operate. They require acquiescence from human rights systems that are closer to the people and instituted by them. The obsession with legality or legal order at the expense of good quality of life for the people can be a distraction, especially where the power relations are not equitable and international capital is implicated in the contradictions of extremities of poverty and wealth. It has been argued that oil business exemplifies market capitalism at its vilest, most brazenly selfish and least socially-concerned caricature.[48] The interface of business with human rights, and particularly that of human rights with oil business in Nigeria, are in desperate need of a radical overhaul.

47 Niall Crowley, 'Roadmap to a Strengthened Equality and Human Rights Infrastructure in Ireland' *Equality and Rights Alliance*.

48 Jahangir Amuzegar, *Managing the Oil Wealth: OPEC's Windfalls and Pitfalls* (St. Martin's, 2001).

Part III

African perspectives on contemporary challenges of investment dispute settlement

10

Quo vadis international investment law in Africa?

Francis N. Botchway and Mohamed Salem Abou El Farag*

Introduction

Global law on investment appears to be in a state of flux. The old debates of States' intervening to protect their investors as the primary mode of investor protection appears settled in favor of individualized protective mechanisms in the form of host State national laws, bilateral investment treaties (BITs) and private dispute resolution mechanisms. The reasons for this shift are many. It includes the so-called 'Washington Consensus' in the later decades of the twentieth century and the triumphalism of neo-liberalism and the collapse of the Eastern bloc.[1] It is also due to the fact that the distinction between capital exporting and capital importing or receiving countries is now blurred with several European and North American countries becoming recipients of investments and therefore susceptible to being pursued as violators of the rights of investors.[2] Another debate that appears settled is

* I am grateful to the editor Professor Yenkong Ngangjoh Hodu for his support and encouragement. My part of the work is part of a portfolio of research made possible by NPRP grant NPRP 7-1815-5-272 of the Qatar National Research Fund (a member of the Qatar Foundation). The comments made herein are solely the responsibility of the authors.

1 The Washington Consensus is broadly a set of ten policy prescriptions by the leading international economic institutions, particularly the International Monetary Fund (IMF) and the World Bank. See John Williamson, 'The Washington Consensus as Policy Prescription for Development' *Peterson Institute for International Economics* https://piie.com/publications/papers/williamson0204.pdf, accessed 12 June 2019. See also Ben Fine and Alfredo Saad-Filho, 'Politics of Neoliberal Development: Washington Consensus and Post-Washington Consensus' in H. Weber (ed), *The Politics of Development: A Survey* (London: Routledge, 2014).

2 See Julian Donaubauer and Peter Nunnenkamp, 'EU Investors versus EU States: International Arbitration of Investment Disputes' (2018) 56 (6) *Journal of Common Market Studies*.

the dichotomy between the Hull and Calvo Doctrines on remedies for the violation of the rights of foreign investors, particularly expropriation and compensation.[3]

Notwithstanding these apparent settlements, there appears to be serious controversies on international investment generally. First is the raging controversy over multilateral investment treaties. Following the debacle of the Multilateral Agreement on Investment in the late 1990s, many had thought the issue of a universalized investment regime was done.[4] In many ways, it was. However, the apparent similarities in BITs, national investment codes and the near uniformity of the culture of arbitration has led some to call for what they see as 'fact' into 'law'.[5] Sometimes this call for a multilateral investment treaty is characterized as lex mercatoria, lex arbitriti, or any other Latinized jargon.[6] The problem is that within each of the areas of the call for conformity there are significant differences among the players, texts, academics and countries.[7] For example, in BITs, it is argued that there is a lack of uniformity and that it is more accurate to talk about *lex specialis* rather an emerging customary law.[8] State practice regarding investment codes also varies considerably.[9]

3 Ahmed Kamal El-Din Izzeddin, *The Calvo Doctrine and the Hull Formula: Prospects for Harmony* (Book Venture Publishing LLC, 2017).

4 See Rainer Geiger, 'Towards a Multilateral Agreement on Investment' (1998) 31 (3) *Cornell International Law Journal* https://scholarship.law.cornell.edu/cgi/viewcontent.cgi?article=1427&context=cilj, accessed 12 June 2019.

5 For a taste of the debates, see Anders Aslund, 'The World Needs a Multilateral Agreement on Investment' (2013) 13 (1) *Peterson Institute for International Economics Policy Brief*; and Berger Axel, 'Do We Really Need a Multilateral Investment Agreement?' (2013) *German Development Institute Policy Briefing Paper 9/2013* www.die-gdi.de/en/briefing-paper/article/do-we-really-need-a-multilateral-investment-agreement/, accessed 12 June 2019.

6 See Mert Elcin, 'Lex Mercatoria in International Arbitration: Theory and Practice' (Unpublished PhD thesis presented to the European University Institute, 2012); Ralf Michaels, 'The True Lex Mercatoria: Law Beyond the State; (2007) 14 (2) *Indiana Journal of Global Legal Studies*; Alastair Henderson, 'Lex Arbitri, Procedural Law and the Seat of Arbitration' (2014) 26 *Singapore Academy of Law Journal* 886. On Latin in international law, see Aaron X. Fellmeth and Maurice Horwitz, *Guide to Latin in International Law* (Oxford University Press, 2009).

7 See Shaun Donnelly, 'Let's Get Realistic About a Multilateral Agreement on Investment' www.uscib.org/lets-get-realistic-about-a-multilateral-investment-agreement/, accessed 12 June 2019.

8 See M. Sornarajah, *The International Law on Foreign Investment* (Cambridge University Press, 2009).

9 *Ibid.* See also Emmanuel T. Laryea, 'Evolution of International Investment Law and Implications for Africa' in Francis N. Botchway (ed.), *Natural Resource Investment and Africa's Development* (Edward Elgar Publishing, 2011).

Many countries do not even have comprehensive or self-contained investment codes, strictly speaking. The countries that have specialized investment regimes or codes also do not adopt uniform provisions or principles. This is to be expected, as their respective circumstances are different. Even when placed in similar economic circumstances, competition for investments naturally mean that the provisions, specifically the investment incentives offered, will differ.

The next controversy comes broadly under investment dispute settlement. At the turn of the century, arbitration of investment disputes took off. For example, for the first three decades of its existence (between 1965 and 1995), the International Centre for Settlement of Investment Disputes (ICSID) had a total caseload of less than 30; however, in 2018 it had registered a record 56 cases in that single year.[10] Similar statistics exist in other well-known arbitration institutions.[11] Although this rapid elevation symbolizes confidence in arbitration as a means of investment dispute resolution, it has also engendered enormous disquiet. The concerns surround the quantum of the claims and awards, the cost of arbitration, particularly counsel cost, the delays in the process and the apparent exclusivity of arbitration business to a few Western lawyers.[12]

Beyond these 'external' concerns, there are serious questions regarding the jurisprudence of arbitral tribunals. The cardinal principle of each arbitration award being limited to the parties in that dispute with no precedential anchorage has also led to significant diversity of awards and opinions regarding the law in arbitration. The *Société Générale de Surveillance SA* (SGS) cases, the Vivendi cases, the Argentinian cases and others illustrate a certain level of uncertainty and confusion in the jurisprudence.[13] The invention or definition of concepts such as 'investment', 'legitimate expectations', and 'fair and equitable treatment' generated so much contention and

10 ICSID, *The ICSID Caseload – Statistics (Issue 2019-1)* https://icsid.worldbank.org/en/Documents/resources/ICSID%20Web%20Stats%202019–1(English).pdf, accessed 12 June 2019.

11 See, for example, London Court of International Arbitration (LCIA), *2018 Annual Casework Report* www.lcia.org/News/2018-annual-casework-report.aspx, accessed 12 June 2019.

12 See Corporate Europe Observatory, 'Profiting from Injustice' https://corporateeurope.org/en/international-trade/2012/11/profiting-injustice, accessed 12 June 2019.

13 *SGS Société Générale de Surveillance S.A.* v. *Islamic Republic of Pakistan* (2005) ICSID Case No. ARB/01/13, 8 *ICSID Reports* 383; *SGS Société Générale de Surveillance S.A.* v. *Republic of the Philippines* (2005) ICSID Case No. ARB/02/6, 8 *ICSID Reports* 515; *Suez, Sociedad General de Aguas de Barcelona, S.A. and Vivendi Universal, S.A.* v. *Argentine Republic.*

consternation in many academic and governmental quarters. Orrego Vicuña, a former Chilean Ambassador under Augusto Pinochet and a prolific arbitrator, in his American Society of International Law (ASIL) lecture, for instance, first invented the doctrine of legitimate expectations.[14] The problem with the doctrine of legitimate expectations as applied by its champions is that it is not reciprocal.[15] States do not have the right legitimately to expect that the investment should contribute to economic development or any form of corporate social responsibility.[16] Besides, it overrides a longstanding common law position of normal business risks as articulated under the doctrine of frustration, force majeure and impracticality of performance.[17] Apart from legitimate expectations, there are issues of privity of contract, third party participation in arbitration, interpretation of umbrella clauses, etc.[18]

African countries are caught up in the middle of the foregoing controversies. Unlike the immediate post-independence era, particularly the 1960s and 1970s, when under the umbrella of groups such as the Group of 77, African Caribbean and Pacific Group of States (ACP), and the Non-Aligned Movement (NAM), and galvanized by the United Nations Conference on Trade and Development (UNCTAD), United Nations Centre on Transnational Corporations (UNCTC), United Nations Educational, Scientific and Cultural Organization (UNESCO) and the United Nations (UN) itself, particularly the General Assembly, African countries and developing countries in general, pushed for the recognition and enactment of ideas and concepts such as permanent sovereignty over natural resources, the right to development, the Generalized System of Preferences,[19] International Convention on the Elimination of All Forms of Racial Discrimination, doctrines such as *rebus*

14 M. Sornarajah, 'Evolution or Revolution in International Investment Arbitration? The Descent into Normlessness' in Chester Brown and Kate Miles (eds) *Evolution in Investment Treaty Law and Arbitration* (Cambridge University Press, 2011).

15 See Yenkong Ngangjoh Hodu and Collins Ajibo Chikodili, 'Legitimate Expectations in Investor State Arbitration: Re-Contextualizing a Controversial Concept from a Developing Country's Perspective' (2018) 15 (1) *Manchester Journal of International Economic Law.*

16 *Ibid.*

17 See Professor Sir Guenter Treitel, *Frustration and Force Majeure* (Sweet & Maxwell, 2014).

18 See M. Sornarajah, *The International Law on Foreign Investment.*

19 See Norma Breda dos Santos, Rogério Farias and Raphael Cunha, 'Generalized System of Preferences in General Agreement on Tariffs and Trade/World Trade Organization: History and Current Issues' (2005) 39 (4) *Journal of World Trade*, 637. See Veronica Stracqualursi and Donna Borak 'Trump removes India from special trade status' *CNN Politics* https://edition.cnn.com/2019/06/01/politics/trump-india-trade-status/index.html, accessed 12 June 2019.

sic stantibus, uti posseditis, etc.[20] African leaders, since the annunciation of the Washington Consensus, appear to have surrendered policy formulation, advocacy and enactment to the IMF, World Bank and a coterie of non-governmental organizations (NGOs), aid agencies and consultants.[21] The result is that there is hardly any coherent or unified development or investment policy framework or document representative of developing countries in general, and African countries in particular. What exists are a motley of regional, bilateral or national agreements or initiatives that do not always evince an original and authentic African experience.

1 Regional economic institutions and blocs

Regional organizations such as the East African Community (EAC), Economic Community of West African States (ECOWAS), Southern Africa Development Community (SADC) and the Common Market for Eastern and Southern Africa (COMESA), Arab Maghreb Union,[22] have taken initiatives and fostered agreements that seek to advance the economic interests of their respective Member States. Even in these cases, the initiatives by these institutions have had a bit of a checkered and somewhat debilitating history.

The original document that established SADC set out its key objectives as reducing the dependency of the Member States on other countries, particularly the apartheid regime in South Africa at the time; fostering serious linkages between the economies of the Member States, mobilizing the resources of Member States to implement national, inter-State and regional policies and development.[23] When they sought international cooperation, it had to be 'within the framework of the strategy

20 See Anthony Carty (ed) *Law and Development* (New York University Press, 1992).

21 IMF, 'Africa and the Washington Consensus: Finding the Right Path' (2003) *Finance and Development* 18. See also Carlos Lopes, 'Economic Growth and Inequality: The New Post-Washington Consensus' (2012) 4 *RCCS Annual Review* https://journals.openedition.org/rccsar/426, accessed 12 June 2019.

22 For the treaties and related documents establishing these regional institutions, see Francis Botchway, *Documents in International Economic Law* (Taylor & Francis, 2006).

23 The Southern African Development Coordination Conference (SADCC), which preceded the SADC, was a coordinating bloc of frontline States set up to confront the Apartheid regime in South Africa. See SADC, *History and Treaty* www.sadc.int/about-sadc/overview/history-and-treaty/, accessed 12 June 2019. See also SADCC, 'The Southern African Development Coordinating Conference' 18 (6) (1987) *The Black Scholar* www.tandfonline.com/doi/abs/10.1080/00064246.1987.11412783?journalCode=rtbs20, accessed 12 June 2019.

for economic liberation'.[24] This is in contrast with what the revised and consolidated treaty provides for. The consolidated treaty reflects the language and ethos of the Washington Consensus and the pervasive influence of neo-liberalism.[25] The preamble opens with 'poverty alleviation' and 'meeting the challenges of Globalization' and enlisting the support of 'development partners'.[26]

The principles of SADC, as outlined in Article 4, did not even mention economic development. It has no direct provisions on corporate social responsibility, on equitable investment and much muted provision on dispute resolution.[27] It is entirely acceptable that the SADC evolved with generational changes and is reflective of contemporary trends.

SADC was established originally to coordinate the efforts of the States that bore the brunt of the brutal apartheid regime and to help lessen their respective dependence on that political pariah yet economic giant, ultimately to see to its demise.[28] It was therefore a political effort with economic imperatives. It was not necessarily so with other regional organizations in Africa.

ECOWAS was established to facilitate the economic integration of the West African States who signed on to it.[29] One of the remarkable themes that run through the ECOWAS Treaty is uniform policies, particularly in the area of trade and investment.[30] For example, Article 3(2)(I) calls for the harmonization of national investment codes leading to the adoption of a single community investment code.[31] It did not give any indication of what would be the features of the envisaged community investment code, and as at the time of writing, there is no such code. Moreover, investment regimes in Member States vary significantly. As will be seen in the discussion below on BITs, Nigeria, a key member of ECOWAS, appears to be signaling a new radical investment regime as seen in the BIT it entered into with Morocco in 2016.

24 *Ibid.*

25 *Ibid.* See the preamble to the consolidated Treaty text of the SADC.

26 *Ibid.*

27 *Ibid.*

28 For more information, see SADC, *Declaration and Treaty* www.sadc.int/files/8613/5292/8378/Declaration__Treaty_of_SADC.pdf, accessed 12 June 2019.

29 See Falilou Fall, Blandine Vachon and Cosimo Winckler, 'Regional Integration: Comparison Between SADC and ECOWAS' in Diery Seck (ed) *Regional Economic Integration in West Africa* (Springer International Publishing, 2014) 213.

30 *Ibid.*

31 See ECOWAS, Revised Treaty of ECOWAS www.ecowas.int/wp-content/uploads/2015/01/Revised-treaty.pdf, accessed 12 June 2019.

All the same, the ECOWAS Treaty is, in many ways, one of the most progressive regional economic pacts entered into by African States.[32] It is the aim of ECOWAS to 'promote co-operation and integration, leading to the establishment of an economic union in West Africa in order to raise the living standards of its peoples, and to maintain and enhance economic stability, foster relations among Member States and contribute to the progress and development of the African continent'.[33] To achieve this, socio-economic policies are to be harmonized; environmental policies to be coordinated; the free movement of goods, people and services enhanced; and a common market established.[34] All these are founded on the fundamental principles of ECOWAS, including solidarity and collective self-reliance, equality and inter-dependence of Member States, accountability, economic and social justice and popular participation in development, as well as equitable and just distribution of the costs and benefits of economic cooperation and integration.[35]

In practical terms, the revised Treaty creates eight Commissions primarily in economic sectors.[36] Of course, there is a Commission on Law and Regional Security, which are important bedrocks for development.[37] The Treaty also mentions cooperation or relations with other regional, continental and international economic institutions.[38] What it did not do is give clear guidelines or guideposts for investment in the region.

Presumably any foreign investment in the West African region will have to be consistent with the expressed ideals of ECOWAS. However, given that the Treaty addresses nation State parties, there is no legal obligation for private investors to comply with the ECOWAS Treaty. It is only when State parties implement the principles of ECOWAS in their respective national legislation that they can oblige all investors to comply indirectly with the ECOWAS requirements.[39]

An example of the inconsistent or confusing signals given by regional economic organizations and nation States in Africa about the philosophy or principles that guide and underpin investment law on the continent, is the ECOWAS Energy

32 See the comparison done by Falilou Fall, Blandine Vachon and Cosimo Winckler, 'Regional Integration: Comparison Between SADC and ECOWAS'.

33 ECOWAS, Revised Treaty of ECOWAS. See Article 3 and the preamble.

34 *Ibid.*

35 *Ibid.*, see Article 4.

36 *Ibid.*, Articles 6 and 22.

37 *Ibid.*, Article 58.

38 *Ibid.*, Articles 78–9.

39 See Richard Frimpong Oppong, *Legal Aspects of Economic Integration in Africa* (Cambridge University Press, 2011).

Protocol of 2003.[40] It was largely motivated by and based on the original European Energy Charter Treaty (ECT) of 1994.[41] The ECT was put in place to usher in the former Communist, mainly Eastern European, countries into the market economies of the West.[42] It was to set clear market principles by which the former Communist countries and their appendages were to operate, and to protect the expected investments from the West.[43] It was a clear reflection of Washington Consensus neo-liberalism.[44]

The ECOWAS Energy Protocol acknowledges that it is 'convinced that adherence to the terms and principles of the Energy Charter Treaty by Member States of the Community will demonstrate to international investors and capital markets that the ECOWAS Region is a very attractive region for investing in energy projects and infrastructure'.[45] The Protocol then goes on to adopt both the ideas and language of the ECT, by for example, seeking to remove what it calls market distortions and 'anti-competitive behavior.[46] Many West African countries like Ghana, the Gambia and Nigeria do not even have competition laws to date and so the jurisprudence on market distortions and anti-competitive behavior will necessarily have to be foreign, most likely European.[47]

More than that, the Protocol gives two directions for the resolution of any disputes that are not based on the dispute resolution mechanism established in the ECOWAS Treaty itself.[48] The two options are ad-hoc arbitration under Article 27 of the Protocol and World Trade organization (WTO) dispute resolution processes that are otherwise exempted from the ECOWAS Protocol's prescribed dispute

40 See ECOWAS, ECOWAS Energy Protocol www.energy.gov.sl/EcowasProtocol.pdf, accessed 12 June 2019.

41 James Chalker, 'Article 17(1) of ECOWAS Energy Protocol' (2008) *Oil, Gas and Energy Law* www.ogel.org/article.asp?key=2816, accessed 12 June 2019.

42 See Thomas W. Wälde (ed) *The Energy Charter Treaty: An East-West Gateway for Investment and Trade* (Kluwer Law International, 1996).

43 *Ibid.*

44 See Nathalie Bernasconi-Osterwalder, 'How the Energy Charter Treaty Could Have Costly Consequences for Governments and Climate Action' *International Institute for Sustainable Development* www.iisd.org/library/how-energy-charter-treaty-could-have-costly-consequences-governments-and-climate-action, accessed 12 June 2019.

45 ECOWAS, ECOWAS Energy Protocol. See the preamble.

46 *Ibid.*

47 See Francis N. Botchway, 'Mergers and Acquisitions in Resource Industry: Implications for Africa' (2010) 26 (1) *Connecticut Journal of International Law* 51.

48 ECOWAS, ECOWAS Energy Protocol. See Articles 26–8.

resolution by means of ad hoc arbitration.[49] Furthermore, the Protocol deliberately or subconsciously omits reference to the resolution of the UN General Assembly on Permanent Sovereignty over Natural Resources (PSNR) and instead refers to State sovereignty in what can be described as a PSNR 'light'. In the end, there is no clear signal to researchers, practitioners and the investment community of where the countries of Africa stand when it comes to international investment law.

Similar arguments can be made of the ECA. The ECA makes it clear that its ultimate goal is the economic and political union of the 'Partner States': Burundi, Kenya, Rwanda, South Sudan, Uganda and the United Republic of Tanzania.[50] It also uses words like 'fast' and 'equitable development' of the Partner States and calls for greater interdependence on each other. Yet, at the same time it uses what it terms market principles' as a litmus test for membership and as a marker to its policies. It is perhaps an effort to combine the extremes of the 1960s and 1970s on the one hand, and the 1990s and beyond, on the other, that the treaty appears to have objectives that are 'people-centred and market driven'.[51] This is not only pragmatic but also a reflection of the history of the ECA from colonial times to the immediate post-colonial period and contemporary times. Yet, as far as this chapter is concerned, it has not signaled clearly the direction of the African perspective on international investment law. The provisions on dispute resolution are further evidence of this. The Treaty enshrines the principle of peaceful settlement of disputes as one of the cardinal principles of the ECA.[52]

As in the case of ECOWAS, it offers three options for dispute resolution. These are referral to the EAC Court for disputes regarding the interpretation and application of the Treaty and its accompanying protocols.[53] Secondly, the Treaty envisages the use of arbitration to resolve disputes involving the Community, its organs and Partner States.[54] In such arbitration-related matters, the Parties to the arbitration

49 *Ibid.*

50 See 'What Regional Integration Means to You' *East African Community* www.eac.int/, accessed 12 June 2019.

51 Article 7(1) of the ECA Treaty, 2008 www.eala.org/uploads/The_Treaty_for_the_Establishment_of_the_East_Africa_Community_2006_1999.pdf, accessed 12 June 2019.

52 *Ibid.*, Article 6(c).

53 Articles 23 and 27. This will include matters referred to it by the organs of the ECA and Heads of the Partner States.

54 *Ibid.*, Article 32.

agreement can designate the ECA Court as the supervisory or enforcement court.[55] Thirdly, there is the option of resorting to the national courts of the Partner States to resolve disputes arising from or related to the Treaty. Article 33 states that 'Except where jurisdiction is conferred on the Court by this Treaty, disputes to which the Community is a party shall not on that ground alone, be excluded from the jurisdiction of the national courts of the Partner States.' The language of Article 33 suggests that national courts are to function as usual and will not be disabled by a claim that an issue relates to or arises from the ECA Treaty. Except that, the interpretation of relevant treaty provision by the ECA Court will take precedence over national courts jurisprudence.[56]

The COMESA regional treaty appears to follow the model of the ECA and ECOWAS regional treaties.[57] COMESA was established to incorporate and supersede the Preferential Trade Area for Eastern and Southern Africa.[58] COMESA is perhaps the most expansive economic area in Africa next to the African Union. Its membership spans from North African countries, such as Tunisia and Egypt, to Southern African countries such as Swaziland and Lesotho, an area of over 12 million km^2, with a population of more than half a billion people trading in USD 235 billion trade relations.[59] Its objectives include the attainment of sustainable growth and development of the Member States through the promotion of a more balanced and harmonious development of its production and marketing structures.[60]

Indeed, the entire treaty can be described as a more balanced and nuanced paradigm than many others on the continent. It calls for interdependence and support for more economically depressed areas. Its specific investment protection principles such as those on macroeconomic policies, natural resources, monetary and fiscal stability, human rights and trade are directed at both 'domestic' and foreign investment. This is somewhat summed up in Article 6(f) of the Treaty when it states that the treaty is founded, *inter alia*, on the 'accountability, economic justice and popular participation in development'.

55 *Ibid.*
56 Articles 33(2) and 34.
57 See Padamja Khandelwal, 'COMESA and SADC: Prospects and Challenges for Regional Trade Integration' *International Monetary Fund Working Paper No. 04/227* (2004).
58 See 'Overview of COMESA.' *Common Market for Eastern and Southern Africa* www.comesa.int/overview-of-comesa/, accessed 12 June 2019.
59 *Ibid.*
60 Article 3 of the COMESA Treaty.

At the same time, the chapter devoted to investment promotion and protection has some of the same language and ethos of most of the BITs that countries on the continent have entered into and reflects the Washington Consensus, as well as the dominant discourse in international arbitration.[61] For example, Article 159 of the Treaty states that '[i]n order to encourage and facilitate private investment flows into the Common the Market, Member States shall: (a) accord fair and equitable treatment to private investors'.

The concept of fair and equitable treatment has been a cause of disagreement in the jurisprudence of arbitral tribunals. Many deem it a nebulous and opaque concept, which allows some arbitrators to grant remedies to claimants and investors for almost any plaint. More than that, the Treaty calls for the acceleration of deregulation, 'reasonable period of stability of investment climate … required to refinance the investment', and a prohibition of expropriation or nationalization.

It defines expropriation in the most liberal terms:

> [Expropriation] shall include any measures attributable to the government of a Member State which have the effect of depriving an investor of his ownership or control of, or a substantial benefit from his investment and shall be interpreted to include all forms of expropriation such as nationalization and attachment as well as creeping expropriation in the form of imposition of excessive and discriminatory taxes, restrictions in the procurement of raw materials, administrative action or omission where there is a legal obligation to act or measures that frustrate the exercise of the investors rights to dividends, profits and proceeds of the right to dispose of the investment.

In terms of dispute resolution, the COMESA Treaty provisions are somewhat similar to those discussed earlier.[62] There is the COMESA Court whose jurisdiction can be invoked both vertically by States and horizontally by citizens of Member States, except that there is a requirement for the exhaustion of local remedies.[63] It also has the power to give advisory opinions and to oversee arbitration proceedings. The Treaty calls for the accession to the ICSID Convention yet, it grants the ICSID a very limited role in dispute settlement, mainly through the Additional Facility process.[64]

61 See Chapter 26 of the COMESA Treaty.

62 See COMESA, COMESA Investment Agreement, Articles 26–8, Annex A. Also see Peter Muchlinski, 'The COMESA Common Investment Area: Substantive Standards and Procedural Problems in Dispute Settlement' (2010) 11 *SOAS School of Law Legal Studies Research Paper Series* https://eprints.soas.ac.uk/22042/, accessed 12 June 2019.

63 *Ibid.*

64 *Ibid.*

2 Continental level initiatives

The African Union (AU) is the continental organization that is supposed to be the umbrella for all the regional economic blocs.[65] Its objectives and principles are both a reflection and an encapsulation of those of the regional economic organizations. It makes this clear by stating that one of its goals is to 'coordinate and harmonize the policies between existing and future regional economic communities'.[66] Its objectives include the acceleration of the political and economic integration of the continent, promote and defend African common positions on issues of interest to the continent and its peoples, promote sustainable development and 'establish the necessary conditions which enable the continent to play its rightful role in the global economy and in international negotiations'.[67] These objectives call for a greater, more coherent and sustained role for the continent in international economic discourse and in the jurisprudence of international and comparative investment law. Unfortunately, eighteen years after the creation of the AU, there is little sign that these noble ideals have been translated into concrete action. One important development under the aegis of the former Organization of African Unity (OAU), and now the AU, is the signing of the Treaty Establishing the African Economic Community (AEC) in 1991.

The AEC was the key platform for continental economic advancement. Its principles include solidarity and collective self-reliance; inter-State cooperation; harmonization of policies and integration of programmes; accountability; economic justice; and popular participation in development. The objectives of the AEC reflect its principles. A key objective is to achieve economic and social self-reliance, endogenous sustainable development in an increasingly integrated Africa. This is particularly important in the light of the fact the AEC was considered an integral part of the OAU, and now the AU. For the purposes of this chapter, Article 94 is of crucial importance. It provides for Member States to coordinate and take common positions within the AEC and present a united front in international economic negotiations in order to promote and safeguard Africa's interest. Member States are enjoined to take steps to bring their international economic agreements and relations in line with the AEC.[68]

65 For an overview of the AU and its work, see https://au.int/, accessed 12 June 2019.

66 Article 3(i).

67 See The Constitutive Act of the African Union, Article 3(i) https://au.int/sites/default/files/pages/34873-file-constitutiveact_en.pdf.

68 Article 93 of the AEC.

It is quite surprising that the AEC does not take a clear and specific stance in international economic discourse that is vital to Africa's development. Some of the areas that dog discourse on Africa's economic development include migration, flow of investment, dumping of industrial waste from the developed world, liberalized trade, etc. It is gratifying, therefore, that seventeen years after the signing of the AEC, the leaders of the continent have adopted an African continental free trade agreement (ACFTA).

The ACFTA enunciates the largest free trade area in the world since the formation of the World Trade Organization (WTO).[69] It aims to liberalize trade, generate jobs and synchronize the various regional economic blocs and agreements on the continent.[70] This is a momentous development that should point clearly to the direction of African Economic law, including the discourse on investment law. The fact is that AFCTA is fundamentally a free trade agreement in goods and services and therefore only has a sprinkling of provisions or mention of investment. Its general objectives include the promotion of the movement of capital and industrial development. Article 4 more specifically calls for cooperation on investment, intellectual property and the establishment of a mechanism for the settlement of disputes. Unlike the WTO, Article 6 of the AFCTA makes it clear that the scope of the AFCTA covers not only trade in goods and services, but also investment, intellectual property and competition. However, unlike trade and services, the investment provisions are to be negotiated as a second phase, which will start subsequent to the coming into force of the ACFTA on the ratification of the twenty-second State. It means that, at the time of writing, we are to await the outcome of the envisaged negotiations to glean what the direction African position would be on the evolving law of international investment.

Given that that AFCTA generally follows the principles of the WTO, and in some instances prioritizes the principles, policies and ideals of the IMF,[71] a radical departure from the existing ethos of the international investment regime is not to be expected. In many ways, this is simply a realistic judgment on the history of failure of many new initiatives since the 1960s, including the New International Economic Order (NIEO), the right to development, permanent sovereignty over natural resources, fundamental

69 Abdi Latif Dahir, 'Africa Moved the World Closer to its Largest Free Trade Area since WTO in 2018' *Quartz Africa* https://qz.com/africa/1507273/africas-free-trade-agreement-was-signed-in-2018/, accessed 12 June 2019.

70 *Ibid.* See also Article 3(c) of the AFCTA.

71 Article 14(2)(b) of the ACFTA Protocol on Trade in Services. See also the ACFTA Protocol on Trade in Goods, for example, Article 28.

change in circumstances, etc.[72] On the other hand, it could be the absence of serious thought, capacity and resources to formulate and see through a pioneering direction for the world in terms of international investment law.

Radical thought on international investment law appears to be somewhat left to individual countries. The rest of this chapter will look at emerging regimes and laws from Tanzania on natural resources and dispute resolution, followed by an examination of the recent Nigeria–Morocco BIT.

3 National and bilateral regimes

In this section, we look at various initiatives and legal developments that appear to depart from the rudderless direction of the African position on international investment law. Tanzania appears to have taken a stance on international investment law that can be considered quite radical in contemporary times, but in many ways it is a reflection of the immediate post-independence arguments, as well as recent concerns about dispute resolution trends. In the summer of 2017, the Tanzanian Parliament passed three pieces of legislation on natural resources – the Natural Wealth and Resources (Permanent Sovereignty) Act, the Natural Wealth and Resources Contracts (Re-Negotiation of Unconscionable Terms) Act and the Written Laws (Miscellaneous Amendments) Act.[73] Other related pieces of legislation were also passed, which have an impact on international investment.[74]

A key feature of these new statutes is the revision of the fiscal regime for resource investment. Royalties have been increased to 6% from the previous 5%for hard rock mining.[75] Fossil fuel royalty remains unchanged, but it is to be calculated prior to the posting of cost and profits. In a bid to discourage transfer pricing, a tax rate of 100% is slated for benefits from tax avoidance schemes and transfer pricing.[76] Depreciation or capital allowances are limited to 10 years after the start of

72 See, for example, Thomas Wälde, 'A Requiem for the "New International Economic Order" The Rise and Fall of Paradigms in International Economic Law' *Oil, Gas and Energy Law* www.ogel.org/article.asp?key=816, accessed 12 June 2019.

73 See Nicola Woodroffe, Thomas Scurfield and Matt Genasci, 'Tanzania's New Natural Resources Legislation: What Will Change?' *National Resource Governance Institute* https://resourcegovernance.org/sites/default/files/documents/tanzania-new-natural-legislation-what-will-change.pdf, accessed 12 June 2019.

74 *Ibid.*

75 *Ibid.*

76 *Ibid.*

production.[77] This is aimed at discouraging the practice of capital allowances ad infinitum by 'expansions' or 're-developments'. Additional profits tax is introduced when a specific recovery of initial costs and rate of return has been attained. Finally, the State is guaranteed a 16% carried equity in any natural resource undertaking.[78]

Apart from the fiscal changes enacted by the Tanzanian Parliament, the laws also made significant changes to the institutional, contractual and dispute resolution regimes for natural resource exploitation.[79] Institutionally, the President, the Parliament and the Cabinet's hand has been strengthened in the negotiation and approval of resource contracts. The power and discretion of the responsible government minister has been reduced mainly to monitoring and seeking prospective renewals of operational licenses. Natural resources are vested in the President in trust for the people; Parliament now has to approve resource contracts. It is unlawful to make any arrangement or have an agreement on natural resources without fully securing the interests of the citizens. This is in addition to the expectation that citizens should be offered the opportunity to participate in the equity ownership of the natural resource company. Furthermore, the law requires that any natural resource contract must guarantee 'returns into the Tanzanian economy'.

Under the new provisions for parliamentary review of resource contracts, Parliament is mandated to question whether the new contract contains 'unconscionable' terms, whether the interest of the State is secured, whether it can make significant returns to the economy. The criteria for determining unconscionable terms include whether the resource is to be exported in its raw form, whether the dispute resolution provisions have been externalized, and whether the laws of the country are broadly frozen indefinitely for the purposes of or at the behest of the investor. In any contract negotiations or renegotiations, the principles of transparency, equity in the distribution of benefits, upholding the national interest, accountability and respect for permanent sovereignty over natural resources must be met.

Many of the provisions and principles are very vague. For example, what is 'guaranteed returns to the economy'? Would this return be in terms of money, jobs, social advancement, internationalization of the economy, etc.? What would amount to 'unconscionable' terms? It is expected that implementing regulations will be enacted that will clarify a number of ambiguous provisions in the new laws. If this is not done with care, the country may be mired in international disputes.

77 *Ibid.*
78 *Ibid.*
79 *Ibid.*

The laws attempt to avoid this multiplicity of disputes scenario by exempting prior existing contracts and projects from its ambit.[80] They are, however, to be subject to the Resources Contracts (Re-Negotiation of Unconscionable Terms) Act. It is made clear that natural resource investment or contractual disputes must be resolved through the national legal system.[81] Internationalization of dispute settlement is not encouraged by the law. As with general resource contracts, the new dispute resolution provisions will be prospective and not retroactive. Therefore, existing BITs, including internationalized dispute resolution provisions, entered into by Tanzania remain valid.[82]

Overall, the reforms can be structured into domestic and international or fiscal and general. Most of the fiscal measures are domestic – focused to the extent that the processes for assessment and collection of taxes are to be transparent and streamlined. For example, the replacement of the weak and duplicative agencies, like the Mining Advisory Board, the Commissioner of Minerals, Zonal Mines Offices and the Tanzania Minerals Audit Agency, with the 'one-stop shop' Mining Commission.

The domestic or fiscal changes do not signal any strong change in the conception of and direction of investment law that other African countries can follow. The fiscal regimes for natural resource exploitation in Africa since the 1980s have been very liberal. The reforms in Tanzania do not make a radical break from the existing regimes on the continent.

What is different in the new Tanzanian legal regime is the international aspects of the reforms. Even the idea of reintroducing sovereignty over natural resources signals a radical departure from the neo-liberal economic orientation that has eclipsed the world since the 1980s, notwithstanding the fact that it is a throwback or an offspring of the 1960s UN resolution on and the discourse of NIEO. The emphasis on domestic beneficiation of raw resources, local content, citizenship participation, corporate social responsibility and advancing the national interests are all significant signs of dissatisfaction with the old regime that failed to alter the developmental trajectory of the people in the countries endowed with resources. It is not enough to have these ideas codified, it is important to build sustainable human capacity that will ensure their effectiveness.

80 See Winston & Strawn LLP, 'Tanzania's Legal Reform of the Natural Resources Sector Threatens Extractive Industries.' www.winston.com/en/thought-leadership/tanzania-s-legal-reform-of-the-natural-resources-sector.html, accessed 12 June 2019.

81 *Ibid.*

82 *Ibid.*

At a first glance, some foreign investors may not be encouraged by the signals the laws give, but on deeper analyses, the laws do not change the fiscal regime radically.[83] The law seeks to restore some balance of interests of national and international stakeholders, which had largely been lost since the 1990s. Moreover, deep thinking investors prefer balanced and predictable legal regimes. Such investors will not be dispirited by the reforms. The provisions are not radically different from what exists in the United States of America, resource-rich Arab countries, etc. Furthermore, Tanzania is one of the most stable and peaceful countries in Africa with rich natural resources, the most important factor in any resource company's investment location.

What would be worrying to investors is the new legal regime's emphasis on domestic dispute resolution. It effectively outlaws international arbitration as an option in resolving resource disputes. As with many countries, Tanzania was alarmed by its experience in the *TANESCO* and *Biwater Gauff* arbitrations, where the companies sought about a billion dollars from the State in claims.[84] It was also alarmed by the threats or the multibillion dollar arbitrations initiated against neighboring Uganda and Kenya, and concluded that international arbitration offered foreign companies opportunities to intimidate poor countries over investments in their countries.[85] If that is the case, the move to domestic dispute resolution could be an overreaction. Be that as it may, there are options to all stakeholders, including foreign investors, and Tanzania has about eleven BITs that are in force. Many of the foreign investors have residence in these countries and therefore may be able to use the dispute resolution options afforded to investors under the BITs. Besides, mediation, third party neutral evaluation and many other methods of resolving disputes are available and which the Government should be amenable to engage in to resolve investment disputes.

One BIT involving two African countries that offers a signpost as to the direction of BITs involving African countries and beyond is the Morocco–Nigeria

83 The rate of investment flows into the country has not reduced in the wake of the new laws. See Jason Mitchell, 'Mining Overhaul Fails to Dent Tanzania's Investment Appeal.' *FDI Intelligence* www.fdiintelligence.com/Locations/Middle-East-Africa/Tanzania/Mining-overhaul-fails-to-dent-Tanzania-s-investment-appeal, accessed 12 June 2019.

84 See Njiraini Muchira, 'Tanzania cites bias as it changes laws governing arbitration' www.theeastafrican.co.ke/business/Tanzania-cites-bias-as-it-changes-laws-governing-arbitration/2560-4763234-timkl6z/index.html, accessed 12 June 2019.

85 *Ibid.*

BIT.[86] The preamble immediately draws the attention of interested stakeholders to the somewhat unusual objectives of and motivations for the agreement. The Parties 'recogniz[e] the important contribution that investment can make to the sustainable development of the state parties, including the reduction of poverty … the transfer of technology, furtherance of human rights and human development'. This is a rare context for a BIT, since some BITs and model BITs expressly forbid technology transfer as an element in investment. Furthermore, whereas sustainable development has become fashionable in recent international instruments, human rights and human development are not the stated objectives of most BITs. Moreover, the Nigeria–Morocco BIT consciously reaffirms 'the right of the State Parties to regulate and to introduce new measures relating to investments in their territories in order to meet national policy objectives and tak[e] into account any asymmetries with respect to the measures in place, the particular need of developing countries to exercise this right; [and seek] an overall balance of the rights and obligations among the State Parties, the investors, and the investments under this Agreement'. The right of State Parties to regulate is what stabilization or development agreements often seek to prevent. It is interesting that a BIT will open with a reassertion of the State's right to regulate and to seek equity or balance in the rights and obligations of all the stakeholders. This clearly is a signal of a new direction in international investment law.

This signal is concretized in the substantive articles of the Treaty. Article 23 stipulates that the 'the Host State has the right to take regulatory or other measures to ensure that development in its territory is consistent with the goals and principles of sustainable development, and with other legitimate social and economic policy objectives'. The caveat that this must be done in accordance with customary international law and other general principles of international law appears to douse the radicality of this provision. It is further weakened by the subsequent clause that clarifies the right to regulate should be seen in the context of the balancing of the rights and obligations of investors in the host State. All the same, Clause 3 of Article 23 reinforces the provision by saying that discriminatory measures taken by the

86 For an overview of the BIT, see Busola Bayo-Ojo, 'Morocco-Nigeria BIT: A Departure or More of the Same?' www.mondaq.com/Nigeria/x/765460/Inward+Foreign+Investment/MoroccoNigeria+BIT+A+departure+or+more+of+the+same+by+Busola+BayoOjo, accessed 12 June 2019.

host State under the agreement shall not be seen or interpreted as a violation of the agreement.[87]

Article 24 also renders efficacious the preamble's call for social responsibility by investors. This provision is no doubt novel. However, its sharpness is blunted by the language used in its formulation. Investors are to 'strive' to make the maximum 'feasible' contributions to the sustainable development of the host State. This is to be based on the size, capacity, national priorities, UN and International Labour Organization (ILO) goals and standards, etc. It is difficult to measure or assess when an investor is meeting this requirement. Could it be by shares in the investing company? Could it be social contribution or intervention programmes or employment of local workers? The lack of precise language can engender disputes.

Dispute settlement is another important innovative development arising from the Treaty.[88] Dispute settlement is organized into four main forms. The first is dispute prevention. Here, a joint consultative committee comprising representatives of the Parties is established and one of its key functions is to preempt disputes, receive complaints about measures that could trigger disputes, and take steps to resolve the disputes. If it could not resolve the dispute within six months, the investor is at liberty to go to the second stage, which is international arbitration. However, international arbitration under the ICSID or ad hoc is to be initiated only after the exhaustion of local remedies. There is no time restraint on the resort to local remedies. The third arm of the dispute resolution structure is the usual mechanism for the settlement of disputes between the State Parties, that is, diplomatic channels followed by inter-State arbitration at The Hague. The final part of the dispute settlement structure is on consolidation of claims or processes. When investor-State and/or inter-State disputes arise and are submitted to arbitration, a claimant can apply to a tribunal for the consolidation of the arbitration, provided the disputes arise from the same or similar set of circumstances and have a common question of law or facts. This can be a very complicated procedure, as issues of consent and choice of tribunal have to be dealt with. Yet, the Treaty leaves the procedure to the Joint Committee of the Parties to figure out.

There are other provisions that are unique to the Treaty. These include provisions on corruption, transparency, environmental regulation, and the assessment of the

87 See Tarcisio Gazzini, 'The 2016 Morocco–Nigeria BIT: An Important Contribution to the Reform of Investment Treaties' *Investment Treaty News* www.iisd.org/itn/2017/09/26/the-2016-morocco-nigeria-bit-an-important-contribution-to-the-reform-of-investment-treaties-tarcisio-gazzini/, accessed 12 June 2019.

88 *Ibid.*

environmental and social impact of investment projects. There is little doubt that the Nigeria–Morocco BIT is very different from traditional BITs. Given the fact that it is between two African States makes it very interesting to Africa but perhaps of lesser importance to Europe and North America, except if African countries were to insist on the Nigeria–Morocco BIT model in their new or renegotiated BITs. This could be a tectonic shift in the formulation of BITs and the settlement of investor State disputes.

Conclusion

There has been some movement in reforming the investment regime in various African countries. At the national level, countries are seeking to incorporate more social and environmental imperatives to the laws on investment. As seen in the case of Tanzania, they are also seeking to limit their exposure to international arbitration as the means of resolving investment disputes.[89]

Although the Nigeria–Morocco BIT is the most significant indication yet of shifts in the thinking of African countries regarding the international investment regime, countries such as South Africa have indicated their unwillingness to continue with or enter into new BITs. Many reasons account for these apparent shifts. In the case of South Africa, the immediate cause was the *Foresti* v. *The Republic of South Africa* (2007),[90] which sought, in an anticipatory manner, to restrain the country's efforts to address the legacy of apartheid by giving Africans, who had been the victims of the racist apartheid regime, the opportunity to get into positions which were not open to them during the apartheid era. In the case of Tanzania, the *TANESCO* and the *Biwater Gauff* cases where they were made to pay costs, although the merits of the award appeared to be in favor of the country and pressures from NGOs influence the reforms. Overall, there is a feeling on the African continent that resource exploitation agreements between the 1970s and the time of writing have not helped the continent. The reforms are being undertaken in this broad context.

Some of the provisions in the revised laws and agreements are vague and hortatory. Others make miniscule changes to rates of fiscal reposts. Even so, the changes

89 Other countries such as Namibia and South Africa have similar limitations on their exposure to international investment dispute settlement. In the case of Angola and Libya, they have refused to be parties to the ICSID.

90 See *Piero Foresti, Laura de Carli* et al. v. *The Republic of South Africa* www.wits.ac.za/media/wits-university/faculties-and-schools/commerce-law-and-management/research-entities/cals/documents/programmes/bhr/in-court/Foresti%20and%20Others%20v%20Republic%20of%20South%20Africa%20judgment%204%20August%202010.pdf, accessed 12 June 2019.

have drawn the ire of some foreign investors and Western law firms looking to represent investors in potential arbitrations.[91]

Whether at the regional, continental or national levels, the reforms do not appear coherent or grounded in deep philosophical thinking. They are mainly very few countries taking the lead to change their laws and investment agreements. For the reforms to be sustainable and avoid unnecessary litigation or legal wrangling, they must be based not only on national concerns, but also on broad regional and continental consensus with a clear vision on the expected results. They must also take account of and provide avenues for the representation of all stakeholders, including foreign investors.

91 See, for example, Baiju S. Vasani *et al.*, 'Tanzania Overhauls Mining Laws, Fines Investor US$ 190 Billion: Is your Investment Protected?' *Jones Day* www.jonesday.com/files/Publication/3aa70a15-44f4-42d5-a001-8c8a5e61e13b/Presentation/PublicationAttachment/ab7bad52-3c5c-4623-8b89-9553ab5a741e/Tanzania%20Overhauls%20Mining%20Laws.pdf, accessed 12 June 2019.

11

Les avantages pour l'Afrique de l'arbitrage transnational, moyen prioritaire de règlement des différends relatifs aux investissements directs étrangers[1]

Richard Albert Makon Ma Mbeb

Introduction

L'arbitrage[2] mixte[3] est inscrit dans la plupart des instruments juridiques qui encadre des investissements directs étrangers, qu'il s'agisse des législations

1 Au-delà de la controverse doctrinale sur la définition de l'investissement direct étranger, celui-ci peut être perçu, en empruntant au Fonds Monétaire International (FMI), comme: « the category of international investment that reflects the objective of a resident entity in one economy obtaining a lasting interest in an enterprise resident in another economy ». Cependant, la définition la plus partagée reste celle proposée par l'Organisation de cooperation et de développement économiques (OCDE), voir OCDE, *Benchmark Definition of Foreign Direct Investment*, (4e édition) (2008).

2 L'arbitrage est communément défini comme « un mode privé de règlement des litiges fondé sur la convention des parties ; il se caractérise par la soumission d'un litige à de simples particuliers choisis par les parties, directement ou indirectement » (Paul-Gérard Pougoué, Jean-Marie Tchakoua, Alain Fénéton, *Droit de l'Arbitrage dans l'Espace OHADA* (Yaoundé: Presses Universitaires d'Afrique, 2000)) 8. Cette définition, bien que brève, permet de mettre en relief deux aspects importants: le premier, l'arbitrage à fonction juridictionnelle, car il a pour but le règlement d'un litige ; le second, l'arbitrage a une origine conventionnelle, en d'autres termes c'est la volonté des parties qui est non seulement au fondement de l'arbitrage, mais aussi du choix des arbitres, de l'étendue de leur pouvoir et de la détermination des règles applicables au litige (soit un arbitrage en droit, soit un arbitrage en équité lorsque les parties permettent à l'arbitre, si nécessaire, d'être amiable compositeur). Il convient de souligner ici qu'en matière d'arbitrage international, il existe des *summa divisio* qui distinguent l'arbitrage ad hoc de l'arbitrage institutionnel ; l'arbitrage interne de l'arbitrage international (« [c']est international l'arbitrage qui met en cause les intérêts du commerce international » (Civ., 18

nationales,[4] des accords interétatiques d'investissement[5] ou des contrats mixtes Etat/investisseur.[6] Généralement, le but poursuivi à travers ces inscriptions normatives est de rassurer l'investisseur privé sur l'existence d'une voie de recours juridictionnelle en cas d'atteinte, par l'Etat d'accueil, à son investissement.[7]

février 1930, *Mardelé* c. *Muller & Cie*, S. (1933) 1. 41, note Niboyet) ; et plus proche de nous, l'arbitrage commercial international de l'arbitrage d'investissement. Le champ de l'arbitrage international est en expansion. En effet, avec la montée en puissance par exemple de l'arbitrage sportif, ce dernier est dorénavant considéré comme l'une des branches de l'arbitrage international. Voir Achille Ngwanza, « L'Essor de l'Arbitrage International en Afrique Sub-saharienne: les Apports de la CCJA », (2013) 3 *Revue de l'ERSUMA* 30.

3 L'arbitrage mixte ou transnational est celui qui oppose un Etat à un investisseur privé. Le premier arbitrage de ce type, opposant une personne privée à un Etat à propos du traitement d'un investissement, est l'affaire *Compagnie Universelle du Canal de Suez* c. *Vice-Roi d'Egypte*, sentence du 21 avril 1864. L'arbitre unique choisi, comme il était de pratique courante à cette époque, était un monarque, dans le cas d'espèce Napoléon III. Toutefois, malgré le fait que ce litige soit typique du droit des investissements, les parties (surtout l'investisseur privé) n'avaient pas pris la précaution d'insérer une clause compromissoire. C'est sur la base d'un compromis d'arbitrage ultérieur, entre la Compagnie Universelle et l'Egypte, que ce litige a été porté devant l'arbitre.

4 En l'occurrence les codes ou chartes des investissements, les codes des activités économiques, les codes de commerce, les codes gaziers, pétroliers, miniers, entre autres.

5 Le plus généralement, il s'agit des traités bilatéraux d'investissement (TBI). Un TBI est un accord conclu entre deux Etats, destiné à favoriser la promotion et la protection des investissements en provenance de chacune des parties. Ce traité est avant tout un accord international au sens où l'entend le droit international.

6 Il s'agit ici de ce que la doctrine dominante en droit des investissements a convenu de désigner les contrats d'Etat. Voir Charles Leben, « La théorie du Contrat d'Etat et l'Evolution du Droit International des Investissements (Volume 302) » dans *Collected Courses of the Hague Academy of International Law* (2003) 213–4.

7 Il faut dire que divers modes de règlement pacifique de différends sont prévus, faisant intervenir successivement la négociation à l'amiable, la conciliation puis l'arbitrage si les deux premiers modes n'ont pas apporté satisfaction à la partie demanderesse. Dans le cas de l'arbitrage, le droit applicable sera généralement constitué, comme le pose la Société Inter-arabe de Garantie des Investissements prévue et organisée par une convention signée au Koweït le 27 mai 1971, s'inspirant de la pratique dominante en la matière, par « les principes communs aux droits des parties contractantes et les principes reconnus du droit international, les parties ayant la possibilité de demander à l'arbitre de statuer ex aequo et bono ». Voir Dominique Carreau *et al.*, « Chronique du Droit International Economique » (1971)17 *Annuaire Français de Droit International* 657–701, 684. Toutefois, il faut toujours présumer que les arbitres ont l'obligation de statuer en droit, même si les faits les enclins très souvent à préférer les solutions douces qu'offre le recours

Dans la pratique, en effet, un désaccord majeur opposant les parties à l'opération d'investissement peut survenir à l'une des étapes de celle-ci, le plus souvent au sujet de l'interprétation ou de l'application d'une ou de plusieurs dispositions, soit d'un instrument conventionnel,[8] soit d'un texte du droit positif de l'Etat hôte.[9] Cependant, si certains désaccords peuvent être résolus par les parties elles-mêmes, par voie de négociation par exemple, d'autres par contre exigent des moyens de résolution externes.[10] Dans cette dernière hypothèse, les investisseurs peuvent demander directement à l'Etat d'accueil réparation des dommages causés à leurs investissements,[11] soit devant des instances arbitrales, soit devant les juridictions dudit Etat.

Force est de souligner que le contentieux transnational des investissements étrangers présente la particularité d'opposer un Etat et le ressortissant d'un autre Etat,[12] en l'occurrence ici un investisseur privé étranger. Aussi, le règlement juridictionnel d'un différend survenant entre ces parties au sujet d'un investissement ouvre-t-il la voie à un possible recours, soit au juge interne de l'Etat d'accueil de l'investissement, soit à une instance arbitrale. A l'analyse, cependant, le recours à l'arbitrage transnational semble être aujourd'hui l'option priorisée par les parties, affaiblissant ainsi

à l'équité. Aussi, « les pouvoirs d'amiables compositeurs doivent donc être expressément donnés aux arbitres par les parties à l'arbitrage », dans Paul-Gérard Pougoué, Jean-Marie Tchakoua, Alain Fénéon, *Droit de l'arbitrage dans l'espace OHADA* 15.

8 Il peut s'agir soit du traité d'investissement (bilatéral ou multilatéral) auquel sont parties l'Etat de nationalité de l'investisseur privé et l'Etat d'accueil de l'investissement, soit du contrat d'Etat liant l'investisseur privé à l'Etat hôte.

9 Dans la plupart des cas, il s'agit de la réglementation relative aux investissements.

10 Carmen Rodica Zorila dirait à cet effet que « la présence des mécanismes efficaces pour la résolution des conflits est ainsi l'ultime garantie de protection pour les investisseurs étrangers » Carmen Rodica Zorila, *L'Evolution du Droit International en matière d'Investissements Directs Etrangers*, Thèse de Doctorat, Faculté de Droit et de Sciences Politiques, Ecole Doctorale des Sciences Economiques, Juridiques et de Gestion, Université d'Auvergne Clermont-Ferrand 1, 20 novembre 2007 309, citant T.L. Brewer, « International Dispute Settlement Provision: the Evolving Regime for Foreign Direct Investment » (1995) 26 *Law and Policy in International Business* 633.

11 Emmanuel Gaillard, « L'Arbitrage sur le Fondement des Traités de Protection des Investissements » (2003) 3 *Revue de l'Arbitrage* 854.

12 Claire Crépet-Daigrement, « L'Extension Jurisprudentielle de la Compétence des Tribunaux Arbitraux du CIRDI » dans Philippe Kahn and Thomas Wälde (dirs), *Les Aspects Nouveaux du Droit des Investissements Internationaux*, Académie de Droit International de la Haye (Leiden/Boston: Martinus Nijhoff Publishers, 2007) 453.

la compétence des juridictions de l'Etat hôte en matière de règlement des différends d'investissements.[13]

Pourtant, dans les faits il faut bien admettre que c'est davantage l'investisseur privé que l'Etat hôte qui priorise le moyen de l'arbitrage sur le règlement par le juge interne. L'Etat d'accueil semble plutôt subir la voie arbitrale que la prioriser en réalité. Aussi, l'usage de la notion de 'priorisation' peut paraitre quelque peu excessif. Toutefois, puisque la disposition d'un mécanisme d'arbitrage immédiatement ouvert à l'investisseur privé, sans par exemple la contrainte de l'épuisement des voies de recours internes,[14] constitue pour l'investisseur une garantie de sécurité juridique et juridictionnelle, l'Etat, par calcul, se dote[15] d'un tel mécanisme pour améliorer, d'une part la perception que les investisseurs ont de lui, d'autre part, les flux d'investissements en direction de son territoire. C'est donc l'importance de cette dynamique d'ouverture à l'arbitrage, au vu des législations nationales et des

13 En droit de l'arbitrage, à travers le recours au principe de l'*effet négatif de la clause d'arbitrage*, on considère que la conclusion d'un accord arbitral (à travers une clause compromissoire en l'occurrence) interdit aux juridictions étatiques le règlement de tout différend visé par ledit accord. Autrement dit, en application de ce principe, le juge du for se déclare incompétent sans aucune analyse du droit applicable au litige, voir Walid Ben Hamida, « L'Arbitrage Transnational face à un Désordre Procédural: la Concurrence des Procédures et les Conflits de Juridiction » (2005) 51 *Annuaire Français de Droit International*. Voir aussi Philippe Fouchard, Emmanuel Gaillard and Bernard Goldman, *Traité de l'Arbitrage Commercial International* (Editions Litec, 1996) 416. Dans l'optique d'une meilleure compréhension de la relation instances arbitrales/juridictions nationales, il faut cependant préciser que même en intentant une action devant le juge du for ou en se défendant devant lui en cas d'action introduite par l'Etat d'accueil devant ses propres juridictions, l'investisseur ne renonce pas pour autant à l'offre publique d'arbitrage exprimée par cet Etat dans un traité international. Dans la mesure où les deux procédures ne contrôlent pas les mêmes normes, rappelle Ben Hamida, l'investisseur peut recourir aux deux mécanismes. Il peut en effet saisir le juge interne pour contester une violation du droit interne, et saisir simultanément un tribunal arbitral statuant sur le fondement du traité d'investissement, pour contester une violation du droit international. Voir dans ce sens Walid Ben Hamida, « L'Arbitrage Transnational face à un Désordre Procédural: la Concurrence des Procédures et les Conflits de Juridiction » 203.

14 Comme c'est le cas en Afrique du Sud avec l'Article 13 de sa loi portant sur protection de l'investissement (Protection of Investment Act 22 of 2015) qui conditionnent l'accès à l'arbitrage au recours préalable à la médiation ; puis au juge interne ; ensuite à un tribunal indépendant ou à un organe statutaire de l'Etat ; et enfin seulement à l'arbitrage, sous réserve de l'épuisement des voies de recours internes.

15 Soit en créant une instance arbitrale nationale, comme le Togo (Cour d'Arbitrage, de Médiation et de Conciliation du Togo (CATO)); soit en étant partie d'un mécanisme

instruments conventionnels et contractuels auxquels sont parties les Etats, qui fait de l'arbitrage aujourd'hui le moyen prioritaire de règlement des différends d'investissements. Il n'est dès lors pas exagéré d'affirmer que « l'arbitrage transnational est devenu progressivement une institution 'mondialisée '».[16]

Il est juste de relever que pendant longtemps, l'arbitrage n'a joué qu'un rôle très limité en matière de règlement des différends relatifs aux investissements étrangers.[17] Cette fonction juridictionnelle était pour l'essentiel assurée par l'Etat contractant à travers l'office du juge interne. Toutefois, d'importantes évolutions favorables à l'expansion de l'arbitrage surviennent dès le début du 20e siècle.[18] Du point de vue juridique *stricto sensu*, l'« expansion de l'arbitrage comme mode privilégié de règlement des différends »[19] ne peut être détachée, d'une part, du succès de la jurisprudence des commissions mixtes arbitrales,[20] d'autre part, de l'apparition dans les années 1930 des contrats d'Etat, contenant des clauses compromissoires prévoyant la possibilité pour les investisseurs d'attraire leur cocontractant étatique devant un tribunal arbitral international.[21] Du point de vue politico-idéologique, l'expansion de l'arbitrage exprime la victoire du libéralisme dans le champ des investissements

arbitral international ad hoc ou institutionnel, tel que la Cour Commune de Justice et d'arbitrage (CCJA) de l' Organisation pour l'Harmonisation en Afrique du Droit des Affaires (OHADA).

16 Eric Loquin, « Où en est la *Lex Mercatoria* » dans Charles Leben, Eric Loquin, Mahmoud Salem, *Mélanges en l'Honneur de Philippe Kahn, Souveraineté Etatique et Marchés Internationaux à la fin du 20e Siècle. A propos de 30 ans de Recherche du CREDIMI* 20 (Editions Litec – CREDIMI, 2000) 44.

17 Charles Leben, « Droit International des Investissements: un Survol Historique » dans Charles Leben (dir), *Droit International des Investissements et de l'Arbitrage Transnational* (Paris: Editions Pedone, 2015) 55.

18 S'il est vrai que le contexte du 20e siècle sera favorable à l'expansion de l'arbitrage, ce mécanisme de règlement des différends est déjà très usité dans les litiges économiques au Moyen Age. Voir à ce propos Jean Bart, « La *Lex Mercatoria* au Moyen Age: Mythe ou Réalité » dans *Mélanges en l'Honneur de Philippe Kahn, Souveraineté Etatique et Marchés Internationaux à la fin du 20e Siècle.* A propos de 30 ans de Recherche du CREDIMI 20.

19 *Ibid.*

20 Bien que ce soit le Traité de Jay entre les Etats-Unis de l'Amerique et le Royaume-Uni qui inaugure, en 1794, la pratique des commissions mixtes, les plus emblématiques sont celles instituées par les Etats-Unis et les Etats européens, d'une part, et plusieurs Etats d'Amérique Latine, en particulier le Mexique et le Vénézuéla, d'autre part, entre le début et le milieu du 20e siècle. Voir Arnaud de Nanteuil, *Droit International de l'Investissement* (Paris: Editions Pedone, 2014) 20–2.

21 Charles Leben, « Droit International des Investissements: un Survol Historique » 56.

internationaux[22] et marque, dans le rapport de force Nord–Sud, l'échec des partisans du nouvel ordre économique international, en l'occurrence sur son aspect contentieux, lesquels partisans « souhaitaient réinsérer le contentieux avec les investisseurs étrangers dans l'ordre juridique étatique ».[23]

Toutefois, de nos jours, si pour les pays développés cette priorisation de l'arbitrage transnational peut aisément s'expliquer,[24] l'abandon progressif de leur compétence juridictionnelle par les Etats en développement, en l'occurrence les pays africains, peut interroger.[25] Au-delà de la généralisation du libéralisme, l'expansion de l'arbitrage transnational semble être favorisée par les divers avantages que les pays africains trouvent à ce mode de règlement des différends. Aussi, la question que l'on peut se poser est celle de savoir quels avantages les pays africains tirent-ils de l'arbitrage transnational des différends relatifs aux investissements ?

Cette question est d'un intérêt scientifique certain. Elle permet d'abord de relever la volonté des Etats africains de renforcer la sécurité juridique et juridictionnelle due aux investissements étrangers. Ensuite, elle met en lumière l'harmonisation en Afrique des législations nationales et leur adaptation progressive aux standards juridiques internationaux en matière de protection de l'investissement direct étranger. Enfin, cette question permet de souligner le rôle joué par des techniques comme celle du consentement dissocié dans la facilitation de l'expansion de l'arbitrage transnational d'investissement.

Aussi, afin d'interroger cette priorisation de l'arbitrage transnational, choix calculé des pays africains s'il en est, nous convient-il d'envisager, d'une part, les avantages juridiques de l'arbitrage transnational (Section 1), d'autre part, ses avantages économiques et politiques (Section 2).

22 *Ibid.*, 55. L'auteur reconnait dans ce sens que « c'est le règlement arbitral international des litiges entre Etats et investisseurs qui a été le mécanisme essentiel par lequel l'interprétation libérale du droit international des investissements s'est maintenue et s'est même amplifiée ».

23 *Ibid.*, 58.

24 La plupart des pays développés sont exportateurs de capitaux et la majeure partie des investisseurs étrangers opérant sur le continent africain sont ressortissants des Etats du Nord. Pour ces Etats, comme pour leurs ressortissants, l'arbitrage transnational est une garantie d'une procédure juridictionnelle impartiale et équitable. En outre, ces pays sont pour la plupart des démocraties, ayant des ordres juridiques solides, et habitués à être litigants dans des procédures d'arbitrage à la fois comme demandeurs et défendeurs.

25 D'autant plus lorsque l'on rappelle l'arrière-plan historique et idéologique de ce changement dont les point d'orgue sont, entre autres, la Doctrine Calvo et Doctrine Drago. Voir Charles Leben, « Droit International des Investissements: un Survol Historique » 13–8.

1 Les avantages juridiques de l'arbitrage transnational pour les Etats africains

On peut recenser plusieurs avantages juridiques de l'arbitrage mixte Etat/investisseur privé pour les pays africains. Parmi ceux-ci figurent en bonne place, d'un côté, le renforcement de la sécurité juridique et juridictionnelle des investissements directs étrangers (Section 1(a)), et de l'autre, l'harmonisation des législations africaines aux standards juridiques internationaux (Section 1(b)).

(a) Le renforcement de la sécurité juridique et juridictionnelle des investissements directs étrangers

Les Etats africains gagnent assurément dans le renforcement de la sécurité juridique et juridictionnelle des investissements directs étrangers. Il convient de rappeler que la sécurité est, avec la justice et le progrès,[26] l'une de ces valeurs classiques sur lesquelles repose le droit.[27] S'agissant singulièrement de la sécurité, davantage la sécurité juridique (Section 1(a)(i)) et juridictionnelle (Section 1(a)(ii)), son renforcement en matière d'investissements directs étrangers constitue le premier avantage juridique de l'arbitrage transnational.

(i) Le renforcement de la sécurité juridique

La sécurité juridique est une notion extrêmement riche qui se prête à des sens ou à de contenus divers.[28] Elle correspond à la production de toute une série de garanties propres, d'un côté, à assurer la sécurité des transactions des sujets de droit,[29]

26 Il faut cependant bien réfléchir sur la bonne mesure de ce progrès du droit, le système juridique étant toujours écartelé entre statisme et dynamisme.

27 Laurent Leveneur, préface à la thèse de Thomas Piazzon dans Thomas Piazzon, *La Sécurité Juridique Collection de Thèse dirigée par Bernard Beignier, Tome 35* (Paris: Editions Defrenois, 2009).

28 Il peut s'agir de la sécurité juridique envisagée de manière subjective, c'est-à-dire comme un sentiment ou de la sécurité juridique envisagée de manière objective, en tant qu'une réalité donc. Voir Thomas Piazzon, *La Sécurité Juridique* 2–3.

29 Paul-Gérard Pougoue, « Les Figures de la Sécurité Juridique » (2007) 4 (1) *Revue Africaine des Sciences Juridiques* 1. Voir également Jean-Louis Atangana Amougou, « Multiplication des Juridictions Internationales et Sécurité Juridique en Afrique » dans Matthieu Fau-Nougaret, *La Concurrence des Organisations* (L'Harmattan, 2012) 135–52; Patrick Edgard Abane Engolo, « La Notion de Qualité du Droit » 1 (1) *Revue Africaine de Droit et de Science Politique* (Editions Le Kilimandjaro, 2013) 87–110.

de l'autre, à rassurer ces derniers qu'ils peuvent faire valoir leurs droits dans les meilleures des conditions.[30] Dans la première approche, « la sécurité juridique est perçue comme finalité du droit ».[31] Dans la seconde, « la sécurité juridique devient une composante de la notion d'Etat de droit ».[32]

Il faut préciser somme toute que dans les deux approches, la sécurité dont il est question est la sécurité par le droit.[33] Cependant, celle-ci ne peut être garantie que par le respect de trois principales exigences, à savoir, l'*accessibilité* du droit ;[34] la *stabilité* du droit, des droits et des situations individuelles régulièrement constituées[35] et la *prévisibilité* du droit, parce que le droit doit être respectueux des prévisions juridiques des sujets de droit qu'il ne doit pas déjouer.[36] Ce triptyque commande donc, entre autres, l'existence de la norme, sa libre disposition à l'investisseur étranger, sa clarté et sa lisibilité, sa permanence, sa durabilité, et la possibilité pour l'investisseur de la prévoir, c'est-à-dire de pouvoir l'intégrer de manière durable dans une projection juridique et/ou économique.

En matière d'investissement direct étranger justement, la disponibilité de l'arbitrage transnational participe du renforcement de la sécurité juridique de l'investisseur à plusieurs égards.

Premièrement, en termes d'accessibilité du droit, la jurisprudence arbitrale constitue une source du droit des investissements.[37] Bien qu'en la matière il n'y

30 Thomas Piazzon, *La Sécurité Juridique* 3.

31 Paul-Gérard Pougoue, « Les Figures de la Sécurité Juridique ».

32 Thomas Piazzon, *La Sécurité Juridique.*

33 Thomas Piazzon, *La Sécurité Juridique* 6.

34 Elle commande que celui-ci soit clair et lisible, parce que les sujets de droit doivent être en mesure de connaitre et de comprendre le droit applicable pour pouvoir agir avec certitude.

35 Un droit instable risque de ruiner les attentes des sujets de droit et leur confiance même dans le droit.

36 Thomas Piazzon, *La Sécurité Juridique.*

37 Arnaud de Nanteuil, *Droit International de l'Investissement* 125. L'auteur précise à ce propos que la jurisprudence fait partie du dispositif général de protection que le droit international offre aux investisseurs étrangers, qu'elle ait été développée dans le cadre de la discipline ou en dehors. En cela, il ne semble pas exagéré, selon lui, de penser que le droit international des investissements présente de ce point de vue une certaine singularité par rapport au droit international général. En effet, alors qu'au sein de ce dernier, la jurisprudence est clairement considérée comme une source subsidiaire, son importance au sein du premier est telle « qu'elle se présente véritablement comme une composante à part entière de l'ordre normatif qu'est le droit de l'investissement … La

ait pas obligatoirement de *binding precedent* ou *stare decisis*,[38] c'est-à-dire la règle du précédent, « les références de jurisprudences volontaires »[39] de plus en plus fréquentes,[40] faites par les arbitres à la faveur d'autres procédures arbitrales, au-delà de constituer pour certains doctrinaires une sorte de « ongoing conversation between arbitrators »[41] permettent de construire une stabilité des solutions juridiques à des problèmes de droit donnés. Cette tendance a le mérite d'orienter l'édiction des règles de droit national devant encadrer les investissements directs étrangers dans le sens d'une meilleure protection des intérêts des investisseurs.

Deuxièmement, l'arbitrage favorise l'accessibilité et la prévisibilité du droit des investissements à travers la clarification du droit applicable au fond du litige.[42]

jurisprudence arbitrale en matière d'investissement s'est si considérablement développée … qu'elle semble être devenue partie intégrante de la protection que le droit international propose aux opérateurs économiques » (125–6). À l'observation du contentieux, en effet, on relève que les parties au litige n'invoquent pas que les normes en la matière, mais également l'interprétation qui en est proposée par la jurisprudence arbitrale, au point que celle-ci, comme le souligne Arnaud de Nanteuil, parait être devenue sinon autonome, tout au moins un élément indispensable de cette protection (126).

38 Mathias Audit, « La Jurisprudence Arbitrale comme Source du Droit International des Investissements » dans Charles Leben (dir), *Droit International des Investissements et de l'Arbitrage Transnational* 119.

39 *Ibid.*, 131. L'auteur relève à ce propos que « si les arbitres ne sont pas sensibles à la règle du binding precedent propre à la doctrine du stare decisis, ils n'hésitent pas en revanche à s'appuyer volontairement sur des sentences antérieures pour étayer la motivation de leur sentence ». Ces références jurisprudentielles volontaires peuvent être vues, estime l'auteur, comme une application en droit des investissements de la doctrine du *persuasive precedent* connue des systèmes de *common law.*

40 *Ibid.* L'auteur, reprenant Jeffery P. Commission, (« Precedent in Investment Treaty Arbitration –A Citation Analysis of a Developing Jurisprudence » (2007) 24 (2) *Journal of International Arbitration* 129–58), souligne qu'entre 1990 et 2006, près de 80% des sentences rendues sous l'égide du Centre international pour le règlement des différends relatifs aux investissements (CIRDI) font référence dans leurs motifs à des sentences antérieures. Les exemples suivants sont abondement cités: l'affaire *Mondev International Ltd.* c. *Etats-Unis*, Affaire ICSID No. ARB(AF)/99/2 (Sentence du 11 octobre 2002), paras 141–4, *ICSID Report* (2004) 192 et l'affaire *Técnicas Medioambientales Tecmed, S.A.* c. *The United Mexican States*, Affaire ICSID No. ARB(AF)/00/2 (Sentence du 29 mai 2003), para. 122.

41 Florence Sauvé-Lafrance, *L'Arbitrage International entre Investisseurs et Etats. Incohérence et Manque de Légitimité* (Université d'Ottawa, 2010) 23.

42 Compte tenu du consensualisme prégnant dans les procédures CIRDI, les parties à une procédure de conciliation ou d'arbitrage peuvent se mettre d'accord sur les règles de procédure à appliquer. Toutefois, si les parties n'ont pas pris cette précaution, le Règlement

Troisièmement, la sanction fréquente par les arbitres de l'inflation normative[43] conforte la stabilité des droits nationaux, favorisant la solidité des prévisions

de conciliation et le Règlement d'arbitrage du CIRDI s'appliquent (Articles 33 et 44 de la CIRDI). En vertu de la , le tribunal arbitral est tenu d'appliquer le droit désigné par les parties. À défaut d'un tel accord, le tribunal appliquera le droit de l'Etat partie au différend (sauf si le droit de cet Etat prévoit l'application d'un autre droit), et toute règle de droit international applicable en l'espèce. Précisons que le terme « droit international » doit ici être interprété au sens de l'Article 38(1) du Statut de la Cour Internationale de Justice (CIJ), bien que cet Article soit destiné à s'appliquer à des différends interétatiques. Quant à l'OHADA, s'agissant des règles applicables à la procédure et loi applicable au fond, l'Article 16 du Règlement d'arbitrage CCJA (cette disposition s'inspire largement de l'Article 15 du Règlement de la Chambre de Commerce Internationale (CCI), traitant des règles applicables à la procédure, dispose que « les règles applicables à la procédure devant l'arbitre sont celles qui résultent du règlement et, dans le silence de ce dernier, celles que les parties, ou à défaut l'arbitre, déterminent, en se référant ou non à une loi interne de procédure applicable à l'arbitrage ». Quant à la détermination du droit applicable au fond, l'Article 17 du Règlement CCJA consacre l'autonomie des parties en la matière. Il précise toutefois, qu'« à défaut d'indication par les parties du droit applicable, l'arbitre appliquera la loi désignée par la règle de conflit qu'il jugera appropriée en l'espèce ». Cette disposition reprend ainsi le contenu de l'Article 13.3 du Règlement CCI de 1988, lequel diffère de l'Article 17.1 du Règlement CCI de 1998 qui dispose qu'à défaut de choix par les parties des règles de droit applicables, l'arbitre appliquera « les règles de droit qu'il juge appropriées ». Le Règlement CCJA n'a donc pas retenu l'approche plus libérale énoncée dans le Règlement CCI de 1998 qui permet à l'arbitre d'utiliser la méthode dite de la « *voie directe* », laquelle consiste pour l'arbitre à déterminer le droit applicable au fond du litige sans être obligé de recourir à l'utilisation des règles traditionnelles de conflit. Voir à ce sujet G. Kenfack Douajni et C. Imhoos, « L'Acte Uniforme Relatif au Droit de l'Arbitrage dans le Cadre du Traité OHADA » (1999) 5 *Revue Camerounaise de l'Arbitrage* 2–9. Comme en arbitrage CCI, le tribunal arbitral CCJA tiendra compte, dans tous les cas, des dispositions du contrat et des usages du commerce (Article 17.2 du Règlement d'arbitrage CCJA, identique à tout point de vue à la disposition correspondante du Règlement CCI). Voir aussi René Bourdin, « Le Règlement d'Arbitrage de la Cour Commune de Justice et d'Arbitrage » (1999) 5 *Revue camerounaise de l'arbitrage* 10–9.

43 Sanctionnée par exemple lorsque les arbitres, envisageant une modification d'une législation interne à l'Etat d'accueil de l'investissement faisant grief à l'investisseur étranger, la sanctionne sur le fondement d'une expropriation indirecte (ou mesures équivalentes à une expropriation), voir à ce sujet Ferhat Horchani, « Rapport Introductif » dans Ferhat Horchani (dir), *Où va le Droit de l'Investissement? Désordre Normatif et Recherche d'Equilibre*, Actes du Colloque Organisé à Tunis les 3 et 4 mars 2006, (Editions Pedone, 2007) 13. Dans le même ouvrage, lire Sébastien Manciaux, « Les Mesures Equivalentes à une Expropriation » dans l'Arbitrage International Relatif aux Investissements » dans Ferhat Horchani (dir), *Où va le Droit de l'Investissement? Désordre Normatif et Recherche d'Equilibre* 73–94. À titre comparatif, l'Article 201 de L'Accord de

juridiques et économiques des investisseurs étrangers.[44] À ce propos, on semble noter un véritable « *contrôle de la légalité* » des agissements étatiques au regard du droit international, comparable à celui dont sont soumises les juridictions administratives.[45]

Il faut reconnaitre que l'instabilité du droit est une cause d'insécurité juridique et une limite à l'attraction des investissements directs étrangers. Cette insécurité juridique est renforcée pour les investisseurs dont leur pays de nationalité n'ont pas conclus de TBI avec les Etats africains au sein desquels ils localisent leurs capitaux. Il semble important de rappeler que dans le cas de l'existence d'un TBI, les Etats parties s'engagent réciproquement à une protection optimale à l'endroit des investisseurs de leurs cocontractants, par le biais d'une kyrielle de garanties. Ces garanties viennent conforter considérablement la solution généralement envisagée par l'Etat d'accueil et l'investisseur étranger, qui est celle de l'insertion dans le contrat d'investissement les liant, des clauses dites de « stabilisation ».[46] Ces « clauses ont pour but de neutraliser

Libre-Echange Nord-Américain (ALENA), s'agissant des « mesures équivalentes à une expropriation », précise qu'il faut entendre par mesure « toute législation, réglementation, procédure, prescription ou pratique » ayant l'effet de déposséder l'investisseur. On peut citer à titre d'exemples de sentences arbitrales sanctionnant l'avènement d'une nouvelle loi comme mesure de dépossession de l'investissement étranger, l'affaire *Middle East Cement* c. *Egypte* Affaire ICSID No. ARB/99/6 (Sentence du 12 avril 2002) ; l'affaire *Ethyl Corp* c. *Canada* (Décision sur le compétence du 24 juin 1998 (procédure arbitrale de la Commission des Nations Unies pour le Droit Commerciale Internationale (CNUDCI) (1999) 16 (3) *Journal of International Arbitration* 149 et suivant, para. 728) ; l'affaire *Société Rialet* c. *Ethiopie* (Sentence ad hoc du 15 janvier 1929) (1929) 8 *Recueil des Décisions des Tribunaux Arbitraux Mixtes* 742 et suivant, spéc. 749 ; l'affaire *B&B* c. *Congo* Affaire ICSID No. ARB/77/2 (Sentence du 8 août 1980).

44 Voir l'affaire précitée *Middle East Cement* c. *Egypte*, née à cause d'un décret du gouvernement égyptien interdisant la poursuite de l'opération économique constitutive de la seule activité de l'investisseur, Affaire ICSID No. ARB/99/6 (Sentence du 12 avril 2002) para. 178.

45 *Ibid.* L'auteur reprend Emmanuel Gaillard qui s'exprime en ces termes: « il n'est pas exagéré d'affirmer que l'on assiste aujourd'hui à la naissance d'un contrôle de la légalité des agissements des Etats au regard des exigences du droit international d'une importance comparable à celle qui a vu, au XIX XXXX, la transformation, dans le seul ordre juridique français, du rôle du Conseil d'Etat d'organe de conseil en véritable juge de la légalité des actes de l'administration » dans Emmanuel Gaillard, 1 *Journal du Droit International* (2004) 214.

46 Charles Leben, « L'Evolution du Droit International des Investissements », dans *Un Accord Multilatéral sur l'Investissement: d'un Forum de Négociation à l'Autre? Journée d'études, Société Française pour le Droit International* (Paris: Editions Pedone, 1999) 18.

le pouvoir normatif de l'Etat »,[47] car elles sont destinées à geler le droit national à une date donnée et, par ce fait même, d'éviter d'appliquer à l'investisseur tout texte désavantageux qui viendrait à être adopté par la suite.[48]
Mais avec ou en l'absence d'un TBI, l'arbitrage transnational reste un instrument essentiel de garantie de la sécurité juridique des investissements étrangers.[49] Cette sécurité juridique qui est la seule à même d'assurer la satisfaction de leurs « attentes légitimes »[50] est confortée par la sécurité juridictionnelle des investissements directs étrangers.

(ii) Le renforcement de la sécurité juridictionnelle

La possibilité du recours à l'arbitrage transnational prévue dans les codes des investissements, les TBI ou les contrats d'Etat rassure les investisseurs sur l'existence des voies de recours échappant au contrôle des Etats africains en cas de différend.[51] C'est la raison pour laquelle on estime que « pour sécuriser réellement l'investissement, encore faut-il mettre à disposition [de l'investisseur] un mécanisme fiable de règlement des différends ».[52]

Aujourd'hui, la majorité des Etats africains opte pour l'arbitrage transnational comme moyen prioritaire de règlement des différends relatifs aux investissements. Pour preuve, on peut relever au moins deux éléments importants qui en attestent. D'une part, le fait que la plupart de ces Etats est à la fois partie, par exemple, au

47 *Ibid.*
48 *Ibid.*
49 Arnaud De Nanteuil, *Droit International de l'Investissement* 126.
50 Selon le dictionnaire de droit international, dans le contexte des contrats économiques internationaux de longue durée, notamment dans le domaine des investissements, les « attentes légitimes » sont définies comme des avantages et bénéfices économiques qu'une partie, principalement l'investisseur, peut raisonnablement escompter de l'exécution du contrat (Jean Salmon (dir), *Dictionnaire de Droit International Public, Préface de Gilbert Guillaume* (Bruxelles: Bruylant, 2001)). Parfois la notion est traduite à tort en l'anglais par l'expression « *expectatives légitimes* » (*Ibid.*).
51 C'est le cas dans toutes les conventions d'investissement conclues par le Cameroun: Accord entre le Cameroun et la Chine du 10 mai 1997, Article 9 ; Traité entre le Cameroun et les Etats-Unis du 6 avril 1989, Article 7 ; Accord entre le Cameroun et l'Egypte du 24 octobre 2000, Articles 8 et 9 ; Accord entre la République de Maurice et le Cameroun du 3 août 2001, Articles 9 et 10, entre autres.
52 Gabrielle Kaufmann-Kohler, « L'Arbitrage d'Investissement: entre Contrat et Traité – entre Intérêts Privés et Intérêt Public » (2004) *Revue Libanaise d'Arbitrage Arabe et Internationale*.

CIRDI[53] et à l'OHADA.[54] D'autre part, tous ces Etats prévoient systématiquement la possibilité du recours à l'arbitrage transnational dans leurs textes nationaux régissant l'investissement,[55] les TBI[56] et les contrats d'Etat auxquels ils sont partis.

Plusieurs raisons peuvent favoriser ce choix. Il s'agit, entre autres, de la neutralité de l'arbitrage qui permet une résolution impartiale et indépendante des litiges ; la confidentialité de la procédure arbitrale ; son économie en temps, en argent et autres ressources internes des Etats ; du degré important de contrôle que les parties conservent sur tout le processus d'arbitrage.[57] D'ailleurs, même les critiques formulées contre ce moyen de règlement des différends, telles que la faible transparence des procédures,[58] le manque de cohérence[59] et l'absence de

53 Le Cameroun, par exemple, d'une part, est parti, comme il le rappelle lui-même à l'Article 11 alinéas 1 et 2 de sa Charte des investissements du 19 avril 2002, au CIRDI, à l'OHADA (qui dispose d'un mécanisme d'arbitrage tant ad hoc qu'institutionnel, le Centre d'arbitrage de la CCJA) et au mécanisme d'arbitrage pour le règlement des différends entre Etats d'Afrique, Caraïbes et Pacifique (ACP) et entrepreneurs, fournisseurs ou prestataires des services, liés à un financement du fonds européen de développement, conformément à l'accord de partenariat ACP–Union Européenne du 23 juin 2000.

54 Cette dernière dispose d'un mécanisme d'arbitrage tant ad hoc qu'institutionnel, à travers son Centre d'arbitrage de la CCJA.

55 Charte des investissements du 19 avril 2002, Article 11.

56 Accord d'investissement du 3 août 2001 entre l'Ile Maurice et le Cameroun, Article 10, ou Accord du 18 mai 2001 entre le Cameroun et la Guinée, Article 10.

57 Susan D. Franck, « Challenges Facing Investment Dispute: Reconsidering Dispute Resolution in International Investment Agreements » dans Karl P. Sauvant et Michael Chiswick-Patterson (dir), *Appeals Mechanisms in International Investment Disputes* (New York: Oxford University Press, 2008) 156–7.

58 Gabrielle Kaufmann-Kohler, « L'Arbitrage d'Investissement: entre Contrat et Traité – entre Intérêts Privés et Intérêt Public » 19.

59 Voir les développements proposés par Catherine Kessedjian, « To Give or Not to Give Precedential Value to Investment Arbitration » dans Roger P Alford et Catherine A. Rogers (eds), *The Future of Investment Arbitration* (Oxford University Press, 2009) 43 et Susan D. Franck, « The Legitimacy Crisis in Investment Treaty Arbitration: Privatizing Public International Law Through Inconsistent Decisions » (2005) 73 (4) *Fordham Law Review* 1521. La proposition de Norah Gallager quant à la systématisation de la consolidation des cas similaires à titre de solution à l'incohérence des sentences arbitrales est aussi intéressante, dans Norah Gallager, « Parallel Proceedings, Res Judicata and Lis Pendes: Problems and Possible Solutions » dans Loukas A. Mistelis and Julian D.M. Lew (dir), *Pervasive Problems in International Arbitration* (Alphen anden Rijn, Kluwer Law International, 2006) 329 ; ou encore celle de l'octroi par les Etats d'un caractère contraignant aux sentences arbitrales de Stephan W. Schill, *The Multilateralization of International Investment Law* (New York: Cambridge University Press, 2009) 282. Sur ce

légitimité[60] n'annihilent pas son importance pour les diverses parties à l'opération d'investissement.

L'arbitrage transnational joue également un rôle majeur dans l'harmonisation aux standards juridiques internationaux des législations des pays africains.

(b) L'harmonisation des législations africaines aux standards juridiques internationaux

Le droit international des investissements, à l'image du droit international économique, connaît une sorte d'affaiblissement de l'emprise des souverainetés dans les processus d'édiction de ses règles. Malgré l'importance sans cesse croissante de l'économie dans les dynamiques fonctionnelles des Etats,[61] on constate une accélération des dynamiques de déréglementation[62] qui ne sont pas pour déplaire les opérateurs privés. En conséquence, la tendance observée de la priorisation de la *soft law*[63] et des standards juridiques dans l'encadrement des biens, des services, des opérations et des activités économiques. Si l'on peut relever une progressive harmonisation des législations nationales à ces standards juridiques internationaux, le rôle qui y est joué par l'arbitrage transnational est essentiel. Cette harmonisation est

dernier point, il est juste toutefois de souligner que l'OHADA fait exception, et c'est là une des singularités de l'arbitrage CCJA. C'est le caractère régional de l'exequatur des sentences portant son onction, accordé par le Président de la CCJA ou un juge désigné par lui à cet effet (Article 30.2 du Règlement d'arbitrage) qui impose aux autorités nationales du lieu d'exécution d'apposer la formule exécutoire (Article 31.2 du Règlement d'arbitrage).

60 Voir à cet effet la réflexion de Daniel Bodansky, « The Concept of Legitimacy in International Law » (2008) 194 *Beiträge zum ausländischen öffentlichen Recht und Völkerrecht* 315.

61 Dominique Carreau et Patrick Juillard, *Droit International Economique (3e édition)*, (Paris: Dalloz, 2007) 2.

62 Eric Loquin estime à cet effet que « le passage de l'économie multinationale à l'économie globale a provoqué une accélération du mouvement de libéralisation des échanges et un mouvement sans précédent de déréglementation du commerce. Le marché perd en l'Etat son 'grand horloger' », Eric Loquin, « Où en est la *Lex Mercatoria* » 27.

63 À titre d'illustration, l'échec de l'Accord Multilatéral sur l'Investissement (AMI) sous l'égide de l'OCDE, au-delà de l'importante influence des acteurs non-étatiques sur les négociations, a mis en lumière l'opposition entre Etats et les réticences de plusieurs quant à l'évènement d'un accord général contraignant sur l'investissement. Voir Patrick Juillard, « L'Accord Multilatéral sur l'Investissement: un Accord de Troisième Type? », *Un Accord Multilatéral sur l'Investissement: d'un Forum de Négociation à l'Autre? Journée d'Etudes, Société Française pour le Droit International* (Paris: Pedone, 1999) 47–56.

nécessaire (Section 1(b)(i)) et son processus (Section 1(b)(ii)) va de l'identification, la définition à la consolidation juridictionnelle desdits standards.

(i) La nécessaire harmonisation des législations africaines aux standards juridiques internationaux

Le standard juridique, notion davantage familière aux juristes de *common law*,[64] fait référence à « un étalon de comportement généralement accepté, de nature à entrainer prévisibilité et stabilité de ce dernier ».[65] En droit, on entend communément par « *standard juridique* »,[66] « [un] terme ou locution insérés dans une règle de droit ou un acte juridique quelconque, en référence à un état de fait ou une réalité dont l'identification requiert une évaluation ou une appréciation ».[67]

De façon générale, le standard juridique est envisagé comme une « notion du langage juridique à contenu indéterminé ou variable ; [une] notion floue ».[68] Dans ce sens, il est aisé de noter que l'histoire du droit fournit d'innombrables exemples de « notions floues ».[69]

Laurence Boisson de Chazournes ne partage pas l'avis si rependu d'une assimilation des standards à la *soft law*. En effet, elle regrette qu'au vu du « flou terminologique qui entoure la notion »,[70] et fort de la diversité des catégories

64 Dominique Carreau, « Investissements » dans *Répertoire de droit international* (Dalloz, 2014) 155. L'auteur cite par exemple Philippe Jestaz (« Les Standards Dons les Divers Systèmes Juridiques » dans *Autour du Droit Civil, Ecrits Dispersés, Idées Convergentes* (Dalloz, 2005) 19) en appuie à son argumentation. Il relève d'ailleurs que l'expression même est par exemple inconnue du Code civil français, même si dans son essence, elle n'est pas inconnue des rédacteurs du Code civil quand ils faisaient obligation aux débiteurs de certaines obligations légales de les gérer en « bons pères de famille » (Voir par exemple, Code civil, Articles 601, 627, 1137, 1374, 1728, 1766, 1806 et 1880).

65 *Ibid.*

66 Pour plus d'amples développements, voir, par exemple, Stéphane Rials, *Le Juge Français et la Technique du Standard (Essai sur le Traitement Juridictionnel de l'Idée de Normalité* (Paris: Librairie de Droit Général et de Jurisprudence, 1980).

67 André-Jean Arnaud (dir), *Dictionnaire Encyclopédique de Théorie et de Sociologie du Droit* (Paris: Librairie de Droit Général et de Jurisprudence, 2008) 581.

68 *Ibid.*

69 Charles Leben, « Droit International des Investissements: un Survol Historique ».

70 Laurence Boisson de Chazournes, « Standards et Normes Techniques dans l'Ordre Juridique Contemporain: Quelques Réflexions » dans Vera Gowlland-Debbas, *Le Droit International et la Quête de sa Mise en Oeuvre* (Leiden: Brill Nijhoff, 2010) 352.

d'acteurs qui les édictent, « la tentation est souvent celle d'englober ces standards sous le couvert de la notion de soft law. Les prescriptions issues de modes non classiques d'élaboration du droit international sont souvent visées par cette notion car elle présente la qualité d'être souple et malléable ».[71] Pourtant, fait-elle remarquer pour bien singulariser la notion de standard, « si certains standards internationaux en revêtent des traits, force est de constater que la soft law n'est pas mutatis mutandis un processus de standardisation ou de normalisation internationale. La soft law n'a pas pour caractéristique première d'être technique. Or, la technicité est une marque de fabrique des standards internationaux ».[72]

Bien que le concept de standard soit protéiforme,[73] les standards internationaux constituent effectivement des « normes techniques internationales »[74] qui visent une mesure moyenne de conduite attendue des acteurs dans un domaine donné, et constituant un étalon de mesure, servant en l'occurrence à évaluer le degré de conformité des droits nationaux au droit international auquel ces standards sont incorporés.

Dans le contexte actuel du droit international des investissements, on relève une tendance à l'harmonisation[75] des législations nationales aux standards juridiques

71 *Ibid.*, 353. En effet, selon elle, la notion de *soft law* connait en doctrine diverses acceptions qui s'appuient sur « des critères de formation de la norme ou relatifs à son contenu ». En effet, la notion de *soft law* peut permettre de recouvrir certains standards et normes. Mais pour d'autres, elle ne le pourra pas, à moins de considérer que toute norme est susceptible de relever de la *soft law* et que tout acteur de la société internationale et habileté à générer de la *soft law*.

72 *Ibid.* 354.

73 *Ibid.* 352.

74 *Ibid.* 351.

75 Il est opportun de préciser que l'harmonisation n'est ni l'unification ni l'uniformisation du droit qui sont toutes deux des techniques d'intégration juridiques assez similaires de l'harmonisation. Si l'objectif commun des trois notions est le rapprochement juridique entre les peuples, entre ordres juridiques ou système de droit, la mise en œuvre de l'une comme des autres diffère.

L'unification consiste à adopter un texte de loi unique, une réglementation unique pour tous, qui peut être directement applicable aux Etats membres signataires de la dite loi, et qui ne souffre d'aucune altération dans l'ordre juridique interne. C'est le cas des directives communautaires. L'uniformisation du droit quant à elle est un mécanisme un peu plus stricte et radical de l'intégration juridique. Dans ce cadre, il s'agit en effet d'effacer les différences entre les législations nationales des Etats en leur substituant un texte de loi unique, rédigé en des termes identiques pour tous les Etats concernés. On retrouve mot pour mot le même texte dans les législations internes des Etats concernés, avec force contraignante par respect du principe de supranationalité. Il convient cependant de préciser que cette procédure ne met pas forcement en péril la souveraineté des Etats, ces textes étant généralement soumis à l'approbation des différents parlements nationaux avant leur application. S'agissant maintenant de l'harmonisation, elle désigne « un simple rapprochement

internationaux. En l'absence d'une convention internationale générale sur l'investissement,[76] cette harmonisation participe du souci d'un renforcement de la cohérence normative du droit des investissements. À titre d'illustration, il est aisé de constater aujourd'hui une certaine similitude entre les contenus substantiels des codes d'investissements à travers le continent, précisément les dispositions relatives à l'accueil, au traitement et à la protection de l'investissement.[77] L'inscription des pays africains dans cette dynamique contribue au renforcement de la sécurité juridique et juridictionnelle des investissements étrangers et, à terme, pourrait concourir à l'augmentation des flux d'investissements directs étrangers en direction du continent.

(ii) Le processus d'harmonisation des législations africaines aux standards juridiques internationaux

L'arbitrage transnational favorise une harmonisation aux standards internationaux des législations nationales. Justement, il convient de relever que « quoiqu'imprécises, ces normes n'en sont pas moins de normes véritables mais dont le législateur (en droit interne) ou les Etats (en droit international) ont laissé aux organes d'application du droit le soin de dégager le sens exact, au fur et à mesure des affaires traitées ».[78]

entre deux ou plusieurs systèmes juridiques » afin d'en réduire ou supprimer certaines contradictions (Gérard Cornu, *Vocabulaire juridique* (Paris: Presses Universitaires de France, 2000) 423). Elle peut être entendue principalement de trois manières différentes selon le Professeur Cornu:

- Tout d'abord, l'harmonisation peut être l'opération législative consistant à mettre en accord des dispositions d'origine différente, plus spécialement à modifier des dispositions existantes afin de les mettre en cohérence avec une réforme nouvelle
- Ensuite, elle peut se définir comme l'opération consistant à unifier des ensembles législatifs différents par élaboration d'un droit nouveau empruntant aux uns et aux autres
- Enfin, l'harmonisation peut désigner un simple rapprochement entre deux ou plusieurs systèmes juridiques. Ce dernier étant plus proche du concept de l'Union européenne.

76 Toutes les tentatives d'adoption d'une convention universelle sur l'investissement ayant à ce jour échoué. Voir à ce sujet les réflexions de Patrick Juillard dans Patrick Juillard, « L'Accord Multilatéral sur l'Investissement: un Accord de Troisième Type? »; ou encore Patrick Juillard, « À propos du Décès de l'A.M.I. » (1998) 44 *Annuaire Français de Droit International* 595–612.

77 Voir, par exemple, les dispositions en matière de traitement, de protection et de règlement des différends d'une grande similitude de la *Loi n°006/PR/2008 du 3 janvier 2008* instituant la Charte des investissements de la République du Tchad ; la *Loi n°6-2003 du 18 janvier 2003* portant Charte des investissements du Congo ; la *Loi n° 2004-06 du 6 février 2004* portant sur le Code des investissements du Sénégal ; ou de la *Loi n° 2014-09 du 16 avril 2014* portant sur le Code des investissements en République du Niger.

78 Jean Salmon (dir), *Dictionnaire de Droit International Public* 1049–50.

En effet, les décisions arbitrales, résultats de l'œuvre prétorienne des tribunaux arbitraux, constituent, dans une certaine mesure, des indications et des orientations importantes pour l'amélioration des législations nationales. Le rôle de l'arbitrage transnational semble donc essentiel ici à plus d'un titre. Pour illustration, il existe diverses catégories d'acteurs disposant d'un « pouvoir d'édiction de standards »,[79] ce qui peut participer de l'instabilité des significations. C'est par exemple le cas de la Commission du Codex Alimentarius créée conjointement par l'Organisation Mondiale de la Santé (OMS) et l'Organisation des Nations Unies pour l'Alimentation et l'Agriculture (FAO), qui édicte des standards.[80] C'est également le cas des Etats et des organisations internationales qui peuvent admettre que « la manière, la forme ou la procédure selon lesquelles une norme a été énoncée lui confère un statut de standard international ».[81] D'ailleurs, « le nombre de standards sont contenus dans des instruments négociés et adoptés par des Etats, que ce soient des traités ou des résolutions d'organisations internationales ».[82]

79 Laurence Boisson de Chazournes, « Standards et Normes Techniques dans l'Ordre Juridique Contemporain: Quelques Réflexions ».

80 *Ibid.* L'un des mandats de cette Commission consiste, selon son Article 1er, à « promouvoir la coordination de tous les travaux en matière de normes alimentaires entrepris par des organisations internationales gouvernementales et non gouvernementales [et] établir un ordre de priorité et prendre l'initiative et la conduite du travail de préparation des projets de normes, par l'intermédiaire des organisations compétentes et avec leur aide » (Voir Commission du Codex Alimentarius, « Statuts de la Commission du Codex Alimentarius », Article 1, dans *Manuel de Procédure, 17e édition* (Rome: Secrétariat du Programme mixte FAO/OMS sur les normes alimentaires, 2007) 3 www.codexalimentarius.net/web/procedural_manual_fr.jsp.

81 *Ibid.* Dans ce sens, Boisson de Chazournes donne l'exemple de l'Accord sur les Obstacles Techniques au Commerce qui, dans son Annexe 1, donne la définition de norme (ou standard). Selon son paragraphe 2 de l'Annexe 1 est considérée comme une norme, tout « document approuvé par un organisme reconnu, qui fournit, pour les usages communs et répétés, des règles, des lignes directrices ou des caractéristiques pour des produits ou des procédés et des méthodes de production connexes, dont le respect n'est pas obligatoire. Il peut aussi traiter en partie ou en totalité de terminologie, de prescriptions en matière d'emballage, de marquage ou d'étiquetage, pour un produit, un procédé ou une méthode de production donnés ».

82 *Ibid.* 353. Comme exemple de traité, l'auteure évoque l'Annexe III 'Evaluation des risques' du Protocole de Cartagena sur la prévention des risques biotechnologiques relatif à la Convention sur la diversité biologique. D'ailleurs, pour une discussion sur la nature de standard international de l'Annexe III, elle est co-auteur avec Makane Mbengue d'un article à la *Revue Générale de Droit International Public* en 2007 de la page 605 à la page 638, intitulé « A propos du Principe de Soutien Mutuel. Les Relations entre le Protocole de Cartagena sur la Prévention des Risques Biotechnologiques et les Accords de l'OMC ».

Cependant, c'est aussi le cas des entités non-étatiques englobant des acteurs publics, privés, des partenariats public-privé qui énoncent des standards par des instruments dont l'appréhension et la qualification en droit ne sont pas aisées, voire malaisées.[83] C'est même aussi le cas des ensembles composites réunissant Etats, organisations internationales et acteurs non-étatiques.[84]

Ce caractère diffus du pouvoir d'édiction des standards internationaux rend nécessaire l'intervention de l'arbitre pour assoir leur signification et leur contenu. À cet effet, dans le débat relatif à la charge normative de la notion de standard, un auteur rappelle que le traitement juste et équitable, ou la pleine et entière protection et sécurité, sont « des notions aux contours imprécis qui ne prendront corps que progressivement, grâce à l'œuvre prétorienne des tribunaux arbitraux ».[85] L'auteur reconnait très clairement là le rôle important, sinon décisif, des tribunaux dans la consolidation des standards. D'ailleurs, il est reconnu que « ce ne sera pas la première fois que les tribunaux arbitraux ou judiciaires auraient à se prononcer à partir de notions floues, et seraient amenés à préciser la signification des règles coutumières imprécises ».[86]

En réalité, cette précision de la signification des standards ne constitue que la première étape de leur consolidation. La seconde est constituée de leur prise en compte par les Etats, dans un premier lieu à l'occasion de l'adoption de leurs législations, en l'occurrence celles relatives aux investissements directs étrangers,[87] dans un second lieu, à la faveur de la conclusion de leurs conventions d'investissement.[88] C'est la raison pour laquelle, dans cette même optique, une auteure précise que « les dispositions relatives au règlement des différends offrent les moyens de s'assurer que les standards de traitement et de protection accordés par un traité sont obligatoires

83 *Ibid.*

84 *Ibid.*

85 Patrick Juillard, « L'Evolution des Sources du Droit des Investissements », Recueil des cours - Académie de Droit International de La Haye (1994) 131. Voir aussi Charles Leben, « L'Evolution du Droit International des Investissements ».

86 *Ibid.*

87 On peut se référer par exemple ici à l'engagement du Cameroun à « établir un cadre institutionnel et réglementaire approprié, garantissant la sécurité des investissements, l'appui aux investisseurs et le règlement équitable et rapide des différends sur les investissements et les activités commerciales et industrielles » qui n'est autre qu'une prise en compte du standard de la pleine et entière protection et sécurité de l'investissement étranger.

88 Voir l'éventail des standards inscrits dans le Traité entre la République du Cameroun et les Etats-Unis concernant l'*encouragement et la protection réciproques des investissements,* signé le 26 février 1986, ratifié le 6 avril 1989.

et effectivement mises en application. De ce fait elles jouent un rôle critique dans les traités bilatéraux ».[89]

Si, *in fine*, nous avons pu souligner l'importance des avantages juridiques de l'arbitrage transnational pour l'Afrique, les développements qui suivent nous permettent de démontrer que les avantages économiques et politiques de ce moyen de résolution des différends ne sont pas moins importants.

2 Les avantages économiques et politiques de l'arbitrage transnational pour les Etats africains

L'arbitrage transnational a des avantages économiques et politiques importants pour les Etats africains. Il favorise, dans un premier lieu, la confortation de l'ouverture économique et l'amélioration de l'attractivité économique de ces pays (Section 2(a)), c'est l'avantage économique ; dans un second lieu, l'amélioration de la gouvernance internationale de l'investissement (Section 2(b)), c'est l'avantage politique.

(a) L'avantage économique : l'amélioration de l'ouverture et de l'attractivité économique

Du point de vue économique, le premier avantage que tire l'Afrique de l'arbitrage transnational est la confortation de l'ouverture économique des Etats (Section 2(a)(i)) et l'amélioration de leur attractivité économique (Section 2(a)(ii)).

(i) La confortation de l'ouverture économique des Etats africains

L'espace marchand international actuel est le résultat du décloisonnement des marchés nationaux.[90] C'est à partir des années 60 que commence à se développer une économie multinationale,[91] que participe à consolider et à étendre ces décloisonnements des marchés. Dans cette dynamique, les marchés nationaux africains, leviers principaux d'une meilleure intégration du continent à l'économie mondiale, ne sont pas en reste.

Dans ce monde de plus en plus libéral, l'arbitrage transnational permet de conforter l'ouverture des économies et le développement du commerce mondial. C'est ici en fait qu'il convient de rappeler l'approche pragmatique, c'est-à-dire fonctionnelle,

89 Carmen Rodica Zorila, *L'Evolution du Droit International en matière d'Investissements Directs Etrangers* 309.

90 Éric Loquin, « Où en est la *Lex Mercatoria* » 43.

91 *Ibid.*

suivie en matière d'investissements internationaux, qui consiste à « *réglementer sans définir* ».[92] Cette approche, « si elle est sans doute peu satisfaisante pour l'esprit, présente cependant des avantages certains de souplesse: appliquée au domaine des investissements internationaux, elle permet – et a permis – de privilégier un certain nombre de transactions en les dotant d'un régime protecteur ».[93]

En matière d'arbitrage des différends relatifs aux investissements, on note également cette approche pragmatique. L'arbitre saisi du règlement d'un différend d'investissement, au-delà de l'obligation de dire le droit, est soucieux de contribuer par son office à l'ouverture des économies nationales et au développement du commerce mondial. Lorsqu'il qualifie, par exemple, une nouvelle réglementation adoptée par l'Etat d'accueil de protectionnisme,[94] ou estime qu'une législation déjoue les prévisions économiques légitimes des investisseurs en impactant négativement sur leur rentabilité,[95] il se positionne en réalité comme un défenseur de l'ouverture des territoires économiques. Analysant le recours par les arbitres à la « méthode comparative » dans le choix des dispositions applicables à un litige, un doctrinaire fait remarquer la tendance des juridictions arbitrales à procéder à une analyse économique du droit.[96] Dès lors, la règle retenue par les arbitres sera celle qui optimise sur le plan économique le rapport juridique.[97] L'efficacité des relations économiques internationales n'est évidemment possible que dans un contexte d'ouverture et de décloisonnement des marchés nationaux.

L'arbitrage d'investissement devient dans cet environnement un levier important de la libéralisation des économies et des marchés. La preuve, la tendance bien

92 Dominique Carreau, *Investissements*, paragraphe 16. En effet, cette approche est surtout envisagée à la faveur du débat sur la définition de la notion 'd'investissement' et d'autres notions fondamentales du droit économique en général et du droit des investissements en particulier. Le constat qui est fait ici est qu'en matière économique, le droit international ne s'est pas attaché à donner des définitions précises correspondant à l'analyse économique, mais à poser un régime juridique particulier, en général de faveur, comme le con l'auteur.

93 *Ibid.*

94 Voir, par exemple, l'affaire précitée *Middle East Cement* c. *Egypte*.

95 Comme dans les sentences *Saluka Investments B.V.* c. *République Tchèque*, Sentence CNUDCI/UNCITRAL, 17 mars 2006, para. 255 ; *Methanex Corp.* c. *United States*, Sentence CNUDCI, 3 aout 2005, para. 7, dans lesquelles, malgré la reconnaissance sans ambigüité du droit de l'Etat hôte de réglementer dans un but d'intérêt général, le droit à l'indemnisation en cas d'atteinte aux intérêts légitimes des investisseurs étrangers a été admis.

96 Eric Loquin, « Où en est la *Lex Mercatoria* » 38.

97 *Ibid.* 39.

observée dans les sentences arbitrales rendues par les différents tribunaux, d'une protection davantage renforcée des investisseurs privés et d'un encouragement à l'ouverture des marchés nationaux.[98] C'est pourquoi certains auteurs estiment que le but premier de l'arbitrage transnational est clairement « l'encouragement des investissements internationaux ».[99]

D'ailleurs, partageant ce point de vue lorsqu'il analyse les liens entre le Cameroun et l'arbitrage transnational, un auteur affirme que « l'arbitrage international revêt une importance cardinale dans la volonté d'attirer des investissements étrangers ».[100] Pour lui, en effet, à travers le droit de l'arbitrage transnational, « se dessine en filigrane la politique d'ouverture d'un pays aux capitaux venant de l'extérieur. Plus un Etat souhaite l'arrivée de ces derniers sur son territoire, plus sa législation adopte une conception libérale de l'arbitrage ».[101]

Cette disposition à l'arbitrage, en sus de conforter l'ouverture économique des Etats africains, participe de l'amélioration de leur attractivité.

(ii) L'amélioration de l'attractivité économique des Etats africains

L'arbitrage transnational favorise une meilleure attractivité des pays africains. En effet, on peut aisément noter pour ce qui concerne les Etats membres de l'OHADA,[102] que le souci du développement en général, et celui de l'amélioration de l'attractivité économique en particulier, ont souvent été à l'origine d'importants projets conventionnels. S'agissant de l'OHADA justement, les Etats membres l'ont créé « afin

98 Affaire *Consortium RFCC* c. *Royaume du Maroc*, Sentence arbitrale rendue le 22 décembre 2003, Affaire ICSID No. ARB/00/6 ; Affaire *Antoine Goetz et consorts* c. *République de Burundi*, Sentence arbitrale du 9 février 1999, 15 *ICSID Review – Foreign Investment Law Journal* (2000) 456–8.

99 Florence Sauvé-Lafrance, *L'Arbitrage International entre Investisseurs et Etats. Incohérence et Manque de Légitimité* 10–1.

100 Achille Ngwanza, « Le Cameroun et l'Arbitrage International », dans Jean-Louis Atangana Amougou (dir), *Le Cameroun et le droit international, Colloque des cinquantenaires de l'Indépendance et de la Réunification du Cameroun, Ngaoundéré les 2 et 3 mai 2013* (Editions Pedone, 2014) 86.

101 *Ibid.*

102 À sa création en 1993, l'OHADA est composée des Etats ci-après: Bénin, Burkina Faso, Cameroun, Centrafrique (RCA), Comores (République Fédérale Islamique qui deviendra Union des Comores), Congo, Côte d'Ivoire, Gabon, Guinée Equatoriale, Mali, Niger, Sénégal, Tchad, Togo. Ces Etats sont rejoints par la Guinée Bissau (1995–1996), la Guinée (2000) et la République Démocratique du Congo (RDC) en 2012.

de se doter de règles modernes favorables au déroulement optimal du commerce ».[103] Dans cette dynamique, l'avènement de l'organisation a favorisé la création « des institutions [ayant] la charge de la sécurité juridique et judiciaire dans son espace, notamment la Cour Commune de Justice et d'Arbitrage (CCJA) »,[104] qui subroge aux juridictions nationales suprêmes pour le contentieux des matières régies par l'OHADA, parmi lesquelles l'arbitrage.[105] En effet, la CCJA a vocation à traiter les pourvois en cassation contre les décisions émanant des juridictions nationales en arbitrage, qu'il s'agisse d'annulation ou d'exequatur d'une sentence.[106]

La disposition d'un cadre africain de l'arbitrage transnational à travers les cours nationales d'arbitrage, la CCJA, les autres instances d'arbitrage telles que le CIRDI ou la CCI, a entre autres le mérite d'inciter et d'encourager les investisseurs étrangers à choisir les Etats africains comme destinations privilégiées de leurs capitaux. De ce point de vue, l'attractivité du continent est un enjeu économique et politique capital.

On peut entendre par attractivité, de façon générale, la capacité d'un territoire ou d'un Etat donné à attirer une quantité importante et constante d'activités de production et de capitaux extérieurs à l'économie nationale. Dans un sens plus strict, l'attractivité économique consiste en la capacité d'un Etat à attirer le maximum d'investisseurs sur son territoire, en leur offrant un cadre légal, politique et économique satisfaisant, c'est-à-dire un cadre qui soit plus favorable que celui des Etats concurrentiels, pour l'établissement de leurs projets.[107] Dans ce sens, les stratégies visant à attirer l'investissement direct étranger consistent en la mise à disposition des investisseurs d'un environnement dans lequel ils peuvent mener leurs activités de manière la plus rentable sans courir de risques inutiles.[108] En dehors d'un contexte macroéconomique stable permettant notamment l'accès au commerce

103 Achille Ngwanza, « L'Essor de l'Arbitrage International en Afrique Subsaharienne: les Apports de la CCJA » 30.

104 *Ibid.*

105 *Ibid.*

106 *Ibid.*

107 Evelyne Patience Memphil Ndi, *Attractivité Economique des Investissements Directs Etrangers en zone CEMAC: Harmonisation des Instruments Juridiques aux Règles Internationales*, Thèse pour le Doctorat en Droit présentée et soutenue le 21 octobre 2015, Faculté de Droit et Science Politique, Ecole doctorale D.E.S.P.E.G/Laboratoire G.R.E.D.E.G, Université Nice Sophia Antipolis, 29.

108 Narith Chan, *Institution et Investissement: Impact de l'Environnement Institutionnel sur l'Entrée d'IDE au Cambodge*, Thèse pour le Doctorat en Sciences Economiques, Université Lumière Lyon 2, 17 mai 2011, 17.

international et aux ressources suffisantes et accessibles, l'attractivité économique nécessite, en l'occurrence, la présence d'une infrastructure adaptée, des ressources humaines de qualité, une réglementation prévisible et non discriminatoire, l'absence d'obstacles administratifs à la conduite des activités, un cadre juridictionnel favorable à la résolution équitable des différends.[109]

On peut donc relever à ce sujet que l'attractivité économique d'une zone, d'une région ou d'un pays dépend de leur stabilité, de leur fiscalité, du dynamisme de la demande, des caractéristiques de la main d'œuvre disponible, de la qualité des infrastructures, de leur système normatif et juridictionnel.[110] C'est à ce niveau que l'ouverture à l'arbitrage, moyen de règlement des différends privilégié des investisseurs, constitue un apport essentiel dans l'attractivité économique des Etats africains.

Outre l'avantage économique, nous pouvons également relever l'avantage politique de l'arbitrage, à savoir l'amélioration de la gouvernance internationale de l'investissement.

(b) L'avantage politique: l'amélioration de la gouvernance internationale de l'investissement

La bonne gouvernance internationale de l'investissement direct étranger est un enjeu important pour les Etats africains, parfois impuissants, par exemple, face à certaines dérives des firmes multinationales.[111] L'arbitrage transnational peut dès lors, outre son apport au développement d'un environnement favorable à l'investissement direct étranger en Afrique (Section 2(b)(i)), jouer un rôle important dans la responsabilisation des investisseurs étrangers (Section 2(b)(ii)).

109 Evelyne Patience Memphil Ndi, *Attractivité Economique des Investissements Directs Etrangers en zone CEMAC: Harmonisation des Instruments Juridiques aux Règles Internationales.*

110 *Ibid.* 30.

111 Philippe Kahn, « Investissements Internationaux et Droits de l'Homme », dans Ferhat Horchani (dir), *Où va le Droit de l'Investissement ? Désordre Normatif et Recherche d'Equilibre, Actes du Colloque Organisé à Tunis les 3 et 4 mars 2006* (Editions Pedone, 2007) 101–4.

(i) Le développement d'un environnement favorable à l'investissement direct étranger

La doctrine s'accorde à reconnaitre la montée de vives critiques formulées contre l'arbitrage transnational d'investissement,[112] à la fois par les diverses opinions publiques nationales, les organisations non gouvernementales et autres organisations de la société civile (OSC), les gouvernements et les investisseurs eux-mêmes.[113] Certains auteurs reviennent sur certaines d'entre elles.[114] Il s'agit, entre autres, du manque de transparence dans les procédures d'arbitrage ; de l'absence de cohérence entre les sentences arbitrales sanctionnant les différends d'investissements ; et plus grave souvent, l'absence de légitimité de tout le processus et du système même d'arbitrage, dont certains ont pu qualifier les tribunaux de « gouvernements de l'ombre », ou pis encore, de « terrorisme arbitral ».[115]

Certaines décisions ont peut-être contribué de manière significative à cette dégradation de la confiance envers ce système d'arbitrage. On peut reprendre ici, les exemples de sentences vivement critiquées comme dans les affaires *SGS Société Générale de Surveillance S.A.* c. *Republic of the Philippines* ;[116] *Waste Management, Inc.* c. *United Mexican States,*[117] ou encore *Robert Azinian* et al. c. *United Mexican States.*[118]

Toutefois, l'augmentation sans cesse accrue des conventions bilatérales d'investissements ou des contrats d'Etat, prévoyant quasiment tous, en vertu de leurs dispositions, la possibilité de saisine des tribunaux arbitraux en cas de différends nés de l'opération d'investissement, finit par convaincre de l'importance du système arbitral. On peut énumérer justement pour mémoire, quelques-unes des raisons

112 Walid Ben Hamida, « L'Arbitrage Transnational face à un Désordre Procédural: la Concurrence des Procédures et les Conflits de Juridictions » 195–221.

113 Ces deux dernières catégories, pourtant acteurs majeurs de l'opération d'investissement et, en ce qui est singulièrement des Etats, initiateurs de ce type spécifique d'arbitrage international. Voir Susan D. Franck, « Challenges Facing Investment Dispute: Reconsidering Dispute Resolution in International Investment Agreements » 1544–6.

114 Entre autres,(Gabrielle Kaufmann Kohler, « L'Arbitrage d'Investissement: entre Contrat et Traité – entre Intérêts Privés et Intérêt Public » 26 ; Florence Sauvé Lafrance, *L'Arbitrage International entre Investisseurs et Etats. Incohérence et Manque de Légitimité* 2 ; Emmanuel Gaillard, *Legal Theory of International Arbitration* (Martinus Nijhoff, 2010) 857–8.

115 Michael Goldhaber, *Arbitral Terrorism*, American Lawyer/Focus Europe (2003).

116 Sentence sur la compétence du 29 janvier 2004 www.worldbank.org/icsid/cases/awards.htm.

117 Sentence du 30 avril 2004 www.worldbank.org/icsid/cases/awards.htm.

118 Sentence du 1 novembre 1999 www.worldbank.org/icsid/cases/awards.htm.

qui justifient l'ouverture quasi systématique des Etats à l'arbitrage transnational.[119] Certaines d'entre elles, à savoir la neutralité, la confidentialité des procédures, sa finalité ou encore le contrôle important, qu'exerce les parties sur le déroulement de l'instance en font, assurément, un mécanisme de bonne gouvernance et un important vecteur de paix.[120] Autrement dit, l'arbitrage favorise un environnement propice à l'épanouissement de l'investissement direct étranger, certainement aussi à la responsabilisation des investisseurs étrangers.

(ii) La responsabilisation des investisseurs étrangers opérant en Afrique

Même si l'arbitrage transnational apparait comme un acquis, il semble important que celui-ci prenne en compte certaines des critiques formulées à son encontre afin de se reformer substantiellement. C'est par exemple la nécessaire prise en compte de l'intérêt public ou l'intérêt général dans la procédure et le fond de l'arbitrage.[121] Une auteure affirmait dans le sens des perspectives de l'arbitrage d'investissement, « [qu'] il est indispensable que l'arbitrage, méthode éprouvée pour servir des intérêts privés, s'adapte pour intégrer l'élément d'intérêt public, tant au niveau de la procédure que du droit de fond ».[122] De nos jours, la doctrine reconnait que l'une des évolutions les plus spectaculaires du droit de l'arbitrage transnational est la reconnaissance par les Etats du pouvoir des tribunaux arbitraux de sanctionner les atteintes à l'ordre public[123] dans le but de l'intérêt général.[124] D'ailleurs, le métadiscours en droit des investissements perçoit dans les sentences arbitrales une revendication certaine « d'un ordre public transnational ».[125] On peut, à titre d'illustration, évoquer les nombreuses sentences arbitrales qui ont annulé des contrats entachés de corruption, « au nom d'un ordre public qui serait l'expression des valeurs reconnues par

119 Susan D. Franck, « Challenges Facing Investment Dispute: Reconsidering Dispute Resolution in International Investment Agreements ».

120 *Ibid.*

121 Gabrielle Kaufmann Kohler, « L'Arbitrage d'Investissement: entre Contrat et Traité – entre Intérêts Privés et Intérêt Public » 26–7.

122 *Ibid.*

123 Éric Loquin, « Où en est la *Lex Mercatoria* » 49.

124 *Ibid.*

125 *Ibid.*

la communauté internationale »,[126] ou encore la célèbre sentence CIRDI à la faveur de laquelle les arbitres ont estimé que les activités d'un investisseur menaçant un monument faisant partie du patrimoine commun de l'humanité pouvaient devenir illicites au regard du droit international.[127]

De façon pratique, plusieurs procédés pourraient davantage participer à cette meilleure défense de l'intérêt public. Nous pouvons en retenir au moins deux: d'une part, la procédure d'*amicus curiae* inspirée des pratiques de la Cour Suprême des Etats-Unis,[128] dont l'apport à la transparence des procédures arbitrales est évident, à travers la participation à l'instance de tiers intéressés;[129] d'autre part, le *duty of care*, notion de *common law* qui renvoie à l'obligation coutumière de prendre soin

126 *Ibid.* L'auteur nous partage son analyse des sentences CCI n° 1110, *Arbitration International* (1994) 277 ; CCI n° 3916, *Journal de Droit International* (1984) p. 930 ; CCI n° 7293, *Bulletin ASA* (1993) p. 373; Sentence *Hilmarton* du 19 août 1988, *Revue de l'Arbitrage* (1993) 327.

127 *Affaire du Plateau des Pyramides*, Sentence CIRDI du 16 février 1993, *Revue de l'Arbitrage* (1986) 105. Citée par Éric Loquin, « Où en est la *Lex Mercatoria* ».

128 Gabrielle Kaufmann Kohler, « L'Arbitrage d'Investissement: entre Contrat et Traité – entre Intérêts Privés et Intérêt Public » 26–7. Il faut préciser que cette procédure permet à des tiers, non parties au différend, de produire des observations écrites à la Cour, qui participent des modalités d'informations des arbitres ou des juges dans une procédure contentieuse. Le CIRDI y a fait recours à plusieurs reprises déjà. Les exemples célèbres suivants sont généralement cités à cet effet : *Methanex Corp.* c. *United States of America*, Décision du 15 janvier 2001 sur l'admissibilité des *amicus curiae briefs* www.naftaclaims.com; *United Parcel Service of America Inc.* c. *Government of Canada*, Décision du 17 octobre 2001 sur l'admissibilité des *amicus curiae briefs*, www.naftaclaims.com; *Aguas del Tunari, S.A.* c. *Republic of Bolovia*, lettre du Président du Tribunal de janvier 2003 www.earthjustice.org.

129 Voir Catherine Yannaca-Small dans OCDE, *Droit International de l'Investissement. Un Domaine en Mouvement. Complément aux perspectives de l'investissement international* (Paris: Editions OCDE, 2005) en l'occurrence le Chapitre 1 intitulé « Transparence et Participation des Tiers aux Procédures de Règlement des Différends entre Investisseurs et Etats 9. À titre d'illustration, voir *Aguas Argentinas, S.A., Suez, Sociedad General de Aguas de Barcelona, S.A. et Vivendi Universal, S.A.* c. *la République d'Argentine*, Arrêt répondant à une demande de transparence et de participation à titre d'*amicus curiae* du 19 mai 2005. Si le CIRDI ne prévoit pas dans son Règlement d'arbitrage l'intervention des tiers dans la procédure, la CNUDCI par contre reste le seul règlement arbitral qui le prévoit, bien qu'elle soit conditionnelle (Article 17, alinéa 5).

d'autrui, plus sollicitée dans le droit pétrolier et minier[130] où il peut être invoqué sur le fondement de la *lex petrolea*.[131]

Cette question de l'intérêt public est sans aucun doute d'une extrême importance pour des Etats en développement comme ceux d'Afrique, car il rassurerait la société dans son ensemble, ou tout au moins les OSC, sur la prise en compte et la défense, au cours de l'instance arbitrale, des droits des populations, supposées bénéficiaires des projets d'investissement. En effet, il est admis aujourd'hui que « les projets qui donnent lieu à des procédures d'arbitrage en matière d'investissement revêtent souvent une importance majeure pour l'économie d'un pays, parfois pour une population entière ».[132]

Conclusion

En somme, les investisseurs étrangers en Afrique peuvent, dans de nombreuses situations, demander à l'Etat d'accueil réparation, à la faveur d'une procédure arbitrale, des dommages causés à leurs investissements. Cette possibilité est facilitée lorsqu'il existe un instrument de protection des investissements entre l'Etat territorial et l'Etat

130 Conformément au *duty of care*, même en l'absence d'instruments juridiques de qualité contenant des dispositions pertinentes relatives à la protection des droits des populations riveraines, l'investisseur à l'obligation de prendre soin des populations riveraines, par exemple à travers la remise en l'état des sites après exploitation pétrolière ou minière. Avec le *duty of care*, les Etats comme les investisseurs privés ont des obligations qui vont bien au-delà des prescriptions contractuelles. Aujourd'hui par exemple, la notion de 'société pétrolière' apparait comme une prise en compte, en matière de droit pétrolier, des droits des populations riveraines. En effet, ils font partie aujourd'hui de la 'société pétrolière', au-delà des parties du contrat pétrolier (qui est de deux types: soit *un contrat de concession*, soit *un contrat de partage de production*), entre autres les riverains, les bailleurs de fonds et la société civile. Il y a d'ores et déjà une prise en compte des besoins des riverains dans la négociation et l'exécution du contrat. Cela s'est vu par exemple s'agissant de la négociation du contrat COTCO/Tchad, sur l'incitation de la Banque mondiale, après moult campagnes de revendications des riverains. De plus en plus on parle moins, en matière de contrat pétrolier, de 'parties contractantes' mais de 'parties prenantes' du projet pétrolier ou minier. Voir les différentes analyses des auteurs de Achille Ngwanza et Gilles Lhuilier, *Le Contentieux Extractif* (Paris, ICC, 2015), en l'occurrence Achille Ngwanza, « L'Arbitrage en Matière Extractive » 227–42.

131 La *lex petrolea* peut être entendu comme l'ensemble des bonnes pratiques des sociétés en matière pétrolière.

132 Gabrielle Kaufmann Kohler, « L'Arbitrage d'Investissement: entre Contrat et Traité – entre Intérêts Privés et Intérêt Public » 27.

de nationalité de l'investisseur, ou lorsqu'existe, soit une clause compromissoire insérée dans le contrat d'Etat, soit est signé un compromis d'arbitrage entre l'investisseur et l'Etat hôte après la survenance du litige. Le litigant privé a généralement le choix entre les juridictions des Etats africains et la saisine d'une instance arbitrale transnationale. C'est cette dernière option qu'il priorise, car c'est elle qui semble la plus à même de lui garantir un règlement des plus équitables du litige l'opposant à l'Etat d'accueil de son investissement. Toutefois, l'investisseur privé n'est pas le seul bénéficiaire de ce recours à l'arbitrage transnational, l'Etat d'accueil tire également de nombreux avantages à mettre à la disposition de l'investisseur ce mécanisme juridictionnel de règlement de différend. Les avantages de l'arbitrage transnational pour les Etats africains sont de deux ordres au moins : d'une part, les avantages juridiques, d'autre part, les avantages économiques et politiques.

La présente analyse nous a donné l'occasion de vérifier l'idée dominante en doctrine d'après laquelle l'objectif principal des Etats, africains ou autres, est de « sécuriser les investissements internationaux afin de donner confiance aux investisseurs, et donc augmenter leur afflux».[133] Toutefois, « pour sécuriser réellement l'investissement, il faut mettre à disposition un mécanisme fiable de règlement des différends »,[134] en d'autres termes, accepter l'arbitrage transnational dont la finalité, au-delà de ses limites, est de produire des solutions équitables pour les parties.[135] Malgré certaines ambiguïtés littérales[136] et d'importants revirements normatifs, tel celui de l'Afrique

133 Florence Sauvé Lafrance, *L'Arbitrage International entre Investisseurs et Etats. Incohérence et Manque de Légitimité* 1.

134 Gabrielle Kaufmann Kohler, « L'Arbitrage d'Investissement: entre Contrat et Traité – entre Intérêts Privés et Intérêt Public » 4.

135 Patrick Rambaud, « Des Obligations de l'Etat vis-à-vis de l'Investisseur Etranger: la Sentence CIRDI du 27 juin 1990 , *Société Asian Agricultural Products Ltd (A.A.P.L.)* c. *Sri Lanka* » (1992) 38 *Annuaire Français de Droit International* 510.

136 De nombreux textes africains contiennent des dispositions ambiguës, ou à tout le moins imparfaites, qui ne permettent pas de clarifier la place accordée à l'arbitrage dans règlement des différends d'investissements. On peut citer l'Article 2 du Titre 2 de la Loi n°15/1998 instituant la Charte des Investissements en République gabonaise ou l'Article 17 de la Loi-cadre n° 18–95 du 3 octobre 1995 portant Charte des investissements du Maroc, qui évoque l'arbitrage au passage, dans une disposition ayant pour objet le programme d'investissement des entreprises, à l'intérieur du Titre 3 lui-même traitant des 'Mesures d'ordre financier, foncier, administratif et autres'. Toutefois, à côté de ces dispositions imparfaites on relève un autre type qui tend à prioriser le règlement des litiges d'investissement par les juridictions internes. La formulation de la loi algérienne (Loi n° 2016–09 du 3 août 2016 relative à la promotion de l'investissement)

du Sud[137] qui soumet désormais le recours à l'arbitrage en cas de différend l'opposant à un investisseur étranger à de forte contraintes,[138] l'arbitrage transnational, au vu de l'orientation davantage libérale des droits nationaux et des TBI, restera longtemps encore le moyen prioritaire en Afrique de règlement des différends relatifs aux investissements directs étrangers.

est assez intéressante à cet égard. L'Article 24 de cette loi dispose: « Tout différend né entre l'investisseur étranger et l'Etat algérien, résultant du fait de l'investisseur ou d'une mesure prise par l'Etat algérien à l'encontre de celui-ci, sera soumis aux juridictions algériennes territorialement compétentes, sauf conventions bilatérales ou multilatérales conclues par l'Etat algérien, relatives à la conciliation et à l'arbitrage ou accord avec l'investisseur stipulant une clause compromissoire permettant aux parties de convenir d'un compromis par arbitrage ad-hoc ». Bien qu'il y ait ici chez le législateur, une volonté de prioriser la soumission du différend d'investissement devant les juridictions algériennes, par rapport à la conciliation et à l'arbitrage dont le recours est conditionné à l'existence du convention bilatérale ou multilatérale ou à une convention d'arbitrage entre les parties, on est moins gêné face à une telle disposition lorsqu'on sait l'important réseau de conventions d'investissement auxquelles est partie l'Etat algérien, et lorsqu'on prend en compte le fait de la quasi systématisation des conventions d'arbitrage à l'occasion des contrats d'investissement. Deux éléments décisifs qui rassurent les investisseurs sur le difficile recours au juge algérien.

137 L'adoption d'une nouvelle législation en matière d'investissement à la faveur du Protection of Investment Act 22 of 2015.

138 Voir Article 4 de la Loi. En effet, déjà à partir des dispositions de l'Article 4, le législateur précise que l'objet de cette loi est de protéger les investissements conformément à la constitution et sous réserve de l'intérêt public, du droit souverain de la République de réglementer et des droits et obligations des investisseurs.

On peut s'arrêter aussi un moment sur l'insistance du législateur sur ce droit de réglementer ce qui constitue d'ailleurs l'essentiel de l'Article 12 de la Loi. Ces différentes dispositions renseignent sur l'orientation nouvelle de la politique sud-africaine en matière d'encadrement des investissements, moins libérale et plus protectionniste au prétexte de la promotion d'un certain patriotisme économique. Cette orientation est confirmée par les dispositions de l'Article 13 qui fait de la médiation (paragraphe 1) la modalité première de résolution des différends relatifs aux investissements ; du recours à juge interne, à un tribunal indépendant ou à un organe statutaire de l'Etat les modalités secondes du règlement du litige et finalement de l'arbitrage la modalité troisième, sous réserve de l'épuisement des voies de recours internes. Il faut d'ailleurs préciser que le législateur sud-africain exclut l'investisseur privé de la procédure arbitrale dans la mesure où il précise encore que ledit arbitrage opposera l'Etat sud-africain à l'État de résidence de l'investisseur concerné.

Il ne semble pas exagéré de conr qu'il s'agit là d'un frein à l'expansion de l'arbitrage au vue de la place qu'occupe l'Afrique du Sud dans l'économie mondiale général, et dans la géographie des investissements directs étrangers en particulier.

12

The Investment Court System proposed by the European Union: what does it mean for Africa?

Stefanie Schacherer

Introduction

Just one day after the annual conference of the African Society of International Law (AfSIL), which took place from 28 to 29 October 2016, the European Union (EU) finally signed – after huge internal political struggles – the Comprehensive Economic Trade Agreement (CETA) with Canada.[1] The CETA is a broad economic agreement between two highly developed economies that goes far beyond existing agreements, setting new standards for international economic relations. Due to the significant economic weight in current global trade and investment relations of the EU and Canada, the agreement has been classified as so-called mega-regional.[2] One of the most prominent features of the CETA is its specific chapter on foreign investment, containing rules on the entry of investments, their protection, as well as a stringent dispute settlement mechanism. With respect to the regulation of international investments, CETA seeks to implement a number of reform proposals. One of its most prominent innovations is the establishment of a permanent Investment

1 The signature was in limbo for almost two weeks because the Belgian region of Wallonia refused to give its consent to the Belgium Federal Government to sign the CETA; for more details see Guillaume Van der Loo, 'CETA's Signature: 38 Statements, a Joint Interpretative Instrument and an Uncertain Future' (31 October 2016) *CEPS* www.ceps.eu/publications/ceta%E2%80%99s-signature-38-ments-joint-interpretative-instrument-and-uncertain-future, accessed 23 April 2017. For the full CETA text, see Comprehensive Economic and Trade Agreement between Canada, of the One Part, and the European Union and Its Member States, of the other Part (signed 30 October 2016, not in force at time of writing) http://trade.ec.europa.eu/doclib/docs/2016/february/tradoc_154329.pdf, accessed 23 April 2017.

2 United Nations Conference on Trade and Development (UNCTAD), *World Investment Report 2014* (hereafter referred to as WIR 2014) 118.

Court System (ICS) for the settlement of investor-State disputes arising under the CETA.

Upon the conclusion of the CETA, the EU and Canada started to gather like-minded countries in order to promote the idea of establishing a multilateral investment court. At the time of writing there is no clear evidence on what such a multilateral investment court would look like, but it seems very likely that the EU proposal builds on the ICS mechanism contained in CETA.[3] The goal of such a new court would be to replace ad hoc investor-State arbitration and also the bilateral ICS mechanisms included in EU agreements.[4] Several meetings of interested countries took already place, such as at the World Investment Forum in Nairobi in July 2016, at the World Trade Organization (WTO) in December 2016,[5] or more recently at the World Economic Forum in January and a stakeholder meeting in Brussels in February 2017.[6] In addition to that, the EU held a public consultation on the idea of a multilateral investment court, the results ofwhich were not yet published at the time of writing.[7] The EU presents its proposal of a multilateral investment court as the solution to the many criticisms made about investor-State arbitration over the last years. The European Commission is convinced that a more court-like system moving away from ad hoc arbitration has the potential to better ensure fairness and impartiality. The EU also considers that the idea of creating a more institutionalized and accountable mechanism for investor-State dispute settlement (ISDS) is gaining increased 'interest and momentum'.[8] There seems to have been for quite some time

3 The CETA contains a binding commitment for the EU and Canada 'to pursue with other trading partners the establishment of a multilateral investment tribunal and appellate mechanism for the resolution of investment disputes', see Article 8.29 of the CETA.

4 European Commission, *A Future Multilateral Investment Court* (Brussels, 13 December 2016) http://europa.eu/rapid/press-release_MEMO-16-4350_en.htm, accessed 24 April 2017.

5 International Institute for Sustainable Development (IISD), 'European Union and Canada Co-Host Discussions on Multilateral Investment Court' *Investment Treaty News* (13 March 2017) www.iisd.org/itn/2017/03/13/news-in-brief-26/, accessed 25 April 2017.

6 Cecilia Malmström, *In Davos, Discussing Investment Disputes* (19 January 2017) https://eaccny.com/news/chapternews/in-davos-discussing-investment-disputes/.

7 The European Commission public consultations on a multilateral reform of investment dispute resolution finished on 15 March 2017, but the assessment thereof was ongoing at the time of writing; for more details, see http://trade.ec.europa.eu/doclib/press/index.cfm?id=1610, accessed 12 April 2017.

8 European Commission and the Government of Canada, *The Case for Creating a Multilateral Investment Dispute Settlement Mechanism* (20 January 2017) http://trade.ec.europa.eu/doclib/docs/2017/january/tradoc_155264.pdf, accessed 12 April 2017.

now no doubt about the 'interest and momentum' for reforming ISDS. This fact has incidentally also been confirmed by the participants of the 2016 AfSIL annual conference. However, agreeing on reform is far different from agreeing on how the reform should actually materialize. From an African perspective, one might question whether the EU proposal is the best way forward in reforming ISDS.

Against this background, the present chapter seeks to stimulate discussion on the EU ICS proposal from the point of view of Africa. It asks to what extent the EU ICS is actually innovative and also what the EU proposal means for Africa and African States. Should it or should it not be followed? Is an African reform approach of more interest and more likely to happen? In order to answer these questions, the ICS shall first be contextualized and analysed in greater detail (Sections 1 and 2). Subsequently, the impacts of the EU proposal for Africa and African countries shall be discussed by looking at the pathways of multilateralism and regionalism (Section 3).

1 The Investment Court System: the origins of a new approach

The rise in the number of costly ISDS cases that touched upon sensitive societal issues of States' regulatory powers in areas such as health, environmental protection and labor standards lead to the still ongoing global backlash against investment arbitration. A case that certainly had a tremendous impact on the awareness and the perception of the public on investment arbitration in Europe was the case *Vattenfall AB* et al. v. *Germany II*,[9] initiated in 2012. Vattenfall, a Swedish energy company brought a case against Germany before the International Centre for Settlement of Investment Disputes (ICSID) for alleged violations of investment protection obligations arising under the Energy Charter Treaty with regard to the decision of the German Parliament to shut down all nuclear power plants in Germany. The case illustrates, on the one hand, that cases are now also brought against States whose companies have been rather on the other side of litigation *in casu* Germany. On the other hand, the *Vattenfall* v. *Germany II* case makes clear once again that democratically adopted decisions that seek to ensure certain societal values, in this case to phase out nuclear energy, can be attacked by foreign companies and might become a costly affair for the State. Consequently, civil society started worry that democratic

9 *Vattenfall AB* et al. v. *Federal Republic of Germany* (July 2020) ICSID Case No. ARB/12/12.

principles could be threatened if international investment tribunals were to overturn democratically enacted laws or important governmental action.[10]

This opposition was further strengthened when in 2013 the negotiations of potentially the biggest mega-regional agreement, the Transatlantic Trade and Investment Partnership (TTIP) between the EU and the United States of America (USA), started. The public interest groups were alarmed that the traditional system of investment arbitration would be included in the TTIP and thus the potential for ISDS cases would multiply. Consequently, during 2014 and 2015, ISDS was one of the most controversial topics with respect to the TTIP negotiations. Civil society groups were collecting signatures against the inclusion of ISDS in the TTIP and regularly organized public protests in major European cities. Therefore, the European Commission organized in 2014 public consultations on ISDS in TTIPs. These consultations received a very high number of answers from various stakeholders, including civil society groups and the private sector. It revealed that the majority of Europeans was not in favour of an investor-State arbitration mechanism in any future agreement concluded by the EU. Once these results were published in January 2015, the European Commission was under political pressure to undertake more significant steps in reforming ISDS.[11] The European Commission subsequently submitted in November 2015 a formal proposal to the US Government on a permanent investment court as a basis for further negotiations in the context of the TTIP.[12] As for the CETA, it is worth underlining that the first consolidated CETA text that was published in September 2014 contained traditional investor-State arbitration. In autumn 2015, the European Commission asked Canada to reopen the negotiations, *inter alia*, on the chapter on investment of the CETA. Canada agreed to include a permanent tribunal to the CETA. The revised treaty text containing a

10 Frank Hoffmeister, 'The Contribution of EU Trade Agreements to the Development of International Investment Law' in Steffen Hindelang and Markus Krajewski (eds), *Shifting Paradigms in International Investment Law – More Balanced, Less Isolated, Increasingly Diversified* (Oxford University Press, 2016) 357–8.

11 European Commission, *Investment in TTIP and Beyond – the Path for Reform. Enhancing the Right to Regulate and Moving from Current ad hoc Arbitration towards an Investment Court* (5 May 2015) http://trade.ec.europa.eu/doclib/docs/2015/may/tradoc_153408.PDF, accessed 25 April 2017.

12 European Commission, text proposal for the investment chapter of the TTIP, first published on 16 September 2015 and subsequently submitted to the US Government on 12 November 2015. The proposal is available at http://trade.ec.europa.eu/doclib/docs/2015/september/tradoc_153807.pdf, accessed 12 April 2017. See also, S. Dumanoir, 'Vers une Renégotiation de l'Accord Economique et Commercial Global (AECG) entre l'Union Européenne et le Canada?' (2016) 596 *Revue de l'Union Européenne* 132–4.

permanent investment tribunal for investor-State disputes was released in February 2016. After Canada, Vietnam also accepted to introduce a permanent investment tribunal in the EU–Vietnam Free Trade Agreement(FTA).[13] The EU is currently also seeking to introduce the ICS into treaty texts that are still under negotiation such as the EU–Japan FTA.[14]

The new approach of the EU of putting into place an ICS might have quietened down some of the opponents to traditional ISDS through arbitration. However, the ongoing opposition also to ICS was illustrated by the refusal of the Belgium region of Wallonia to give its final consent to the Belgium Federal Government to sign the CETA. Under EU law, the CETA is considered as a mixed agreement, which means that not only the EU has to sign and ratify the Agreement, but also all the 28 EU Member States. In order to appease the Government of Wallonia, an intra-Belgium statement, as well as a Joint Interpretive Instrument, was negotiated.[15] EU and Canadian authorities then approved the Joint Interpretive Instrument. The Instrument sets out how certain provisions of the CETA should be interpreted, but does not alter the text of the Agreement. Interestingly for the present context is that the Joint Interpretive Instrument mainly addresses concerns related to the ICS. The main focus is on the right to regulate, stating, *inter alia*, that the EU and Canada will 'continue to have the ability to achieve legitimate policy objectives that their democratic institutions set, such as public health, social services, public education, environment'.[16] The Instrument further confirms the Agreement's provisions on sustainable development, environmental protection and labor rights.[17] Thus, the CETA has been finally signed, but, still, it will have to overcome the hurdle of ratifications,

13 See Chapter 8 'Liberalisation of Investment, Trade in Services and Electronic Commerce', (2016) *EU–Vietnam FTA* Articles 12 *et seq*, http://trade.ec.europa.eu/doclib/press/index.cfm?id=1437, accessed 12 April 2017.

14 At the time of writing, the EU and Japan have not yet found a common ground on ISDS, see European Commission, *Report of the Seventeenth EU–Japan FTA/EPA Negotiating Round*, Brussels, 26–30 September 2016, 4–5 http://trade.ec.europa.eu/doclib/docs/2016/october/tradoc_155060.pdf, accessed 12 April 2017.

15 Van der Loo, 'CETA's Signature: 38 Statements, a Joint Interpretative Instrument and an Uncertain Future' 3.

16 Council of the European Union, Joint Interpretative Instrument on the Comprehensive Economic and Trade Agreement (CETA) between Canada and the European Union and its Member States (27 October 2016). The Instrument is available at: https://eur-lex.europa.eu/legal-content/EN/TXT/?uri=CELEX%3A22017X0114%2801%29, accessed 25 April 2017.

17 *Ibid.*

which means on the EU side the ratifications of 28 EU Member States (involving 38 parliaments).[18]

In sum, it can be said that the ICS was born in a very particular political setting in Europe and in the context of the adoption of very comprehensive economic agreements, such as the TTIP and CETA, both of which are expected to have impacts on the everyday life of European societies.

2 The ICS: main features

This section will present the EU ICS as it has been established in the CETA. Some of the main reform objectives will also be discussed and critically assessed.

(a) Structure and organization of the ICS

The CETA ICS is characterized by a two-tier court mechanism composed of a standing tribunal, as well as an appellate tribunal. The dispute settlement system of the CETA establishes the Tribunal of First Instance (hereafter referred to as the Tribunal) and the Appellate Tribunal.[19] The Tribunal is composed of fifteen permanent Members[20] that are elected by the CETA Joint Committee.[21] Five of these Members are to be nationals of a EU Member State, five are to be nationals of Canada and five are to be nationals of third countries.[22] If revealed to be necessary in the future, the CETA Joint Committee can decide to increase or to decrease the number of Tribunal Members by maintaining the same national proportion.[23] The Members of the Tribunal are appointed for a five-year term, which can be renewed once.[24]

18 Van der Loo, 'CETA's Signature: 38 Statements, a Joint Interpretative Instrument and an Uncertain Future' 4. The United Kingdom has been included in the count.

19 Articles 8.27 and 8.28 of the CETA.

20 In comparison with the EU TTIP proposal, the term 'member' has been chosen for the CETA instead of 'judge' in the TTIP proposal (see Article 9 of the text proposal for the investment chapter of TTIP).

21 The CETA Joint Committee is the main organ of the CETA, comprising representatives of the EU and Canada, see Article 26.1 of the CETA.

22 Article 8.27.2 of the CETA.

23 Article 8.27.3 of the CETA.

24 Article 8.27.5 of the CETA; to ensure a differentiated renewal of the Tribunal, seven of the initial Members of the Tribunal shall exceptionally serve for six years instead.

Cases will be heard in divisions of three Members.[25] The Chairperson of the division has to be a third country national.[26] The assignment of cases to divisions operates in a 'random and unpredictable' manner.[27] Members of the Tribunal shall be available and be able to perform their functions.[28] Furthermore, they shall be paid a retainer fee, the amount of which is yet to be determined by the Joint Committee.[29] The EU and Canada pay equally into an account managed by the Secretariat of the ICSID.[30] For the work performed in relation to a case, the amount of fees and expenses will be determined according to the rules applicable under the ICSID Convention.[31] By decision of the Joint Committee, the retainer fee, other fees and expenses can be transformed into a regular salary, in which case the Members would serve on a full-time and exclusive basis.[32] The Tribunal is organized by a President and a Vice-President that shall be responsible for organizational issues and will be appointed for a two-year term and are to be Members of the Tribunal that are nationals of a third country.[33] In addition, the Tribunal may draw up its own working procedures.[34] Nonetheless, the ICSID Secretariat shall act as secretariat for the Tribunal and provide it with appropriate support.[35] This means that no permanent secretariat or registry is created.[36]

Under the CETA, a permanent Appellate Tribunal is also established, which has appellate jurisdiction over awards issued by the Tribunal.[37] The total number of

25 Article 8.27.6 of the CETA.

26 *Ibid.*

27 Article 8.27.7 of the CETA; the President and the Vice-President of the Tribunal shall appoint the division within ninety days.

28 Article 8.27.11 of the CETA.

29 Article 8.27.12 of the CETA; it is interesting to note that the EU suggested in its proposal to the USA a retainer fee of EUR 2000 per month, see European Commission, text proposal for the investment chapter of the TTIP, Article 9.12.

30 Article 8.27.13 of the CETA.

31 Article 8.27.14 of the CETA. The text refers to Article 14(1) of the Administrative and Financial Regulations of the ICSID .

32 Article 8.27.15 of the CETA.

33 Article 8.27.8 of the CETA.

34 Article 8.27.10 of the CETA.

35 Article 8.27.16 of the CETA.

36 It is interesting to note that the future Centre for the Settlement of Investment Disputes of the Union of South American Nations (UNASUR) will most likely have its own secretariat. See Katia Fach Gomez and Catharine Titi, 'UNASUR Centre for the Settlement of Investment Disputes: Comments on the Draft Constitutive Agreement' *IISD Investment Treaty News* (10 August 2016).

37 Article 8.28.1 of the CETA.

Members of the Appellate Tribunal needs to be determined by the Joint Committee.[38] It is then also the Joint Committee that will appoint the Members of the Appellate Tribunal.[39] Divisions of three Members will hear an appeal.[40] The competences of the Appellate Tribunal is to uphold, modify or reverse a Tribunal's award based on errors in the application or interpretation of applicable law, on manifest error in the appreciation of the facts, including the appreciation of relevant domestic law, and finally on grounds set out in Article 52 of the ICSID Convention.[41] The Appellate Tribunal can also '[refer] issues back to the Tribunal for adjustment of the award'.[42] It is important to underline that administrative and organizational matters regarding the functioning of the Appellate Tribunal are not addressed in the CETA text, but will be decided upon by the Joint Committee later on.[43]

(b) Independence and impartiality[44]

One of the objectives of establishing a permanent tribunal with pre-elected Tribunal Members is to mitigate criticisms that have been made about investment arbitration due to a perceived lack of independence and impartiality of arbitrators.[45] Under the CETA, investors have no say in the determination of the Tribunal Members deciding their claim. This is so with respect to the election process of the Members of the Tribunal and the Appellate Tribunal and with respect to the appointment or assignment of the elected Members to a division deciding a dispute.[46]

38 Article 8.27(f) of the CETA.

39 Article 8.28.3 and 4 of the CETA.

40 Article 8.28.5 of the CETA.

41 Article 8.28.2 of the CETA.

42 Article 8.28.7(b) of the CETA.

43 Article 8.28.7 of the CETA.

44 The two terms 'independence' and 'impartiality' are related, but different, as has been described by the Chairman of ICSID's Administrative Council: 'Impartiality refers to the absence of bias or predisposition towards a party. Independence is characterized by the absence of external control. Independence and impartiality both "protect parties against arbitrators being influenced by factors other than those related to the merits of the case"'. *Abaclat* et al. v. *The Argentine Republic* (4 February 2014) ICSID Case No. ARB/07/5, Decision on the Proposal to Disqualify a Majority of the Tribunal, para. 75.

45 See also Kate Miles, 'Investor-State Dispute Settlement: Conflict, Convergence, and Future Directions' in: Marc Bungenberg *et al.* (eds) *European Yearbook of International Economic Law* (Springer, 2016) 290.

46 For the sake of clarity, the following analysis will only refer to 'Tribunal Members'. This is without prejudice to the fact that some of the aspects will apply *mutatis mutandis* to the Appellate Tribunal, see Article 8.28 of the CETA.

Firstly, the Joint Committee elects the Tribunal Members.[47] Decisions of the Joint Committee are taken on the basis of mutual consent of the contracting parties, Canada and the EU.[48] The fact that the decision is taken by Canada and the EU (i.e. potential respondents in an investment dispute) leads arguably to the appointment of Tribunal Members that could be more sympathetic to the States' positions than to the investors' positions.[49] However, Canada and the EU elect the Tribunal Members before any dispute arises and thus the prediction of a Tribunal Member being more likely to decide in favour of the respondent are of a rather abstract character. In addition, both Canada and the EU have an interest in also electing Tribunal Members that are sympathetic to the investors' interests, since it will potentially be one of their investors acting as claimant in a dispute before the Tribunal.

The idea that investors should have a say in the election process through business organizations could be interesting.[50] Yet, since the beginning of ICSID, it has never been controversial that the ICSID Convention entitles each Member State to designate up to four persons to the Panel of Arbitrators and up to four persons to the Panel of Conciliators without business having a say.[51] A pre-designation of arbitrators by States is thus not a new practice. More significant is that in order to ensure objectivity and to foster the legitimacy of the selection, it seems to be more important that the election procedure is transparent and susceptible to being clearly monitored by all stakeholders.[52]

47 Members of the Appellate Tribunal will be elected by the Joint Committee after the entry into force of the CETA, Article 8.28.3 of the CETA.

48 Article 26.3 of the CETA.

49 European Federation for Investment Law and Arbitration, *Task Force Paper regarding the Proposed International Court System (ICS)* (1 January 2016) http://efila.org/wp-content/uploads/2016/02/EFILA_TASK_FORCE_on_ICS_proposal_1-2-2016.pdf, accessed 12 April 2017 15.

50 Kaufmann-Kohler and Potestà generally favor the idea of business having a say in the selection process. See, Gabrielle Kaufmann-Kohler and Michele Potestà, 'Can the Mauritius Convention serve as a Model for the Reform of Investor-State Arbitration in Connection with the Introduction of a Permanent Investment Tribunal or an Appeal Mechanism? Analysis and Roadmap' *CIDS – Geneva Center for International Dispute Settlement* (3 June 2016) www.uncitral.org/pdf/english/commissionsessions/unc/unc-49/CIDS_Research_Paper_-_Can_the_Mauritius__serve_as_a_model.pdf, accessed 25 April 2017 61.

51 Articles 12 and 16 of the ICSID .

52 Gabrielle Kaufmann-Kohler and Michele Potestà, 'Can the Mauritius Convention serve as a Model for the Reform of Investor-State Arbitration in Connection with the Introduction of a Permanent Investment Tribunal or an Appeal Mechanism? Analysis and Roadmap' 60.

Secondly, in the event of an investor's claim, it is the competence of the President of the Tribunal to assign cases to the Members on a rotation basis, ensuring that the composition of a division is random and unpredictable, while giving equal opportunity to all Tribunal Members to serve.[53] The introduction of a method based on an objective rotation seems to better ensure that there is no direct link between the Tribunal Members and the disputing parties, as well as that there is no direct link between them and the specific issues of the case. It is more suitable to clearing suspicions of bias than it used to be under the case-by-case appointment by the disputing parties in traditional investment arbitration. Interestingly, the CETA sticks to the traditional number of three adjudicators sitting in a division, which has been the standard number in investment arbitration.[54] One might question why this has been maintained, since most international courts decide in larger compositions.[55] A higher number of adjudicators with respect to the CETA Tribunal might have enhanced the legitimacy and the credibility of its decisions.[56]

A further interesting aspect regarding the CETA Tribunal is the nationality of the individuals who will compose the division hearing a case. The division of three Tribunal Members is composed of one national of the EU and one of Canada, and the Chairperson is a national of a third country. This constellation means that one person in a division is from the respondent State – a circumstance that can raise suspicions as to the impartiality and independence of this person. Under the DSU of the WTO, for instance, a Panel Member cannot be a national of the disputing States unless otherwise decided by the disputing parties.[57] Under the Statute of the ICJ, in

53 Article 8.27.7 of the CETA.

54 Three arbitrators being the default rule under Article 37.2(b) of the ICSID .

55 The International Court of Justice (ICJ) is composed of fifteen to seventeen judges (Articles 3.1 and 31.3 of the Statute of the ICJ). The European Court of Human Rights is composed of chambers of seven to seventeen judges (Article 26 of the European on Human Rights).
The Court of Justice of the EU is composed of chambers of three, five or fifteen judges (Article 16 of the Statute of the Court of Justice of the EU, and Article 60 of the Rules of Procedure of the Court. The Appellate Body of the WTO is composed of seven members and sits in formations of three (Article 17 of the Dispute Settlement Understanding (DSU) and Rule 4 of the Working Procedures for Appellate Review.

56 For a more detailed discussion on the appropriate number of judges/arbitrators, see Gabrielle Kaufmann-Kohler and Michele Potestà, 'Can the Mauritius Convention serve as a Model for the Reform of Investor-State Arbitration in Connection with the Introduction of a Permanent Investment Tribunal or an Appeal Mechanism? Analysis and Roadmap' 64–5.

57 Article 8.3 of the WTO DSU.

theory it is possible that nationals of the disputing parties sit on the Bench of the ICJ and a State party to a case, which does not have a judge of its nationality on the Bench, may choose a person to sit as judge ad hoc in that specific case.[58] However, the influence of the national judges in proceedings before the ICJ is largely relativized, taking into account that fifteen to seventeen judges decide the case. In an investment dispute under the CETA, the division is composed of only three adjudicators and thus the influence of the nationality of the respondent State might be much higher. In addition, the national of the home State of the investor can also be perceived as being biased in favor of the investor of its country. It occurs that only the Chairperson of the division, who is a third country national, can be perceived as fully neutral. One might question whether this tendency to concentrate a significant amount of power in one individual is a desirable situation and also it brings the ICS back into the same difficulty, yet to a lesser extent than investment arbitration, resulting in a process with potentially one 'pro-investor' adjudicator and one 'pro-State' adjudicator.[59]

A further issue that has received a lot of attention in the debate on independence and impartiality is the interplay of roles or the 'changing of hats', the situation in which an individual acts both as counsel and arbitrator in different proceedings.[60] The CETA addresses this issue, thus responding to one of the major public and doctrinal concerns.[61] The CETA contains an exclusion for Tribunal Members to act as counsel or as party-appointed expert or witness in any pending or new investment

58 Article 31.2 and 31.3 of the Statute of the ICJ.

59 On the special role of the presiding arbitrator, see International Council for Commercial Arbitration (ICCA), *Report of the ASIL-ICCA Joint Task Force on Issue Conflicts in Investor-State Arbitration. The ICCA Reports No. 3* (17 March 2016) www.arbitration-icca.org/media/6/81372711507986/asil-icca_report_final_5_april_final_for_ridderprint.pdf, accessed 12 April 2017 13.

60 Philippe Sands, 'Conflict of Interests for Arbitrators and/or Counsel' in: Meg Kinnear *et al.* (eds) *Building International Investment Law – The First 50 Years of ICSID* (Alphen aan den Rijn: Kluwer Law International, 2016) 655.

61 European Commission, *Online Public Consultation on Investment Protection and Investor-to-State Dispute Settlement (ISDS) in the Transatlantic Trade and Investment Partnership Agreement (TTIP)* (13 January 2015) http://trade.ec.europa.eu/doclib/docs/2015/january/tradoc_153044.pdf, accessed 12 April 2017 103. See also, August Reinisch and Christina Knahr, 'Conflict of Interests in International Investment Arbitration' in Anne Peters and Lucas Handschin (eds), *Conflict of Interest in Global, Public and Corporate Governance* (Cambridge University Press, 2012) 103; ICCA, *Report of the ASIL-ICCA Joint Task Force on Issue Conflicts in Investor-State Arbitration.*

dispute under CETA or any other international agreement.[62] This new restriction is a positive development, since situations where the '*dédoublement fonctionnel*' of an individual as an adjudicator in one case and as counsel (or expert or witness) in another case can give rise to a perception of bias, in the sense that his or her role in one case might be perceived to inform actions in the other case.[63]

Furthermore, the CETA foresees a number of qualifications and ethical requirements that apply to the Tribunal Members.[64] They shall have the qualifications required in their respective countries for appointment to judicial office, or have to be jurists of recognized competence.[65] In particular, they have to demonstrate expertise in public international law.[66] The express reference to public international law has been welcomed, since it underlines the fundamental character of investment treaties as inter-State agreements.[67] Tribunal Members have to be independent and shall not be affiliated with any government nor shall they take instructions from any organization or government.[68] In order not to be seen to be affiliated to any institution or State, Tribunal Members should disclose all relevant information.[69] Moreover, the CETA expressly opts-in to the International Bar Association (IBA) Guidelines on Conflicts of Interest in International Arbitration.[70] It is worth highlighting that the CETA does not yet contain a code of conduct for the Tribunal Members.[71] Such a

62 Article 8.30.1 of the CETA.

63 Philippe Sands, 'Conflict of Interests for Arbitrators and/or Counsel' 655–6; Sands refers to such a situation as 'role confusion'.

64 The same requirements will apply to the Members of the Appellate Tribunal (Article 8.28.4 of the CETA).

65 Article 8.27.4 of the CETA.

66 Article 8.27.4 of the CETA; it is also desirable that Members of the Tribunal have expertise in international investment law, in international trade law and the respective dispute resolution.

67 Ingo Venzke, 'Investor-State Dispute Settlement in TTIP from the Perspective of a Public Law Theory of International Adjudication' (2016) 17 *The Journal of World Investment & Trade* 393–4.

68 Article 8.30.1 of the CETA.

69 Rules on the duty of disclosure can be found in all arbitral rules, Article 6 of the ICSID Arbitration Rules (2006), Article 11 of the United Nations Commission on International Trade Law (UNCITRAL) Arbitration Rules (2010).

70 IBA, *IBA Guidelines on Conflicts of Interests in International Arbitration* (23 October 2014) www.ibanet.org/Publications/publications_IBA_guides_and_free_materials.aspx, accessed 12 April 2017.

71 Article 8.44.2, last paragraph, of the CETA: 'The Parties shall make best efforts to ensure that the code of conduct is adopted no later than the first day of the provisional application or entry into force of this Agreement, as the case may be, and in any event no later than two years after such date'.

code could further set out rules on the duty of disclosure, on duties of fairness and diligence, and the duties to avoid creating appearances of bias or to be guided by personal interests.[72] In the Joint Interpretative Instrument that was pushed for by the Belgium region of Wallonia, the EU and Canada have agreed 'to begin immediately further work on a code of conduct to further ensure the impartiality of the members of the Tribunal,' the code had to be finalized before the entry into force of the CETA.[73]

If there remain issues relating to the behaviour or relations of a Tribunal Member, either the President of the Tribunal or the Joint Committee can remove the Tribunal Member if his or her behaviour is inconsistent with his or her obligations and incompatible with his or her continued membership.[74] In addition, challenges by the disputing parties to Tribunal Members sitting in a case division are possible under CETA.[75] In the event that a disputing party considers that a Tribunal Member sitting in a division hearing the case has a conflict of interest, the disputing party shall send to the President of the ICJ a notice of challenge to the appointment and if after 15 days the appointed Tribunal Member does not resign from the division, the President of the ICJ shall issue a decision within 45 days after having considered the submissions of the parties.[76] Given that the CETA has pre-selected Tribunal Members randomly assigned to cases, it might lead to the outcome that challenges are less likely. Moreover, the rather strict rules on the 'ethics' of Tribunal Members gives some cause for hope to further prevent the issue of conflicts and thus prevent challenge proceedings.[77] However, this still needs to be seen in practice since the outcomes of challenge cases are indeed 'highly fact-dependent'.[78]

72 See European Commission, text proposal for the investment chapter of the TTIP, Annex II, 'Code of Conduct for Members of the Tribunal, the Appeal Tribunal and Mediators'.
73 EU–Canada Joint Interpretative Instrument, Part 6(f).
74 Article 8.30.4 of the CETA.
75 Article 8.30.2 and 8.30.3 of the CETA.
76 *Ibid.*
77 Ingo Venzke, 'Investor-State Dispute Settlement in TTIP from the Perspective of a Public Law Theory of International Adjudication' 394.
78 ICCA, *Report of the ASIL-ICCA Joint Task Force on Issue Conflicts in Investor-State Arbitration* 64–5, para. 183. The ICCA Task Force is of the view that hard rules would be unlikely to be fruitful.

As a last point, the remuneration of the Tribunal Members should also be discussed, since it is a further aspect that affects their independence and impartiality.[79] With regard to the Tribunal Members, they receive a monthly retainer fee that still needs to be determined.[80] The rules under the ICSID Convention apply in order to determine the amount of fees and expenses a Tribunal Member receives for sitting in a division.[81] It has been argued that the mechanism of case-related remuneration maintains the financial interest of Tribunal Members in future claims.[82] Yet, given that Tribunal Members are randomly assigned to cases on a rotating basis means that they cannot influence being appointed more often. Arguably they could be interested in having a huge number of cases so that the rotation goes in quicker circles. However, if the caseload increases, the Joint Committee might likely put to use its mandate to transform the retainer fee and other fees and expenses into a regular salary.[83] Yet, a fixed salary would be preferable, since in this way Tribunal Members would not have a financial interest in a high number of cases and they would have no financial incentives to have long proceedings.[84] Such incentives can again potentially call into question the independence and impartiality of the Tribunal Members.[85]

Taking all these elements into account, it can be concluded that the ICS remedies some of the concerns regarding conflicts and might thus avoid challenges to Tribunal Members. ICS also addresses some of the concerns raised regarding the need for institutional safeguards that mitigate the perceived lack of independence and impartiality of adjudicators in investor-State disputes.

79 Gus van Harten, 'The European Commission and UNCTAD Reform Agendas: Do They Ensure Independence, Openness, and Fairness in Investor-State Arbitration?' in Steffen Hindelang and Markus Krajewski (eds) *Shifting Paradigms in International Investment Law: More Balanced, Less Isolated, Increasingly Diversified* (Oxford University Press, 2016) 129.

80 The remuneration of the Members of the Appellate Tribunal has to be determined completely (Article 8.28.7(f) of the CETA).

81 Article 8.27.14, referring to Regulation 14.1 of the Administrative and Financial Regulations of the ICSID .

82 Gus Van Harten, 'Key Flaws in the European Commission's Proposal for Foreign Investor Protection in TTIP' (2016) *Osgoode Legal Studies Research Paper Series*.

83 Article 8.27.15 of the CETA.

84 Ingo Venzke, 'Investor-State Dispute Settlement in TTIP from the Perspective of a Public Law Theory of International Adjudication' 394.

85 *Ibid.*

(c) Consistent awards

The EU picked up the idea of an appeal mechanism, which has been discussed by legal scholars for quite some time. The EU seeks to better ensure consistent outcomes, to make dispute settlement more predictable for States and investors, and to render it therefore more legitimate.[86] The CETA introduces a possibility for appeal through the so-called Appellate Tribunal, which is inspired largely by the institutional setup of the Appellate Body of the WTO, with some adaptations to make it specific to ISDS.[87]

The CETA Appellate Tribunal has jurisdiction to review awards rendered by the Tribunal.[88] The scope of jurisdiction is to uphold, modify or reverse a Tribunal's award based on three different grounds.[89] First, the award can be appealed for errors in the application or interpretation of applicable law. Second, an award can be appealed on manifest errors in the appreciation of the facts, including the appreciation of relevant domestic law. Under the CETA, appeals are possible on issues of fact. It is worth noting that the Appellate Body of the WTO is in principle restrained to reviewing questions of law.[90] However, in a few cases the Appellate Body also reviewed the facts where a panel failed to objectively assess the facts.[91] For both grounds, it is not explicitly stated in the CETA text, whether the Appellate Tribunal reviews these issues *de novo* or whether it has to accord some degree of deference to the findings of the Tribunal.[92] The reference to 'manifest' errors regarding the appreciation of the facts, suggests that the Appellate Tribunal should accord some deference to the factual assessment of the Tribunal. As a third category of ground of appeal, the CETA

86 European Commission, *Investment in TTIP and Beyond – the Path for Reform. Enhancing the Right to Regulate and Moving from Current ad hoc Arbitration towards an Investment Court* 8.

87 *Ibid.* 9.

88 Article 8.28.1 and 8.28.2 of the CETA.

89 Article 8.28.2 of the CETA.

90 Article 17.6 of the WTO DSU.

91 Article 11 of the WTO DSU. See *European Communities — Measures Affecting Importation of Certain Poultry Products*, WT/DS69/AB/R, para. 133; *European Communities — Measures Concerning Meat and Meat Products (Hormones)*, WT/DS26/AB/R (WT/DS48/AB/R) para. 133; *Australia — Measures Affecting Importation of Salmon*, WT/DS18/AB/R.

92 For a definition of the standard of review and its distinction from grounds for review and method of review, see Caroline Henckels, *Proportionality and Deference in Investor-State Arbitration: Balancing Investment Protection and Regulatory Autonomy* (Cambridge University Press, 2015) 29–34. See also Jan Bohanes and Nicolas Lockhart, 'Standard of Review in WTO Law' in Daniel Bethlehem *et al.* (eds) *The Oxford Handbook of International Trade Law* (Oxford University Press, 2009) 378–436.

text explicitly refers to the grounds for annulment under the ICSID Convention, that is, the Tribunal was not properly constituted, the Tribunal has manifestly exceeded its powers, there was corruption on the part of the Tribunal Members, there was serious departure from fundamental rules of procedure or the award failed to state the reasons on which it was based.[93]

At this stage, it is difficult to know whether the CETA Appellate Tribunal will lead to a more consistent and coherent jurisprudence. An aspect of the ICS as a whole, which in principle should better ensure consistency, is the fact that under the CETA a group of the same adjudicators will decide the cases.[94] This has been referred to as 'personal and institutional continuity', which is generally beneficial for more consistency in case law.[95] As mentioned above, Tribunal Members will serve five years, which already allows in the first instance more personal continuity.[96] It might be reasonable to have a longer period for the Appellate Tribunal Members in order to further emphasise personal and institutional continuity.

Linked to the question of consistency is the question of precedent. Interestingly, the CETA text does not specifically provide that the decisions of the CETA Appellate Tribunal would have the force of binding precedent or *stare decisis* on subsequent awards rendered by the Tribunal.[97] Whether a clear rule of precedent would have been preferable in the context of the CETA Appellate Tribunal can be discussed. It is true that judges of other permanent international courts and tribunals usually stick more or less to precedent for the purpose of legal certainty.[98] For instance, neither the ICJ nor the Appellate Body of the WTO have a rule on *stare decisis*[99] but both repeatedly referred to their precedent in their respective case law.[100]

93 Article 8.28.2(c) of the CETA; Article 52 of the ICSID .

94 Christian J. Tams, 'An Appealing Option? The Debate About an ICSID Appellate Structure' (2006) 57 *Essays in Transnational Economic Law Working Paper* 26.

95 *Ibid.*

96 The number of years that an Appellate Tribunal Member will serve is not yet definitely fixed (Article 8.28.7(f) of the CETA).

97 Article 8.41.1 of the CETA. As for awards of the first Tribunal, decisions of the Appellate Tribunal are binding between the parties, but have no third party effect.

98 Gilbert Guillaume, 'The Use of Precedent by International Judges and Arbitrators' (2011) 2 (1) *Journal of International Dispute Settlement* 5–23.

99 Article 59 of the Statute of the ICJ; Article 3.2 of the WTO DSU.

100 For an overview of ICJ cases on precedent, see Gilbert Guillaume, 'The Use of Precedent by International Judges and Arbitrators' 7–13; for the Appellate Body of the WTO, see 'Japan — Taxes on Alcoholic Beverages' (4 October 1996) *WTO Appellate Body Report* 13, 'United States — Final Anti-Dumping Measures on Stainless Steel from Mexico' (30 April 2008) *WTO Appellate Body Report*, para. 160. Consider that seven ICJ judges

Despite the criticism on inconsistent awards in investment arbitration, it is fair to say that tribunals relied many times on previous cases in their decision-making.[101] A certain 'persuasive precedent' occurred based on the idea that a well-established line of cases should be followed.[102] While acknowledging that ISDS through arbitration established a certain level of *jurisprudence constante,* the CETA Appellate Tribunal has the potential to better guarantee that a truly CETA *jurisprudence* will be developed. Furthermore, the decisions of the CETA Appellate Tribunal are likely to have a quasi *stare decisis* effect, since it can be assumed that each time the Tribunal is not following previous decisions of the Appellate Tribunal, the losing party will immediately appeal against the award and the award then has good chances of being overturned by the Appellate Tribunal.[103]

Nevertheless, noteworthy is the fact that the CETA contracting parties do not intend to confer any 'law-making' function. This is underlined by that fact that the CETA contracting parties retain some control over the interpretations of the CETA provisions, since the Joint Committee can issue binding interpretative notes, which would of course also bind the Appellate Tribunal.[104]

The benefits of an appeal mechanism under the CETA also has its drawbacks. The biggest drawback is certainly that the possibility for appeal adds costs and time to an already highly cost- and time-intensive dispute settlement. In order to tighten up the process, the CETA provides that the appeal decision has to be taken within

made it very clear by stating that the ICJ 'must ensure consistency with its own past case law in order to provide predictability' and adding '[c]onsistency is the essence of judicial reasoning', see Joint Declaration of Vice-President Ranjeva, Judges Guillaume, Higgins, Kooijmans, Al-Khasawneh, Buergenthal and Elaraby, *Legality of Use of Force (Serbia and Montenegro* v. *Portugal)* (2004) Preliminary Objections, Judgment, *ICJ Reports* 1160, 1208, para. 3; see also R. Bernhardt, 'Article 59' in Andreas Zimmermann *et al.* (eds) *The Statute of the International Court of Justice: A Commentary* (Oxford Commentaries on International Law, 2019) 1244, Article 59, MN 48.

101 Andrea Bjorklund, 'Investment Treaty Arbitral Decisions as Jurisprudence Constante' in Colin Picker, Isabella D. Bunn and Douglas Arner (eds) *International Economic Law: the State and Future of the Discipline* (Hart Publishing, 2008) 265.

102 Christian J. Tams, 'An Appealing Option? The Debate About an ICSID Appellate Structure' (2006) 57 *Essays in Transnational Economic Law Working Paper* 19; see *El Paso Energy International Company* v. *The Argentine Republic*, ICSID Case No. ARB/03/15, para. 39; *Saipem S.p.A.* v. *The People's Republic of Bangladesh,* Decision on Jurisdiction and Recommendation on Provisional Measures, (21 March 2007) ICSID Case No. ARB/05/07, para. 67.

103 Christian J. Tams, 'An Appealing Option? The Debate About an ICSID Appellate Structure' (2006) 57 *Essays in Transnational Economic Law Working Paper* 24.

104 Article 8.31.2 of the CETA.

90 days after issuance of the award.[105] Likewise, the Appellate Body of the WTO provides for an expedited appellate process that normally takes 60 to 90 days.[106] It is argued that appeals would become the rule, since a losing party might always have the hope of convincing the Appellate Tribunal of the soundness of its arguments.[107] However, as decisions become more consistent, the Appellate Tribunal could have the effect that there will be fewer revisions instead of more, since the content of the norms crystallizes and thus the chance to win or lose becomes more predictable for the disputing parties.

With respect to the CETA Appellate Tribunal, it can be held that these drawbacks are outweighed by the achievement of consistency and predictability, which, in turn, correlate with the important considerations of trust and legitimacy that the EU seeks to gain among all stakeholders.[108]

(d) Improved procedural aspects under the ICS

As has been pointed out in the previous section, the CETA's ICS constitutes to some extent a 'break with the past'.[109] However, when analysing the procedure more closely, it becomes also clear that many of the ICS procedural aspects are still similar to those of traditional investment arbitration.[110] This becomes evident when considering that proceedings under the ICS are governed by arbitration rules, spanning from the UNCITRAL Arbitration Rules to the ICSID Convention and Additional

105 Article 8.28.9(a) of the CETA.

106 Article 17.5 of the WTO DSU.

107 Gabrielle Kaufmann-Kohler and Michele Potestà, 'Can the Mauritius Convention serve as a Model for the Reform of Investor-State Arbitration in Connection with the Introduction of a Permanent Investment Tribunal or an Appeal Mechanism? Analysis and Roadmap' 48.

108 European Commission, *Investment in TTIP and Beyond – the Path for Reform. Enhancing the Right to Regulate and Moving from Current ad hoc Arbitration towards an Investment Court* 8.

109 European Commission, *Investment Provisions in the EU-Canada Free Trade Agreement (CETA)* (February 2016) http://trade.ec.europa.eu/doclib/docs/2013/november/tradoc_151918.pdf, accessed 25 April 2017.

110 For a discussion on the hybrid form of the ICS and its implications for the enforcement of the awards, see August Reinisch, 'Will the EU's Proposal Concerning an Investment Court System for CETA and TTIP Lead to Enforceable Awards? — The Limits of Modifying the ICSID and the Nature of Investment Arbitration' (2016) 19 (4) *Journal of International Economic Law* 761.

Facility Rules to any other rules agreed upon by the disputing parties.[111] For the enforcement of the award, the ICS relies on existing rules on enforcement of arbitral awards contained in the ICSID and the New York Arbitration Convention on the Recognition and Enforcement of Foreign Arbitral Awards.[112] Moreover, the ICS allows for direct access to the international fora for the investor without requiring the exhaustion of local remedies.

Yet, the EU claims that, in order to optimize the procedure, the ICS implements many proposals that have been made in the ongoing discussion on global reform.[113] They seek on the one hand to render the proceedings less time- and cost-intensive (Section 2(d)(i)); and on the other hand to ensure full transparency of the proceedings (Section 2(d)(ii)).

(i) Avoiding time- and cost-intensive proceedings

In order to reduce the number of potential cases, the CETA limits the scope of disputes covered by the relevant ISDS.[114] The CETA also seeks to dismiss unfounded claims and claims outside the Tribunal's jurisdiction through an expedited process for review. The CETA indicates the obligation for the Tribunal to address the issue at its first session or promptly thereafter.[115] Moreover, under the CETA, proceedings for the same dispute in different fora shall be avoided through a 'no-U-turn' clause.[116] The 'no-U-turn' categorization is relatively new and used in particular by the EU.[117] The provision stipulates that once the investor has opted for the respective ISDS under the CETA, it cannot go back to domestic courts or any other dispute settlement procedure.[118]

A very interesting feature of the CETA is the introduction of the 'loser pays principle'. This principle means that the disputing party who loses has to pay all the

111 Article 8.23.2 of the CETA.

112 Article 8.41.3–4 of the CETA.

113 UNCTAD, *World Investment Report 2015* (WIR 2015) http://unctad.org/en/PublicationsLibrary/wir2015_en.pdf 147–9.

114 Article 8.18 of the CETA. See also UNCTAD, *World Investment Report 2016* (WIR 2016) https://unctad.org/en/PublicationsLibrary/wir2016_en.pdf 113. The majority of the bilateral investment treaties (BITs) concluded in 2015 contain limitations to the scope of disputes.

115 Articles 8.32 and 8.33 of the CETA.

116 UNCTAD, WIR 2015, 86–90.

117 Article 8.18 of the CETA.

118 Article 8.22.1(f) and (g) of the CETA.

costs of the legal proceedings, including the litigation cost of the other disputing party.[119] A provision on how the Tribunal has to allocate the costs of proceeding is not common in arbitration. All of the arbitral rules leave discretion to the tribunals on the decision on the allocation of costs.[120] The ICSID Convention for instance provides that unless the parties agree otherwise, the tribunal should assess the expenses incurred by the parties in connection with the proceeding and should decide how and by whom these expenses and the costs of the arbitration should be paid.[121] Since arbitral rules give no further guidance as to how to allocate costs there has been no uniform approach in investment arbitration.[122] Taking a new approach, the CETA makes the 'loser pays principle' the default rule. Yet, the CETA Tribunal retains some power as to the allocation of costs since it can 'in exceptional circumstances, apportion the costs between the disputing parties if it determines it appropriate in the light of the claim'.[123]

Finally, the CETA defines the types of remedies a tribunal may accord; these are monetary compensation and restitution of property.[124] Yet, it does not provide further guidance on interpretation of the calculation of compensation.

(ii) Transparency

The lack of transparency of the proceedings has been among the first criticisms raised against investment arbitration.[125] First steps had been taken by the North American Free Trade Agreement (NAFTA) Free Trade Commission in 2001, clarifying that there was no general duty of confidentiality in investment arbitration under the NAFTA.[126] The amendment of the ICSID Arbitration Rules in 2006 was

119 Article 8.39.5 of the CETA.

120 Articles 59–61 of the ICSID; Article 42 of the UNCITRAL Arbitration Rules (2010); Article 37 of the International Chamber of Commerce (ICC) Arbitration Rules (2012); and Article 44 of the Stockholm Chamber of Commerce (SCC) Arbitration Rules (2012 version).

121 Article 61.2 of the ICSID .

122 Christoph H. Schreuer, *et al.*, *The ICSID – A Commentary (2nd edition)* (Cambridge University Press, 2009) 1228–35.

123 Article 8.39.5 of the CETA.

124 Article 8.39.1 of the CETA.

125 Loretta Malintoppi and Natalie Limbasan, 'Living in Glass Houses? The Debate on Transparency in International Investment Arbitration' (2015) 2 (1) *BCDR International Arbitration Review* 31.

126 NAFTA Free Trade Commission, *Notes of Interpretation of Certain Chapter 11 Provisions* (31 July 2001) www.sice.oas.org/tpd/nafta/Commission/CH11understanding_e.asp, accessed 25 April 2017.

a further important step towards more transparency in investment arbitration.[127] Afterwards, the USA and Canada incorporated provisions on transparency in their model BITs.[128] From then on, transparency provisions have been included into almost all treaties.[129] The current most progressive global action towards more transparency are the UNCITRAL Rules on Transparency in Treaty-based Investor-State Arbitration,[130] as well as the related United Nations Convention on Transparency in Treaty-based Investor-State Arbitration, referred to as the Mauritius Convention.[131] CETA perfectly reflects the global trend towards more transparency. The CETA expressly opts-in the UNCITRAL Rules on Transparency for all the proceedings before the Tribunal and the Appellate Tribunal, which means also for proceedings, governed by the ICSID Arbitration Rules.[132]

First, the CETA sets out rules to make available to the public any document related to the proceedings. The CETA contains the same requirements as the UNCITRAL Transparency Rules but additionally requires the agreement to mediate to be publicly available.[133] CETA also adds exhibits to the documents that can be requested by any person to the Tribunal.[134] The CETA contains a slight derogation from the UNCITRAL Transparency Rules, as to who has to publish the relevant document prior to the constitution of the Tribunal, which is not the registry but the respondent State.[135]

Second, under the CETA, hearings are to be public.[136] Interestingly, the CETA again goes a step further than the UNCITRAL Transparency Rules, since the disputing parties cannot be opposed to having the hearing in public. In fact, the parties or the

127 Rule 37.2 of the ICSID Arbitration Rules (2006).

128 Loretta Malintoppi and Natalie Limbasan, 'Living in Glass Houses? The Debate on Transparency in International Investment Arbitration' 38–40.

129 UNCTAD, *Transparency* (UNCTAD, 2012) 37.

130 UNCITRAL, *Rules on Transparency in Treaty-based Investor-State Arbitration* (2014) www.uncitral.org/pdf/english/texts/arbitration/rules-on-transparency/Rules-on-Transparency-E.pdf.

131 The United Nations Convention on Transparency in Treaty-based Investor-State Arbitration was adopted on 10 December 2014 and opened for signature on 17 March 2015 (United Nations, United Nations Convention on Transparency in Treaty-based Investor-State Arbitration, General Assembly, sixty ninth session, A/69/116, 18 December 2014.

132 Article 8. 36.1 of the CETA.

133 Article 8.36.2 of the CETA; Article 3.1 of the UNCITRAL Transparency Rules.

134 Article 8.36.3 of the CETA; Article 3.2 of the UNCITRAL Transparency Rules.

135 Article 8.36.4 of the CETA; Article 2 of the UNCITRAL Transparency Rules.

136 Article 8.36.5 of the CETA.

Tribunal cannot decide that it would be for any reason unfeasible to hold the hearings in public.[137] The Tribunal only has the power to consult with the disputing parties in order to consult on the appropriate logistical arrangements.

Third, the CETA allows for *amicus curie* briefs after consultation with the disputing parties.[138] The CETA applies in this respect the UNCITRAL Rules on Transparency without amending them. The ICSID Convention provides that the Tribunal, after consulting with the parties, may allow a non-disputing party to file a written submission within the scope of the dispute.[139] Likewise, the CETA Tribunal takes into account a number of elements in deciding the relevance of an *amicus curie* brief. Such elements are whether the third person has a significant interest in the proceedings and whether the third person's submission would assist the Tribunal in the determination of a matter of fact or law within the scope of the dispute.[140] The allowing for *amicus curie* briefs underline that this has become a firmly accepted element of investor-State disputes.[141]

With respect to the process under the ICS, it can be summarized that the EU introduced a couple of refinements and improvements. In particular, the CETA provides for a high degree of transparency and for an early discharge of frivolous and manifestly unmeritorious claims. Yet, many procedural aspects are not court-like, but remain arbitration-like.

3 The ICS: what does it mean for Africa?

After having highlighted the main features and the claimed innovations of the ICS, this last section shall ask what this new approach to ISDS means for Africa and African States. The answer to this question is certainly not easy or straightforward. In order to attempt to tackle the question, the scenarios of multilateralism and enhanced regionalism in international investment law shall be discussed.

137 Article 6 of the UNCITRAL Transparency Rules, in particular para. 3 thereof.

138 Article 4.1 of the UNCITRAL Transparency Rules by reference of Article 8.36.1 of the CETA.

139 Rule 37.2 of the ICSID Arbitration Rules (2006); See also Article 4.1 of the UNCITRAL Transparency Rules.

140 Article 4.3 of the UNCITRAL Transparency Rules.

141 M Zachariasiewicz, 'Amicus Curiae in International Investment Arbitration: Can It Enhance the Transparency of Investment Dispute Resolution?' (2012) 29 (2) *Journal of International Arbitration* 221.

(a) The Multilateral pathway to reforming ISDS

Until today, international investment law has been predominantly enshrined in BITs, which count currently over 3 200. It all started with the very first BIT concluded in 1959 between Germany and Pakistan, which then was followed by a wave of BITs being adopted. The vivid adoption phase of BITs was predated by various efforts to find a multilateral consensus on an international agreement on the protection of investment, including a dispute settlement mechanism.[142] Since they have ultimately all failed, the system that developed was based on bilateralism. Without going into too much detail, it shall be recalled that the very first attempts to establish multilateral rules on investment protection have been made in the context of the negotiations for an International Trade Organization (ITO) from 1945 to 1948. The final text of the so-called Havana Charter did not contain substantive investment protection provisions because no consensus could be found. Yet the Havana Charter and the ITO ultimately failed, which has been said to be the first shift away from multilateralism within the international investment law regime.[143]

In the years after, the Director-General of the Deutsche Bank, Mr Hermann Abs argued for a multilateral treaty. He first helped to elaborate a draft code titled the 'International Convention for the Mutual Protection of Private Property Rights in Foreign Countries' in 1957. It is interesting to note that this instrument suggested the establishment of a permanent arbitration tribunal, yet the details of which would have had to be set out in a separate instrument.[144] The draft convention received little attention,[145] which then led to the more famous 'Abs-Shawcross Draft Convention on Investments Abroad' elaborated by Mr Abs and Lord Shawcross published in 1959. The Abs-Shawcross Draft Convention consisted of ten articles and an annex, which provided for the establishment of an arbitral tribunal.[146] However,

142 Chester Brown, 'International Investment Agreements – History, Approaches, Schools' in Marc Bungenberg *et al.* (eds) *International Investment Law – A Handbook* (C.H. Beck/Hart/Nomos, 2015) 153–185, 154.

143 Jürgen Kurtz, *The WTO and International Investment Law – Converging Systems* (Cambridge University Press, 2016) 41.

144 Rudolf Dolzer and Christoph Schreuer, *Principles of International Investment Law (2nd edn)* (Oxford University Press, 2012) 8.

145 Chester Brown, 'International Investment Agreements – History, Approaches, Schools' 162–3.

146 Chester Brown, 'International Investment Agreements – History, Approaches, Schools' 163.

this draft also did not garner sufficient support to serve as a basis for a multilateral treaty. In the early 1960s, two further instruments sought to provide a basis for a multilateral agreement on investment protection. First, the 1961 'Harvard Draft Convention on the International Responsibility of States for Injuries to Aliens' prepared by Professors Louis Sohn and Richard Baxter. Second, the Organisation for Economic Co-operation and Development (OECD) elaborated in 1962 the 'OECD Draft Convention on the Protection of Foreign Property'. The Abs-Shawcross Draft Convention, the Harvard Draft Convention, as well as the OECD Draft Convention, all provided for the possibility for nationals to bring a claim against a State directly[147] and hence set the basis for the future consolidation of investor-State arbitration, as these drafts served as a template for several national model BITs.

The only multilateral agreement for which sufficient consensus could be found was indeed the ICSID Convention. It was the idea of the General Counsel of the World Bank, Aron Broches, to develop an agreement that 'only' set out a facility for the settlement of international investment disputes. The approach of Broches was held artificial since logic would dictate that any system of dispute settlement would have to be based on substantive rules, which could be applied.[148] In the eyes of Broches, such an axiomatic approach was neither 'necessary nor productive'.[149] At any rate, his idea was successful, as the ICSID Convention entered into force in 1966 and by the end of the 1990s, the ICSID had become the main forum for the settlement of investment disputes.[150]

There has been one further attempt by the OECD, from 1995 to 1998, through the negotiation on the Multilateral Agreement on Investment (MAI). After the East–West conflict was settled, global trade and investment liberalization was the general political agenda and the possibility for the adoption of a multilateral investment agreement seemed to be attainable. Yet, this project also ultimately failed due to, as has been argued, a multiple set of reasons among which a newly established opposition coming from civil society. After the failure of the MAI, there was only one further attempt to take a multilateral approach. It was made in the context of the WTO Doha Round, where it was initially intended to launch negotiations on international investment. However, the plan was also abandoned due to the strong opposition from some developing countries.[151]

147 Article 7(b) of the OECD Draft Convention (1962).

148 Rudolf Dolzer and Christoph Schreuer, *Principles of International Investment Law (2nd edn)* 9.

149 *Ibid.* 9.

150 *Ibid.* 9.

151 *Ibid.* 357.

(i) The EU proposal on a multilateral court

In the light of the many unsuccessful multilateral approaches, one might ask why does the EU attempt to take multilateral action? For the EU, the opportunity to make another attempt lies within the legitimacy crisis of the international investment regime and the investment arbitration system in particular.[152] As mentioned before, international investment arbitration attracted growing criticisms. Since the increase in costly ISDS cases, governments around the world have started to question the traditional ISDS mechanism. Consequently, most countries are reforming and revising their investment law policies. The result of this is that regional and national approaches to international investment law are today very diverse and looking at ISDS the differences can be rather stark. For instance, Bolivia, Ecuador and Venezuela already denounced membership of the ICSID Convention. South Africa and Indonesia have terminated a couple of their old BITs. South Africa no longer accepts ISDS. Foreign investors in South Africa will have to settle their disputes before South African courts. Brazil embarked on a new way of investment law making by adopting cooperation and facilitation agreements that do not provide for investor-State arbitration and rather set out a cooperative mechanism in order to ensure the enforcement of the parties' obligations, and provide for State-State arbitration as a last resort.

Despite the different reform approaches, the argument of the EU is to say that there is a global reform on ISDS ongoing and this fact already creates a suitable environment to start multilateral negotiations. The EU underlines that a coherent set of rules would be most beneficial for investors, governments and other stakeholders.[153] The EU recognizes that the ideal solution would be a multilateral reform on substantive provisions, as well as dispute settlement. Yet an all encompassing reform seems unrealistic today. Therefore, the EU is suggesting that a multilateral reform approach of the investment dispute settlement system would already constitute an important step in increasing the legitimacy and acceptance of the international investment regime as a whole.[154]

152 European Commission and the Government of Canada, *The Case for Creating a Multilateral Investment Dispute Settlement Mechanism*.

153 *Ibid.* para. 5. UNCTAD is also in favor of multilateral approaches, see UNCTAD, WIR 2016, 115.

154 *Ibid.* paras 5 and 6.

Multilateral action and approaches are a central element of the EU international investment policy and the EU expressed its objective to take the lead for global action towards reforming ISDS.[155] Thus, the EU seeks to pursue its reform on ISDS that it started bilaterally with Canada and Vietnam at the international level. The CETA for instance contains a specific provision stating a binding commitment for the EU and Canada to 'pursue with other trading partners the establishment of a multilateral investment tribunal and appellate mechanism for the resolution of investment disputes'.[156] This individual commitment in a bilateral setting was a first signal of the EU and Canada taking multilateral action on ISDS. As mentioned at the beginning of this chapter, the EU and Canada are currently seeking to gather further like-minded countries that wish to establish a multilateral investment court.

The reactions from third countries so far do not allow an optimistic future for the EU proposal. Argentina, Brazil, India, Japan and other nations reportedly rejected the initiative, which Canada and the EU presented at the 2017 World Economic Forum.[157] The Indian Commerce and Industry Minister Nirmala Sitharaman said that 'India summarily rejected' the idea that the CETA, incorporating an ISDS mechanism, could be the template for a multilateral agreement. In the occasion, Minister Sitharaman also emphasized India's position in favor of requiring investors to exhaust local remedies before resorting to international tribunals.[158] The requirement to exhaust local remedies forms part of India's current model BIT that was adopted in 2013.[159]

At the present stage, it is however impossible to make concrete predictions of how such a multilateral court could look. At the last meeting, in February 2017, European stakeholders discussed many potential aspects of the court, which do not

155 See Statement of EU Trade Commissioner Cecilia Malmström available at https://ec.europa.eu/commission/commissioners/2014-2019/malmstrom/blog/proposing-investment-court-system_en, accessed 23 April 2017.

156 Article 8.29 of the CETA.

157 IISD, 'European Union and Canada Co-Host Discussions on Multilateral Investment Court'.

158 IISD, 'European Union and Canada Co-Host Discussions on Multilateral Investment Court'.

159 See Government of India, Model Text for the Indian Bilateral Investment Treaty (2015), Article 15, http://investmentpolicyhub.unctad.org/Download/TreatyFile/3560, accessed 25 April 2017.

necessarily follow the ICS as contained in the CETA.[160] For instance, it had been discussed whether the court should allow claims based solely on international investment treaties or also on investment contracts and domestic law. The profile of adjudicators, in particular their independence, has also been touched upon and also whether decisions taken by the multilateral court would be effectively enforceable, that is, have a level comparable to the enforcement under ICSID Rules. Two further highly interesting topics came up: one, whether there should be a requirement for the exhaustion of local remedies. This approach would be contrary to the current CETA ICS. Two, the idea has been mentioned that the court should not be restricted to investors but could also be open for claims from States and third parties.[161]

(ii) Alternative current multilateral reform proposals to ISDS

It is not only the EU and Canada that are currently discussing a multilateral reform approach towards ISDS. Academia and non-governmental entities started to do so too.[162] For instance, the Geneva Center for International Dispute Settlement (CIDS) suggests concluding a multilateral convention that would establish a permanent international tribunal for investment (ITI), which would be competent to resolve investment disputes concerning as many States as would ratify the convention.[163] Under this proposal, States, after their ratification of the convention, would be subject to the compulsory jurisdiction of the ITI for the settlement of their investment disputes with foreign investors.[164] This means that when the investor's home State and the respondent State have both ratified the said convention, the investment dispute at stake would be resolved before the ITI.

160 European Commission, *Stakeholder Meeting on a Multilateral Reform of Investment Dispute Resolution Including the Possible Establishment of a Multilateral Investment Court*' (27 February 2017) http://trade.ec.europa.eu/doclib/docs/2017/march/tradoc_155418.pdf, accessed 25 April 2017.

161 *Ibid.*

162 For an earlier proposal, see Gus van Harten, 'A Case for an International Investment Court' (2008) *Society of International Economic Law Working Paper no. 22/08*.

163 Gabrielle Kaufmann-Kohler and Michele Potestà, 'Can the Mauritius Convention serve as a Model for the Reform of Investor-State Arbitration in Connection with the Introduction of a Permanent Investment Tribunal or an Appeal Mechanism? Analysis and Roadmap' 5.

164 *Ibid.*

The International Institute for Sustainable Development (IISD) is working on an interesting proposal for an investment-related dispute settlement, which seeks to be more inclusive by allowing other stakeholders than investors to submit claims.[165] According to the IISD, any new international mechanism on investment-related conflicts should address the variety of legal and actual relationships, such as between the government and the investor, the investor and the community (or citizens), and the government and the community (or citizens). Moreover, such a mechanism should have a broader base of law that includes next to international investment treaties and investment contracts also international and domestic law related to human rights, labor law and environmental law.[166]

To conclude, the pathway of multilateralism is a difficult one. Another, more general question, however, is whether a more institutionalized ISDS mechanism is the proper means to improve the international investment system as a whole. Strong concerns have already been raised that an international investment court would not cure the illegitimacy of the regime, but on the contrary would consolidate even more the neoliberal and investor-friendly substantive investment rules.[167]

(b) The regional pathway to reforming ISDS

Even though the main sources of international investment law are BITs, States also frame their international investment agreements within larger regional arrangements. It began most prominently with the NAFTA in 1992. Over the past ten years, we have witnessed the adoption of major regional arrangements in Asia, Africa and Latin America.

165 IISD, *Investment-Related Dispute Settlement: Towards a Comprehensive Multilateral Approach* (23–4 May 2016) www.iisd.org/event/investment-related-dispute-settlement-towards-comprehensive-multilateral-approach, accessed 25 April 2017.

166 For more details on the IISD proposal for an investment-related dispute settlement, see www.iisd.org/library/investment-related-dispute-settlement-towards-inclusive-multilateral-approach, accessed 25 April 2017.

167 M. Sornarajah, 'An International Investment Court: Panacea or Purgatory?' (15 August 2016) 180 *Columbia FDI Perspectives*. Rather in favor of multilateral approaches, see Eduardo Zuleta, 'The Challenges of Creating A Standing International Investment Court' in Jean E. Kalicki and Anna Joubin-Bret, *Reshaping the Investor-State Dispute Settlement System – Journeys for the 21st Century* (Leidin: Koninklijke Brill Nijhoff, 2015) 403.

Comprehensive economic regional agreements have the primary objective to foster economic integration in the specific region. They often contain a chapter on investment promotion and protection.[168] The adoption of foreign investment regulation that would apply in the specific region allowed the regions to engage in shaping investment rules according to their vision and need, and to implement certain reform proposals. This includes the shaping or reshaping of ISDS.

The halt on WTO negotiations has been regarded as one of the reasons for the regionalization of international economic law. The EU and Canada had precisely the objective of setting rules that go beyond the WTO agreements when starting the negotiations on the CETA. As the CETA was to include a fully-fledged chapter on investment, the two contracting parties had the opportunity to reshape certain investment provisions and to reform ISDS.

Regionalism became increasingly important in the last years in international investment law. This last section will therefore discuss two points of regionalism. It will firstly highlight the specific phenomenon of mega-regionals, before looking more closely on regional approaches in Africa.

(i) Mega-regionals and their impact on third countries

In the reform process of international investment law, the negotiations of mega-regionals have received a lot of attention since these agreements were set up, due to their economic size, are potential 'rule-setters' for the future shape of substantive and procedural international investment standards.[169] One of the often cited examples is the Trans-Pacific Partnership Agreement (TPP) between the USA, Australia, Brunei Darussalam, Canada, Chile, Japan, Malaysia, Mexico, New Zealand, Peru, Singapore, and Vietnam.[170] It makes up around 40% of global gross domestic product (GDP) and tops the list in terms of global foreign direct investment inward stock.[171] The second example is the TTIP between the USA and the EU.[172] The TTIP would have the potential to be the most important mega-regional

168 For instance Chapter 11 of the NAFTA.

169 UNCTAD, WIR 2014, 118.

170 The TPP text was concluded on 5 October 2015. At the time of writing the text was under national reviews in the twelve Contracting States to the TPP. The text is available at https://ustr.gov/trade-agreements/free-trade-agreements/trans-pacific-partnership/tpp-full-text, accessed 25 April 2017.

171 UNCTAD, WIR 2014, 120.

172 European Commission, text proposal for the investment chapter of the TTIP.

with regard to GDP by representing 45% of global GDP.[173] As mentioned before, the CETA is also considered to be a mega-regional because of the significant economic weight of the EU and Canada in international trade and investment relations.[174]

Thus, it is not surprising that in 2014, UNCTAD pointed out '[o]nce concluded, these [mega-regionals] are likely to have a major impact on global investment rule making and global investment patterns'.[175] This is to say that mega-regionals would become the template of future international investment law making for countries that are not parties to any mega-regional, as well as for countries that are. The emergence of mega-regionals has been seen as 'a new and quite promising opportunity for a kind of mega-consolidation' in the field of international investment law'.[176]

When comparing the content of the TPP and the CETA, it becomes easily evident that these two mega-regionals differ starkly with respect to the mechanism for investor-State dispute resolution.[177] The TPP, which mainly follows the US Model BIT of 2012, contains the traditional mechanism of investor-State arbitration, maintaining the disputing parties' autonomy to choose their arbitrators. The CETA, as has been presented before, introduces the ICS. Be that as it may, politically the two treaties received a severe blow, in particular from the new US Administration. The negotiations on the TTIP have been stalled since the end of 2016 and it is unclear when or whether they will be reopened at some point. In the same vein, the US Administration decided not to ratify the already finalized text of the TPP. The TPP might of course still enter into force thanks to the ratifications of the remaining States, but without the USA its economic and political importance certainly decreased.

The aforementioned agreements might lead to de facto multilateralization in other areas of international economic law, but it seems that this is not the case for the future shape of ISDS. The TTIP negotiations might have been decisive for international investment law governance with respect to ISDS, since the TTIP could have exemplified which of the two approaches to ISDS – US or EU – would be more

173 UNCTAD, WIR 2014, 120.

174 UNCTAD, WIR 2014, 117–8.

175 WIR 2014, 118.

176 Karsten Nowrot, 'Of "Plain" Analytical Approaches and "Savior" Perspectives, Measuring the Structural Dialogues between Bilateral Investment Treaties and Investment Chapters in Mega-Regionals' 10 (2017) *Rechtwissenschaftliche Beiträge der Hamburger Sozialökonomie* 11.

177 Stefanie Schacherer, 'TPP, CETA and TTIP Between Innovation and Consolidation – Resolving Investor-State Disputes under Mega-Regionals' (2016) 7 (3) *Journal of International Dispute Settlement* 628–53, 630.

successful. However, there is little hope left that the TTIP will be adopted or negotiations will be pursued any day soon. Given these factors and the latest political developments, it is unlikely there will be something like the de facto multilateralization through mega-regionals concerning ISDS.

(ii) The Africanization of ISDS

In the past, Africa has not been a decisive actor in international investment law making. African countries used to be considered as 'rule takers' in general and thus also with respect to ISDS. The reason for this is that from the mid-1990s onwards, African countries accepted to adhere to the traditional system of BITs.[178] These BITs were initially concluded with capital-exporting countries mainly from Europe.[179] The content of the majority of these agreements follows the traditional approaches of treaties elaborated by capital-exporting countries and all include ISDS through arbitration without noteworthy safeguards.[180] African countries were also among the first to ratify the ICSID Convention.[181]

However, as regards treaties that are adopted between African countries in the context of African Regional Economic Communities (RECs), Africa appears to be innovative and has even been considered as a 'laboratory' of international

178 By January 2017, African countries had signed 881 BITs or international investment agreements IIAs. There are 722 agreements signed with non-African countries and 159 intra-African BITs (UNCTAD, Investment Policy Hub International Investment Agreements Navigator http://investmentpolicyhub.unctad.org/IIA, accessed 17 February 2017).

179 Alfredo Crosato, Evin Durmaz and Aliki Semertzi, 'Africa's Investment Regime: Assessing International Investment Agreements in the Light of Current Trends and Needs in Africa' *The Graduate Institute: Trade and Investment Law Clinic Papers* (2016) 26: Germany (52) and Switzerland (46). They are followed by China (36), Belgium–Luxemburg Economic Union (32), Italy (32), the Netherlands (30), France (25), the United Kingdom (24), Portugal (21) and Spain (19).

180 Hamed El Kady, 'Towards a more Effective International Investment Policy Framework in Africa' (2016) *Transnational Dispute Management* 4.

181 African countries that signed the ICSID Convention in 1965 are: Benin, Burkina Faso, Cameroon, Central African Republic, Côte d'Ivoire, Ethiopia (never ratified), Gabon, Ghana, Liberia, Morocco, Niger, Nigeria, Sierra Leon, Somalia, Tunisia (ICSID, Database of ICSID Member States https://icsid.worldbank.org/en/Pages/about/Database-of-Member-States.aspx, accessed 23 April 2017).

investment law making.[182] In fact, most of the RECs adopted legal instruments concerning the regulation of foreign investment.[183] For instance, COMESA elaborated an investment agreement in 2007, which reflects a first shift with the traditional model BIT negotiated with capital-exporting countries, since it pays more attention to sustainable development goals and introduces a provision on investor obligation.[184] The ISDS provision in the COMESA Investment Agreement foresees next to international arbitration also the possibility for an investor to start proceedings under the COMESA Court of Justice.[185] This suggests a certain intention to regionalize ISDS in the context of COMESA.[186] However, the Agreement had not entered into force at the time of writing, since the required threshold of ratification by at least six Member States has not been met.

Another example is the SADC region that adopted a model treaty in 2012, which expresses even more clearly African development concerns.[187] The purpose of this non-binding instrument is to enhance harmonization of investment regimes in the region and to provide an effective tool for the future conclusion of investment agreements by SADC Member States. The SADC Model Treaty suggests as a preferred option not to include ISDS.[188] In fact, all SADC Member States are meanwhile opposed to ISDS as is evidenced by the amendments of August 2016 to the SADC

182 Alfredo Crosato, Evin Durmaz and Aliki Semertzi, 'Africa's Investment Regime: Assessing International Investment Agreements in the Light of Current Trends and Needs in Africa' 30.

183 The eight RECs that were identified as the pillars of the future African Economic Community (AEC) are: the Arab Maghreb Union (AMU), the Economic Community of West African States (ECOWAS), the East African Community (EAC), the Intergovernmental Authority on Development (IGAD), the Southern African Development Community (SADC), the Economic Community of Central African States (ECCAS), the Common Market for Eastern and Southern Africa (COMESA), and the Community of Sahel-Saharan States.

184 See UNCTAD, Investment Agreement for the COMESA Common Investment Area (signed 23 May 2007) https://investmentpolicy.unctad.org/international-investment-agreements/treaty-files/3092/download, accessed 17 February 2017.

185 Article 28.1(b) of the COMESA Investment Agreement (2007).

186 Makane Moïse Mbengue, 'Special Issue: Africa and the Reform of the International Investment Regime – An Introduction' (2017) 18 (3) *The Journal of World Investment & Trade* 371.

187 SADC, SADC Model Bilateral Investment Treaty Template with Commentary (2012) www.iisd.org/itn/wp-content/uploads/2012/10/sadc-model-bit-template-final.pdf, accessed 17 February 2017 (hereafter referred to as SADC Model BIT).

188 SADC Model BIT, Commentary, 55.

Protocol on Finance and Investment, where ISDS has been deleted from Annex I.[189] The amended version no longer contains any reference to ISDS and only provides for State-State dispute resolution.[190]

The EAC region adopted a first model investment code in 2006, which was revised in 2015.[191] Interestingly, the EAC model like the SADC model suggests that ISDS should not be included into a future treaty of EAC Member States. In June 2015, the regions of SADC, COMESA and EAC signed the Agreement on a Tripartite Free Trade Area (TFTA).[192] A protocol on cross-border investment had not yet been adopted at the time of writing, which might set new trends with respect to international investment law and ISDS.[193]

The fact that we are today witnessing a regionalization of international investment law and approaches to ISDS in Africa, that is, an Africanization as has been stated by several authors.[194] African RECs, by adopting their investment rules, can play a role in the current global reform process and the future shape of ISDS.[195] Looking at the RECs, it seems that there are two main approaches towards ISDS,

189 See SADC, Protocol on Finance and Investment (signed 18 August 2006) http://investmentpolicyhub.unctad.org/Download/TreatyFile/2730, accessed 17 February 2017. In August 2016, SADC Member States adopted an amended version of the Protocol on Finance and Investment, which at the time of writing is yet to be ratified. For more details, see Luke Eric Peterson, 'Investigation: In Aftermath of Investor Arbitration Against Lesotho, SADC Member-States Amend Investment Treaty so as to Remove ISDS and Limit Protections' *IAReporter* (20 February 2017) www.iareporter.com/articles/investigation-in-aftermath-of-investor-arbitration-against-lesotho-sadc-member-s-amend-investment-treaty-so-as-to-remove-isds-and-limit-protections/, accessed 21 February 2017.

190 *Ibid.*

191 Makane Moïse Mbengue, 'Special Issue: Africa and the Reform of the International Investment Regime – An Introduction' 372.

192 See COMESA, EAC and SADC, Agreement Establishing a Tripartite Free Trade Area among COMESA, EAC and SADC www.tralac.org/images/docs/7531/tfta-agreement-june-2015.pdf, accessed 17 February 2017. A protocol on cross-border investment will be adopted in a second negotiation phase, see Article 45 of the TFTA Agreement.

193 Makane Moïse Mbengue, 'Special Issue: Africa and the Reform of the International Investment Regime – An Introduction' 372.

194 Makane Moïse Mbengue, 'Special Issue: Africa and the Reform of the International Investment Regime – An Introduction'.

195 Alfredo Crosato, Evin Durmaz and Aliki Semertzi, 'Africa's Investment Regime: Assessing International Investment Agreements in the Light of Current Trends and Needs in Africa' 26.

consisting of those that want to replace ISDS altogether and those that seek to maintain ISDS by introducing new features.

At the continental level, it is the African Union (AU)[196] that is in the position to put forward continent-wide regional economic agreements. One of the most important integration endeavours currently undertaken by the AU is the Continental Free Trade Area (CFTA).[197] The CFTA is intended to include a comprehensive chapter on investment.

Also under the auspices of the AU, a Pan-African Investment Code (PAIC) was finalized in 2016. The PAIC contains a variety of innovative provisions intended to ensure the sustainable development of African States. It was finally agreed that the PAIC serve as a model investment treaty and, as such, will have impacts on the future negotiations of the chapter on investment of the CFTA.[198]

At the present stage, the PAIC is so far a unique instrument in reflecting an African consensus on international investment law. During the negotiations there were problems, however, in finding common ground between AU Member States on ISDS. The final version of the PAIC foresees the possibility of ISDS, but keeps the provisions in brackets for the time being. It is interesting to note that during the negotiations a majority of African countries expressed a need for having ISDS in the PAIC in order to render their countries attractive for foreign investors.[199] The countries in favour of ISDS through arbitration shared the consensus that the provisions on ISDS should be shaped in a manner so as to avoid the shortcomings of this mechanism.

Consequently, the ISDS provisions of the PAIC include a couple of important reform approaches. A critical question is the exhaustion of local remedies. The traditional approach of IIAs is to provide for direct access to international arbitration

196 The AU is a continental organization consisting of 55 African States. The AU was founded in 2001. Its headquarters are located in Addis Ababa, Ethiopia (see Article 3 of the Constitutive Act of the African Union (signed 11 July 2000) www.achpr.org/instruments/au-constitutive-act, accessed 17 February 2017).

197 See Ilmari Soininen, 'The Continental Free Trade Area: What's Going On?' (24 October 2014) *International Centre for Trade and Sustainable Development* www.ictsd.org/bridges-news/bridges-africa/news/the-continental-free-trade-area-whats-going-on, accessed 17 February 2017.

198 Makane Moïse Mbengue and Stefanie Schacherer, 'The 'Africanization' of International Investment Law: The Pan-African Investment Code and the Reform of the International Investment Regime' (2017) 18 (3) *The Journal of World Investment & Trade* 446.

199 *Ibid.* 441–5.

for a foreign investor, usually after a 'cooling-off period'.[200] It was for a long time considered that in many countries an independent judiciary could not be taken for granted and that the defending State might influence the outcome of investor-State disputes in its own courts.[201] However, it can be argued today that the situation in most African countries has changed; consequently, the exhaustion of local remedies could and should revive.[202] The drafters of the PAIC decided to include the requirement for foreign investors to first exhaust local remedies in the Member State where their investment is located before a request for arbitration can be submitted.[203] In this way, investor-State arbitration becomes a remedy of last resort under the PAIC.

In addition, the current version of the PAIC contains an important limitation to the investors' access to ISDS. The State's consent for arbitration is given on a case-by-case basis or on the basis of national law: '[T]he dispute may be resolved through arbitration, subject to the applicable laws of the host State and/or the mutual agreement of the disputing parties.'[204] This rather peculiar provision implies that if the host State's law does not allow for ISDS, such as in the case of the South African Investment Bill,[205] ISDS cannot take place, and even if the host State's law provides for ISDS, the investor would still need the agreement of the host State to initiate ISDS proceedings. Last but not least, even in case of silence in the host State's law, ISDS can only take place upon the mutual agreement of the disputing parties.

A further important aspect of the ISDS provisions of the PAIC is the express possibility for a State to file a claim against an investor in an investor-State arbitration,

200 A number of IIAs require pursuing local remedies for a period of time, see, for example, Agreement between the Belgium–Luxembourg Economic Union and the Republic of Botswana on the Reciprocal Promotion and Protection of Investments (signed 7 June 2006, not in force at time of writing) https://investmentpolicy.unctad.org/international-investment-agreements/treaty-files/331/download Article 12.2; Agreement between the Government of the Republic of Korea and the Government of the Republic of Argentina on the Promotion and Protection of Investments (signed 17 May 1994, entered into force 24 September 1996) https://investmentpolicy.unctad.org/international-investment-agreements/treaty-files/102/download Article 8.3(a).

201 Rudolf Dolzer and Christoph Schreuer, *Principles of International Investment Law (2nd edn)* 235.

202 M. Sornarajah, 'An International Investment Court: Panacea or Purgatory?' 190.

203 Article 42.3 of the PAIC.

204 *Ibid.* Article 42.3.

205 Government of the Republic of South Africa, Promotion and Protection of Investment Bill of South Africa (2015). The Bill has not yet entered into force. The current draft is available at www.thedti.gov.za/gazzettes/39514.pdf, accessed 17 February 2017.

a so-called 'counterclaim'. It is worth mentioning that the COMESA Investment Agreement[206] and SADC also provide for the possibility of counterclaims.[207]

Interestingly, the PAIC contemplates the possibility of establishing an AU Court of Arbitration that would have jurisdiction to deal with investor-State disputes.[208] The PAIC generally seeks to regionalize investment arbitration also by suggesting that the Permanent Court of Arbitration Centres in Africa, and African regional courts where they exist, should be used in order to settle investment disputes.[209]

The law making of African RECs together with the innovations of the PAIC show that Africa is adopting its own approaches to ISDS. Yet, a big question is whether these African approaches might have any impact on non-African countries? Recently concluded BITs between African States and a third State still show that African States are keen to accept the suggested model investment treaty of an economically more powerful contracting party. This circumstance can quite clearly be proved by the BITs that African countries have concluded with Canada in recent years,[210] all of which contain ISDS through arbitration. Other African countries, such as Angola, Malawi and Mozambique, have subscribed to the new approach adopted by Brazil and concluded 'investment cooperation and facilitation agreements' with Brazil without suggesting any adaptation.

Conclusion

The way in which future international investment disputes will be settled will remain a hot topic for the coming years. Countries and regions only seem to be at the beginning of the implementation of the many reform ideas that have been discussed for some time now. Africa through its RECs developed clearer positions

206 UNCTAD, Investment Agreement for the COMESA Common Investment Area, Article 28.9: 'A Member State against whom a claim is brought by a COMESA investor under this Article may assert as a defence, counterclaim, right of set off or other similar claim, that the COMESA investor bringing the claim has not fulfilled its obligations under this Agreement, including the obligations to comply with all applicable domestic measures or that it has not taken all reasonable steps to mitigate possible damages'.

207 SADC, SADC Model Bilateral Investment Treaty Template with Commentary, Articles 19 and 29.19.

208 Article 42, para. 4 of the PAIC.

209 *Ibid.*

210 J. Anthony VanDuzer, 'Canadian Investment Treaties with African Countries: What Do They Tell Us About Investment Treaty Making in Africa?' (2017) 18 *Journal of World Investment and Trade* 556–84.

on ISDS, including the position not to have ISDS at all. The adoption of the PAIC should have allowed African States to be aware of the many reform possibilities and also to better integrate sustainable development concerns into the way in which the ISDS mechanism could be shaped or whether it is even necessary to include it at all.

The EU is still in the unique position to have implemented into the treaties with Canada and Vietnam, a reform approach that institutionalizes traditional investment arbitration by establishing the ICS. The CETA between the EU and Canada constitutes the starting point for the EU and Canada of gathering interested countries together in order to explore the idea of a multilateral investment court. The precise shape of this court is not yet known. It can be assumed that the EU intends to build it in a similar way to the CETA ICS.

This chapter looked more closely at the ICS of the CETA. It has been pointed out that the new institutional safeguards are likely to be more favourable for the independence and impartiality of the Tribunal Members than is the case in traditional investment arbitration. The main reason is that there is no link between the disputing parties and the Tribunal Members sitting in a division thanks to their pre-selection by the Joint Committee, as well as the fact that Tribunal Members are randomly assigned to sit in a case. Additionally, the CETA adds new standards on the ethics of Tribunal Members, thus further ensuring their independence and impartiality. A welcoming feature introduced by the CETA is the prohibition for Tribunal Members to act as counsel or as party-appointed expert or witness in any pending or new investment dispute.

The Appellate Tribunal of the CETA is intended to enhance consistency and coherence among the awards rendered under the ICS. As argued in this chapter, the decisions by the Appellate Tribunal will likely provide guidance for the subsequent reasoning of the Tribunal, which is thus likely to render the CETA case law consistent and to enhance the predictability of the law for the various stakeholders.

The adoption of the ICS and the related policy agenda of the EU to promote a multilateral investment court means for Africa and African States that clear positions on ISDS are important to have for potential upcoming multilateral negotiations. Whether the EU proposal will receive sufficient support is yet soon to know. As mentioned before, several countries already declared that they were not interested in following the CETA ICS as a model for the multilateral investment court.

If multilateralism was to fail once again, what then could still be fostered are regional approaches. Regionalism might be seen as the more realistic pathway for the next years. For the EU, regionalism might look like 'the best we could get'. Yet, with respect to Africa and African countries, regionalism can have the advantage of integrating more specifically broader development concerns in their investment regulations.

Conclusion

Laurence Boisson de Chazournes

The discussions we had during the Fifth Annual Conference of the African Society of International Law were rich and dense. They highlighted that the relationships between the promotion and protection of foreign investment and law in its various dimensions are multifaceted. It is through this prism that I will address the three following themes: first, investment and its relationship with disciplines other than law (Section 1); then, investment and the law (Section 2); and, finally, investment in the law (Section 3).

1 Investment and its relationship with disciplines other than law

The topic of investment promotion and protection is interdisciplinary. Indeed, other social sciences have explored their relationship with investment. Some of the contributions to the conference dealt with political science approaches, others gave an economics perspective on the topic, while some approached it through a historical lens, in particular as regards the impact of colonization in Africa. It is interesting to note that the issue of investment promotion and protection has become a key topic in many disciplines. It has taken the place of the issue of international financial institutions and their provision of public financing in the context of structural adjustment programmes, a topic which attracted a lot of attention in the 1980s and 1990s. The attention has moved from public investment to private investment and the role the private sector plays in development processes.

The perspective of political science can imply thinking about investment as a means to bolster the elemental functions of a State. There are calls in this area for a reformist approach: with this, what is meant by this is that a State should have adequate policy space for providing public goods, fulfilling its task according to the social contract it is bound by or discharging its commitment as a trustee for a community to ensure its basic needs are met. Investment promotion and protection, while acknowledging this policy space, should provide the means to this end.

As can be seen, this way of thinking is not only about investment protection, but it is also about the benefits that should derive from investment protection, that is, good governance, respect for human rights, technology transfer and the sharing of benefits among the various components of the population. The reformist stance is less about the finer nuances of investment law, but more about a claim for the proper functioning of the welfare state, as understood from a contemporary political science perspective.

Interestingly, this perspective is different from the understanding that practitioners have of the functioning of a State in the context of investment protection. Access to justice, due process and transparency are some of the recurrent claims made under the concept of fair and equitable treatment to the benefit of foreign investors. They are supported by many doctrinal articles and awards which have framed what should be a 'good system of justice' in the context of ensuring respect for the rule of law to foreign investors.

These two 'State model' discourses are not alike but it is important to consider whether they are reconcilable.

This interdisciplinary perspective also prompts a focus on research methodology. Pleas have been made for empirical research that brings law outside its box. There is indeed a need for serious empirical studies, particularly because many assumptions have not yet been tested. Such is the case with the value added of dispute settlement in terms of investment promotion and investment protection.[1]

2 Investment and the law

Investment promotion and protection entertain many links with law, at least when assessing whether there has been a breach of a treaty or a contract. Let us first deal with investment law *stricto sensu*. This body of law encompasses treaties, be they bilateral, regional or multilateral, as well as national legislation, contracts and other international agreements. At the outset, it is interesting to note the dynamics between domestic law and international law. The interconnections between these bodies of law are multifaceted in investment law. Article 42 of the Convention on the Settlement of Investment Disputes between States and Nationals of Other States

1 See Lauge N. Skovgaard Poulsen, *Bounded Rationality and Economic Diplomacy: The Politics of Investment Treaties in Developing Countries* (Cambridge University Press, 2015) 247.

(ICSID Convention) illustrates some of these facets.[2] Some of the contributions place an emphasis on constitutional law[3] and other domestic legislation. Indeed, domestic law has a role to play, especially when disputes can only be brought before domestic jurisdictions. This body of law also has a role to play when fundamental rights are at stake in a dispute. Tribunals have referred to it using the concept of transnational public policy, and have acknowledged it in their interpretation of investment law provisions.[4]

While investment law has relationships with other rules of international law, there has been a tendency to isolate investment law. However, it should be interpreted and applied together with other rules, especially when a treaty expressly refers to these rules. There is no contracting out effect, except under a *lex specialis* provision. The *Peter A. Allard* v. *the Government of Barbados* case offers an insight into how a principle of international law such as the due diligence principle can help assess the fulfilment of a treaty provision by a host State, in that case a full protection and security standard.[5] In another case, it was also found that respect for the principle of good faith finds application when assessing if an investment could receive protection under an investment treaty.[6]

Some of the contributions to the proceedings of the conference have dealt with aspects of human rights and international water law. More attention should be given to the relationships of these bodies of norms and principles with investment rules in the wake of previous awards, such as that of *SAUR International SA* v. *Republic of*

2 Article 42 of the ICSID Convention reads as follows: '(1) The Tribunal shall decide a dispute in accordance with such rules of law as may be agreed by the parties. In the absence of such agreement, the Tribunal shall apply the law of the Contracting State party to the dispute (including its rules on the conflict of laws) and such rules of international law as may be applicable. (2) The Tribunal may not bring in a finding of *non liquet* on the ground of silence or obscurity of the law. (3) The provisions of paragraphs (1) and (2) shall not prejudice the power of the Tribunal to decide a dispute *ex aequo et bono* if the parties so agree.'

3 More generally on this issue, see Laurence Boisson de Chazournes and Brian McGarry, 'What Roles Can Constitutional Law Play in Investment Arbitration?' (2014) 15 (5–6) *The Journal of World Investment and Trade* 862–88.

4 *World Duty Free Company Limited* v. *Republic of Kenya* (4 October 2006) ICSID Case No. ARB/00/7, Award.

5 *Peter A. Allard* v. *the Government of Barbados* (27 June 2016) PCA Case No. 2012–06, Award.

6 *Plama Consortium Limited* v. *Republic of Bulgaria* (27 August 2008) ICSID Case No. ARB/03/24, Award, paras 143–4.

Argentina.[7] Incidentally, the same can be said about trade and intellectual property rights. There will be more and more overlaps between these bodies of norms.[8]

Other rules include corporate social responsibility standards and codes of conduct, also referred to as technical and social responsibility rules. They are elaborated and endorsed by various stakeholders, including, *inter alia*, representatives of the private sector. These often self-regulatory instruments can produce legal effects. They are important in the light of the pleas for making investors more responsible. They could help, for instance, to 'rebalance' the understanding of the concept of fair and equitable treatment. In this context, it is interesting to note that it has been suggested that States could also claim legitimate expectations.[9]

3 Investment in the law

I would now like to refer to the point discussed in Chapter 1 above by Professor Maurice Kamto, when he mentioned the subjective and objective criteria for defining an investment, in particular the criterion of a contribution to development. I submit that the concept of sustainable development is relevant in this context. Sustainable development rests on three pillars: economic development, environmental protection and social development. The Sustainable Development Goals[10], as agreed upon by all Member States of the United Nations and endorsed by international institutions, the private sector and non-governmental organizations, could help assess the contribution to development, as understood in the area of investment promotion and investment protection. They are defined around criteria and parameters which can help to evaluate contributions of foreign investments to sustainable development.[11]

7 *SAUR International SA* v. *Republic of Argentina* (6 June 2012) ICSID Case No. ARB/04/4, Decision on Jurisdiction and Liability.

8 For an insight of possible overlaps, see *Menzies Middle East and Africa S.A. and Aviation Handling Services International Ltd.* v. *Republic of Senegal* (5 August 2016) ICSID Case No. ARB/15/21, Award.

9 Karl P. Sauvant and Güneş Ünüvar, 'Can Host Countries Have Legitimate Expectations?' (26 September 2016) 183 *Columbia FDI Perspectives*. For further discussion of this issue, see also Yenkong Ngangjoh Hodu and Collins C. Ajibo, 'Legitimate Expectation in Investor-State Arbitration: Re-contextualising a Controversial Concept from a Developing Country Perspective' (2018) 15 (1) *Manchester Journal of International Economic Law*.

10 See United Nations, *Sustainable Development Knowledge Platform* https://sustainabledevelopment.un.org, accessed 30 October 2018.

11 See Frank Anthony Fariello, *et al.* (eds), 'Financing and Implementing the Post-2015 Development' Agenda, 7 *The World Bank Legal Review* (Washington: World Bank Group, 2016) 194.

Another issue concerns the legality of the investment. Should the investment be legal when it is initially established? Should the investment be conducted lawfully during its operation? These questions were discussed in the *Metal-Tech* v. *Uzbekistan* case,[12] which limited itself to interpreting the explicit words of the bilateral investment treaty that applied. In other awards, tribunals have considered that protected investments should always abide by the laws of the host country. For example, in *David R. Aven* et al. v. *Costa Rica* a tribunal rejected claimants' contentions that Costa Rica had breached its obligations under the Dominican Republic–Central America Free Trade Agreement (CAFTA-DR) by interfering with their investment in a local tourism project. It noted that the claimants had not complied with environmental laws and that Costa Rica's response was thus justified under the laws of Costa Rica.[13] Finally, some tribunals have suggested that this legality condition should be considered implicit even when not expressly stated in a bilateral investment treaty.[14]

Should it not be considered that the requirement of compliance with host State laws is grounded in respect for the rule of law? This legality component should be understood as an incentive for States to develop their legal framework and for it to be predictable, substantial and explicit in its content.

A lot has been said about the balance between the rights and obligations of States and investors. There is a need in this context to better articulate the investor's obligations in domestic law, as well as in investment treaties.[15] Together with this balance comes the issue of remedies. There is a need to think about how to make the investor accountable. Where can this be done? Before domestic courts? Before investment tribunals? Compromissory provisions inserted in bilateral and other investment treaties, as well as in domestic legislation, need to be drafted in such a manner as to allow the relevant governing law to find application, and for counterclaims to be exercised. Indeed, counterclaim mechanisms can play a role. These are not sufficiently

12 *Metal-Tech Ltd.* v. *The Republic of Uzbekistan* (4 October 2013) ICSID Case No. ARB/10/3, Award.

13 *David R. Aven* et al. v. *The Republic of Costa Rica* (18 September 2018) DR-CAFTA Case No. UNCT/15/3, Award, paras 447–587.

14 *Phoenix Action, Ltd.* v. *The Czech Republic* (6 April 2007) ICSID Case No. ARB/06/5, Award, para. 101.

15 Laurence Boisson de Chazournes, 'Changes in the Balance of Rights and Obligations: Towards Investor Responsibilization' in Tarik El Ghadban, Charles-Maurice Mazuy and Alexandre Senegacnik (eds), *La Protection des Investissements Etrangers, vers une Réaffirmation de l'Etat ? Actes du Colloque du 2 juin 2017* (Editions Pedone, 2018) 83–96.

developed in investment law and, when applied, they obey conditions which have so far been understood in a rather restrictive manner. Further reflection is needed on the framing of provisions dealing with the offer to arbitrate. It would also be important to give more thought to the notion of connexity in its legal sense, particularly in investment law where domestic, transnational and international principles are intertwined.

This shows that, besides substantive norms, attention should also be paid to procedural law. Not enough attention has been given to procedural devices looked at from an international law perspective.

I do not yet have a clear opinion on the need to set up an investment court. The only comment I would like to make, somewhat tentatively, is in relation to the overly certain attitude of some about the necessity of establishing such a court. This attitude emerged when Western States started to be brought before investment tribunals as respondents. The establishment of an investment court could be perceived as both an act of redemption as well as a shield. However, we must ask: redemption from what? Protection from what? Those are the questions I would like to end with.

Table of cases

International Centre for the Settlement of Investment Disputes (ICSID), International Chamber of Commerce (ICC) and United Nations Commission On International Trade Law (UNCITRAL)

Abaclat *et al.* v. The Argentine Republic, ICSID Case No. ARB/07/5, Decision on the Proposal to Disqualify a Majority of the Tribunal (4 February 2014).

ADC Affiliate Limited and ADC & ADMC Management Limited v. The Republic of Hungary, ICSID Case No. ARB/03/16, Award (2 October 2006).

Aguas del Tunari, S.A. v. Republic of Bolovia, Letter of the President of the Tribunal (29 January 2003).

Antoine Biloune and Marine Drive Complex Ltd v. Ghana Investments Centre and the Government of Ghana, Ad Hoc Arbitration, UNCITRAL, Awards (27 October 1989 and 30 June 1990).

Antoine Goetz *et al.* v. The Republic of Burundi, ICSID Case No. ARB/95/3 (10 February 1999).

Asian Agricultural Products Ltd v. The Republic of Sri Lanka, ICSID Case No. ARB/87/3, Final Award (27 June 1990).

Banro American Resources, Inc. and Société Aurifère du Kivu et du Maniema S.A.R.L. v. Democratic Republic of the Congo (2002) 17 ICSID Rev. 8 FILJ 382, para 15.

Barizaa Manson Tete Dooh *et al.* v. Royal Dutch Shell Plc.

Bayindir Insaat Turizm Ticaret Ve Sanayi A.S. v. Islamic Republic of Pakistan, ICSID Case No. ARB/03/29 (14 November 2005).

Biwater Gauff (Tanzania) Ltd v. United Republic of Tanzania, ICSID Case No. ARB/05/22, Award (24 July 2008).

Burlington Resources Inc. v. Republic of Ecuador, ICSID Case No. ARB/08/ 5 (formerly Burlington Resources Inc. *et al.* v. Republic of Ecuador and Empresa Estatal Petróleos del Ecuador (PetroEcuador)), Decision on Stay of Enforcement of the Award (31 August 2017).

Table of cases

Ceskoslovenska Obchodni Banka, A.S. v. The Slovak Republic, ICSID Case No. ARB/97/4 (1 December 2004).

CMS Gas Transmission Company v. The Argentine Republic, ICSID Case No. ARB/01/8.

Consortium Groupement L.E.S.I.-DIPENTA v. People's Democratic Republic of Algeria, ICSID Case No. ARB/03/08, Award (10 January 2005).

David R. Aven *et al.* v. The Republic of Costa Rica, DR-CAFTA Case No. UNCT/15/3, Award, paras 447–587 (18 September 2018).

Desert Line Projects LLC v. The Republic of Yemen, ICSID Case No. ARB/05/17, Award (6 February 2008).

El Paso Energy International Company v. The Argentine Republic, ICSID Case No. ARB/03/15, para 39.

Emilio Agustín Maffezini v. The Kingdom of Spain, ICSID Case No. ARB/97/7, Award (13 November 2000).

Fedax N.V. v. The Republic of Venezuela, ICSID Case No. ARB/96/3, Award (9 March 1998).

Fidelis Ayoro Oguru *et al.* v. Royal Dutch Shell Plc.

Friday Alfred Akpan v. Royal Dutch Shell Plc.

Gas Natural SDG, S.A. v. The Argentine Republic, ICSID Case No. ARB/03/10 (17 June 2005).

Helnan International Hotels A/S v. Arab Republic of Egypt, ICSID Case No. ARB/05/19 (17 October 2006).

Holiday Inns S.A. *et al.* v. Morocco, ICSID Case No. ARB/72/1.

Joy Mining Machinery Limited v. Arab Republic of Egypt, ICSID Case No. ARB/03/11 (16 December 2005).

Klöckner Industrie-Anlagen GmbH *et al.* v. United Republic of Cameroon and Société Camerounaise des Engrais, ICSID Case No. ARB/81/2.

Lanco International Inc v. The Argentine Republic, ICSID Case No. ARB/97/6, Jurisdiction of the Arbitral Tribunal (8 December 1998).

Malaysian Historical Salvors, SDN, BHD v. The Government of Malaysia, ICSID Case No. ARB/05/10, Award on Jurisdiction (17 May 2007).

Menzies Middle East and Africa S.A. and Aviation Handling Services International Ltd. v. Republic of Senegal, ICSID Case No. ARB/15/21, Award (5 August 2016).

Metal-Tech Ltd. v. The Republic of Uzbekistan) ICSID Case No. ARB/10/3, Award (4 October 2013).

Methanex Corporation v. United States of America, Final Award of the Tribunal on Jurisdiction and Merits, UNCITRAL (3 August 2005).

Middle East Cement Shipping and Handling Co. S.A. v. Arab Republic of Egypt, ICSID Case No. ARB/99/6, Award (12 April 2002).

MTD Equity Sdn. Bhd. and MTD Chile S.A. v. Republic of Chile, ICSID Case No. ARB/01/7, Award (25 May 2004).

Noble Ventures, Inc. v. Romania, ICSID Case No. ARB/01/11, Award (12 October 2005).

Parkerings-Compagniet AS v. Republic of Lithuania, ICSID Case No. ARB/05/8, Award (11 September 2007).

Patrick Mitchell v. Democratic Republic of the Congo, ICSID Case No. ARB/99/7, Decision on the Application for Annulment of the Award (1 November 2006).

Peter A. Allard v. the Government of Barbados, PCA Case No. 2012–06, Award (27 June 2016).

Phoenix Action, Ltd. v. The Czech Republic, ICSID Case No. ARB/06/5, Award, para 101 (6 April 2007).

Piero Foresti, Laura de Carli *et al.* v. The Republic of South Africa, ICSID Case No. ARB(AF)/07/01.

Plama Consortium Limited v. Republic of Bulgaria, ICSID Case No. ARB/03/24, Award, paras 143–4 (27 August 2008).

Pope & Talbot Inc. v. The Government of Canada, UNCITRAL (November 2002).

Rabi Abdullahi *et al.* v. Pfizer, Inc.

Robert Azinian *et al.* v. United Mexican States.

RSM Production Corporation v. Central African Republic, ICSID Case No. ARB/07/2, Decision on Jurisdiction and Liability (7 December 2010).

Rumeli Telekom A.S. and Telsim Mobil Telekomunikasyon Hizmetleri A.S. v. Republic of Kazakhstan, ICSID Case No. ARB/05/16 (29 July 2008).

Saipem S.p.A. v. The People's Republic of Bangladesh, Decision on Jurisdiction and Recommendation on Provisional Measures, ICSID Case No. ARB/05/07, para 67 (21 March 2007).

Salini Costruttori S.p.A. and Italstrade S.p.A. v. Kingdom of Morocco [I], ICSID Case No. ARB/00/4, Decision on Jurisdiction (23 July 2001).

SAUR International SA v. Republic of Argentina, ICSID Case No. ARB/04/4, Decision on Jurisdiction and Liability (6 June 2012).

Sempra Energy International v. The Argentine Republic, ICSID Case No. ARB/02/16 (28 September 2007).

SERAP v. Federal Republic of Nigeria, Judgment No. ECW/CCJ/JUD/18/12 (14 December 2012).

Serbia and Montenegro v. Portugal.

SGS Société Générale de Surveillance SA v. Islamic Republic of Pakistan, ICSID Case No. ARB/01/13, 8 *ICSID Reports* 383 (2005).

SGS Société Générale de Surveillance SA v. Republic of The Philippines, ICSID Case No. ARB/02/6, 8 *ICSID Reports* 515 (2005).

Siemens A.G. v. The Argentine Republic, ICSID Case No. ARB/02/8, Award (17 January 2007).

Spyridon Roussalis v. Romania, ICSID Case No. ARB/06/1, Award (7 December 2011).

Técnicas Medioambientales Tecmed, S.A. v. The United Mexican States, ICSID Case No. ARB (AF)/00/2, Award (29 May 2003).

Total S.A. v. The Argentine Republic, ICSID Case No. ARB/04/01, Liability (27 December 2010).

Tulip Real Estate and Development Netherlands B.V. v. Republic of Turkey, ICSID Case No. ARB/11/28, Decision on Annulment (30 December 2015).

Tza Yap Shum v. The Republic of Peru, ICSID Case No. ARB/07/6, Decision on Jurisdiction (19 June 2009).

United Parcel Service of America Inc. v. Government of Canada, Decision of the Tribunal on Petitions for Intervention and Participation as Amici Curiae (17 October 2001).

Vattenfall AB *et al.* v. Federal Republic of Germany ARB/12/12, case pending.

Victor Pey Casado and President Allende Foundation v. Republic of Chile, ICSID Case No. ARB/98/2, Award (8 May 2008).

Waste Management, Inc. v. United Mexican States, ICSID Case No. ARB(AF)/00/3.

Wena Hotels Ltd. v. Arab Republic of Egypt, ICSID Case No. ARB/98/4, Award (8 December 2000).

World Duty Free Company Limited v. Republic of Kenya ICSID Case No. ARB/00/7, Award (4 October 2006).

African Court on Human and Peoples' Rights (ACHPR) and other international courts

Application of the Convention on the Prevention and Punishment of the Crime of Genocide (Bosnia and Herzegovina v. Serbia and Montenegro) (13 September 1993) Provisional Measures (Separate Opinion of Judge ad hoc Lauterpach), *ICJ Reports* (1993) 325 [102].

Asylum (Colombia v. Peru), *ICJ Reports*, Judgment (20 November 1950).

Balkan Energy (Ghana) Limited v. The Republic of Ghana, PCA Case No. 2010-7, Interim Award (22 December 2010).

Elettronica Sicula S.p.A. (ELSI) (United States of America v. Italy), *ICJ Reports*, Judgment (20 July 1989).

Ilesanmi v. Nigeria (Communication No. 268/2003) ACHPR 66 (11 May 2005).

Land and Maritime Boundary between Cameroon and Nigeria (Cameroon v. Nigeria: Equatorial Guinea intervening), *ICJ Reports*, Judgment 303 (10 October 2002).

Lohé Issa Konaté v. The Republic of Burkina Faso, ACHPR (16 February 2016).

Domestic jurisdictions

Adofo v. Attorney-General, Supreme Court of Ghana, 1 GLR 239, paras 245–6 (2003–2005).

Amidu *et al.* v. The Attorney-General *et al.*, Supreme Court of Ghana, Writ No. JI/15/2012, Judgment (21 June 2013).

The Attorney-General v. Faroe Atlantic Co. Ltd, Supreme Court of Ghana, SCGLR 271 (SC) (2006).

Banco Nacional de Cuba v. Sabbatino, 376 U.S. 398 (1964).

Beckingham v. Boksburg Liquor Licencing Board, TPD 280, 282 (1931).

Bodo Community *et al.* v. Shell Petroleum Development Company of Nigeria Ltd, EWHC (TCC) (June 2014).

His Royal Highness Emere Godwin Bebe Okpabi *et al.* v. Royal Dutch Shell Plc and Shell P.D.C. of Nigeria Ltd, EWHC 89 (TCC) (2017).

Johannesburg Liquor Licencing Board v. Kuhn (4) SA 666 (A) at 671C (1963).

Kiobel *et al.* v. Royal Dutch Petroleum Co. *et al.*, 569 U.S. 108 (2013).

Larry Bowoto *et al.* v. Chevron Corporation *et al.* (2010) 621 F.3d 1116, United States Court of Appeals, Ninth Circuit.

Marbury v. Madison 1 Cranch (US) 137, 176–7 (1803).

The Ministry of Defense and Support for the Armed Forces of the Islamic Republic of Iran, as Successor in Interest to the Ministry of War of the Government of Iran, Petitioner, v. Cubic Defense Systems Inc., as Successor in Interest to Cubic International Sales Corporation, Respondent. Civ. No. 98-1165-B. United States District Court, S.D. California. (7 December 1998).

New Patriotic Party v. Attorney-General, Supreme Court of Ghana, 1 GLR 378 (SC) (1998).

The Republic v. High Court *Ex Parte* Attorney-General, Supreme Court of Ghana, Case No. J5/10/2013, ILDC 2547 (20 June 2013).

Table of cases

Romak S.A. (Switzerland) v. The Republic of Uzbekistan, UNCITRAL, PCA Case No. AA280 (26 November 2009).

Sosa v. Alvarez-Machain 621 F.3d 111 Court of Appeals (Second circuit, 2010)

Tuffuor v. Attorney-General, Supreme Court of Ghana, GLR 637 (1980).

Wiwa v. Royal Dutch Petroleum Company (2001) 226 F. 3d 88 (Second circuit, 2000) Cert. denied 532 U.S. 941.

Index

Index

Index

Index

Index

Index

EU authorised representative for GPSR:
Easy Access System Europe, Mustamäe tee 50,
10621 Tallinn, Estonia
gpsr.requests@easproject.com

www.ingramcontent.com/pod-product-compliance
Lightning Source LLC
Chambersburg PA
CBHW051953270326
41929CB00015B/2644

* 9 7 8 1 5 2 6 1 8 2 4 7 0 *